{Woman Jesus land to eledins time at Great Awakenir revival of American religion history — perhaps Jon Butler will conte that it is a myth,

Just read Maniso Toni

AFTER REDEMPTION

I hate flying physically, but I love it intellectually. Away from email, google, and all of the other distractions, I set to do 2 things: pray and read. Since I hardly pray anymore, it is nice to have the proverbial fear of God (or the gods) instilled as my rational brain (more likely to die in a car accident on the way to the airport than on the plane) battles with my ___ spirit (that wants to be in control). So I pray. Then I read. And on my way to and from the SHA, I read two fabulous new books on religion in the late 19th & early 20th centuries. My trek started with Sister Aimee McPherson as I almost fell in love with her (probably) face-lifted face and ended w/

After Redemption was so interesting that when I ran out of ink in my final pen, I shelled out more th $4 for a pen at the Richmond Airpo

reviews - about my process
of reading - as an
author, as a teacher
and I believe that
ideas still matter.

$\mathcal{A}$FTER
REDEMPTION

Jim Crow and the Transformation of
African American Religion in the Delta,
1875–1915

JOHN M. GIGGIE

OXFORD
UNIVERSITY PRESS

2008

OXFORD
UNIVERSITY PRESS

Oxford University Press, Inc., publishes works that further
Oxford University's objective of excellence
in research, scholarship, and education.

Oxford   New York
Auckland   Cape Town   Dar es Salaam   Hong Kong   Karachi
Kuala Lumpur   Madrid   Melbourne   Mexico City   Nairobi
New Delhi   Shanghai   Taipei   Toronto

With offices in
Argentina   Austria   Brazil   Chile   Czech Republic   France   Greece
Guatemala   Hungary   Italy   Japan   Poland   Portugal   Singapore
South Korea   Switzerland   Thailand   Turkey   Ukraine   Vietnam

Copyright © 2008 by John M. Giggie

Published by Oxford University Press, Inc.
198 Madison Avenue, New York, New York 10016

www.oup.com

Library of Congress Cataloging-in-Publication Data
Giggie, John Michael, 1965–
After redemption : Jim Crow and the transformation of African American religion in the Delta,
1875–1915 / John M. Giggie.
p.   cm.
Includes bibliographical references and index.
ISBN 978-0-19-530403-9; 978-0-19-530404-6 (pbk.)
1. African Americans—Religion. 2. Delta (Miss.: Region)—Religious life and customs. I. Title.
BR563.N4G53 2007
277.62'40808996073—dc22   2007011508

1 3 5 7 9 8 6 4 2

Printed in the United States of America
on acid-free paper

For Marisa

ACKNOWLEDGMENTS

This book has been a long time in coming. Were it not for the steady backing of institutions, friends, colleagues, and family, I would still be at it. To pause here and record my many debts of gratitude hardly seems an adequate gesture for all that I have received, but it is a start.

The research and writing for this book, which began as a dissertation, was generously supported by Department of History and the Office of the Dean of the Graduate School at Princeton University, the Center for the Study of American Religion at Princeton University, the Andrew Mellon Foundation, the Whiting Foundation, the American Historical Association, the Louisville Center for the Study of American Religion at the Louisville Seminary, the Pew Program in American Religion at Yale University, and the Young Scholars in American Religion program at Indiana University-Purdue University of Indianapolis. A faculty fellowship from the National Endowment for the Humanities was critical in completing a series of final revisions. At the University of Texas at San Antonio, summer fellowships and a Faculty Research Award helped put the book into print.

It goes without saying that any history book rises on the backs of archivists. I have been extremely fortunate to work with archivists from across the country, who took a personal interest in my work, tracked down leads for me, and lent their own wisdom and perspective to my project. Their selflessness, to no small degree, made this book possible. In particular, I would like to thank Ann Lipscomb and Clinton Bagley at the

Mississippi Department of Archives and History; Andrea Cantrell at the Division of Special Collections at the Williams Library of the University of Arkansas at Fayetteville; Russell Baker at the Arkansas Historical Commission; Randy Burkett and Teresa Burke at the Manuscript, Archive and Rare Book Library at Emory University Archives; Mary George and Emily Belcher at Firestone Library at Princeton University; Debra MacIntyre at the Cain Archives at Millsaps College; and the late Rev. Peter Hogan at the Archive of the Josephite Fathers in Baltimore, Maryland.

I am also grateful for the level of professionalism and expertise shown to me by archivists and librarians at the University Archives at Louisiana State University; the Amistad Research Center at Tulane University; the University Archives and Records Service and the Southern History Collection at the University of North Carolina at Chapel Hill; the Perkins Library at Duke University; the Archive of the Diocese of Little Rock, Arkansas; the Archive of the Diocese of Jackson, Mississippi; the Special Collections Department of Hendrix College; Mississippi Baptist College; the Special Collections Division of the University of Mississippi; the Special Collections Department and the Mississippi Valley Collection Resources at the University of Memphis; the Tennessee State Archives in Nashville, Tennessee; and the Schomburg Center for Research in Black Culture at the New York Public Library

At the University of Texas at San Antonio, I benefited from the support of my colleagues and the Chairs of the Department of History, Wing Chung Ng and later John Reynolds, as well as the Deans of the College of Liberal Arts, Alan Craven and later Daniel Gelo. Stacy Pena, Paulo Villarreal, Sherrie McDonald, and Andrea Treatise provided critical technical support. Bruce Moses, of the Center for Archeological Research, expertly drafted the maps for the book. Many of my graduate students have helped complete a number of vital tasks, including gathering and analyzing census data, fact checking, reviewing endnotes, and compiling the bibliography. Thanks to Andrea Crossen, Benjamin Domingue, Teresa Gonzalez, Patrick Murphy, Jodi Peterson, Martin Valdespino, and Catherine Wilke. At the University of Alabama, I have been welcomed with open arms by the faculty and staff, especially Dean Robert Olin and history department chair Larry Clayton.

My graduate school professors went far beyond the call of duty in the patience and support they showed me over the years. James McPherson anchored my learning at Princeton, steadily guiding me across the historiographical terrain of nineteenth-century America and steering the direction of the dissertation. Albert Raboteau and David Wills first pushed me to focus on the post-Reconstruction era as a period of research into southern and black culture, and ever since then have selflessly shared their own insights and poured over my drafts. Al generously opened his own research files to me and was a never-ending source of creativity for my work. Special thanks goes to David, who first introduced me to the excitement of studying American religious history as an undergraduate at Amherst College and, through his own work and teaching, continues to do so. Bob Wuthnow, particularly through his weekly workshops on religion and culture in America, was a role model of the interdisciplinary scholar. His ability to traverse disciplines and bring new questions to old fields of knowledge deeply shaped my own intellectual curiosities.

Many, many friends contributed support over the years. The list is very long, and I hope that I have remembered everyone. For reading drafts and offering tips on research and writing, I would especially like to thank Bill Jordan, Steve Kotkin, John Murrin, Phil Nord, Elizabeth Lunbeck, Leigh Schmidt, John Wilson, Sean Wilentz, Christine Stanzell, Vince DiGirolomo, April Masten, Walter Johnson, Steve Kantrowitz, Grazia Lolla, Jerry Podair, Henry Yu, James Hogue, Paul Miles, Jacob Cogan, Bradford Verter, Daniel Sack, Kathleen Joyce, Diane Winston, John Evans, John Smalzbauer, Matthew Lawson, Paul Kemeny, James Bennett, Luis Murillo, Charles Reagan Wilson, William Ferris, Fitz Brundage, Ted Ownby, Vernon Burton, Jonathan Imber, Phil Scranton, Roger Horowitz, Barbara Savage, Jeannie Whayne, Patrick Williams, Laurie Maffly-Kipp, Althea Butler, Clarence Hardy, David Daniels, James Lewis, Nancy Ammerman, David Hackett, James Morehead, John Summerfield, Bruce Dorsey, Peter Williams, Catherine Brekus, Phil Groff, Nick Salvatore, David Morgan, Paul Harvey, Sally Promey, Jon Butler, Ed Blum, James Schneider, Steven Boyd, and Harvey Graff.

The chance to deliver my work to different groups of scholars was fundamental to advancing the overall structure and argument of the book. I would like to acknowledge the many historians who posed important questions about my research and shed new light on it over the years. I presented sections of this book to the Institute for the Study of Religion and Capitalism at Boston University; the Department of History at the University of Arkansas; the Young Scholars Program in American Religion at Indiana University-Purdue University Indianapolis; the Institute for Southern Studies and the Watson-Brown Foundation at the University of South Carolina; the Shelby Collum Davis Center and the Department of History at Princeton University; the Louisville Institute for the Study of American Religion at the Louisville Seminary; the Erasmus Institute of the University of Amsterdam and the Van Gogh Museum, Amsterdam, the Netherlands; the Symposium on Commerce and Commodification at the Hagley Museum and Library and, later, its Faculty Research Seminar in the History of Technology; the Center for Contemporary Studies at the University of California at Los Angeles; the Center for the Study of American Religion at Princeton University; the Valparaiso Art Museum at Valparaiso University; the Winterthur Library and Research Center; and the Pew Conference in Religion and American History at Yale University.

The book draws from materials published in a book that I coedited, *Faith in the Market: Religion and the Rise of Urban Commercial Culture* (New Brunswick: Rutgers

University Press, 2002), used with the permission of Rutgers University Press, and several of my essays: "The African-American Holiness Movement," *SOCIETY* (*Social Science and Modern Society*), vol. 43, no. 7 (November/December 2006), 50–59, used with the permission of Transaction Publishers; "Preachers and Peddlers of God: Ex-Slaves and the Selling of African-American Religion in the South, 1865–1917," in Susan Strasser, ed., *Commodifying Everything: Consumption and Capitalist Enterprise* (New York: Routledge, 2003), 168–190, used with the permission of Routledge; "'Disband Him From the Church': African Americans and the Spiritual Politics of Disfranchisement in Post-Reconstruction Arkansas," *Arkansas Historical Quarterly*, vol. 60, no. 3 (Fall 2001): 245–264, used with the permission of the Trustees of the University of Arkansas; "Introduction" (with Diane Winston), *Journal of Urban History*, special edition, "Urban Commercial Culture and Religion in Modern North America," (May 2002): 395–397, used with the permission of Sage Publications; and "'When Jesus Gave Me a Ticket': Train Travel and Spiritual Journeys Among African Americans, 1865–1917," in David Morgan and Sally Promey, eds. *The Visual Culture of American Religion* (Berkeley: University of California Press, 2001), 249–266, 356–359, used with the permission of the University of California Press.

I had the good fortune of bumping into Susan Ferber at Oxford University Press years ago while searching for a book to purchase at the annual meeting of the American Historical Association. That chance meeting became the first of many conversations about the profession and my work in specific. Her unflagging zeal for my project and uncanny sense of knowing just what an argument needs propelled the book through its final stages; her friendship over the years made writing it all the more enjoyable. Gwen Colvin, my production editor, combed through the manuscript with a steady hand and greatly improved it.

My three children, Julia, Alexandra, and Christian, were born during the research and drafting of this book. They did their best to keep me from working at it, and for their constant distraction I am eternally grateful. Their every breath continues to beckon me to rediscover the curiosity of childhood and explore the wonders of parenthood. Other family members were also important. Jack and Irene Giggie enthusiastically backed the project from the start. Sandy and Louisa Arico flung upon their doors whenever I visited Mississippi, and their warmth and support always steadied my path.

My wife, Marisa, and I have lived much of our lives together. For over twenty years we have shared life's adventures and miracles, none more special than our children. I have been made wiser by her humor and intelligence; emboldened by her own steady ascent through graduate school, medical school, residency, and fellowship training; and blessed by her love and compassion. It will surprise no one that it is to she that I dedicate this book.

Contents

Abbreviations

———◦———

ADJ   Archives of the Catholic Diocese of Jackson, Miss.

AG   *Arkansas Gazette*

AHC   Arkansas Historical Commission

AHQ   *Arkansas Historical Quarterly*

AHR   *American Historical Review*

ADLR   Archives of the Catholic Diocese of Little Rock, Ark.

AME   African Methodist Episcopal

Amistad   Amistad Research Center, New Orleans, La.

BV   *Baptist Vanguard*

Cain   Cain Archives, Millsaps College, Jackson, Miss.

CH   *Church History*

CME   *Colored Methodist Episcopal*

CI   *Christian Index*

CR	*Christian Recorder*
DU	Duke University Archives, Perkins Library, Durham, N.C.
Emory	Special Collections, Emory University, Atlanta, Ga.
JAH	*Journal of American History*
JFA	Archives of the Josephite Fathers, Baltimore, Md.
JMH	*Journal of Mississippi History*
JNH	*Journal of Negro History*
JSH	*Journal of Southern History*
LSU	Louisiana State University Archives, Baton Rouge
MDAH	Mississippi Department of History and Archives, Jackson
ME	*Methodist Episcopal*
Schomburg	Schomburg Library, New York Public Library, New York City
SWCA	*Southwestern Christian Advocate*
TSLA	Tennessee State Library and Archives, Nashville
UAK-F	Special Collections, University of Arkansas at Fayetteville
WPA-HRS	Work Project Administration—Historical Records Survey

PROLOGUE

LIFE AND DEATH IN THE DELTA

I . . . tells my Father all about my trials here below. We are free, but we can't stop praying; we must keep on. . . . We have been let loose, and now we are just marching on to a better land.

—*Octavia V. R. Albert, The House of Bondage,*
or Charlotte Brooks and Other Slaves, p. 5

———⟫●⟨———

I n June 1893, Reverend S. A. Moseley gave one of the most important speeches of his young life to a crowd of several hundred fellow black Baptists, mostly share-croppers and tenant farmers drawn like him from the Arkansas Delta. Born about the time of the outbreak of the Civil War, Moseley was pastor of St. Paul's Baptist Church in Pine Bluff, a cotton town nestled on the banks of the Arkansas River in the southwestern corner of the state. Tall, thin, mustachioed, and gifted with a silver tongue, he was a rising star in his denomination when he addressed the annual meeting of the Arkansas Sunday School Convention held that year outside of the state capitol. He attemped to make sense of the strange plight of southern African Americans since the signing of the Emancipation Proclamation thirty years earlier, drawing upon his life in the Delta for insight.[1]

The preacher opened on a triumphant note, proudly reminding his audience that since slavery "[m]any have been our trials, great our conflicts, and bitter our experiences; but out of them the Lord has brought us safe. . . ." His upbeat tone quickly sunk, however, as he turned his attention to the recent upheavals in local and regional politics and blamed them for unleashing a "sectional, selfish, and partial" pestilence that was "more dreadful than the yellow fever, small pox, cholera or any other ever visited upon human beings." Fast spreading across the South, this contagion wore a white face and carried an insatiable appetite for black victims. "Its emblems," continued Moseley, "[we]re the Winchester, Smith & Wesson pistols, double action revolvers of other factories, etc." Its name was "mob violence" and it was giving rise to African-American communities composed of "broken-hearted widows, fatherless children, heart sickening friends and relatives, and discouraged citizens who have lost all hope for protection, even for life."[2]

Moseley evoked a crisis afflicting not only freed people from Arkansas and its Delta but all black southerners at the end of the nineteenth century, that of living after "redemption." Despite its rosy gloss and cheerful evocation of their emancipated status, the phrase shone darkly for them. It referred to the period of their lives beginning roughly in the mid-1870s, when Reconstruction collapsed and white Democrats broadened their political campaigns to thwart black freedoms and recent social advances. Ever since then, these self-proclaimed white leaders of the "New South" had slowly but successfully birthed a modern world born of their racist dreams, one that, as they loved to call it, had "redeemed" their beloved homeland from the clutches of Union victory and the political empowerment of former slaves and their descendants. African Americans had labored ceaselessly and, for the most part, futilely to stop them. The southern "redeemers" had steadily and ruthlessly stripped them of the franchise, the right of due process, the chance to attend adequately funded public schools, the ability to travel freely, and, most basically, the daily hope of living without the threat of being scorned, mocked, raped, beaten, or killed because of the color of their skin. They had bequeathed a South that, by 1893, shared much in common with the depredations of slavery and little with the first years of emancipation, when Confederate defeat had unloosed waves of joy and optimism among African Americans about a future as fully fledged citizens. Indeed, they had brought into being a South that left blacks groping for answers about the meaning of freedom won and lost.

In his address, Moseley offered no immediate solution to the problem of living after redemption. Instead, this reverend framed the tragic turn of history as part of a necessary if heartbreaking stage in a slow African American passage toward freedom. Not surprisingly, he turned for inspiration to the familiar story of the ancient Hebrews recorded in the book of Exodus in the Bible. Like generations of black Americans slave and free before him, he saw in the journey of the Israelites from the Egypt of bondage to the Canaan Land of liberty a historical model for his own people to follow.[3] "We have left the borders of Egypt, and are now between the [Red] Sea and the Jordan. We have quite a long way to reach Canaan. We are not without a Moses nor a Joshua . . . [and] the Walls of Jericho will be made to bow before us. We are only to be strong and courageous and the victory is sure." Like their predecessors in the Old Testament who wandered in the desert for forty years after being manumitted, blacks in the Delta also dwelled in a time of transition between slavery and freedom, only they were battling whites over their claims to unobstructed citizenship and physical safety. In this modern struggle, Moseley counseled that they were far from helpless. They had their new and growing networks of churches, religious schools, and presses to turn to for support and guidance. In comparison to any other point in black history, the minister asserted, "[w]e are much better organized.... We can touch more people and secure prompter responses from a larger number of persons...."[4]

What follows is a story about the spiritual lives of African Americans living after redemption in the violent and uncertain world of the Arkansas and Mississippi Delta. It is a story about how blacks found in their sacred beliefs and practices a mediating space through which to respond to the ambiguities, horrors, and hopes of life in the New South. It is about a reinvention of southern black religion during the late nineteenth and early twentieth centuries, about newly formed independent black churches confronting white supremacy and sweeping changes in technology and the consumer market, and about the spiritual dimensions of the Great Migration. It is about the development of African American religious ideologies and movements at the local level, about how they assumed a popular and institutional expression, and about how they changed communities. It is about coercion and freedom, racial intimidation and attempts to minimize it, and disillusionment with the democratic promise of America and resilient devotion to it. It is, to no small degree, a story about the tragedies and triumphs of Southern culture. For when Reverend Moseley strained to make sense of his earthly fate and that of his people's, he implicitly raised a question that affected all black southerners—namely, how would they negotiate their place in the modern era and what role would their faith play in it.

AFTER REDEMPTION

{add this +
Butler to
themes (559)}

INTRODUCTION

AFRICAN AMERICAN RELIGION
IN THE AGE OF SEGREGATION IN THE DELTA

Against this landscape, variable, heat-tortured, shifting; amid swamps dark and mysterious and lost; in the presence of the mighty river rolling onward to the Mexican Gulf, under sudden suns and swarming stars, never far from the Negro speech and the Negro singing; within American and yet withdrawn from it, whites and Negroes, in the strangest mass relationship of men on this continent, painfully tried to work out their singular destiny together

—David L. Cohn in *The Mississippi Delta and the World:*
The Memoirs of David L. Cohn, ed. James C. Cobb, p. 5

This is a book about religious transformation in the lives of ex-slaves and their descendants living in the Arkansas and Mississippi Delta between the end of Reconstruction and the start of the Great Migration. My interest in this subject first took shape when I came across an interview with a former bondsman recorded by graduate students at Fisk University in Nashville, Tennessee, as part of that institution's broad effort from 1927 to 1929 to chronicle the history of black Americans' lives during and after slavery. When asked to reflect on the trials of his religious life, this poor elderly sharecropper, never named in the surviving interview, pointed to a moment shortly after his eighteenth birthday when he "began to think seriously about the salvation of my soul." Likely harkening back to the mid-1870s, he recalled an image of a railroad station, where he stood nervously next to Jesus. Suddenly, he remembered, "my knees got weak, and I knelt to pray. As I knelt Jesus handed me a ticket. It was all signed with my name. I arose to my feet and handed it in at the window and was told to take my place with the three men standing on the platform and wait."[1] The symbolic meaning of receiving a ticket from Jesus and waiting at the railroad station was immediately plain to this black Christian: he was saved.

What caught my attention in the ex-slave's account was his staging of spiritual transformation as a train journey. He subtly incorporated images of and experiences with contemporary technology and travel into his sacred life to fashion a distinctly modern narrative of conversion. By reimagining a vehicle of segregated transportation as an agent of spiritual deliverance, he also integrated current politics into his conversion experience and muted their racist overtones, at least temporarily. I found that the interviewer had captured dimensions of an African American religious culture deeply enmeshed in the sights, sounds, and signs of everyday life and one thick with implications about how we tell the history of the New South. This striking account pointed to the presence of black sacred ideas and institutions that confounded older popular and scholarly assumptions that this was an era when African American southerners acceded, reluctantly, to the overwhelming power of segregation. It invited new questions about historical categorization. Given the racial cruelty and terror of the late nineteenth and early twentieth centuries, how could we explain the development of this type of vision and the spiritual organizations that obviously supported it without dismissing them as interesting but ultimately aberrant to the study of southern culture and its religious facets? And how would such an explanation affect our conception of African American life after Reconstruction?

This book is an attempt to answer these inquiries and explore more broadly the meaning of W. E. B. Du Bois' 1903 insight, offered in *Souls of Black Folk,* that "the study of Negro religion is not only a vital part of the history of the Negro in America, but . . . of American history."[2] I hope to suggest the need to reperiodicize African American religious history after slavery. Similar to Steven Hahn's recent call to notice the development of a sophisticated political culture among rural black Southerners that originated during bondage and extended up to the start of World War I, I seek to establish the post-Reconstruction era as a moment of far-reaching novelty in southern black spiritual life and refigure its traditional historical chronology. In the normal temporal schema, there are two watershed periods: Reconstruction, when freed people built independent denominations and established their churches as vibrant centers of black education, politics, and racial pride; and, nearly four decades later, World War I, when southern migrants flooded northern cities and introduced new styles of music and worship to black urban congregations, formed Holiness-Pentecostal "store-front" churches, and tested ideas about racial self-help made famous through the philosophy of Marcus Garvey. The years in between have been commonly portrayed as a time when southern blacks struggled with scant success to contain the damage wrought by burgeoning racism and made only marginal advances in their religion, politics, and social life. In contrast, I argue that African Americans developed a surprisingly rich and complex sacred culture during the late nineteenth and early twentieth centuries. It was a time of intense religious transformation, when blacks experimented with new symbols of freedom and racial respectability, forms of organizational culture, regional networks of communication, and popular notions of commodification and consumption that enabled them to survive, make progress, and at times resist white supremacy. These innovations, in turn, shaped the arc of black culture during and after the Great War.

After Redemption also seeks to introduce new theoretical perspectives to three overlapping academic disciplines: American religious history, African American history, and southern history. First, the book adopts a conceptual point of view that blurs traditional analytical boundaries within the study of American religion in order to craft a history that reflects the full range of meanings and experiences ascribed to it by Delta blacks. It employs an expanded definition of what many scholars normally consider "religious" because African Americans from the Delta possessed a popular sense of the divine and the supernatural that was not easily contained by creed or doctrine; it threaded its way into the tapestry of everyday life.[3] They based their religious beliefs and practices as much on visions and dreams as they did on any report published by a denominational conference or edict announced by a bishop or local preacher. They were as likely to pray, experience conversion, or gain a sense of religious calling while riding a train as standing in a pew or at a pulpit. And they frequently imparted spiritual significance to the purchase of a new suit of clothes for themselves or a new set of lights for their churches.

Relatedly, I blend different historical models and methodologies to bring to light the array of human stories and personalities embedded in the records left behind by Delta blacks. I do not closely adhere to any formal theory of religion and dutifully follow its diagnostic cues and interpretive prescriptions, even though my topic is religious history. Like traditional church historians, I devote substantial consideration to the evolution of black denominations and the leadership of important religious figures. Official church rules and regulations embody beliefs about the nature of divinity, sacred polity, and the definition of religious authority, while the writings of major preachers offer a bird's eye view of institutional controversies, successes, and debacles. Similar to students of theology and the more expansive category of myth and ritual, I study the birth of new ideas about God and spiritual experiences that mark one as "being saved." I also dedicate extensive attention to the development of new rites of consumption, decoration, and personal dress as a way of illuminating how the home and the individual body became sites for registering religious conviction. Most regularly, though, I mix these analytical approaches and concentrate on the interplay of sacred belief and practice in the daily lives of individual men and women. Delta blacks expressed their spiritual tensions, convictions, doubts, and fantasies most readily and consistently when they cooked, cleaned, farmed, played, read, wrote, argued, fought, and cared for families and themselves. Tracking and decoding individual behavior and action offers the best way of understanding how African American religion operated in the Delta. This is not to say that church was unimportant as a focal point of their spiritual lives, for of course it was, but rather that Delta blacks, like most southerners, also articulated and manifested their faith in many other settings.[4]

By offering a working definition of religious history that finds the divine in prosaic locations and focuses on individual experience as the key site for analysis, I seek an approach to the study of African American history that refines—rather than discards or disproves—earlier ones. In this field, students traditionally tend to examine black religion by assuming the presence of "the black church," a general term that refers to a collective institutional expression of black faith. It is an idea that stretches back at least to the nineteenth-century black philosopher and abolitionist Martin Delany, who, in an 1849 account of black religion, wrote that, "[a]mong our people generally, the church is the Alpha and Omega of all things. It is their only source of information-their only acknowledged public body—their state legislature. . . ."[5] The notion of the "black church" as the center of black life arguably received its fullest scholarly expression in 1963 in the work of the black sociologist, E. Franklin Frazier. In *The Negro Church in America,* Frazier pronounced that the black church was a "nation within a nation" and the crucial source for the maturation not only of black sacred culture but also black literature, education, social life, and politics.[6] Yet Delany and Frazier, followed by generations of intellectuals, conceptualized "the black church" in ways that simplified the conflicts and complexities that lay at the heart of African American religion and generally based their conclusions on the words and deeds of male ministers. As a result, their portrayals were often incomplete. It is certainly possible to speak of theologies, social goals, and political interests shared by black churches, but not without acknowledging and probing the equally important themes of dissent, disagreement, and the leadership of women.[7]

I hope to modify the most current and widely held scholarly formulations of "the black church." The term still persists today, but largely as shorthand for organized forms of black religion, especially its Protestant dimensions. Recently, scholars have defined it by stressing its different sociological purposes for African Americans, such as liberating, prophetic, and "dialectical" (as in moving between a series of opposite functions over time, such as a worldly and otherworldly focus). The most sophisticated model of the black church, though, avoids any rigid classification. Evelyn Brooks Higginbotham, in her work on black Baptist women from 1880 to 1920, has argued that the black church was an intermediary between the government and the black community and a type of black public "sphere." It simultaneously structured contact between blacks and the outside world and provided a physical place for worship, civic conversation, and political activity. The black church lacked any one major function but instead was a "dialogic" arena in which congregants, often through heated conflict and debate, created new notions, policies, and regulations about religion, race, gender, and politics.[8]

Higginbotham's model, while helpful in capturing the historical role of doctrinal controversy and especially black women in African American religion, pays little attention to supernatural items of faith that so strongly informed common belief and both connected and disconnected church and everyday life among Delta blacks. By focusing nearly exclusively on the most successful African Americans, it also leaves open the question of how their less fortunate brethren imagined religion. To portray the extensive scope of sacred life and different dimensions to the "black church" in the Delta, among a population overwhelmingly poor, rural, and lacking a formal education, I investigate multiple forms of religious expression. They include dreams, nightmares, disembodied voices, and phantasmagoric visions but also the bits and pieces of material culture that Delta blacks stamped with spiritual significance, such as pencils sold by their ministers, sketches of African American leaders published in their denominational newspapers and hung inside their homes, articles of clothing, and pieces of furniture.

Reconceptualizing the analytical definition of the black church to include dimensions of popular religion ultimately makes it easier to see how Delta blacks developed a supply of religious resources that enabled them to blunt—but never completely banish—the prescriptive power of white supremacy. Such an observation, at first glance, might seem to be already a part of the recent literature in southern history that deals with the rise of Jim Crow and segregation. Much of it has successfully destabilized older beliefs about the immutable and suffocating nature of white supremacy as it evolved during the late nineteenth century. It has done so primarily by illuminating how blacks worked the edges of segregation to their maximum advantage and at times shaped its very character.[9] Yet much of this literature has generally centered on the lives of well-off African Americans who lived in larger towns and cities—those who, not coincidentally, left the densest supply of personal diaries, letters, autobiographies, and printed books and articles. The world of rural blacks is mostly uninvestigated.

New South historians certainly have tackled the topic of black religion as well. They have correctly pointed out that African American preachers and churches historically minimized the debilitating effect of racism by identifying blacks as God's chosen people, financing schools and presses, teaching literacy, providing job skills, organizing protests, and steadfastly demanding racial equality and justice.

But they usually study black religion by focusing on "the black church" as it has been traditionally defined and do not explore the rich connections between religion and technology, commerce, or consumer culture.[10]

Largely unexplored, then, is the topic of the religious culture of rural blacks. Yet it is one that promises fresh insights into the historical relationship between segregation and southern society. Delta blacks mediated the construction of social hierarchy based on skin color during the years of Jim Crow by drawing on their sacred beliefs and practices in often-unanticipated ways. For example, black Baptists and Methodists incorporated their experiences with the color line into revelations, prophecies, visions, ditties, hymns, and early blues music, reenvisioning them as something other than deadly or debasing. Combining the social and psychological resources of fraternal orders with those of their churches, they created a new institutional culture of black religion that better responded to the popular need for jobs, insurances, and articulations of racial pride. Church leaders took advantage of the expanding railroad infrastructure to evangelize, build new houses of worship, and distribute religious literature. They also tapped the growth of the commercial economy to raise money and public enthusiasm for their emerging local networks of churches, schools, and newspapers and to fashion new aesthetics of dress and decoration.

It is, to be sure, a bit curious to postulate that blacks living in the Delta reinvented their religious lives during the post-Reconstruction era in ways that helped them neutralize the corrosive effects of segregation. Indeed, at first glance such an assertion seems difficult even to sustain, especially given that the era has long been dubbed "the nadir" of modern black cultural achievement and civil rights and witnessed a level of state-backed violence against African Americans realistically unmatched during the previous century.[11] Adding to the challenge of credibility is that, during this time of intense racial conflict in the South, the Delta ranked as one of the bloodiest areas. Indeed, the promise of full citizenship that accompanied the Confederacy's defeat was shorter lived here than in most other places. Arkansas Democrats wrestled control of the legislature and governorship from Republicans in October 1874. Through violence, voter intimidation, electioneering, and skillful manipulation of their party's factions, many of the white politicians who had run the state before and during the Civil War recaptured power. As officeholders, they repudiated much of the state's debt, cut property taxes, slashed appropriations for public institutions like schools, and dismantled blacks' right to vote and enjoy due process.[12] The tale was much the same in Mississippi. In 1875, white Democrats began a bid to regain political dominance over the state by implementing the "Mississippi Plan," which was a systematic campaign of election fraud and racial intimidation designed to disfranchise African Americans. Predictably, black

Mississippians were outraged when white Democrats physically tried to prevent them from casting ballots. Some fought back and race riots broke out. Black and white Republicans pleaded with Governor Adelbert Ames to deploy the state militia and restore order but Ames refused, fearful that the sight of African-American troops training their guns on white citizens would only make matters worse. Instead he begged President Ulysses Grant to send federal soldiers, but his appeal fell on deaf ears. Facing only local opposition, champions of the Mississippi Plan soon got their wish. White Democrats seized most statewide offices and, like their political brethren in Arkansas, quickly reduced taxes, lowered public expenditures, and openly sanctioned racial violence as a means of restricting African American liberties.[13]

In both Arkansas and Mississippi, the clearest sign of the new political regimes' disregard for blacks—and the main reason for why the era as a whole has been labeled the nadir for so long—was the steep rise of extralegal violence visited upon African Americans daring to violate any aspect of the complex codes governing segregation. Like all black southerners, Delta blacks risked being spit upon, beat, knifed, shot, or raped when they, for example, failed to address white adults by their formal titles or as "Mr." and "Mrs.," to enter white homes or stores through a rear door, to doff their hats in the presence of a white person, or to step aside and let a white person pass by in the street. Worse still, they faced the strong possibility of being lynched if their transgression involved accusations of sexual contact with or physical harm of a white person, particularly of a white woman. The matter of lynching in the Delta was especially severe: the area hosted more lynchings than almost any other in the nation. From 1889 to 1917, eighty-six blacks were lynched in the Arkansas Delta; during roughly the same period, eighty-eight blacks were lynched in the Mississippi Delta.[14] Mississippi itself was first among all states in the nation in the overall number of lynchings during the decades after Reconstruction and, in the 1880s alone, recorded twice as many as any other state.[15]

While statistics limn the magnitude of the problem of racial violence in the Delta, they only hint at how its savagery and randomness poisoned interactions between blacks and whites. The account of a lynching in Doddsvilles, in Sunflower County, Mississippi, is instructive on this point. In 1904 Luther Holbert was the prime suspect in the killing of James Eastland, a prominent white planter, and a black man. Holbert had worked as a sharecropper on Eastland's 2,300-acre plantation and apparently committed the murders in response to threats against him and his wife. Aided by friends and members of a local black fraternal organization, the couple escaped to a nearby swamp. They hid for four days until discovered by a 200-man posse, which dragged them back to Doddsville and lynched them in the shadow of their church. Before fastening the noose, and much to the delight of a boisterous crowd that numbered about 1000, vigilantes forced the Holberts to hold out their hands, chopped their fingers off, and distributed the severed digits to the audience. According to an account published by the Vicksburg *Evening Post,* they then sliced off the Holberts' ears and repeatedly bore a large corkscrew into their arms, legs, and torsos, "tearing out big pieces of raw, quivering flesh every time it was withdrawn." It was a story that haunted Delta blacks for decades.[16]

Significantly, by claiming that the recovery of black religious history for this violent time reveals the need to rethink the accuracy of its longstanding historical moniker, I am not seeking to substitute a new monolithic narrative of black cultural triumph for an older one that stressed its absence. It is certainly not my intention to craft a history that obscures the cruelty, frustrations, and failures that blacks confronted when building their communities; nor is my goal to minimize the bitter intra-racial tensions over spiritual authority, politics, and gender roles that divided African Americans. For along with the advances blacks made, their struggles are also central to the warp and woof of their spiritual life. That said, one of my main objectives is to demonstrate how Delta blacks constantly remade their sense of the sacred as they came into intimate and sustained contact with the shifting constraints upon their citizenship and, in turn, show how this reality reframes our understanding of the complexity of black religion and its role in confronting segregation. By doing so, I hope to draw a portrait of the period as one of severely constrained freedom for blacks, but one in which they also made strides toward building a world of their own design.

Perhaps no area of the nation during the post-Reconstruction era saw greater change in the religious culture of its black residents than the Arkansas and Mississippi Delta. Much of the reason stemmed from its historical status as a focal point of African American and southern life. During slavery, the Delta's counties contained some of the highest concentrations of slaves and largest plantations in the country; during the Civil War, they were military and cultural strongholds of the Confederacy. Throughout Reconstruction and up until World War I, blacks steadily moved to the area in massive numbers, chasing the dream of land ownership and the seductive promises wafted by unscrupulous labor agents. These agents, employed by white Delta landowners and speculators desperate for a new and bigger workforce after slavery, rode by horse and rail to every state that once flew the Confederate flag and dangled wondrous tales of cheap plentiful land and high wages to any black person who would come and work. Thousands did, and sowed their ambitions in the soil of the Delta. From 1870 to 1910, when 90 percent of all black Americans lived in the South, the Delta had an overall population that was about 75 percent black.[17] It ranked first nationally in the total number of black-majority counties, some of which possessed a ratio of blacks-to-whites that ran as high as 15:1.[18]

The migration account of John J. Morant was typical. In the 1870s, he moved from Alabama to the Delta with his family after speaking with a labor recruiter. Though only a young boy at the time, this future minister recalled being deeply "impressed by the migration agents, who circulated fantastic stories about the richness of the Delta. It was said that cotton grew so tall that one could pick it from the back of a horse, while riding, and that money could be gathered from the trees." Morant, however, soon discovered that the reality of life in the Delta was far from its advertised version. His family joined the ranks of black sharecroppers, men and women too poor to buy or rent land and who instead pledged to "share" a portion of their crop to a landowner in exchange for farm acreage, tools, and seed. "[M]y father was soon disillusioned. While the land was fertile, the money went into the coffers of the white[s]. . . ."[19] Other black migrants to the Delta in the 1870s and 1880s also cut trees, built levees and roads, and laid railroad tracks as part of a massive effort to transform the Delta, much of which was boggy marshland and dense forests in 1860, into an area suitable for farming.[20]

The blackness of the Delta made it a topic of intense interest for a nation hungry for details and stories about the aftermath of slavery. Travelers, adventure-seekers, humanitarians, reporters, writers, and others thronged to the area in the hope of catching sight of a slice of the "authentic" South. A columnist for the *New York Evening Post,* Clarence Deming, visited in the early 1880s ostensibly to investigate southern planters and their politics. He dutifully catalogued the "obstacles in the work of upbuilding the South," singling out the "havoc of war, the loss of slave-property, the transition to a system of free labor, and the carpet-bag era." Yet for Deming, as for his fellow chroniclers, the real journalistic promise of the Delta lay in the thrilling chance to glimpse the world of former bonds people and their descendants. Deming eventually got his voyeuristic wish and, peering through the race-tinged spectacles worn by most of his ilk, breathlessly reported that "[t]he Negroes here . . . are probably the purest types of their race to be found this side of Africa. . . . Huddled together on their plantation settlements, rarely leaving home, and working out for themselves the simple problems of their lowly lot, they form a class whose life and habits reveal the lower phases of the Negro character most faithfully, most amusingly, and in certain aspects, most sadly."[21]

When Deming described black life in the Delta, however, he confined his observations to the Mississippi Delta and ignored its Arkansas complement. Historians of the Delta typically analyze either its Mississippi or its Arkansas section, but I look at both to draw conclusions about African American religion. My decision to do so reflects the reality that, during the post-Reconstruction era, blacks from each part of the Delta shared an overlapping network of religious education, communication, literature, and beliefs. They frequently heard the same itinerant preachers,

attended the same revivals, and, most significantly, read the same religious newspapers, books, and tracts. In 1894, L. A. Rankin of the Mississippi Delta penned a
short note to the editors of the *Arkansas Vanguard,* the weekly newspaper of the
Arkansas Baptists, thanking them for their hard work. "I love to read letters from
good thinking men and active workers in the Baptist cause. It seems to me like the
Baptists of Mississippi are sleeping away our time, while the Baptists of Arkansas are
going about their Father's business." He closed by promising to send a donation to
Arkansas Baptist College in Little Rock.[22]

United by the common cultural activities of their black residents, the Mississippi
and Arkansas Deltas also share a geologic history, topography, and climate that
further make it possible to conceptualize and study them as a whole. The Delta was
formed about fifteen thousand years ago during the last phase of the Ice Age, when
the Mississippi River and its major tributaries, the St. Francis, White, Arkansas, and
Red Rivers, sliced deep vales and gorges into the Lower Gulf Coastal Plain. When
the glaciers melted and flooded the waterways, the rivers overflowed their boundaries and covered the area with a dense alluvium of fine sand, clay, silt, and organic
material that ran hundreds of feet deep.[23] Over the course of thousands of years, the
regular flooding of the Mississippi River and its tributaries created a thick, deep,
loamy soil that was as fertile as any in the world. The river and the soil it created
became literary and environmental symbols for the region, evoked most passionately
and famously by William Alexander Percy, a native son of the Mississippi Delta and
member of a prominent family of white landowners from Greenville, in the opening
lines from his classic memoir, *Lanterns on the Levee,* published in 1941.[24] "Every few
years it rises like a monster from its bed and pushed over its banks to vex and sweeten
the land it has made. For our soil, very dark brown, creamy and sweet-smelling,
without substrata of rock or shale, was built up slowly, century after century, by
sediment gathered by the river in its solemn task of cleansing the continent and
depositing in annual layers of silt."[25] Percy' soil was the perfect setting for raising
crops, especially in the Delta's subtropical climate. And blacks, first as slaves and
then as freed people, provided the agricultural muscle that eventually made the Delta
a national center for cotton production.

The map of the Delta that I use reflects the full scope of its cultural and physical
history and so includes both its Mississippi and Arkansas regions (map I.1). The Delta
is divided by the Mississippi River. Its westerly section consists of the Arkansas Delta
and its smaller easterly segment is composed of the Mississippi Delta.[26] The foothills
of the Ouachita and Ozark mountains, which slope from the northeastern corner of
Arkansas to Little Rock, form the northern boundary of the Arkansas Delta. From
Little Rock, the boundary extends south-southeast to Wilmot, just north of the
Louisiana border, reflecting a natural landscape division between the alluvial Delta

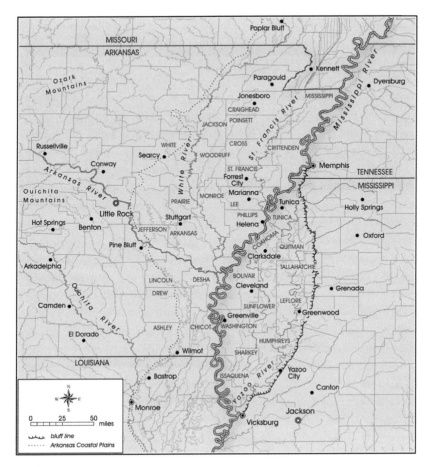

Map I.1. The Delta

soil and the piney woods of the Arkansas Coastal Plains.[27] A steep line of bluffs that reaches heights of two hundred feet defines the Mississippi Delta. It begins below Memphis, Tennessee, bulges eastward and follows the meandering path of the Yazoo River to its confluence with the Mississippi River at Vicksburg.[28] The total area of the Delta is about one and one-half million acres and encompasses twenty-seven counties in whole.[29] During the late nineteenth and early twentieth centuries, it was a rural region but not an isolated one because on or near its perimeter sat major towns and small cities, including Little Rock and Pine Bluff, Arkansas; Memphis, Tennessee; and Jackson, Mississippi. This book will concentrate on the Delta counties with black-majority populations, which includes the entire Mississippi Delta and most of the Arkansas Delta, except for a few parts of its northeastern and central areas.[30]

Although this is a book about black religion in the Delta after Reconstruction, it really begins during the Civil War, when blacks suddenly controlled the shape and style of their spiritual lives to a hitherto unprecedented degree and established goals and priorities, as well as tensions and controversies, that would persist for decades.[31] A few independent black churches existed during the antebellum era, but most slaves worshipped under the watchful eye of the master and white preacher or, more privately, by themselves in hush harbors and secret meeting places. They widely interpreted the defeat of the Confederacy as a providential event in which God, through the act of battle and the brute force of the Union Army, cleansed the nation of its original sin of human bondage, punished slaveholders, and freed his chosen people. "When the war was over," recounted O. W. Green, a former bondsman from Arkansas, "de people just' shout for joy. De Men and women jus shouted for joy. Twas' only because of the prayers of the culled people, dey was freed, and de Lawd worked through Lincoln."[32] After the war, blacks forged a religious culture that, above all, reflected their desire for autonomy. To be sure, some initially joined the church of their former masters and experimented with biracial worship, but they usually abandoned their efforts because white southern denominations generally balked at incorporating ex-slaves as members on equal footing with whites.[33] Instead, most became a member of one of the new black denominations, such as the Colored Methodist Episcopal Church (later the Christian Methodist Episcopal Church) and the National Baptist Convention, Inc. Others joined southern branches of established northern black denominations, such as the African Methodist Episcopal Church and the African Methodist Episcopal Zion Church, or northern white denominations with sizeable southern black populations, such as the Methodist Episcopal Church. Few became Catholic, Presbyterian, Congregationalist, or Episcopalian.[34] As they built their churches and communities, blacks stressed five overlapping aims: managing their own ecclesiastical affairs with little or no involvement from former masters; worshipping in their own churches; being led by black preachers; building schools; and soliciting and welcoming the advice and financial aid of northern white and black denominations, so long as they controlled their own budget.[35]

The construction of this new landscape of African American religion during the first years of freedom, however, occurred in fits and starts as blacks responded to changes in politics, the economy, race relations, and their own communities. They struggled to drum up money and sustain high levels of public support for their fledgling schools and newspapers. Churches found it difficult to meet the many spiritual and social needs of their congregants, especially providing money during times of financial hardship and illness. Preachers were few and far in between in the most rural stretches of the Delta, compelling residents to set aside denominational differences on Sundays and simply worship with whatever minister happened to be hosting services nearby. Among Baptists in particular, congregations quarreled over the best ways to balance their desire to control worship and liturgy within their local churches against the need to create denominational structures of authority and discipline. The end of Reconstruction only exacerbated many of these challenges and disagreements and added new ones, such as disfranchisement and the dramatic rise in racial violence.

Picking up the telling of this history in the mid-1870s, I focus only on a select group of religious bodies that, while distinguishable by dogma and doctrine, collectively embodied the major social tensions and internal divisions driving the evolution of African American spiritual life in the Delta and the South more generally. First, I study the four most popular and powerful black religious bodies in the Delta. They are, in descending order of membership totals: the black Baptist churches, the African Methodist Episcopal (AME) Church, the Colored Methodist Episcopal (CME) Church, and the black conferences of the Methodist Episcopal (ME) Church. Statistics on African American religious affiliation during this era are difficult to come by and not always reliable, but it is still possible to gain a rough sense of the size of churches. In 1919, the US Census Bureau published the best set of statistics based on data culled from the 1910 Census and research undertaken during the mid-1910s as part of a comprehensive study of religion in the United States. Relying in part on this body of research, William Harris calculated that among blacks living in the Mississippi Delta, 101,792 identified themselves as members of the National Baptist Convention, Inc., which was formally organized in 1905 and served as the principal denomination for black Baptists; 13,788 the AME Church; 5,394 the CME Church; and 5,830 the ME Church. The Census Bureau itself revealed that among blacks living in the Arkansas Delta, 89,184 identified themselves as members of the National Baptist Convention; 11,451 the AME Church; 7,232 the CME Church; and 3,061 with ME Church.[36]

These black denominations represent a diverse historical sample of African American Protestantism. Two were headquartered in the North. The AME Church held its first General Conference at Bethel Church in Philadelphia in 1816. The ME Church convened its first General Conference in Baltimore in 1784, though it traced its North American origins to the 1730s and John and Charles Wesley's successful effort to import Methodism from England to the colonies. White bishops directed the ME Church, but they successfully recruited black congregants after the Civil War with invitations to join a church without racial boundaries. They never built such a community, though, and instead organized segregated conferences. The other two Delta churches were southern based. The CME Church originated in 1870 as an all-black offshoot of the Methodist Episcopal Church, South. The black Baptist churches were loosely modeled, both theologically and organizationally, on white Baptist churches. Their popularity rested largely in their decentralized denominational structure, which allowed local communities a great deal of freedom to form churches, select ministers, and design and implement by-laws.

Mindful of the internal diversity of African American religion in the South and the historical tendency to homogenize black churches, I pay particular attention to quarrels between and among these churches over the proper definition of worship, sacred space, spiritual authority, and consumption. The most significant result of these disputes, and the most conclusive evidence proving the lack of the existence of any seamlessly unified "black church" during this era, was the birth of the African American Holiness movement in the Delta during the late 1880s. Emerging partly as a popular rejection of Baptist and Methodist churches that many feared had grown too large and worldly, it strove to recapture an idealized version of the simplicity and intimacy of the early Christian church. I analyze the evolution of the three Delta churches during the late-nineteenth century that initially formed the organizational core of the African American Holiness movement: the Church of the Living God, the Church of God (Holiness), and the Church of God in Christ. Though far smaller than the other black Delta churches, they represent an essential but often neglected dimension of the black religious experience. The Church of God in Christ, more-over, grew rapidly from its Delta origins and became the fastest growing black religious body during the twentieth century.

I base my understanding of black spiritual life in the Delta on a series of interlocking historical and literary sources. Some are familiar to scholars but can be seen in a different light when interrogated for evidence about rural black religion. Others are less well known yet critical in answering the question of how African American religion developed during the post-Reconstruction period. All remind us that we should speak of this period as the nadir of black cultural achievement with irony; it is the inattention to sources by scholars that has been the chief reason for this interpretation.[37]

African American newspapers remain the best source for the history of black religion in the Delta and, more generally, the South during this era. These public records are a thick, multilayered, and much understudied resource. I read every surviving black newspaper published in the Delta between 1870 and 1916 and many from outside of its boundaries but which enjoyed a strong readership there. The best preserved and most complete were the denominational newspapers, probably because members were required or at least strongly encouraged to buy them. Of these the most useful were *The Southwestern Christian Advocate,* the voice of the black church embedded within the Methodist Episcopal Church, begun in 1876 in New Orleans, Louisiana; *The Christian Index,* the official organ of the Christian Methodist Episcopal Church, begun in 1868, and published in two Tennessee cities, first

Memphis and then Jackson; and *The Baptist Vanguard,* the newspaper of the Arkansas Baptists, founded in 1884 and printed in Little Rock. Each was predominantly a small regional newspaper that included the Delta as a target area of coverage and distribution. Also invaluable was the *Christian Recorder,* published by the African Methodist Episcopal Church continuously since 1854 in Philadelphia, Pennsylvania. The *Christian Recorder* was national in scope but devoted significant attention to its southern churches. It was the only AME newspaper that served the Delta.

These black denominational newspapers, which were typically published weekly or biweekly, catalogued a variegated cross section of rural black life. In addition to reports about regional and national politics, they printed short stories and poems by local authors, train schedules, crime reports, pictures of ministers and churches, land sales, the fluctuating price of cotton, corn, and mules, and advertisements for clothing, Bibles, church bells, and sewing machines. Particularly valuable was the "Letters to the Editor" section, found in every newspaper, which effectively functioned as a site of printed public testimony. It was not uncommon for an issue to feature a dozen letters to the editors, which ranged in size from a twenty-word blurb to a four-column missive and usually included the name and address of the author. This form of historical record, of course, is not without its problems. Editors certainly censored the letters that landed on their desks, weeding out those broadcasting harsh sentiments about their denomination or inflammatory appeals that might excite white supremacists, such as a public call for blacks to seek physical retribution after a public lynching. But beyond these obvious cases, the editors had little reason to limit what they published.

The letters to the editor remind us that, in the rural Delta, a large part of the public dimension to religion was epistolary. Indeed, many isolated church communities had a main existence in the form of letters: people isolated by geographic distance knew each other's travails, values, fears, and wishes through their writings.[38] In print, preachers detailed the topic and content of their sermons, the look and decoration of their churches, the size and history of their congregations, and the reasons members were disciplined. Likewise, male and female congregants described their hopes and dreams, what they read, how they spent their money, what social issues demanded their attention, and what they thought about their church. These letters, then, represented a type of black print-culture that facilitated the task of nurturing religious and racial identity across the region.

In addition to black newspapers, I relied heavily on the published ex-slave interviews conducted between 1934 and 1936 as part of the New Deal's Works Project Administration (WPA).[39] Though commonly used in slave studies, these interviews, when read carefully, also offer insights into black life during the generations after the Civil War. They present challenges of reliability and accuracy, of course, especially on the issues of how honestly and accurately former bonds people recalled aspects of their lives while being questioned by someone who was usually a white male stranger. It was a problem captured pithily by David Cohn in his book about growing up as the son of a white merchant from the Delta town of Greenville, Mississippi, during the late 1800s. Cohn remembered blacks "practicing the language of caution and secretiveness in the presence of the white man."[40] Yet fortunately this interpretative issue and others raised by scholars about the trustworthiness of the WPA interviews—the racial biases of the interviewer, the lack of a universal training for interviewers, the absence of a consistent methodology, the possibility of transcription errors[41]—are less serious in the case of many of the interviews of African Americans from the Arkansas Delta. Two Arkansas interviewers, Samuel Taylor and Pernella Anderson, were black, a rarity among any state's team of workers. Taylor conducted nearly one-quarter of all of the state's interviewers and was reportedly the best interviewer in the entire federal project. Irene Robinson, a white woman, performed 286 of the 696 total interviews for Arkansas, making her the most prolific WPA interviewer in the country. Their sustained experience arguably produced more consistent interviewing techniques and trustworthy transcripts.[42]

More important for this book, though, were the hundreds of unpublished WPA investigations and interviews conducted specifically to gain information about black religious life in Arkansas. These records still exist in their original form, only now yellowed and crinkled with age. They are a collection of handwritten and typed transcripts of interviews with black preachers and congregants from Arkansas, many of who lived in the Delta. Conducted during the mid-1930s, the interviews— loosely organized by denomination, usually unedited—are remarkable in their intimate detail about churches. Some contained lengthy church histories, rough architectural sketches, maps, lists of wall hangings and modern amenities, and membership rolls. Others included brief biographical accounts of important congregants. When viewed collectively, they open a rare window onto the organizational and visual culture of black religion in the Delta.[43]

Black autobiographies make up the third main body of sources for this project. The growth of the black denominational and secular presses in the 1870 and 1880s created new opportunities for the publication of books, tracts, pamphlets, and articles detailing the life of prominent ministers, businessmen, politicians, fraternal leaders, and, occasionally, women. Newspapers also published short autobiographical vignettes of black preachers and politicians. Yet as a genre of self-representation, these narratives are by definition incomplete because they typically tell only of those who rose far above the poverty, violence, and segregation of the Delta at a time when few did. They are also scrubbed clean of any element of luck or patronage and leave the false impression that local fame and fortune was readily available to any one willing to work hard, save, shun temptation, and believe in God. Despite their lack of widespread representativeness, though, these autobiographies can still instruct us about pathways of upward mobility and structures of community organization in the Delta. To avoid viewing them transparently, I have read them in conjunction with travel accounts produced by visitors to the Delta, articles published by black journalists, letters to the editors printed in black newspapers, WPA interviews, and visual images. By situating the narratives in a comparative context, I have been able to clarify the accuracy of the history they represent.

Finally, I have used early recordings of black musical culture and oral expression to evoke the religious lives of Delta blacks. The field shouts, work hollers, chants, hymns, and early blues music, of course, contain their own interpretative challenges. Most recordings in the Delta and the South as a whole occurred after 1910 and did not always identify the performers or their homes. The earliest observers and recorders, most of whom were white but not southern, also tended to transcribe lyrics by attempting to replicate precisely what they heard. The result, particularly when they strove to reproduce unfamiliar local dialects, was sometimes a jumble of words and literary images difficult to decipher. In light of these problems, I have restricted my use of recordings to those that clearly label the performer, his home, and the date of production. When the lyrics are unclear, I study them in tandem with other recordings by the same performer or by a contemporary in an effort, usually successful, to decode them as accurately as possible.

The discursive nature of these different types of sources was both a blessing and a curse when I sat down to write up my research. It made it difficult to build a traditional historical narrative along conventional plot lines, such as political or economic change. Yet at the same time it invited a focus on the daily experience of social and religious change in the Delta that ultimately helped to shine a light on hidden or little glimpsed acts of community formation and statements of theological novelty. As a result, *After Redemption* is not a straightforward story of "change over time" that opens in 1875 and marches steadily forward to 1915. Instead, it is arranged as a series of overlapping historical investigations into how Delta blacks struggled day by day with the shifting meanings of religion and freedom as they experienced the growth of Jim Crow. In some chapters, Delta blacks labor to adapt to new technologies sweeping the area. In others, they test how to build religious communities and how to define the place of the consumer market in their lives. And in others, they fight bitterly over the legitimacy of religious rituals and doctrines. What unite the chapters is the relentless efforts of these rural African Americans, through their spiritual lives, to conceptualize, transform, assimilate, or reject the history to which they were sadly joined.

After Redemption opens with the interplay of black religion and modern technology. The first chapter studies how Delta blacks confronted the rapid growth of the railroad as the one of the most important and visible engines of economic progress and racial segregation in the region. It shows how they integrated the sensory experience of traveling by rail into their spiritual lives and created new words, visions, songs, and sermons based upon it; converted forsaken depots into houses of worship and waiting platforms into revival stages; and took advantage of train travel to organize regional gatherings of individual churches and spread news and gossip about leaders and movements. By popularizing railroad travel as a metaphor for African American freedom, Delta blacks eventually refigured its symbolism as a vehicle of racial restriction.

Chapter two explores how blacks expanded the organizational basis of their religion during the late 1800s by integrating dimensions of African American fraternal culture into their spiritual lives. Thousands of Delta black men joined the Masons, Odd Fellows, and Knights of Pythias in order to tap into their health and burial insurances, employment opportunities, social functions, and ritual life. The popularity of these groups, however, angered many churchgoers. Black women complained that fraternal orders represented a new black civic culture open only to men. Many clerics feared a loss of financial support and moral authority as their male congregants devoted much of their time and money to local fraternal orders. Conflict died down by 1900, though, as fraternal leaders openly stressed subservience to churches in spiritual matters and some lodges fell into financial ruin. But churches changed, too. In a bid to boost their popular appeal, churches began to incorporate the most salient and attractive features of fraternal life, such as life and burial insurance, while most women and preachers grudgingly accepted the role of lodges as a new and legitimate source of African American religious life.

The slow emergence of consumer capitalism in the post-Reconstruction South, as chapter three analyzes, went hand-in-hand with the evolution of black religion. As the growth of the railroad made possible the rapid flow of commodities between urban and rural areas and the South and the North, and as fraternal culture stressed the ritual and racial importance of wearing uniforms and dressing properly, blacks increasingly relied on the market to construct fresh expressions of sacred and racial identity. They turned to it to raise money for their churches, schools, and newspapers and to expand their access to consumer goods. Some preachers began to serve as peddlers to their congregations, advertising and selling domestic consumer goods produced by northern white manufacturers and netting a small commission every time they sold a bolt of cloth, a set of tableware, a pair of shoes, a stove, a bike, or an organ. Religious newspapers counseled readers on what to buy and where to buy it. The effect was to change the character of relationship between the consumer market and black religion in the South: consumer capitalism spread to blacks partly through their own networks of religious leaders and institutions and, in turn, black Baptists and Methodists integrated the language and practices of the market more directly into their spiritual lives.

As religion and the consumer market intertwined in the Delta, Baptists, and Methodists developed a rich material culture of religious experience. As seen in chapter four, the purchase and display of certain types of consumer goods became crucial elements of new ideas about respectability, domesticity, and the "black Christian home." They also shaped a new aesthetic of personal and corporate consumption. Congregants purchased staid clothes, lithographs of church leaders, and religious wall hangings of black leaders to model self-restraint and racial pride. Preachers symbolized progress by purchasing drapes, upholstered altar chairs, pipe organs, and electric chandeliers for their houses of worship. Central to these new consumer and spiritual practices was the shifting association between politics, black women, and black churches. As disfranchisement laws expelled all blacks from the political arenas, Baptist and Methodist churches tightened their rules of excluding women from traditional positions of leadership, and fraternal orders evolved as new centers of community affairs run only by men, women, in an attempt to capture a new measure of social authority, defined themselves as the curators of home decoration. With the support of male clerics, they openly championed themselves as the market's arbiters of public taste and domestic consumption.

During the 1890s, growing numbers of black congregants found distasteful and even sacrilegious a number of the new facets to black religion, including the important role that fraternal orders played in churches, the sight of ministers hawking market wares in person and in print, the popular stress on worldly goods as a sign of spiritual worth and success, and the marginalization of women from many traditional roles of religious authority. They profoundly disagreed with other recent changes to religion in the Delta, too, such as efforts by younger Baptist and Methodists leaders to strip worship practices of any vestiges of "slave religion," by which they meant spontaneous singing, shouting, and dancing, and uneducated men and women serving as preachers. As chapter five demonstrates, the disenchanted turned to a new breed of religious leader, men such as William Christian, Charles H. Mason, and Charles P. Jones, one-time Baptist ministers from the Delta who preached the need for blacks to recapture the spirit of early Christianity. Each was a founding father of the African American Holiness movement and criticized black denominational churches as too materialistic, rational, and hostile to ecstatic dimensions of worship and divine inspiration. Yet within twenty years of its founding, the Holiness leaders, ironically, embraced some of the very denominational practices they had previously castigated, revealing not only the limits to their calls for religious reform but also some of the modern characteristics of Delta black religion as a whole.

African Americans who made their home in the Delta during the late nineteenth and early twentieth centuries were forced to confront the boundaries of citizenship in the post-Reconstruction South. Living in a wilderness littered with broken promises and scattered dreams, many wondered how far they had really traveled since slavery. To a degree unrivaled in most southern communities, the laws and customs of segregation in the Delta resurrected the memory of slavery in painful detail, lynchings mocked any pretense of civil liberty, and unsteady crop prices and unreliable access to financial credit cut short ambitions for long-term economic self-sufficiency. But here, too, blacks transformed their spiritual lives, formulating new ideological and institutional resources that braced community life against the pressures of Jim Crow. These developments collectively form the heart of a crucial episode in African American religion and southern history that bridges Reconstruction with the Great Migration. They reveal the period to be one of unexpected novelty, when blacks integrated sacred life with many of the defining features of life in the New South and limited the power of white supremacy to sculpt African American culture according to its racist imperatives. In laying bare how Delta blacks strove relentlessly to recapture the democratic promise of the nation, despite being persistently and violently excluded from it, they remind us as well of both the heroic and tragic character of the era.

I

Train Travel and the
Black Religious Imagination

I saw a pretty white train coming like lightening. I looked and saw myself on the train. I don't know how I got on, but when that train passed through, I was on it. God shows me these things to let me know that he is well pleased with me.

—*Mama, "Slavery Was Hell without Fires," in* God Struck Me Dead:
Religious Conversion Experiences and Autobiographies of Ex-Slaves,
ed. Clifton H. Johnson, pp. 162–163, 167

———◦———

The railroad always enchanted Ruby Hicks. As a young white girl living in the heart of the Mississippi Delta in the 1890s and 1900s, she believed that the Yazoo and Mississippi Valley Railroad (Y. & M.V.R.R) was omnipresent. In her autobiography, she recalled that "[e]very depot, train engine, coal car, box car, baggage car, passenger coach and caboose, railroad crossing and cattle gap bore the sign, Y. & M.V.R.R. Every store and [cotton] gin in those little towns displayed that sign. . . ." She loved to watch and study the faces of "people getting off and others boarding the train; people going places; and people just waiting to see the train come in at Winona, Greenwood, and Moorhead." Even when she couldn't see the train, she could still hear it and be magically transported by it. "[G]rowing up, I listened to its whistle and dreamed of places far away." The rapid development of the railroad in the Delta transformed Hick's sleepy community into a local center of commerce and logging and injected it with a new level of worldliness and excitement.[1] For her, the railroad's emergence as a common visual and aural feature of life in the post-Reconstruction era was thrilling, wondrous, and unequivocally positive.[2]

Hick's black neighbors in the Delta shared much of her wide-eyed fascination with the railroad. They frequently greeted their first glimpse of a train with great anticipation. The day one finally passed near to his rented plot of land in Crittenden County, in the middle of the Arkansas Delta, ex-slave Mose [*sic*] Banks made sure that he was there to see it. He rode all day to catch a glimpse of it and, when he finally pulled up to the track, breathless, joined a throng of excited farmers and sharecroppers. No one was disappointed when the train came. "It was a great show to me and we all had something to talk about for a long time. People all around went to see it and we camped out one night going and coming and camped one night at the railroad as we could see the train the next day."[3]

Banks, like white residents of the Delta, thrilled at the sight of a train because it symbolized raw physical power and man's technological prowess. It offered the chance to migrate to new areas of opportunity, proselytize and distribute religious literature in distant counties, and hope for better markets for goods, services, and employment. "We are to have a new railroad" in our county, boasted one group of black Arkansas sharecroppers in the early 1890s, "and, of course, we are all glad, because we think of cheaper coal, horse feed, etc."[4] As railroad lines expanded into new counties, they usually offered jobs to whites and blacks that, while menial and backbreaking, often paid better than many found on a farm.[5]

Delta blacks, however, marveled at the railroad for reasons all their own. It promised a fresh start to locate friends and loved ones uprooted during slavery or the Civil War. It linked them directly to distant regions of the country and, during times of heightened racial violence, sustained hopes of fleeing the Delta.[6] More significantly, the ability to board a train and travel to a destination of one's own choosing was a significant act of liberty for a people only recently emancipated and still subject to laws crafted to limit their mobility.[7] At the turn of the century, Arkansas legislators voted to punish black "vagrants" by imprisoning them from thirty to ninety days, fining them between five and thirty dollars, and forcing them to work on public roads.[8] Mississippi lawmakers similarly authorized sheriffs to roundup suspected vagrants and jail them. White planters in both states tried to chain black agricultural workers to their land by strictly regulating the use of farm animals, especially mules.[9] As a result, blacks riding their first train often experienced a heady sense of mastery over the world around them. In 1890, Reverend I. H. Anderson, a minister with the CME Church and an editor of its denominational newspaper, the *Christian Index,* chronicled his inaugural trip over the rails. As the train sped across the landscape, Anderson, traveling with other first-time black passengers, enthusiastically reported that "we would look around and [each] felt for once that I am monarch of all I survey. . . ."[10]

Delta blacks viewed the growth of the railroad with greater suspicion and alarm than most whites, as well. The railroad was one of the region's most important and universal emblems of change, of course, but also of unsettling continuity with the slave past. While its development announced a new era of economic modernization and black mobility, this was accompanied by a perpetuation of racial caste. As railroad workers, blacks were restricted to the ranks of fireman, brakemen, porters, redcaps, waiters, and the crews that laid ties, performed track maintenance, and cleaned and repaired locomotives and boilers. They were barred from applying for the best-paying jobs, serving as engineers and conductors, and joining railroad unions. As passengers, they routinely faced the threat of being harassed, bludgeoned, shot, or lynched because of their skin color. Black women who rode the rails commonly confronted the added burden of sexual advances and assaults by white men. And if they traveled alone they also endured criticism from ministers and fellow congregants for the danger and impropriety of their behavior. By the 1890s, the courts forced all black travelers to use waiting rooms, toilets, and cars that were separate from and vastly inferior to those enjoyed by whites. Even if they purchased first-class tickets, black riders journeyed in the baggage car, the smokers' car, or the back section of a sleeper car.[11] "There is not in the world a more disgraceful denial of human brotherhood," grimly submitted W. E. B. Du Bois writing in 1921 on the topic of black life after Reconstruction, "than the 'Jim Crow' car of the southern United States."[12] As Du Bois intimated, the train powerfully shaped and symbolized the public limits of black liberty and democracy during the late nineteenth and early twentieth centuries.

Not surprisingly, then, the cultural meaning of the railroad as a vehicle of religious and racial deliverance among Delta blacks was always ambiguous and in flux. During slavery, trains were not a major part of their religion or politics largely because the railroad industry was small. Individual companies struggled to survive and many fell into ruin. To be sure, slaves occasionally portrayed escaping to freedom as a train ride and at times literally did so, by stealing away on the Underground Railroad. But such representations and experiences were far from universal. The story of the railroad's limited presence in black life was much the same immediately after the end of slavery. The Civil War devastated southern railroads. Few companies emerged intact; none were financially strong. Entrepreneurs built new lines during Reconstruction, but they were typically small, poorly run, and prone to failure. Freed people sometimes worshiped in abandoned boxcars and a few black missionaries proselytized among black railroad workers. But in general the relationship between the railroad and African American spiritual life after emancipation was minimal until the mid-1880s, when it began to change dramatically.

Triggering the shift was a series of economic and political events: northern investors purchased and successfully propped up flagging southern railroads, southern politicians declared the expansion of the railroad as the key to the economic rebirth of the region, and jurists legalized the segregation of train passengers by race. As the pace of railroad construction quickened and many lines became profitable, trains became a common feature of urban and rural landscapes and an important arena for the enactment of racial hierarchy. As a result, the representation of the railroad among blacks gathered in complexity and public visibility and ultimately developed as a modern crossroads where black hopes and ambitions for a better life intersected with social customs and legislation that would constrain them.

Beginning in the late 1890s, for example, Delta blacks hosted prayer meetings at depots and depicted individual spiritual journeys as train journeys. They evangelized and constructed new churches near railroad stations. And they experienced private moments of religious conversion and fantasies of racial freedom while taking the train or envisioning doing so. These new practices and rituals, in turn, contradicted the popular wish among white Southerners that the railroad represented an instrument of modernity that would reinscribe racial hierarchy onto black-white interactions and provide lasting relief from the cultural tensions swirling around the question of how the races would live together in the post-Reconstruction South. Eventually many Delta blacks embedded the train into stylized versions of the biblical narrative of the Exodus, in which the train was the contemporary vehicle carrying them to the Promised Land. Tens of thousands would take these literary and religious uses of the railroad a step further during the 1910s and 1920s and physically board trains bound for cities like Chicago and St. Louis in what they prayed was a journey to greater freedom.

Making a case for the peculiar nature of the historical connection between the railroad and southern black religion, however, may seem a bit of a stretch at first glance. Indeed, it is tempting to view rural black Protestants in the Delta as reacting similarly to the growth of the railroad as white Protestants. Both groups developed the theme of the "spiritual railroad," or the representation of an individual's earthly life as a train trip ending at either heaven or hell, in a range of literary and musical settings. They sang versions of the same songs, such as "The Gospel Train Is Coming" and "This Train." Both races employed identical images to symbolize being saved, such as a train whisking the faithful to heaven or the purchase of a special ticket on a train bound for God's kingdom. And poor blacks and whites alike interpreted the phrase "taking the train to heaven" to include being liberated from the shackles of poverty.[13]

Still, important differences existed that bear witness to the particular ways that African Americans imagined and experienced train travel. These differences help make it possible to think of the railroad as operating in distinctive ways in the evolution of black spiritual life after Reconstruction. During the late 1800s, many white farmers lobbied to force railroads to regulate their rates and pay more taxes. They perceived unresponsive railroad executives as emblems of corporate greed and monopolistic power.[14] Yet this political quality was far less prevalent among blacks in the Delta, possibly because of their declining faith in large-scale white-run organizations, be they a government or a private company, to ever treat them fairly. Promotional literature published by railroad companies regularly depicted modern travel as a setting where the values of Victorian gentility flourished. White gentlemen and ladies who rode the rails enjoyed many of the same luxuries and conveniences of a fine home, including private dining areas, sumptuous meals, richly upholstered reading chairs, sleeper beds with linen sheets, and a trusty uniformed black porter. White popular culture also added the portrayal of white women as incapable of navigating the rails alone and easily seduced by charming commercial salesmen.[15] In contrast, most blacks were forbidden to enjoy the amenities and services featured on many passenger trains. Black female passengers were constantly on the lookout for lechers and predators among the ranks of white male riders and workers. The most significant dissimilarity, though, was symbolic. Even if black and whites chanted the same tune and told the same story about the railroad, African Americans typically infused their lyrics, images, memories, and rhythms with specific meanings that fit their own particular historical experience with segregation. When blacks sang of or imagined a conversion experience as going to heaven on a train, they understood the train as a vehicle of both spiritual and racial transformation bringing them to a time and place where salvation included an end to racism.

The African American appropriation of train travel to frame expressions of racial and religious deliverance began during slavery, where it developed slowly and unevenly. Bonds people sometimes invoked the train as a means of liberation in their spirituals, despite the small scale of the railroad industry.[16] Most famously, "Git on Board, Little Children" urged listeners to prepare for the heaven-bound "Gospel Train," where the fare was cheap and no distinction drawn between first- and second-class passengers. The only requirement for passage was a strong and steady faith. As slaves sang in the chorus and verses two and three:

> Git on board, little children
> Git on board, little children
> Git on board, little children
> Dere's room for many a more.
> De Gospel train's a comin,'I hear it jus' at han'
> I hear de car wheels rumblin,'An rollin' thro' de lan'
> De fare is chap an' all can go, De rich an' poor are dere
> No second class a board dis train, No difference in the fare.[17]

Slaves also married the idea of riding a train to personal freedom in their stories about the Underground Railroad or, if they were lucky enough, through their experience of actually taking it. Hundreds of slaves, mostly from the Border States, escaped their masters by following "conductors" such as Harriet Tubman who escorted them to "stations" plotted along secret routes toward freedom in northern cities and Canada.[18] Black and white abolitionists sometimes struck their antislavery message by representing the drive toward emancipation as a train ride. For example, the 1844 cover illustration of the sheet music to the popular antislavery ballad "Get off the Track!" prominently featured a locomotive whose wheel cover bore the title "Liberator," a reference to the abolitionist newspaper founded in 1831 by William Lloyd Garrison, and a passenger car emblazoned with the movement's war cry of "Immediate Emancipation." Its lyrics reinforced the notion of the railroad as a symbol of racial deliverance. As verse seven read:

> All True Friends of Emancipation
> Haste to Freedom's Rail Road Station
> Quick into the Cars get seated
> All is ready, and completed
> Put on the Steam! All are crying
> And the Liberty Flag Flying.[19]

Most slaves, though, did not draw a strong association between the railroad and emancipation. More commonly they linked trains with white power and social dominance, as exemplified in the case of wealthy white Arkansan John Dockery, who owned the Mississippi, Red River, and Ouachita Railroad. He publicized his financial and racial status in extravagant and rather grotesque fashion, by naming each of the quadruplets born to one of his slaves in the late 1850s after a section of his company's title. Accordingly, he called the first child "Mississippi," the second "Red River," the third "Ouachita," and the fourth "Railroad."[20]

Immediately after slavery, the popularization of the railroad as a source of imagery and inspiration in African American religion in the Delta continued to be haphazard, though now the main reason was that trains were simply too scarce to be a major part of white or black culture. The Civil War had ruined over half of the South's railroad. Damage estimates ran as high as twenty-eight billion dollars. Few terminal facilities, shops, or passenger stations remained standing. The main route connecting farmers in northern Mississippi to the markets of Memphis was nearly completely destroyed. In the Arkansas Delta, no line tied the major towns and cities to regional commercial centers.[21] People traveling from Little Rock to Memphis took a combination of stagecoach, riverboat, and train in a trip that collectively lasted up to thirty-two hours. The time decreased only marginally when the area's first railroad, the Memphis and Little Rock, opened in 1871.[22]

The slow pace of rebuilding the South's railroads after the Civil War reflected the shortsightedness of railroad executives, high operating costs, and national economic tensions. Striving to be frugal, railroad leaders frequently attempted to restore crippled lines by ordering workers first to smooth and straighten twisted tracks and then relay them. These repairs were speedy but hazardous; even as total track mileage neared prewar levels in the South by 1870, cars running on warped rails often spun off the tracks. Fares were expensive, too. Passengers paid six to ten cents per mile shortly after the war and only slightly less, four or five cents per mile, by 1870. Southern farmers shipped their crops at a cost of four to five cents per ton-mile, a rate that was two to three times higher than what northerners paid. During the financial depression that lasted from 1873 to 1877, many southern railroads funded by publicly issued bonds failed to meet interest payments and collapsed. By 1876 nearly 43 percent of all southern railroads were in default or receivership and about 33 percent of all southern track miles were in the possession of the courts due to foreclosure proceedings. New construction practically stopped; in 1875, only fifty miles of new track were laid in the entire South, none of them in Mississippi or Arkansas.[23]

As in the South as a whole during the fifteen years after the Civil War, railroads developed slowly in the Delta. By 1880 there were only two lines operating in the Mississippi Delta: the thirty-nine mile Mobile and Northwestern, which curved across the northern counties; and the Greenville, Columbus, and Birmingham Railroad, which ran thirty-one miles on narrow-gauge tracks east from Greenville to Johnsonville. Opened in 1877, this line was infamous for its rough ride and workers' blatant disregard for punctuality. Cars pitched and lurched with such force that passengers frequently took ill. Travelers were never quite sure when they might arrive at their destination because the crews often made unannounced stops to collect firewood for the engine and water to cool it.[24] Similarly, by 1880 only two main lines operated in the Arkansas Delta: the Cairo and Fulton traversed its northwestern counties as cars ran from St. Louis, Missouri to Texarkana, Texas, while the Memphis and Little Rock cut through its interior counties.[25] Riders on the Memphis and Little Rock sometimes feared for their lives. Catholic missionary Father Peter Benoit sensed his trip would be harrowing because, as he left the station in Memphis, "[o]ne of the Dominican Fathers in bidding me good-bye wished me with much emphasis a *safe* journey. . . ." His intuition was correct. As Benoit recorded in his diary, some of "[t]he railroad is constructed for 40 miles on a swampy ground, which as it is now, is frequently under water, while the ground 10 miles higher is quite safe. The train has to advance very slowly over the uneven rails & even so the rocking is such that these w[oul]d be no great wonder if the whole train rocked itself into the water."[26]

The difficulties in establishing widespread, dependable rail transportation during this period temporarily preserved riverboats as the preferred mode of conveyance in the Delta and especially in its interior counties. As they had during the antebellum era, steamboats and larger flat-bottomed watercrafts trafficked the Mississippi River while rafts, keel boats, and skiffs moved men and materials across the hundreds of smaller rivers, creeks, lakes, and bayous that veined the region. Fierce competition between riverboat companies historically kept freight rates down and ensured that bigger towns and plantations near a large body of water received regular visits. In the 1870s, Pine Bluff enjoyed biweekly service up the Arkansas River to Little Rock and weekly service for the longer run to Memphis. Several years later the Anchor Steamboat Line began to shuttle freight and passengers between the Arkansas ports lining the Mississippi River. Water transportation in general, however, was far from reliable. Nature tended to render smaller waterways impassable during the autumn harvest, just when river transport was most urgently needed. As summer waned and water levels dropped, overturned trees and partially submerged logs left behind by the annual spring floods made riverboat passage all but impossible. Exacerbated planters found themselves with crops ready for the market but with no way to get them there. They were forced to wait for new rain or to travel overland to the nearest town on the Mississippi River, where riverboat transportation was more consistent.[27]

The early failures of the railroad during Reconstruction and the unpredictability of transportation by watercraft did surprisingly little to focus public effort on improving the conditions of local roads and thoroughfares in the Delta. Overland travel remained much as it was before the Civil War. Wagons drawn by horses or oxen followed the edges of rivers and bayous on slender dirt roads that were hard and cracked in the summer and slushy in the winter. Drivers seeking to cross a river occasionally benefited from a manually operated ferry, though mishaps were frequent. They traversed swamps and bogs only by hewing to one of the few man-made pathways, jerry-built of wooden slabs, cross-lays, and low rickety bridges, which sometimes stretched for miles.[28]

The financial struggle of railroad companies in the Delta from 1865 to the mid-1880s, not unexpectedly, constrained any widespread evolution of trains and train travel as major factors shaping the development of black religion. Water travel, however, never captured the black religious imagination during these years. A key reason was the general resistance to organized religion displayed by most African American river workers. They tended to be hard drinkers, poker players, brawlers, and skirt chasers who mocked preachers and rarely set foot in a church.[29] The industry of water transportation, moreover, never became central to the state of race relations.

Even though few African Americans described their dreams of success and liberty by invoking images of the railroad at this time, many still sought to profit from the economic misfortunes plaguing lines, especially when making decision about where to worship and proselytize. Cash-starved black congregants often converted discarded train cars and deserted depots into churches. Members of the Macedonia Baptist Church who lived in rural outskirts of Little Rock, for instance, held their first service as a congregation in a forsaken railroad shop in 1883.[30] W. E. B. Du Bois noted that this habit was widespread among black southerners in his broad survey of their spiritual life, which he conducted during the late 1800s. He wrote that "when the colored people were in their bitter struggle for the necessities of life . . . the race worshiped in box cars frequently, for they could not always obtain houses."[31] Ambitious missionaries also kept a close eye on the growth of local railroads. They anticipated that the construction of a new terminus or depot, even if it eventually failed, would at least initially draw blacks looking for work and who would need a new place to worship. In 1876, Reverend Andrew Williams of Little Rock based his decision about where to start a new church on a discussion with a group of black railroad workers. He learned about nearby Coal Hill, which "was soon to be a division point on the railway[.] It was already a proven coal field, surrounded by rich agricultural and horticultural lands. These glowing prospects convinced the enterprising young negro minister that Coal Hill was eutopia [sic]." Williams moved to there and founded the Bethel AME church.[32]

The railroad industry played a more important role in religious lives of Delta blacks beginning in the mid-1880s, when it developed a dense network of trains, tracks, and terminals that reshaped local transportation, politics, and economics. The pace of railroad growth accelerated at this time due to several factors. First, most of the white Democrats who dominated southern governments by 1880 believed that renewed financial prosperity for their states depended on the rapid construction of a modern railroad. They followed the lead of the railroad's biggest booster in the South, Henry Grady, the white editor of the *Atlanta Constitution*. In print and on the stump, Grady tirelessly promoted a vision of regional economic rebirth that literally saw the locomotive as the engine of change. He argued that the South desperately needed a state-of-the-art transportation infrastructure based on an expanded railroad in order to improve its manufacturing capacity and successfully compete with the industrial North. With the backing of powerful Democrats, he convinced many northern capitalists to invest heavily in southern railroad companies; by 1881, according to his own calculations, six northern firms had already invested $100 million dollars.[33]

While white politicians tied the future of the South to the growth of an improved nexus of rail transportation, railroad executives scrambled to learn from the Panic of 1873 and develop more efficient corporations. Seeking to bolster the financial strength of the industry as a whole by consolidating its resources, they incorporated local lines into regional and national networks, shifted to standard time in 1883, and conformed their tracks to the national standard gauge at four feet, eight and one-half inches in 1886—a massive task that meant refitting nearly 80 percent of all southern rail miles. At the same time, northern investors purchased many of the failed southern railroads and radically changed them. They laid track at a record clip, standardized freight rates, shared cars and terminal facilities, built new bridges, and replaced old iron rails with superior steel track. As a result, southern railroads nearly doubled their total track mileage during the 1880s and nearly 90 percent of all Southerners lived in a county with a railroad stop by 1890.[34]

Along with the rest of the South, the state of the railroad in the Delta greatly improved beginning in the 1880s. One key to local success was the building of a new system of levees and drainage basins in Mississippi and Arkansas. Funded by federal and state government during the late 1800s and early 1900s, these public works projects lined the Mississippi River and other major rivers in each state and greatly limited the perennial destruction to railroads and agriculture caused by flooding.[35] Their construction eventually banished much of the popular fear of death and economic ruin that rushed over the area with the rise and fall of the annual spring waters. Ruby Sheppard Hicks wrote of the general sense of alarm that gripped Delta residents during the annual flood season. "I so well remember the uneasiness in the spring as the northern snows began to melt and rains continued to fall in the South. As the water receded after a flood, that black land dried into crevices that were filled with dead snakes, frogs, snails, worms, tadpoles, leaches and a thousand other germ-producing flotsam. Many brave men looked at the devastation and moved back to the hills or westward with the sun."[36]

With the advent of the levees, sustained railroad growth suddenly became more viable. Local politicians and planters now eagerly backed plans to build new lines in the hopes of bettering their transportation system and freeing themselves of dependency on watercraft. Joining them was a new type of railroad booster, the commercial logger. Drawn in the late 1880s to the Delta by stories of rich and plentiful forests, he demanded bigger and better railroads as a dependable way of shipping felled trees to mills and markets.[37]

In the Mississippi Delta specifically, another crucial step in the evolution of the railroad occurred when California capitalist Colis P. Huntington purchased huge swaths of land and built a north-south line that connected Memphis to Vicksburg in 1882 and then to New Orleans in 1884. This line, the Louisville, New Orleans, and Texas (LNO & T), steadily built branches or "dummy lines" to most plantations. As the LNO & T became profitable in the late 1880s, however, it attracted attention from its major competitor, the Illinois Central. Already owning a continuous line that linked Chicago and New Orleans and traversed the central counties of Mississippi, the Illinois

Central now set it sights on purchasing the LNO & T and creating a monopoly on major north-south lines running through the entire state. In 1892, Huntington, in need of cash to cover a series of investment losses, sold the LNO & T to the Illinois Central, which promptly renamed it the Yazoo & Mississippi Valley Railroad.[38]

As in the Mississippi Delta, northern businessmen played a vital role in spurring railroad growth in the Arkansas Delta. The St. Louis and Southwestern Railroad, which ran from St. Louis through the eastern and southern part of Arkansas and to Texas, was placed in receivership twice during the 1880s. Then northern investors bought it and made it one of the area's most important railroads. It operated the vital "Cotton Belt" that connected plantations in Clay County to Pine Bluff and provided branches into Little Rock. More significantly, the Missouri Pacific Railroad Company opened two lines that provided direct shipping routes between Little Rock, Helena, and many of the towns and plantations lining the Mississippi River in the southeastern half of the Arkansas Delta.[39]

Between 1875 and 1900, railroad executives successfully webbed the Delta in new track (maps 1.1, 1.2). They changed the nature of life in the Delta by transforming their industry into a dominant economic and political force and establishing train transport as ever-more reliable, economical, and extensive. Shipping costs now dropped dramatically, effectively ending the use of boats to move crops between markets by waterways, with the exception of the large steamers that continued to ply the Mississippi River. Passenger fares decreased, too, to about half of what they cost in the 1870s. In a bid to boost the overall number of black travelers, railroad lines regularly permitted black community leaders like ministers to ride at a reduced fare when on official business as well as large groups of blacks traveling to meetings and conventions.[40] New towns and villages sprung up around railroad stations and villages. Official representing the LNO & T, for instance, contracted with black Mississippi entrepreneur Isaiah Montgomery to sell parcels of surplus land in the Delta to his friends and associates. Montgomery eventually purchased 840 acres of land in Bolivar County for himself and with them founded the all-black township, Mound Bayou, in 1887.[41]

Delta blacks reacted quickly to these changes as they constructed religious communities. Most basically, they turned to railroad companies for direct aid in building churches. The sheer size and wealth of some corporations often made them more important than local banks or creditors to black congregations desperate for land and money to build a church. By the turn of the nineteenth century, the Illinois Central Railroad owned more than six hundred thousand acres and was the largest corporation in Mississippi, while the Missouri Pacific and Iron Mountain Railroad owned more than one million acres in Arkansas.[42] It made perfect sense, then, for farmers in Searcy, Arkansas, a small community northeast of Little Rock, to sell a small plot of land to the nearest railroad company in 1897 as a way of financing the cost of a new church.[43]

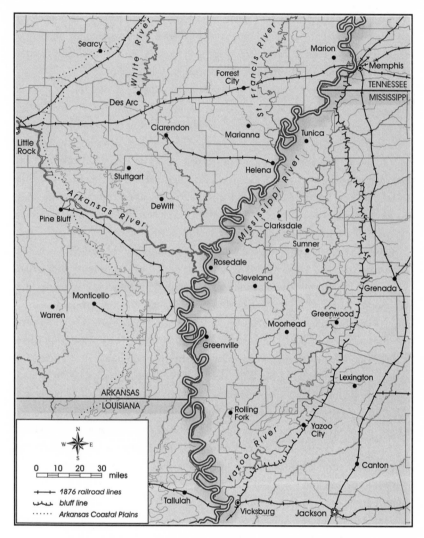

Map 1.1. Railroad in the Delta, 1876

At other times Delta blacks migrated along corridors of railroad expansion. Convinced that prosperity followed the rails, many moved near a new railroad station or crossing juncture; once settled, they founded new churches or relocated old ones closer to them. In the early 1890s black agricultural workers scattered throughout Saline County, Arkansas, heard about the construction of a line connecting the area to Little Rock and the small towns springing up along side of the new route. Many built homes in or near these new communities, seeking employment.

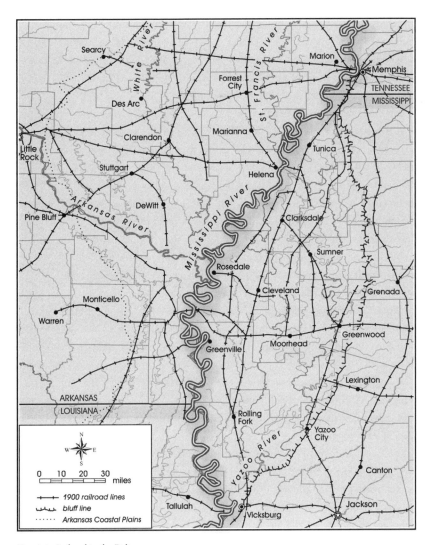

Map 1.2. Railroad in the Delta, 1900

Those who were African Methodist Episcopalian pooled their resources in 1893 and organized a denominational church in Alexander, a town just south of the capitol close to a new railroad depot. Local historians of this church explained the move as an effort "to centralize the location after the R[ail]R[oad] was built, thus causing more of the members to move there."[44]

This pattern of centralizing church communities around a depot or terminal or in a railroad town lessened, though never fully ended, the habit prevalent among blacks living in the most rural parts of the Delta to worship in a different church every Sunday. In areas where great distances separated churches, blacks traditionally had suspended denominational differences and simply attended services at the nearest house of worship that had a preacher on any particular Sunday. This practice of rural ecumenism diminished with the growth of the railroad and was replaced by a new spirit of sectarianism. When Gillett, Arkansas, became a railroad stop in 1895, "Negro workers came along also. [H]aving no place to worship they would congregate in a big barn on one of the farms and have church every Sunday, all together Methodist Baptist & whatever other denomination." But as the number of African Methodist Episcopalians grew, many demanded a separate church. Eventually they built Hay's Chapel AME Church.[45] Still, the habit of ministers serving multiple communities and laypeople attending a different church every week never completely died out. Reverend Ezekiel H. Price took up a Baptist pastorate in the early 1900s in Oak Grove, Mississippi, in Coahoma County. Yet for nearly thirty years he rarely conducted services in the same church in consecutive weekends.[46] Price's sustained itinerancy, though, was increasingly atypical after 1915.

Enterprising missionaries quickly recognized the developing symbiosis between railroad growth, black migration, and church formation. Whereas earlier evangelists like Reverend Andrew Williams had intuitively sensed that the farms and towns surrounding railroad stations were fertile missionary territory, most now widely acknowledged the association by the 1890s. In an article titled "The Southwestern Empire," W. A. Spencer readily identified the railroad as a vital force for reaching not only the unchurched but also the faithful in need of a pastor. "The Missouri Pacific extensions . . . open new sections of rich farming lands to be settled by laborers. . . . Into this field we are pressed by the wants of congregations already organized, some of which have waited a long while [for a preacher]."[47]

Railroad growth, though, was not always a cause for celebration by African Americans or viewed in strictly beneficial terms by them. It frequently sparked tensions within their religious communities. When the local railroad in Kensett, Arkansas, purchased land that it needed to expand, it cared little that a CME church sat on the property and simply expelled the congregation.[48] The lure of well paying railroad jobs broke up families at times. A mother in Arkansas complained that her sons bolted from her and their rented land when "[t]hey heard about the railroad shops and was bound theys [sic] going there to work."[49] A more controversial and pervasive problem was the "excursion" trip, or the inexpensive train ride offered exclusively to blacks by railroad companies. Seeing a way to make additional profits, they ran them usually on Sundays, when most agricultural workers enjoyed a day off and freight and passenger traffic was lightest. Excursion trains, often no more than an open-air platform car, typically ferried Delta blacks between plantations and

Figure 1.1. Excursion Train, Sunnyside Plantation, Sunnyside, Arkansas, circa 1900 (courtesy of the Mississippi Department of Archive and History).

nearby cities for a day of sightseeing, recreation, and visiting with distant relatives (figure 1.1) They were very popular. One of the most heavily traveled routes in the southern counties of the Mississippi Delta was a round-trip from Vicksburg to the state capitol, Jackson.[50]

Predictably, many clerics complained that excursions tempted congregants to ignore God's commandment to "keep holy the Sabbath day." But they also feared that excursions too often turned into debaucheries in which hundreds of blacks crowded into the cars and celebrated boisterously. In 1888 Reverend J. C. Powell, a pastor with a CME church in south Memphis, lambasted the excursions as "where nothing but cursing, swearing, drinking whisky, profaning the day of the Lord in every conceivable way, and sometimes fighting, cursing, and shooting is carried on." Each man and woman who boarded these trains committed an "open and flagrant violation against the laws of the church and God," and Powell openly doubted "the genuineness of that person's conversion."[51] Despite these censures, excursions remained popular and thus a constant irritant for ministers.[52] In 1902, editors at the *Southwestern Christian Advocate* continued to warn readers about "the draft on the moral life of the Negro" caused by the excursion trains, which were "demoralizing to those that participated in them." They begged black Christians to weigh carefully the pleasures of a ride on an excursion train against the temptation to sin faced by so many of the passengers.[53]

To note that the railroad influenced general patterns of evangelization, church growth, and recreation among Delta blacks in the decades following Reconstruction, however, is not to explain why it emerged as a crucial vehicle of their spiritual experience. The answer to that question rests largely in the unusual character of train transportation and its specific relationship to black life. The railroad's dramatic growth in the late 1800s increasingly made the train a regular sight on the physical landscape and train travel a common experience for blacks. And as segregation in public conveyances became the law of the land, the train also became a dominant symbol of blacks' second-class citizenship and a place for coming in contact with it, though in unexpected ways. African American passengers discovered that aboard trains the races mixed and the color line flexed to a degree unrealized in public parks, pools, schools, libraries and restrooms.[54] Despite separate coach laws, south-erners of all types—black and white, male and female, poor and affluent—could never fully avoid the sight, sound, or smell of each other when riding the rails.[55] Once the train departed the depot, it temporarily became a type of self-contained society, where black and white strangers confronted the implications of racial difference in an atmosphere beyond the immediate reach of local authorities. It was this ambiguous, inchoate, and fluid racial quality to train travel that made it so unusual as a public space and so inviting as a modern setting to probe the limits of the color line. Although other forms of public spaces emerged as powerful forces and venues of segregation in the post-Reconstruction South, none at this time rivaled the railroad in popularity or significance as a cultural site where African Americans explored the multiple meanings of racial and religious freedom.

In 1888, the state of Mississippi enacted separate coach laws, which officially divided railroad passengers by race. Modeling its statutes after Mississippi's, Arkan-sas followed three years later.[56] In 1896, the Supreme Court effectively declared the railroad a federally protected location for the public demonstration of racial hier-archy. In the landmark case of *Plessy v. Ferguson,* the Court sided against a group of African Americans from Louisiana seeking to overturn a state law that mandated racial segregation on railroad cars. By a vote of seven to one, the justices rejected the plaintiffs' argument that any citizen who bought a first-class ticket deserved to sit in the first-class car according to the Fourteenth Amendment, which states that "No state shall make or enforce any law which shall abridge the privileges or immunities of citizens of the United States." They affirmed that separation by race was a natural practice necessary to preserve social stability. Blacks enjoyed no legal basis to contest laws of racial division on railway cars, submitted the nation's leading jurists, so long as states provided them with "separate but equal" cars in which to ride.[57]

Yet accommodations for blacks were, of course, very separate and unequal. Southern whites greedily cited local and national court cases to protect and extend their efforts to systematize segregation and through it achieve a new measure of interracial order. They aimed to regulate racial hierarchy by keeping the races apart in every possible space of train travel and making the white "areas" materially superior to the black ones.[58] As a result, whites were served before blacks at the ticket counter. They waited in their own room or cordoned-off area, which was usually much cleaner and better appointed that the one ear-marked for blacks. Before boarding a train in Mississippi, a black newspaper editor protested where he was forced to stand. "I spent two or three hours in the dirtiest, filthiest hole imaginable, called the colored waiting room. There was ample room in the spacious station, but this filthy room, like a pest house, was separated from the main building and devoted to the accommodation of colored people."[59] Matters only worsened when he got on the train. For whether he or any black person purchased first-class tickets or not, they usually sat in the "Negro section." And "[t]he Separate car for colored people," as one black rider complained, "is not in any respect like the one 'for white persons' in appointments. You go up to the same window and pay the same price for a ticket as a white man, but your accommodation is only equal to that provided for stock and baggage."[60] African Americans typically traveled in the baggage car, which, because it was located directly behind the engine, swirled with smoke, soot, sparks, and embers. Or they sat in the smoker car, which was the designated place for men of any color or class to puff cigars, swig whisky, play cards, and rough house. As one black newspaper described it, "[t]he place set apart for Negroes . . . is a little two-by-four pen blocked off f[r]om one end of the smo[k]er, partition[ed] three-fourths of the way up, thereby giving you all the tobacco smoke you wish, four seats, [and] a nasty water cooler. . . ."[61] Curses regularly flew across the room, fights broke out, and money changed hands as drunken white and sometimes black card players settled their scores.[62]

The revulsion felt by black passengers over their inferior treatment and accommodations was more than physical recoil from the dirt and peril of railroad travel. Separate coach laws and practices made painfully clear to blacks that strive as they might to prosper, and as prosperous as they might become, the color of their skin limited their advancement in white society. Every train that rolled across a Delta county or plantation reminded the public that blacks could never earn a permanent "ticket" to first-class citizenship.[63] The problem was particularly acute for those better-off blacks who clung stubbornly to the conviction that their social position and staid behavior entitled them to a modicum of deference and reliable service in all commercial exchanges and services, especially as compared to that received by poorer African Americans.[64] Yet wealth and standing brought them little lasting privilege when traveling by train. More affluent black women grew especially frustrated as their demands for decent accommodations and treatment based on their assumed status and conduct as Victorian "ladies" fell on deaf ears. They quickly discovered that their blackness generally negated any of the social benefits that they supposedly accrued by being a lady.[65] As Anna J. Cooper wrote of herself and other black "ladies" in 1892, "[t]he Black Woman of the South has to do considerable travel. . . . She thinks she is quiet and unobtrusive in her manner, simple and inconspicuous in her dress, and can see no reason why in any chance assemblage of ladies, or even a promiscuous gathering of ordinarily well-bred and dignified individuals, she should be signaled out for any marked consideration."[66]

Black officeholders quickly grasped the grave political overtones emanating from the problem of segregated travel. Writing in 1891 in the *Arkansas Gazette,* the main voice of the state's Democratic Party, Republican state senator George Bell, representing Desha and Chicot Counties and one of the few remaining elected black officials in the Delta, framed the ongoing debate over the legality and morality of separate coach laws as a matter of national identity. Summoning the spirit of the Founding Fathers, Bell argued that "[t]o deny the negro th[o]se rights guaranteed him by the Constitution of the United States and the Constitution and laws of the State of Arkansas, you must first deny Jefferson's proposition, the author and finisher of your faith, that all men are created equal, and are therefore not endowed with certain inalienable rights, nor are they entitled to life, liberty, and the pursuit of happiness."[67]

Similarly, African American journalists understood that the indignities suffered by black rail passengers symbolized the broader crisis of the steady erosion of their liberties. Railroad segregation laws, one writer warned in 1890, demonstrated that "[o]ne by one all the results of the war, secured at such tremendous cost in life and property, are being frittered way. . . ."[68] Another took pen in hand after South Carolina passed a round of separate coach legislation in 1898 and scratched out a lament: "the further we get away from the day of our emancipation, the higher we climb in the scales of knowledge, wealth and moral sentives [*sic*], . . . something transpires to make the impression that the Negro is 'not so much after all.'"[69]

Much of the railroad's special political status in the eyes of blacks, paradoxically, stemmed from its haphazard application of the laws and customs of segregation.[70] Segregation, to be sure, was certainly real for African American riders in the Delta—but it was rarely experienced uniformly or even consistently. The color line, because it was the product of the competing interests of politicians and railroad managers, the varying diligence of train employees, and the mutual suspicions of

[perhaps
too much
time
was for
relisi?]

white and black passengers, was rarely drawn the same way twice. Its plasticity and instability made the depot, the waiting area, and the moving car particularly maddening, frightening, and degrading spaces for blacks to enter and popular targets for their outrage.

Railroad owners played a vital, if inadvertent, role in undercutting separate coach laws. They openly declined to build separate lines for blacks and whites on the grounds that they were too expensive and cumbersome. They purchased freight and passenger cars whose architectural layout typically forced blacks and whites into close proximity when entering or exiting the train and accessing the washroom or dining car. Most importantly, they ordered their conductors and porters, in an effort to maximize profits, to fill every seat in every run. As a result, these employees frequently put African American riders into the white section of a train when the black area was full, thereby creating a color line that fluctuated according to the overall number of passengers.[71] And even when a train carried few passengers, the dividing line between the races was often not an impermeable barrier but a piece of rope hung limply across the center aisle of a car.[72] Sometimes owners had little choice but to suspend strict policies of segregation, as when white policemen escorted black criminals and black servants and nurses attended to white employers.[73]

Further limiting the success of segregation legislation aboard the railroad was "racial passing," or the practice of a light-skinned black person passing as a white one.[74] Riding across the South in the early twentieth century, a northern journalist remarked that "[s]ometimes the motorman makes a mistake and admits a colored man by the wrong door, thinking he is white. . . ."[75] Scott Bond, a successful black farmer of fair complexion from the Arkansas Delta, was repeatedly taken for a white man during railroad trips. In his 1917 autobiography, he recounted laughingly how he sometimes sat in the black section of a train only to be uprooted by a scrupulous conductor and hustled into the "Whites-only" compartment.[76] Less humorously, Arkansan Charles Dortch, a dark-skinned ex-slave and railroad porter, recalled that trouble often followed him when he rode with his black wife, who had a fair complexion, in the "Negro" car. "After I married her, I was bringing her home, and three white men from another town got on the train and followed us, thinking she was white. Every once in a while they would come back and peek in the Negro coach. . . . It seems that they were just buying mileage from time to time and staying on the train to be able to get off when I got off."[77]

The challenge of easily securing and sustaining physical racial boundaries on trains eventually led whites to investigate how visible patterns of individual consumption and comportment could serve as markers of racial difference.[78] White middle-class passengers often dressed expensively as a way of materially representing their identity. They also sat together politely and observed strict codes of manners in their exchanges with each other, seeking to create an area identified as much by their refined behavior as by any official signage: they generally avoided cussing, tippling, betting, or smoking in each other's company. When one or several engaged in these types of illicit activities, they usually did so only in the black areas of the train. This association between blackness and coarse behavior was made clear to one frustrated black minister riding a Mississippi train. He recalled that "[t]he forward car, devoted to colored passengers, had much of the time fully a dozen white men in it and that in spite of the separate coach law of this state. They smoked, they played cards, they swore. We looked appealingly to the conductor, but there he was smoking. . . ."[79]

Ironically, the turn to clothing and comportment by whites as an effort to stabilize the color line created new possibilities for blacks to undermine it. Black professionals frequently carried onto the train their habit of publicly distinguishing themselves from black or white workers by wearing fine vestments and holding themselves in a dignified fashion. Riding the Jim Crow car in 1891 on Abraham Lincoln's birthday, traditionally a day of commemoration in many black communities, J. R. Hand objected to sitting near "low down white men, many of them with no collars on, [who] came in and puffed their dirty tobacco smoke right under the noses of refined men and women of color."[80] Likewise, another black rider complained that, in the "colored car," white men "often throw open the sash . . . letting in a great lot of cinders to . . . to go down the collars of [we] gentlemen."[81] To be sure, these black gentlemen in "collars" resented segregation because it failed to differentiate between themselves and the lower class of both races; better-off blacks often relied on outward signs of class, such as their dress, to mark their status.[82] But these authors also revealed a specific type of class-based protest based on their willingness to endure the sloppy behavior of whites of the lower-sort. Clerics, teachers, lawyers, doctors, and journalists regularly refused to swear, use alcohol or tobacco, or gamble even if surrounded by those who did. Their sophisticated raiment and strict demeanor projected an image of moral propriety that challenged any logic of segregation based on the premise that blacks were unclean or unruly; their bearing reflected a creed of abstemious conduct that defined them as worthy citizens despite the degradation of separate coach laws.

African Americans from the lower classes mocked the color line, too, but usually through more boisterous and physical means. They refused to allow whites to sit quietly by themselves and made their presence felt by speaking loudly, guffawing, and even threatening white passengers and train workers at times. Black and white newspapers registered these behaviors in stories similarly classified as being about black aggression, but framed very differently. Black writers claimed that such actions demonstrated the inability of separate coach laws ever to control black behavior completely. The *Arkansas Mansion*, a black weekly published in Little Rock in the early 1890s, cheered a black couple that sat in the white car while traveling in the Arkansas Delta in 1893. "The conductor and brakeman succeeded in inducing the man to leave, but the woman 'fought nobly' and held her position to Jefferson. . . ." The report ended with an editorial flourish: "the colored woman was clearly entitled to her seat and she paid for it and licked the conductor and brakeman."[83] In contrast, white authors cited such instances of physical resistance to segregation as evidence that the color line needed to be enforced more aggressively in order to protect white passengers from uncivil and abusive African Americans. For example, *The Arkansas Gazette* published stories about blood-thirsty blacks roaming train stations. Two weeks before Christmas in 1891, it detailed the events surrounding a black man's attempt to sit in the white section of the waiting room at the Linwood Depot, about twenty miles outside of Pine Bluff. A law-abiding station agent did his job and expelled the black man, only to nearly lose his life several hours later when a posse of "avenging blacks" descended upon him and chased him from his post.[84] Similarly, in an article titled "Blacks on a Bender," the editors at *The Arkansas Gazette* complained about "the degree of offensiveness borne by respectable [white] people at the hands of . . . insolent blacks. . . ." The target of their anger was a poor black man named John Mitchell who, when denied passage to a train leaving Little Rock, supposedly "drew his pistol and terrorized the crew." The bold disregard of separate coach law and custom by black men like Mitchell, protested the newspaper, revealed that "Negroes seem to think that the road belongs to them."[85]

Throughout the last twenty years of the nineteenth century, then, the railroad emerged as a dominant feature in the overlapping legal, political, and racial cultures in the Delta. Aboard the railroad, Delta African Americans witnessed and tested the shifting parameters of their citizenship and helped to establish it as a distinctive form of modern space defined as much by its capacity for rapid movement as its quality of racial uncertainty. Because trains and train travel were so deeply tied to the meaning and nature of everyday life in the Delta, it is not surprising that blacks eventually incorporated their experience with both into their sacred lives. As more of them saw, heard, thought about, and rode trains, they increasingly relied on them to inform their religious imaginations and rituals.

First, and most elementally, blacks began to depend on the physical coordinates of depots to describe the locations of their houses of worship and important spiritual gatherings. When C. H. Andrews told of his hometown of Leverett, Mississippi, he began by declaring that "[o]ur town is on the edge of the Delta near no railroad. . . ."[86] The printed invitations to the 1888 Annual Meeting of Baptist leaders from Phillips, Lee, and Monroe counties in eastern Arkansas included the date, time, place, and nearest train stop. "Our Association meets Friday before the third Lord's Day in August, at St. Matthew's. Your presence with us is greatly desired. Your nearest point to the church is at Palmer Station."[87] Concurrently, bishops, presiding elders, and other high-ranking religious leaders started to openly identify their pastors and congregations by stating how far they lived from the nearest whistle stop. In a published report on where his ministers labored and churches lay, Presiding Elder J. W. Hudson of the ME Church, who oversaw pastoral activity in Mississippi and parts of Louisiana, ticked off where his charges could be found during the first week of January 1901. "Bro. P. W. Clark, pastor of Wesley Chapel, [is] thirty-five miles from the city of Baton Rouge, and three from the town of Wilson, on the Mississippi Valley Railroad. Vincent Chapel, [is] seven miles from Clinton, on the Mississippi Valley Railroad."[88]

Simple convenience, of course, lay behind publicly identifying the location of churches, meetings, and ministers according to their distance from a railroad stop; the announcement provided future visitors with an easy landmark to navigate their way and gauge how far they needed to travel beyond the depot. Yet part of the meaning of such identifications lay in closely aligning the key institutions of African American spiritual life with the railroad. The act of connecting missions and men to points on an imagined train map encouraged blacks to envision the railroad itself as a setting for organized religious activity. By the turn of the twentieth century, for example, Delta blacks held spiritual services at stations and depots. Reverend E. M. Collet, a conference revivalist with the CME Church in the southeastern states in the late 1890s, often ended his work by hosting the last prayer meeting at the railroad station just before the train pulled away.[89] Similarly, in 1902 Reverend J. W. Reed held his final prayer service with members of his CME church in Forest City, Arkansas, at the local depot. Preparing to move to North Little Rock to pastor a new church, Reed, with the train at his back, offered blessings and goodbyes to his congregation. As the conductor sounded "All Aboard," Reed, deeply saddened by his departure, sang one last song with his now former church members. "I lifted my feeble voice, [and] all joined in chorus."[90]

Delta blacks also began exploring train travel as a general source for new forms of religious anecdote and metaphor, especially those dealing with themes of movement and physical power. In an open letter calling for greater public support for the publishing efforts of the CME Church, David Harrison compared the elements necessary to propel a train to the basic ingredients required to improve and sustain his denominational press. Opening the appeal by asking the reader what caused a locomotive to move, Harrison responded that "[f]irst, we would say it is the steam; if the answer is correct, second, there must be water; third, there must be heat; fourth, we must have fire; fifth, we need coal or wood to make the heat. . . ." Then he drew the analogy between the train and the CME press. "[O]ur own book establishment is stronger than any of the engines used by a locomotive. They need coal or wood to make the fire to push them along. So do our publishing houses need our aid and influence, and our money and orders to push us forward."[91]

More specifically, blacks started to structure religious stories as railroad stories. The most common type was the institutional narrative of church and denominational expansion, which described organizational change through the use of train imagery. In his 1901 report detailing the growth of the CME Church in Mississippi, Reverend J. H. Agnew lauded the evangelical work of Reverend J. W. Nichols by describing him as "the light foot runner... with his hand on the throttle and his eye on the railing, pulling for the round house."[92] Similarly, Agnew's colleague, Reverend J. W. Spearman, penned a letter in 1904 to *The Christian Index* that extolled the dynamic work of early church leaders by comparing it to the building of a new railroad. He referred to the older preachers singularly, as "the old man who has tunneled the mountain ... [and] laid the rails on which [run] the rumbling wheels, the swinging cars and screaming engine of Christianity which is making her schedule...."[93] In the second half of his letter, Spearman inserted his forefathers into the Christian story of salvation, which he represented as a train ride. By doing so, he framed the death of Jesus at Mount Calvary and the redemption of mankind through the spilled blood of Jesus in a contemporary and well-known context. Spearmen told his audience that the development of their denomination depended on the labors of men who, just like "conductors" on a special train heading for heaven, took "passengers who have purchased their tickets at the Calvary's union station stamped with the blood of Christ and the insignia of God to meet Christ the Lord." In this particular example, Spearman presented the germ of an idea that would slowly grow in popularity during the next ten years: the train as a modern vehicle to transport Delta blacks literally to the Promised Land of salvation and freedom.

When Delta blacks explained stories of denominational and church growth as railroad stories, their goal was not always to challenge segregation in a bold and direct manner. Of course, when Spearman told the history of his forefathers by employing different facets to the metaphor of the train ride, he landed a jab against the ability of separate coach laws to regulate black behavior. But explicit protest against discrimination was not part of his missive. Other religious leaders in the 1900s practiced a similar strategy of discussing religious issues by treating segregated travel as more than just an abhorrent fact of life. Some ministers actually stressed the potential benefits of experiencing railroad segregation. In 1904, Arkansas clerics with the CME Church labeled the act of riding a segregated train as a salutary test of the discipline and true desire of any man aspiring to be a minister. After their annual state meeting, one preacher remarked that "accommodations for colored people on railroads is [sic] poor at best, and they are often made to go for many days with a hungry stomach." But such an experience was invaluable for any man hoping to serve

God because he "learn[ed] a lesson of enduring hardships"—namely, that life as a black cleric was fraught with racial degradations. "If any undergraduate enters the Methodist itinerary to have his path-way bedecked with blooming roses and fragrant flowers, he has simply mistaken the profession."[94]

The efforts by these ministers to cast the experience of segregated travel as something other than wicked and unjust was part of a broader cultural moment in which blacks appropriated certain aspects of rail travel, both the thrilling and the denigrating, to depict personal narratives of religious longing and rebirth. Like their institutional counterparts, these individual narratives were not simply morality tales that pitted righteous black passengers against the evil forces of segregation, though undercurrents of such a tension were present at times. Rather, they were more subtle and complex, invoking the railroad as a modern milieu where the realities of modern technology and racial hierarchy entered the sacred lives of blacks and became visions, prayers, fantasies, and songs about religious and racial transformation.

These individual narratives depended heavily on the sensory nature of train travel to communicate spiritual experience. Often the very experience of riding a train or the memory of it triggered bouts of soul-searching and prayer and even individual conversions. This is not to be entirely unexpected given the specific travel conditions endured by most blacks. They suffered the same shaky, unstable ride as white passengers, of course, but often while sitting in the "Negro Car," where they faced a barrage of physical and psychological stressors capable of not only sparking indignation and fear but also firing the religious imagination. In a compartment where the air hung thick with blue-black engine smoke, bits of charred wood or coal, and glowing embers, where the curses of unlucky gamblers and unhappy tipplers ricocheted off the walls, and where the threat of bodily and sexual assault lurked in the shadows, African Americans experienced strain and turmoil that brought many to their knees in a desperate plea for safe passage and, in some, excited episodes of spiritual transformation.

In 1904, for instance, an unnamed man with the CME Church described his participation in a revival and his subsequent conversion by directly evoking the physical dimension of riding a train. In a letter to the *Christian Index*, he labeled the revivalist as the engineer who had "booked the gospel train" for all to board and "thundered [it] along the rail of time." The revivalist worked swiftly. He "didn't carry us very far, before seemingly all the 'blood bought' souls began dashing fuel at the place that makes the steam rise. Then the old train traveled at a rapid rate and soon we were standing at the 'Judgment' seat. After allowing us to hear sentences, some that made us tremble, cry and shout, he landed us back. . . ."[95] In this story, the author evoked the fear, bewilderment, excitement, and ecstasy that accompanied his conversion by evoking the speed, steam, and corporal stress of traveling on a fast-moving train.

In some narratives of individual spiritual experience, the material sensations of riding a train actually became part of the religious event at hand. In these instances, black men and women struggled to distinguish between what was a genuine moment of personal transcendence and what was simply railroad imagery.[96] This was the situation in the deathbed vision of Joe Hutchings. As reported by a black minister with the ME Church, Hutchings underwent what he called "going to heaven" as "going on the train"; for him, religious experience literally flowed through the physical characteristics of rail travel. Lying gravely ill in 1903, with friends and family gathered at his side, Hutchings suddenly "began to shout saying halalujah *[sic]*. I am going into the building. Oh, it is a good thing to serve the Lord. I am going to heaven. . . . I am going on the train. . . . The [rail]road is tedious, you will have troubles of many, but god will be with you."[97]

Like the spiritual stories and prayers of black men, black women also symbolized and experienced the train as a vehicle taking them to heaven. As early as the mid-1880s, New York journalist Clarence Deming observed a black worship service in the Mississippi Delta and overheard a woman pray, "'O lordy, I kno' dat Daniel took de fast express for heaven; I prays yer send down dat train for me too, and give me a free ticket, too."[98] Yet black women represented the railroad as a place of racial and religious transformation in ways distinctive from black men: they more often described it as a setting of spiritual empowerment where they turned back threats of bodily harm.

Violence at the hands of white men was a common element in black women's stories of train travel, especially when they rode alone. Many of the best-known black female writers in the post-Reconstruction South, such as Mary Church Terrell, Ida B. Wells, and Julia Cooper, described being confronted and terrorized by abusive men, always white, while riding a train. They portrayed their experiences as ugly and unfortunate but ultimately educational, teaching them about the arbitrariness of the color line and the specter of danger that threatened all black female passengers. In her autobiography, Terrell, a black woman of money and high social status from Memphis, told of slipping away from her father during a train ride when she was a little girl. She innocently made her way into the first-class car where she soon faced an indignant white conductor. "[He] . . . decided there and then to put me into the coach 'where I belonged.' As he pulled me roughly out of the seat, he turned to the man sitting across the aisle and said, 'Whose little nigger is this?'" Terrell's father quickly rushed to the scene with pistols drawn and freed her. But the incident left no small mark on Terrell: it was "[t]he first time I remember having the Race Problem brought directly home to me." It was not the last time, however. As an adult traveling by herself, she vividly recalled a nighttime encounter with an aggressive white man who "made some ugly remarks." Terrell never confided the nature of the comments but intimated they were sexual in nature, at least in part. "I was terror stricken and started to the door when the train slowed to a stop. He seized me and threw me into a seat and then left the car."[99] Sexual attacks of black women by white men aboard trains, be they verbal or physical, were not atypical though they were rarely disclosed openly or in plain detail. One black newspaper editor, riding the Illinois Central outside of Memphis in 1897, reported the harassment of a young black girl by a white gentleman who, "from the very first, began to prance and chatter. He must talk to her, tug at her clothes, whisper, meddle with her parcels."[100] These types of incidents prompted the editors at the *Christian Index* to write that "[t]here is so much insult offered to colored females, until they have become to feel it is unsafe for them to travel in cars."[101]

Stories of aggressive white men threatening and assaulting black women aboard trains sparked general outcries of anger and concern for their safety among black men. Black clerics of the Upper Mississippi Conference of the ME Church passed a resolution in 1896 condemning the suffering of black women traveling on the railroad. These unfortunate women endured "the presence of vulgar men. . . . Therefore, we . . . deprecate and feel keenly the injustice, and even indecency, heaped on our mothers, wives, and daughters. . . ."[102] The male editors of *The Hornet,* a black newspaper briefly published in Pine Bluff, Arkansas, revealed a similar spirit of alarm in 1900. They went a step further in their published statement, though, and called on black men physically to protect black women. They wrote gravely of the dire need to "[s]ave our wives and children from the ravages of the vulgar white rowdy that infects most Southern railroads."[103]

Yet this black male concern for the safety of black female train riders and the public caution against women riding trains at all also derived from another type of gendered anxiety rooted in the sexual politics of Jim Crow. Disfranchisement, segregation, and especially the widespread lynching of black men accused of violating the strict prohibition against interracial physical and sexual contact with white women left African American men searching for new ways to exert a sense of control over their lives. Part of the solution involved the elaboration of conservative gender roles, which black women implicitly endangered by traveling away from home, especially when they were alone and gone for extended periods. In the late 1800s, most southern black men from every class strove to practice a degree of mastery over their domestic environments. They conceptualized their role in the home as the main breadwinner, decision-maker, and protector; and the women's duty as the primary caretaker of the household and family. They expected their wives, daughters, and sisters to dedicate themselves to building a family loosely along the lines of white patriarchal models and forgoing aspirations for careers and activities that regularly carried them far from the hearth for very long. Women oversaw the cooking, cleaning, washing, sewing, and caring of the children and typically traveled close to home and only to church, the store or market, and any job they held.[104] Thus, when black women boarded a train and moved away from their prescribed duties, they frequently carried the heavy baggage of disapproval from some of the men in their own family and community.

Elements of the racial violence and social censure that accompanied black female passengers consistently appeared in the religious events and imaginings that they experienced while traveling on the railroad, usually as obstacles to be overcome. In relating them, black women frequently described narrowly escaping some confrontation with white men at or near a train station, which they construed as a divine confirmation of their right to travel and, if they were missionaries, to evangelize away from home. Mrs. V. K. Glenn, for example, was a member of the CME Church with a vague inkling that God wanted her to serve as a missionary. Glenn was at the end of a frustrating visit to a rural church. She had hoped to win new converts and finally prove to herself that God really wanted her to labor as a missionary, but doubts remained because she had won few souls. Now she stood at the local whistle stop, tired and broke. Suddenly a group of suspicious white men walked toward her. Her train neared. She grew nervous and started to cry. "I was out among strangers. My heart was heavy and tears came into my eyes." As her anxiety peaked, she had a vision. "Satan caught me and began talking to me, 'Here you are begging, if your husband knew this, he wouldn't like it.'" Another vision immediately followed. "I saw Jesus as he stood watching the birds of the air and the foxes going to their home, and [He] said 'Foxes have holes, birds of the air have nests, but the Son of Man hath nowhere to lay his head.'" Glenn believed that the second vision was a direct message from God that she translated by personally identifying with Jesus' work among the unconverted: much as Jesus had spread the gospel encountering unthankful and skeptical people, so she was to stay her course as a missionary despite the obvious misgivings of her husband and her meager harvest of souls. Any persisting skepticism over the righteousness of her calling as a missionary quickly vanished when she received a more pedestrian sign of God's approval while bracing herself for a confrontation with the men fast approaching her. "Just about train time I looked up and . . . [the men] came up and gave me some money."[105] In Glenn's eyes, God had miraculously transformed the hearts of the men who seemed intent on hurting her and made them into her benefactors.

Like the account given by Glenn, Peggy Lesure, also a member of the CME Church, similarly related how God directly intervened to save her from harm and bless her desire to be a missionary at railroad stations. In one story, Lesure lost her money and found herself standing in a railroad yard, tired and frightened. She cried out, "'O God tell me something.'" A reply came quickly. "I heard that same voice that pilgrims heard in olden times. It said, 'Go right in and tell the Agent to give you a ticket . . . [and] I will see that he gets his money.'" At this point, Lesure probably hesitated: blacks rarely received tickets on credit. Yet she did as she was told and was rewarded for her faith by receiving a free ticket. She persisted in her work. In another incident, Lesure prepared to board a train but suddenly realized that her purse and ticket were still inside the station. There wasn't enough time to retrieve them and still make the train. Daringly, she jumped aboard the train just as it pulled out. While composing herself for the inevitable battle with the white conductor over her missing ticket, an agent appeared from nowhere and "caught the train before it got a good start and threw my purse in the window." To Lesure, "God's hand" had compelled the ticket agent to help her and the whole incident was a divine message indicating that she was to continue as a missionary.[106]

Whereas some black women traveling by rail gained confidence in the certainty of their religious calling, others discovered it for the first time. At a depot in New Orleans, Mississippian Frances Joseph-Gaudet approached an unknown woman who was in tears, intending to give her a simple word of sympathy and a shoulder to lean on. She quickly learned that the stranger wept over the fate of her son, who was on his way by train to a state penitentiary for a crime that he supposedly did not commit. This railroad encounter lasted only a few minutes and was hardly eventful at the time, but the memory of it lingered and soon became the basis for an epiphany for Joseph-Gaudet that changed her life. "That night, as I knelt by my bed to ask God to comfort that aged mother whose only support was locked behind prison walls, it seemed some one was whispering to me, 'You must go to the prison and ask the prisoners to pray that God will help them to resist temptation. . . .'" Joseph-Gaudet interpreted the whisper as God's voice and the chance meeting with the sobbing woman at the train station as a divine sign that she must evangelize among the imprisoned. The next day, she boarded a train for a prison and began a life-long ministry to convert inmates.[107]

The practice of constructing both institutional and individual spiritual journeys from elements of train travel laid the groundwork for the development of a new part of the oral tradition in black religion during the early twentieth century, the chanted railroad sermon. Chanted sermons were a type of folk sermon begun during slavery that consisted of verses, gestures, and stories committed to memory by the speaker and expressed through different oratorical techniques, such as repetition, leitmotif, and parallelism. They followed a common pattern, beginning with spoken prose but swiftly moving to a rhythmic cadence punctuated by cries of encouragement from the audience. They usually climaxed in a near tonal chant, when the preacher successfully brought the listeners to their feet, singing and swaying with him.[108] Beginning in the 1900s, though, ministers included bells, horns, and whistles into their chanted sermons and mimicked the boom of a conductor's voice as devices to enliven their delivery, order its tempo, and pace its lyrics.

It is difficult to pinpoint when black ministers first performed chanted sermons that incorporated railroad images. The first recordings of them, as well as most forms of black oral expression, occurred during the early 1920s. Yet it seems almost certain that railroad chanted sermons began earlier. By the late 1890s the railroad was already an important fund of imagery for the spiritual writings of black Baptists and Methodists. And folklorist Howard Odum, in his work on black culture in Mississippi and other parts of the South, reported in the early 1900s that the railroad was already well established as a popular and widespread source of inspiration for the lyrics and sounds of black singers and guitarists.[109]

One minister who gained fame in the Delta and across the South for his use of railroads in chanted sermons was Reverend J. M. Gates. In "Death's Black Train Is Coming," Gates, who recorded much of his music in Memphis, appropriated visual and aural images of railroad travel to urge his listeners to repent and prepare for the coming of Jesus.[110] He depended on a basic public knowledge about the common stages of a train trip—the waiting at the station, the listening for the bell and whistle that announced the train's arrival and departure, the buying of a ticket—to organize his sermon and lend it a sense of exigency.

Gates opened the chanted sermon by explaining that his purpose was to convert sinners. In a spoken voice, he said, "Ahh, I want to sing us a song tonight, and while I sing I want every sinner in the house to come to the anxious seat and bow, and accept prayer. You need prayer. Subject of this song, 'Death's Black Train Is Coming.' It's coming too." Gates then began to sing, at first softly and slowly. He gradually sang louder and faster, in a manner that suggested the building acceleration of a train. He opened with what would be the four-line refrain followed by a four-line denunciation of backsliders and the unconverted.

> O, the little black train is coming.
> Get all you business right.
> You'd better set you house in order
> For that train may be here tonight.
> There some men and there some women.
> That care nothing for the Gospel Life.
> 'Till they hear the bell ringing and hear the whistle blow.
> O, the little black train in sight (*refrain*).

Gates' voice now assumed a steady chugging rhythm, like that of a train at moving at top speed, and he warned those hoping to enter heaven one day to be ready for the "little black train."[111] Women now joined him in the singing of the refrain.

> If you want to get on the mornin' train
> If you want to go home and live in peace
> You'd better have your ticket in your hand.
> Be standing at the station
> With you ticket in your hand
> For the little black train is coming
> And you goin' to join that band. (*refrain*)[112]

The most famous example of a recorded chanted railroad sermon was "Diamond Express to Hell" by Reverend A. Nix. Originally from Alabama, Nix sold thousands of copies of this sermon in the Delta and across the South, in which he described moral decline as a series of stops along a railroad headed for hell. Nix followed a constant pattern in each verse. He started by announcing the arrival of the Diamond Express at a numbered station, which was always located in a town or on a street named for a specific sin. He then described the unfortunate lives of the men and women who lived there, speaking faster and louder with every word while women from his church joined in, humming, singing, and yelling "amen" and "hallelujah." He ended, in a style also employed by Gates in his chanted sermon, by cadencing his voice to resemble the rhythm of a train as it built up steam and pulled away from the station.

> First Station! Is Drunkards-ville.
> Stop there and all the drunkards get aboard.
> Have a big crowd down there drinking.
> Some city! Some drinkin' shimmy, some drinkin' moonshine, some
> drinkin' white mule and red horse.
> All you drunkards you gotta go to hell on the Black Diamond Train!
> That Diamond starts off for hell now.
> Next station! Is Liar's Avenue.
> Wait there! And let all the liars get on board.
> Have a good crowd of liars down there.
> Have some smooth liars, some unreasonable liars,
> some professional liars,
> some barefaced liars, some ungodly liars, some big liars,

some little liars, some go to be lying, get up lying.
Lie all day! Lie on you and on me!
A big crowd of liars!
You got to go to hell on a Black Diamond Train.[113]

As Delta blacks threaded their experiences of train travel ever more tightly into the fabric of their religious lives, they eventually wove a new image of the train as a vehicle of racial and religious deliverance. During the early twentieth century, they modernized the biblical story of Exodus as the archetypal narrative in black Christian history by envisioning the train as the form of contemporary transportation to carry them to Canaan Land. Although this idea of the railroad as a means of liberation was certainly present in black religious culture before the twentieth century, it only became commonplace after it spread on the wings of a new form of black music born in the Delta sometime around 1900. On plantations and in train stations, churches, and small dancing and drinking houses called "jukes," black men plucked guitars or violins and produced a fresh sound that drew eclectically on traditional forms of southern black folk music, such as spirituals, hymns, levee songs, and field hollers, producing what a later generation of listeners and scholars would call the early blues. These musicians crisscrossed the Delta, usually performed alone, and sang in three-line stanzas in which the first and second lines were often repeated. They drew heavily on the experience of train travel as a major source of inspiration for their music and lyrics.[114] Although their performances and music were rough and bawdy at times, the early blues artists reinforced some of the common literary usages of train travel by Delta blacks in their sacred lives. Their train songs joined the growing assortment of railroad metaphors, narratives, visions, dreams, prayers and chanted sermons through which Delta blacks increasingly expressed their faith by the turn of the century.

One of the earliest and best accounts of these artists and their sound came from a black orchestra leader from the Delta, W. C. Handy, who detailed a chance encounter with a lone black guitar player at a train station in Tutwiler, Mississippi, in 1903. As Handy recalled in his autobiography, he was nodding off while waiting for a train that was nine hours late in this tiny Delta town. He woke up when "a lean, loose-jointed Negro . . . commenced plucking a guitar beside me. . . . His clothes were rags, his feet peeped out of his shoes. His face had on it some of the sadness of the ages. As he played, he pressed a knife on the strings of the guitar in a manner popularized by Hawaiian guitarists who used steel bars. His song, too, struck me instantly: 'Goin' Where the Southern Crosses the Dog.' The singer repeated the line three times, accompanying himself on the guitar with the weirdest music I had ever heard."[115] The place indicated by the phrase "Where the Southern Crosses the Dog" was the Delta town of Moorhead, where the east-west Southern Railroad crossed at right angles to the north-south Yazoo–Mississippi Delta line, popularly known as the "Dog."[116] The "weirdest music" was the buzzing, slurring, and whining made when the guitarist held a knife or piece of polished bone to the throat of the instrument and then quickly scraped a pick along its strings.[117]

The early blues men hardly led religious lives. Nor was their music especially spiritual; most cared little about instilling an awareness of sin and the need for repentance in their audiences. But there were important points of overlap between the blues and black religion. First, many of the early Delta blues men performed in ways that loosely resembled a minister delivering a Sunday church sermon.[118] Their music was protean and improvisational, easily adaptable to the mood of the artist and audience. Their lyrics flowed freely, connecting to a general theme in a loose, associational manner. This flexible structure allowed the performer to seize quickly on his or another person's trouble and turn it into a shared emotion through song and sound. Like a minister chanting a sermon and repeating a favorite verse to the supportive cries of his congregation, the early blues artists often intoned common phrases and sang them back and forth with the audience in a call-and-response pattern. Some of these new musicians also performed at houses of worship and a few were even preachers.[119]

In addition to their performance style, many early blues men deliberately mimicked the sounds of train engines in their music. One type of song favored by them was the "train song," according Howard Odum. He discovered that they frequently imitated trains by "the rapid running of the fingers along the strings, and by the playing of successive chords with a regularity that makes a sound similar to that of the moving train. The train is made to whistle by a prolonged and consecutive striking of the strings, while the bell rings with the striking of a single string." In ways that recalled the use of the railroad by ministers in their chanted sermons, the artists also framed stanzas and individual lines by yelling out orders as would a conductor on a train, such as she "pulls out" from the station. The audience, Odum observed, often joined in the re-creation of the train ride and during the song would burst out and exclaim, "Lawd, God, she's a-runnin' now!" or "Sho' God railroadin'!"[120]

More importantly, the early blues artists from the Delta publicized the concept of the train as a vehicle of escape to freedom and invested it with religious overtones at times. As a young boy, Charley Patton moved with his parents to the cotton plantation owned by Will Dockery in Sunflower County, Mississippi, sometime between 1901 and 1904. Patton recalled a railroad line from his Delta childhood, the Pea Vine, in a blues song of the same title. Nicknamed for the many twists and curves on its route, the Pea Vine stopped once a day at Dockery's and was the primary link to the outside world for the plantation's black workers.[121] In "Pea Vine Blues," a song about a broken relationship, Patton relied on the imagery of a departing train to announce moment of personal change.

> I think I heard the Pea Vine when she blowed
> Blowed just like my rider getting on board.

Patton then confided that "I cried last night" and was now ready to face the consequence of a long life of sin. "But [the] Good Book tells us you got to reap just what you sow." He signaled his intent to start a new life by coupling a verbal promise to change with the sound and visual imagery of the Pea Vine leaving the station.

> Stop your way of livin,' and you won't . . . (*finished by guitar*)
> (*Spoken:* You won't have to cry no more, baby)
> Stop you way of livin' and you won't have to cry no more
> Stop you way of livin' and you won't have to cry no more
> I think I heard the Pea Vine when she blowed
> I think I heard the Pea Vine when she blowed
> She blowed just like she wasn't gonna blow no more.[122]

Like Patton, "Mississippi John Hurt" sang of riding a train as a way of fleeing personal troubles and securing a better life. Hurt was born in 1892 in the central Mississippi town of Teoc, but spent most of his life on the west-central edge of the Mississippi Delta as an agricultural worker in Avalon. In "Got the Blues, Can't Be Satisfied," he portrayed the train as a vehicle of escape from the "blues," denoting in this case personal feelings of anger and violence welling up after discovering his girlfriend with another man.

> Got the blues can't be satisfied
> Got the blues can't be satisfied
> Keep the blues I'll catch that train and ride[123]

Tommy Johnson joined his fellow Delta blues artists in describing the train as a means of escape from dire straits. But he also added an explicit spiritual dimension to his music by gently evoking some the religious imagery of train travel familiar to many Delta blacks by the early 1900s—a reflection, perhaps, of being the son of a part-time preacher. Johnson was born in the Mississippi town of Crystal Springs in 1896 and began playing guitar about 1910. He offered a repertory of what he called his "church songs" as well as a mix of other blues music.[124] In "I Wonder to Myself," loosely modeled on the parable of the prodigal son, Johnson opened by "crying" to the "Lord" and asking will he, a sinner, will "ever be back home" to visit his mother again. The way "home" required him to ride a train and Johnson beseeched God to help him catch one, even if it meant sitting in the black section or "rear of some passenger train."

> Oh, my poor mother, she's standing there already,
> Just a lookin' for her son to make it home.
> Lord, I needs enough to buy me a railroad,
> Got to stagger to the rear of some passenger train.[125]

The song was an individual prayer for family reunion and forgiveness but it contained popular dimensions of African American religious stories styled as train stories in the post-Reconstruction Delta. It featured an appeal to God to secure passage aboard a train; a portrayal of a train ride as a critical way to achieve a goal of personal significance, in this case reuniting with a parent; and only a passing commentary on segregation.

Johnson's music called to mind the partnership between train travel and geographic deliverance more directly in "Delta Slide." In this song, apparently titled for a local train of the same name, he dreamed of hopping a car and leaving behind the Delta and its many hardships for good. Were he to stay, he feared that a thick misery would settle over his life and drive him mad. In the final three lines of "Delta Slide," Johnson evoked the character of this hopelessness by abruptly changing the tone of his voice from the steady alto heard throughout the song to a high-pitched lament.

> Crying, Lord, Lord, Lord, Lord, Lord.
> Lord, I Wonder, I wonder to myself.
> Crying, you know that I wonder, that I wonder to myself.[126]

Like Johnson, Henry "Rag Time Texas" Thomas, an itinerant early blues man and preacher, identified the train with a sense of physical deliverance in his music. But he also sang of the railroad station as a place where Jesus would finally return to earth, coming on a special train to pick up the saved and bring them to heaven. In "When the Train Comes Along," Thomas waited patiently for Jesus' train.

> I may be blind, I cannot see.
> I'll meet you at the station when the train come along.
> The train come along, the train come along.
> I'll meet you at the station when the train come along.

I'm prayin' in my heart, I'm cryin' out of my eyes.
That Jesus has died for my sins.
I will meet you at the station, I'll meet you in the smoke.
I will meet you at the station when the train come a[long].
When the train come along, the train come along.
I'll meet you at the station when the train come along.[127]

Extending Thomas' notion of the train station as a contemporary location where the faithful met their savior, Blind Lemon Jefferson married exodus imagery, the idea of religious and racial liberation, and the railroad. In "All I Want Is That Pure Religion," Jefferson, born in Texas but a visitor to the Delta, described traveling by train across the Jordan River and fearing nothing because "Jesus gonna be my engineer."

When you're journeyin' over Jordan don't have no fear, Hallelu.
When you're journeyin' over Jordan don't have no fear, Hallelu,
Hallelu.
Journeyin' over Jordan don't have no fear,
Jesus gonna be my engineer.
Sayin' you gonna need that pure religion, Hallelu, Hallelu.
Well, your train is comin' round past the curve, Hallelu.
Train is comin' round and it's passin' the curve, Hallelu, Hallelu.
Train is comin' round and it's passin' the curve.
Think I'm leavin' this distressful world.
Sayin' you're gonna need that pure religion, Hallelu, Hallelu
Ride on fast, don't ride slow, Hallelu, Hallelu.
Ride on fast, don't ride slow.
Ride on fast, don't ride slow.

Jefferson represented an example of how Delta blacks reworked and refitted the social meaning of the railroad to answer their own cultural and spiritual needs. By imagining themselves departing the Delta by train to seek out a land of greater opportunity and framing it in the context of the Israelites' journey from slavery to freedom, they synthesized a new source of their spiritual identity with a traditional one and transformed, at least temporarily, the dominant cultural meaning of the railroad in the New South as a vehicle of racial segregation into one of racial and religious liberation. In the process they also made it possible to begin to conceptualize migration to the North and the goal of unrestricted freedom as a fulfillment of their destiny as a religious people.

Recapturing how Delta blacks integrated their experiences with train travel into their spiritual lives reminds us what historians are still learning—that rural African Americans dwelling in the New South were intimately involved in the major technological and racial changes of the day and not merely as quiet, distant observers. Central to this lesson is the subject of religion. Black Baptists and Methodists understood that the growth of the railroad went hand-in-hand with the rise of separate accommodation customs and laws and clearly signaled their fast eroding political status. And they perceived that behind the racialized character of train travel lay the fervent hope of whites that the railroad would help to recreate, finally, a South where racial hierarchy was fixed and respected. But at the same time they saw advantages to be gained from the expanding railroad industry, such as the enhanced ability to move, travel, find better jobs and markets, proselytize, and organize. Train travel also presented them with a distinctive opportunity to expose the flexible and tenuous nature of the color line supposedly governing southern life in strict and unyielding terms. More significantly, it gave them the chance to invest the physical spaces of modern transportation with spiritual value and treat them as both real and imagined sites of personal, racial, and religious transformation that testified to their creativity as human beings. Indeed, by framing religious conversions and journeys as railroad journeys, by creating the train as a rich and dense metaphor for explaining and exploring their faith, and by envisioning spiritual deliverance as a train ride, they defined the meaning of the railroad in ways that validated their quest for a better life.

This is not to say, however, that Delta blacks discovered in their religion a means of completely vanquishing the pain and suffering engendered by the racism that they encountered on trains or in any other part of society. Rather, it is to point out that their behavior in relation to the growth of the railroad ultimately demonstrated that, for them and for every onlooker, segregation was never a static reality but a continuous process of engagement and negotiation that both limited and excited religious metamorphosis. Put another way, the story of the historical association between train travel and the black religious imagination fundamentally concerns how segregation was an unstable culture force in the Delta, at times ruthlessly shaping racial interactions and mocking black longings for full citizenship, while at other moments entering black religious life as a stimulus toward creating modern conceptions of travel, spiritual rebirth, and renewal that dulled the edges of racial hierarchy.

2

FRATERNAL ORDERS, DISFRANCHISEMENT, AND THE INSTITUTIONAL GROWTH OF BLACK RELIGION

The God of Abraham, Isaac, and Jacob has conducted out ship ever since she began to sail over the seas of Odd Fellowship.... Surely the Lord God is pleased with our cause.

—*Rev. Dr. C. H. Phillips, "Sermon on Brotherly Unity," Christian Index,*
March 19, 1887

Some Negroes are that way to-day, they will give up Jesus any time for a Lodge.

—*Rev. Richard Sinquefield, Life and Times of Rev.*
Richard Anderson Sinquefield, p. 34

In 1901, E. P. Jones surveyed the racial landscape of his native state of Mississippi and delivered a bleak assessment to a private gathering of several hundred fellow black men who were, sadly, all too familiar with this particular message. "It is true that murderous onslaughts and high-handed lynching that belong to the dark and bloody past, are enacted sometimes within the sound of the bells of justice.... [They] gnaw at the very vitals of a government for the people and by the people." Yet black southern men, Jones counseled as he shifted the focus of his talk, need not despair. He pointed out, now with rising enthusiasm, that they could draw hope and strength during these years of struggle and hardship from "a figure standing... with one hand extending heavenward, ready to cry 'Eureka! Eureka!' And the other holding a parchment upon which is the scale and balances.... That figure, my Brethren, was none the less than the Vanguard of peace, the hero of the hour, the unequaled and honored Peter Ogden, the founder of Odd Fellowship among the Negroes of America."[1] Fifty-nine years earlier, Ogden, an African American steward on the ship *Patrick Henry,* had organized the first all-black Odd Fellows lodge, in New York City. Previously white Odd Fellows had denied his candidacy because he was black. But, shortly after officially becoming a member of a lodge in Liverpool, England, where his race was not a disqualification, Odgen began recruiting black men to his new organization.[2]

Jones' testimonial formed the heart of an address that he gave as the president of the Mississippi chapter of the black Odd Fellows at their annual gathering. The Odd Fellows were one of the many African American fraternal orders, also called "lodges" and "secret societies," that mushroomed across the Delta and the South after the Civil War. They were private clubs reserved for men, although most formed women's auxiliaries, and organized by local, state, and regional chapters. Fraternal orders typically required successful applicants to secure letters of reference from leading citizens in the local community and lodge brethren in good standing, pass a character and physical exam, and swear to respect the Bible and lead abstemious lives. Famous for their elaborate rituals, Christian beliefs, parades, military-themed uniforms, and rare social benefits that included life insurance and small loans, they were a valuable resource for black men seeking new pathways to financial stability, social authority, and racial pride in the Delta after Reconstruction. Besides the Odd Fellows, the most popular black orders, many of which claimed tens of thousands of members, included the Knights of Pythias, the Mosaic Templars, the United Brotherhood of Friendship, the Grand Compact Masons, and the Prince Hall Masons. Greatly facilitating their expansion was the development of the railroad, which webbed rural areas and urban centers sitting on the periphery of the Delta and quickened the spread of different ideas about the nature of black organization.

In his speech, Jones submitted that African American survival during the Jim Crow years depended in large part on emulating Ogden and joining his fraternal order. He later added the importance of following Jesus and faithfully attending church, but he viewed these other activities as equal complements to—and not as replacements for—a lifelong involvement with the Odd Fellows. For Jones, the local church was emphatically not the main vehicle of moral and material betterment in their communities. Rather, the lodge and the church were partners in a new complex of symbols and resources within southern black spiritual life that offered African Americans an unprecedented range of ways both to deepen their faiths and improve their lives. Jones was not alone in making this assumption: by the 1910s, many Delta blacks shared it as well, be they members of a fraternal order or not. In doing so, they signaled the importance of secret societies to the evolution of their religion during the post-Reconstruction era.[3]

The historical relationship between fraternal orders and African American spiritual life in the Delta, however, was anything but smooth and steady. Although Jones betrayed no hint of the shifting and often tense character of this association in his turn-of-the-century oration, it actually contained three distinct stages— cooperation (1865–early 1880s), conflict (early 1880s–late 1890s), and reform (late 1890s–1910s)—that each shaped, in incremental ways, the development of black religion. In the first stage, fraternal orders expanded rapidly. They worked closely and, for the most part, easily with churches, providing black men with new cultural opportunities that promoted economic enterprise and racial self-help in an environment filled with many of the most familiar and visible elements of southern African American Protestantism.[4] Yet by the early 1880s, as the membership rolls of fraternal orders swelled, many religious leaders started to worry over the possibility that lodges might displace churches as the dominant voluntary institution in black life. Even more alarming was the lurid possibility raised by one member of the Methodist Episcopal Church that "our people are rapidly being led into the idea that the doctrines and teachings of secret societies are equal and as beneficial as the doctrines and teachings of the church of Christ."[5] This was the start of the second phase, which was marked by nearly twenty years of bitter disagreements and public feuds between the two organizations. At the height of the conflict, editors of the *Christian Index* summarized matters for their readers by bluntly stating that "[t]here are two institutions existing among the people, that to some extent are trying to rival one another." Unsure how the competition would conclude and affect the quality of black life, they despaired over whether "the church or the society [would] dominate?"[6] Ultimately the winner was the church, but only after it and fraternal orders underwent radical changes. In the third stage, fraternal orders publicly emphasized their subservience to churches in spiritual matters and banned some of their more objectionable public practices, such as parading on Sundays. These changes made it easier for church leaders to conclude that fraternal doctrines and moral teachings were not heretical but generally supportive of basic Christian theology and precepts. As a result, ministers and congregants previously unnerved by the growth of secret societies now pledged, though still with some degree of hesitancy, to work arm in arm with fraternal orders in a united effort to improve black society. By extending this olive branch, they signaled their realization that most blacks viewed fraternal orders and churches as partners in an emerging structural ecology of their religion. In this popular consensus, black Baptists and Methodists generally saw churches as their primary spiritual institution but relied on fraternal orders to reinforce many of their Christian beliefs and rites and to provide a wealth of new resources critical to their existence and progress during Jim Crow.

Significantly, black fraternal orders surged in popularity at the same time as white ones and shared broad characteristics with them. Both organizations offered members the chance to participate in rituals that affirmed members' dignity and in programs of economic advancement. Both faced withering criticism from churches. And black offshoots of white fraternal orders, such as the Masons, practiced rites similar to those performed by their white counterparts. Yet important differences existed between black and white lodges that permit them to be studied as analogous but independent social organizations.

White fraternal members typically abandoned their churches, forcibly excluded women from all of their activities, and battled a history of virulent anti-Masonic prejudice. White lodges clustered on the East Coast and in the Midwest. Arguably the key reason for their popularity lay in their successful ability to create an androsocial world and promote an aggressive masculinity that collectively provided members with a welcome refuge from the feminizing pressures of Victorian culture and the tensions associated with the rapid transformation from an agricultural to industrial economy.[7] In contrast, black fraternal brethren usually maintained church memberships, created small auxiliaries for women, and initially enjoyed a great deal of cooperation with houses of worship. When their relationships with churches soured, they faced less hostility and for a shorter duration. Their societies were overwhelmingly concentrated in the South. Southern blacks certainly joined fraternal orders to participate in an all-male social universe, but primarily because it was a new type of African American religious and civic space offering avenues of social mobility and power independent of the strictures of Jim Crow.[8] And when they performed rituals loosely resembling ones found in white lodges, they imbued them with distinctive racial meanings. Most obviously, the sight of uniformed black men marching precisely to a strict drum cadence across a town square in the Delta, even if it resembled the pageantry of the parades of white secret societies, reverberated for blacks with the thrilling memory of triumphant black Union soldiers processing after the Civil War. It signaled that they were slaves no more.

When blacks built fraternal orders in the Delta, they were really popularizing an ethic of self-help and a type of black organization whose origins traced back to the urban centers of the post-Revolution North. In 1785, Prince Hall, an African American from Boston, took matters into his own hands shortly after his bid to join a white Masonic lodge was rejected because of his skin color. He founded the all-black Prince Hall Masons, which offered members a series of rituals loosely based on white Masonry and a vow to help them financially during times of need. Three years later in Philadelphia, black clergymen Richard Allen and Absalom Jones began the Free African Society to provide financial assistance to members taken ill and assure them of a proper burial upon death. Shortly thereafter Allen established the AME Church and Jones the Methodist African Church. Both men sustained close ties between their churches and their society.

By the early nineteenth century, many northern cities had black mutual aid societies that worked closely with free black churches in an effort to provide resources vital in strengthening the black community and combating racism. In contrast, most southern societies took root only after the Civil War, when former slaves enjoyed the freedom to form their own associations and meet northern black lodge members who worked among them as missionaries, teachers, and agents of the Freedmen's Bureau.[9] Southern black fraternal orders multiplied slowly during Reconstruction. They only flourished beginning in the late 1880s, when the growth of the railroad facilitated the rapid recruitment of new members and the mounting pressures of Jim Crow fired widespread black interest in organizations that offered alternative routes to dignity and status within their communities.

Reliable data on the number of blacks enrolled in fraternal orders in the Delta during the post-Reconstruction era is hard to come by because of the fragmentary nature of their membership records and the simple fact that blacks commonly joined more than one lodge. Still, the surviving evidence provides a rough outline of their steady growth. In Mississippi and Arkansas, the Knights of Pythias claimed a total of 4,663 members and 169 lodges in 1901; 14,930 members and 480 lodges in 1905; and 23,411 members and 828 lodges in 1909.[10] The Grand Compact Masons totaled 1,594 members and 72 lodges in 1883; 2,391 members and 124 lodges in 1886; and 4,298 members and 205 lodges in 1901.[11] By far the most popular order was the Odd Fellows. In Mississippi alone, it, according to the proceedings of its annual meeting in 1901, had 117,505 members.[12] This statistical portrait of sharply rising membership totals is supported by anecdotal evidence. In the early 1870s, the Catholic Bishop of Mississippi, Reverend William Elder, in a detailed letter on the social condition of blacks in his state, remarked that "[t]he secret societies are drawing many of them into their enclave."[13] Several years later, in 1888, a group of black ministers also from Mississippi tried to estimate the total number of all southern African Americans belonging to a society, and concluded, with astonishment, "there are about 1,000,000 of the Colored people in the South who belong to secret societies . . ." (figure 2.1).[14]

Delta blacks initially embraced the expansion of fraternal orders after Reconstruction warmly because of their many intimate ties to black churches. Most visibly, clerics sometimes served as lodge officials. As an ambitious twenty-two year old studying for his preaching license with the CME Church in 1880, Charles Henry Phillips selected Memphis as the place to prove himself as an up-and-comer in the denomination. Its status as a transportation hub for the Delta and the surrounding region as well as its large black population attracted the young upstart. Yet when

Figure 2.1. Fraternal Organization, Helena, Arkansas, circa 1880 (A. H. Miller Collection, University of Arkansas at Little Rock Archives).

Phillips arrived in the city he brought with him more than an enthusiasm to declare the necessity of repentance and conversion. He also carried a burning zeal to spread the good news about his new fraternal order, the Independent Order of Immaculates. Apparently he was a very persuasive recruiter; he founded ten lodges during that summer in Memphis.[15]

Like Phillips, Reverend Thomas Stringer, pastor of Bethel AME Church in Vicksburg from 1865 to 1893, devoted much of his professional life to building black fraternal orders. Stringer, born a free man in Maryland in 1815, came to the Mississippi Delta after the Civil War and simultaneously spearheaded the local development of the AME church, the Prince Hall Masons, and Negro Knights of Pythias. Stringer established the Most Worshipful Stringer Grand Lodge of the Prince Hall Masons in 1867 and the AME Annual Conference for the state a year later. He served continuously as both the Presiding Elder of the Vicksburg District and as the Grand Master of the Stringer Grand Lodge, which was the wealthiest and most popular Masonic lodge in the state, until his death in 1893.[16] Perhaps the most famous example of a southern black man serving as minister and fraternal leader, though, was J. W. Hood, of North Carolina. He directed the growth of the African Methodist Episcopal Zion Church after the Civil War as a presiding bishop of the state while guiding the expansion of the Prince Hall Masons as Grand Master of the North Carolina lodge.[17]

The example of these high-profile black leaders organizing churches and lodges encouraged lesser-known, everyday African American men to do the same. In another public demonstration of the initial cooperation between the two institutions, black male Baptist and Methodist congregants often claimed memberships in both a lodge and church at the same time. In 1883, a cleric in the AME Church noted that "[s]ome of the best blood of the church"—namely "[m]insters, exhorters, class-leaders, stewards, trustees and members"—filled the benches of black fraternal lodges.[18] In 1884, Reverend R. S. Williams, a cleric with the CME Church, traveled down the Mississippi River and stopped for a meal in Friars Point, Mississippi, a small cotton community on the banks of the river near about seventy miles south of Memphis. He noted matter-of-factly that the proprietor, W. H. Allen, "was grand treasurer of the Masonic Grand Lodge of his State for a long time and stands in the councils of his lodge and his church-AME."[19] And when Mississippian Lot Hill, a CME congregant and former slave originally from North Carolina, died in 1897, the *Christian Index* ran an obituary that revealed his dual institutional affiliation. "He leaves a wife and 5 children, 2 girls and 3 boys, to mourn his loss, as well as the church, the Odd Fellows and a host of friends."[20]

Further encouraging a close working relationship between churches and lodges during the years immediately following Reconstruction was the poverty of many black communities. It forced residents to design and dedicate buildings for use by multiple organizations, such as houses of worship and lodges. In 1883 in Hensley, Arkansas, the congregants of St. Luke's AME Church, "being small and without much finance[,] associated themselves with the members of the Masonic Lodge and agreed to erect a joint building. A two-story frame building was erected; the church congregations using the lower floor and the [M]asonic using the upper floor." As a sign of their appreciation to the black Masons, church congregants unofficially dubbed their church the "Prince Hall."[21] More broadly, nearly one-third of all Missionary Baptist churches in northeastern Arkansas doubled as lodges by the 1880s. As one pastor described it, "our churches are sometimes called lodge rooms, from the fact that the people of God and the people of the world build together."[22]

Besides sharing members and physical space, churches and lodges implemented like strategies of organization that tightened their bonds. Both were rational institutions with a top-down managerial model and were governed according to strict bylaws. Like black churches, black lodges operated through committees: Arkansas Masons, according to one of their handbooks, ordered themselves through committees on credentials, dispensations and charters, grievances, unfinished business, accounts, ways and means, jurisprudence, and correspondence.[23] In both institutions, the annual meetings at the district, state, regional, and national levels were opportunities for delegates to debate policy initiatives or amendments, review cases of misconduct by members, and plan strategies for future growth. These meetings followed a daily order of business, worship, and recreation.[24]

Similar rituals and ethical codes were also sources of the cooperative spirit characterizing the early years of the relationship between churches and secret societies. The two organizations practiced comparable rites of initiation and burial. Christian books, prayers, and songs lay at the heart of the most important traditions in fraternal culture. During their initiation ceremony as the new leaders of the Knights of Tabor, "Chief Mentors," according to the group's manual, received a Bible from a fellow member who delivered a solemn instruction: "I present to you the Holy Bible, the great instructor of the Knights. Open this book in faith, and follow its teachings without faltering or wavering, and you will exert an influence that will be an honor to yourself and a blessing to the Knighthood."[25] Whenever a Knight died, the Palestine Guards, the order's honor unit, gathered at the grave and recited a supplication modeled directly on the words of the Lord's Prayer. With heads bowed, they began: "Our Heavenly Father, in the name of Jesus, our Redeemer, in our sorrow we come unto Thee. . . . O Lord, draw us unto Thee, that we may apply our hearts to holy wisdom, which will in the end bring us to a life of eternal joy and happiness, through the merits of Thy Only Son, Jesus Christ, our Redeemer. Amen! Amen!"[26] Likewise, fraternal codes governing private and public comportment were very similar to the precepts taught and embraced by many Baptists and Methodists. Indeed, lodge leaders explicitly based many of their guidelines for professional conduct on the Christian beatitudes lifted straight from the Gospels of the New Testament. "One of the prime objects of the order," revealed a brief history of the Knights of Canaan in Vicksburg, Mississippi, "is to inculcate and propagate the teachings of Christ and to promote peace, good will, benevolence and charity among its members; to help the sick and feed the hungry, and to do all such works of kindness and humanity as will develop among its members a proper appreciation of the principles of the Christian religion."[27]

Finally, the sympathetic allegiance between black fraternal orders and African American Christianity through the early 1880s in the Delta revealed itself in the religious names and histories claimed by lodges. Many lodges followed the lead of black churches and discovered inspiration for their work in the Exodus story. In 1883, Chester W. Keatts and John E. Bush, two black businessmen from Little Rock, titled their new fraternal order the "Mosaic Templars" for reasons easily grasped by any black Baptist or Methodist. Keatts and Bush wrote that during the years following Reconstruction "[t]he oppressed conditions of the Negro . . . were in such deep resemblance to the conditions of the Children of Israel that, in designing the Mosaic Templars, the founders were moved to make the selection of the life of

Moses as the basis for the principles around which to build the order." They aimed to build "an organization of love and charity" and create "a medium of giving protection and leadership to members of . . . [the black] race as did Moses to the Children of Israel."[28] The Mosaic Templars grew quickly in the Arkansas Delta and enjoyed a strong following. Like them, the Knights of Canaan, based in the southwestern corner of the Mississippi Delta, took their name from the ultimate destination of the ancient Israelites as recorded in the book of Exodus, Canaan Land.[29] More generally, an 1899 survey of Masonic lodges in Arkansas indicated that many took the name of notable figures, events, or phrases found in the Bible or closely associated with it. Masonic lodges in the Arkansas Delta included St. Mark, Japheth, St. Luke, King Solomon, Emanuel, Providence, Golden Diadem, Corinthian, St. Cyprian, Mt. Zion, St. Stephens, St. David, Golden Rule, Star of Bethlehem, St. James, Bethel, St. Andrews, and Pearly Gates.[30]

The early spirit of harmony between black fraternal orders and black churches in the Delta from 1865 to the early-1880s, though, arose not only from what the two institutions had in common: their leaders, members, buildings, rites, ethics, and appellations. It also stemmed directly from the fact that lodges provided opportunities for black men to experiment with ideas about southern African American manhood and black civic culture. Fraternal orders gave members new means of achieving a level of financial and emotional stability otherwise nearly impossible during Jim Crow. This is not to say that secret societies provided the wherewithal for brethren to combat disfranchisement, segregation, and racial violence in full, but instead to suggest that they offered several ways for black men to stabilize their lives to a greater degree than before and achieve a fresh sense of self-reliance and mastery based on them.[31] Specifically, lodges allowed men to purchase sickness and burial insurance, secure small loans for homes and businesses, learn occupational skills, conduct parades that showcased their discipline, and discover institutional histories peopled with powerful black leaders who left their mark on western civilization.

No fraternal benefit was more popular than the opportunity to purchase life and burial insurance. It offered a rare occasion in the post-Reconstruction era for a black man to shield himself and, upon his death, his family from the clutches of debtors' court. E. P. Jones, the Grand Master of the Odd Fellows of Mississippi, pointed out in 1901 that "God grant that there is not living or dead an Odd Fellow whose ambition and ideal of manhood is not found in the great privilege of providing for his family after his death."[32] Outside of fraternal orders, these insurance policies were nearly impossible to acquire in the Delta. Blacks seeking insurance at white-owned banks or insurance companies routinely faced rejection largely because of the common belief that African Americans suffered from abnormally high rates of early mortality and illness.[33] They might have fared better at black banks, but they were few in the Delta and most of them were marginally solvent. Some lucky men joined one of the rare mutual aid societies hosted by a Baptist or Methodist church that, like their predecessors in the Northeast during the early republic era, pledged a modest degree of financial assistance to members burdened by illness and to their families at the time of their deaths. Several of these church societies operated in the Mississippi Delta during the 1870s and 1880s, but they were typically short-lived and cash-strapped.[34] The only other option was to become a member of the Colored Farmers' Alliance, a temporary agricultural club with chapters in the Delta, and take advantage of its modest social welfare benefits. During the late 1880s, some chapters sponsored "Benefit Associations" to care for their needy members.[35] Yet like church-run mutual aid societies, these Benefit Associations were unable to accommodate even a small percentage of the black men interested in obtaining insurance.

The life insurance programs offered by fraternal orders were hugely popular and, at least at first, well run and dependable. They operated in a fairly simple fashion. Brethren seeking to participate usually had only to indicate their willingness to do so and promise to pay the premiums on time; infrequently were they required to sit through a new physical exam. Once enrolled, they typically paid monthly dues or "assessments" calculated according to their age and total years of membership and that ranged in amount from ten cents to one dollar.[36] The money went into a type of endowment fund managed by the financial officers of the lodge; in the case of the Knights of Tabor, officers invested only in "stocks, loans, and securities" and only with the permission of the leadership council.[37] Individual death benefits were guaranteed so long as members paid their premiums on time. One of the largest fraternal programs in the Delta was the Masonic Benefit Association operated by the Stringer Prince Hall Masons. From 1867 to 1899, it claimed to have paid out $260,144.26 to the surviving families of dead members.[38] The accuracy of this figure, like others made by rival lodges, is difficult to verify conclusively and may have been inflated to attract new members. Still, it is clear that, for the benefactor of a deceased brother, the death benefit was sometimes life changing, representing the difference between buying a home and renting one. Cinda Johnson of Pine Bluff, Arkansas, was deeply grateful that her deceased son belonged to a secret society. Standing in the doorway of her home, she told an interviewer in the early twentieth century that "[o]ne of my sons that died belonged to the Odd Fellows and I brought this place with [the] insurance."[39]

Because the opportunity to purchase life insurance through fraternal orders was so highly prized, it was a staple of most successful lodges. Indeed, Delta blacks regularly shunned those societies failing to offer an insurance program. The membership of the Prince Hall Masons, for example, lagged behind other lodges until its leaders began to provide insurance benefits to brethren and advertise them to prospective applicants.[40] Enrolling in a fraternal order's insurance program, although normally a simply matter, was still a proud moment for most members. Successful applicants often received a special certificate of enrollment intended to be framed and hung on the wall as a public testament to the enduring value of membership. In 1910, the Colored Woodmen of Mississippi issued a newly insured brother, Frannie Perry, a handsome golden certificate, twelve inches wide and eighteen inches high, crowned by the image of a bald eagle clutching a quiver of arrows and a shield in its talons. The certificate pledged, in raised Old-English script, to pay one thousand dollars to Perry's benefactors upon his death (figure 2.2).[41]

After insurance, the fraternal benefits that best aided black men in enhancing financial control over their lives and promoting a sense of masculinity were loans and occupational training. The Mosaic Templars of Arkansas, according to its official history, offered loans to members because "[c]olored people find it much harder to get backing, from financial organizations and banks, than do other groups." The order bragged that it "has always come to the rescue of distressed business enterprises" and consequently "[t]housands of farms and homes of members have been saved from going under the hammer."[42] Besides lending money, the Mosaic Templars pointed out that, "through the opportunity to work in the several departments of the Order, many of our young people have been taught to become splendid office clerks. . . ."[43] Similarly, the True Reformers trained members from across the South to work as tellers, accountants, and managers in their Virginia savings bank or as tailors in their uniform and regalia departments.[44]

While black men discovered a new level of monetary security for themselves and their families through fraternal insurances, loans, and employment programs, they also refined a sense of racial pride by participating in secret society rituals, both public and private.[45] Fraternal parades, the most popular communal ritual, openly communicated a vision of black masculinity that celebrated African American discipline.[46] Lodges from the Arkansas Delta regularly trooped through Little Rock and entertained large crowds of blacks with brass bands, drill teams, and picnics.[47] Marchers typically followed a set of precise rules to ensure a public presentation of orderliness. When the Prince Hall Masons of Mississippi conducted a parade, they strove, according to their constitution, to create a procession that "move[d] deliberately in moderate time, with perfect discipline and decorous silence. . . ." The youngest member was to lead, holding high a drawn sword. Next came the band "playing martial music," followed closely by brethren arranged by ascending order of station, including "Apprentices, Fellow Crafts[men], Master Masons, Treasurers and Secretaries, and Wardens." Men who were respected community members but not brethren joined with the highest-ranking lodge officials at the rear.[48]

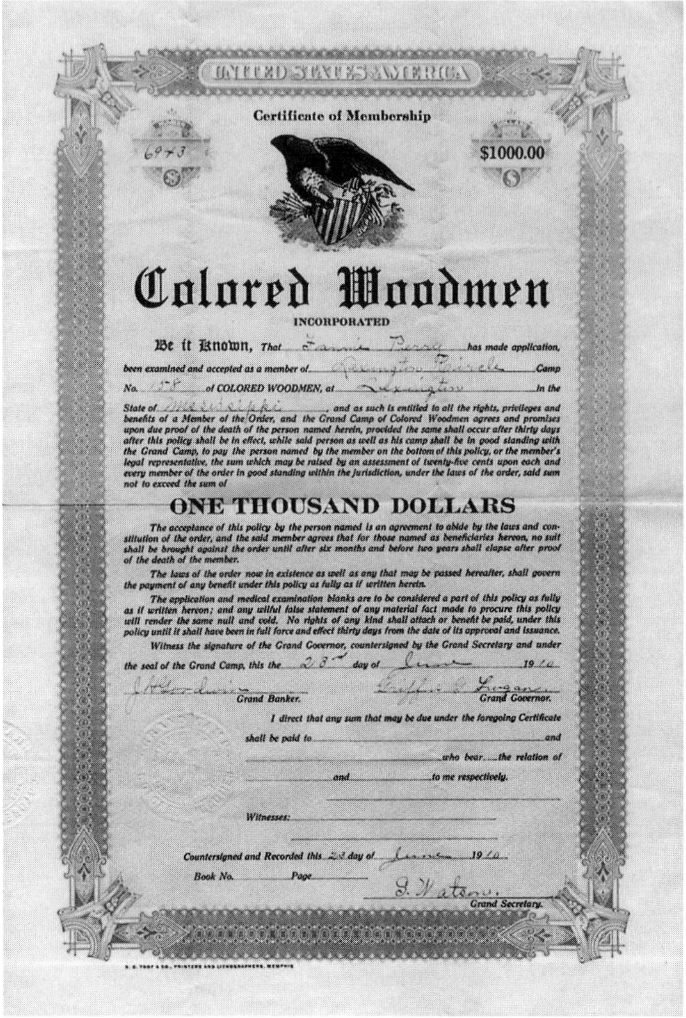

UNITED STATES AMERICA

Certificate of Membership

6973

$1000.00

Colored Woodmen

INCORPORATED

Be it Known, That ________ has made application, been examined and accepted as a member of ________ Camp No. ____ of COLORED WOODMEN, at ________ in the State of ________, and as such is entitled to all the rights, privileges and benefits of a Member of the Order, and the Grand Camp of Colored Woodmen agrees and promises upon due proof of the death of the person named herein, provided the same shall occur after thirty days after this policy shall be in effect, while said person as well as his camp shall be in good standing with the Grand Camp, to pay the person named by the member on the bottom of this policy, or the member's legal representative, the sum which may be raised by an assessment of twenty-five cents upon each and every member of the order in good standing within the jurisdiction, under the laws of the order, said sum not to exceed the sum of

ONE THOUSAND DOLLARS

The acceptance of this policy by the person named is an agreement to abide by the laws and constitution of the order, and the said member agrees that for those named as beneficiaries hereon, no suit shall be brought against the order until after six months and before two years shall elapse after proof of the death of the member.

The laws of the order now in existence as well as any that may be passed hereafter, shall govern the payment of any benefit under this policy as fully as if written herein.

The application and medical examination blanks are to be considered a part of this policy as fully as if written hereon; and any wilful false statement of any material fact made to procure this policy will render the same null and void. No rights of any kind shall attach or benefit be paid, under this policy until it shall have been in full force and effect thirty days from the date of its approval and issuance.

Witness the signature of the Grand Governor, countersigned by the Grand Secretary and under the seal of the Grand Camp, this the 23 day of ________ 1910

Grand Banker. Grand Governor.

I direct that any sum that may be due under the foregoing Certificate shall be paid to ________ and ________ who bear ___ the relation of ________ and ________ to me respectively.

Witnesses: ________

Countersigned and Recorded this ___ day of ________ 19__

Book No. ____ Page ____

Grand Secretary.

Figure 2.2. Colored Woodmen of Mississippi Insurance Certificate, 1910 (Colored Woodmen, Certificate of Insurance, 1910, Black Print Collection, Manuscript, Archive, and Rare Book Library, Emory University).

In addition to promoting racial order, fraternal parades helped to register in the minds of participants and spectators that public life in the South included African Americans. Secret society officials carefully selected the dates and routes of each procession to enhance their political value. They marched on important days not only in the nation's history but also African American history. Thus members commonly paraded both on Independence Day and Emancipation Day, George Washington's birthday and Frederick Douglass' birthday. Tracing routes that wound around courthouses, public schools, libraries, and post offices, they reminded onlookers that the basic institutions of public culture should embrace and serve southerners of every race and do so on a fair and equitable basis.[49]

Like parades, fraternal vestments showcased African American decorum and were much enjoyed by members. Indeed, brethren devoted nearly as much attention to adhering to the strict rules governing the appearance and care of their martial-themed uniforms as they did their parades. Members of the United Knights of Tabor always paraded in "full dress uniforms," which meant wearing "[a] black coat, single-breasted, buttoned up to the neck in military style, yellow metal buttons, with letters 'U.K.T.'; a badge; black pants; helmet trimmed with gold lace . . . a baldric, four inches wide, colors black in the center and scarlet on each side, trimmed with one-half inch gold lace . . . gloves [of] buck skin or lisle-thread. . . ."[50] Those inappropriately attired were sent home.[51] Young fraternal members, whose age at the time of the Civil War had prevented them from donning the blues of the Union Army and fighting against the Confederacy, especially relished the chance to wear society garb. Putting it on and marching in tightly regulated fashion along public streets, they symbolically reenacted African American parades of the early Reconstruction era, when uniformed black veterans celebrated the end of slavery and their newfound power as enfranchised citizens. The "splendid uniforms," noted William Gibson of the United Brothers of Fellowship, gave especially "to the young men of the Order [a] new vigor, life and animation."[52]

An important feature of fraternal uniforms was their shiny and brightly colored adornments. In addition to the braids and brevets signifying a member's rank and status, pins, ribbons, and patches typically bore icons that carried democratic meanings. For example, the Masonic symbols of the "Ruler" and the "Level," commonly stitched into the insignia or etched onto the metal badges covering the uniforms, bore special significance, according to the group's constitution. They reminded blacks and whites alike "that we are descended from the same stock, partake of the s[a]me nature, and share the same hope; 'that we are all children of one common father, heirs to the same infirmities and exposed to the same vicissitudes.'" Eventually, "[a] time will come, and the wisest knows not how soon, when all distinctions but that of goodness shall cease, and death, the grand leveler of all human greatness, reduce us to the same state."[53] These symbols formed a small and highly stylized visual challenge to the ideas of white supremacy, evoking basic human truths about the shared dignity of all people and the constitutional principles of equal citizenship.

Whenever a secret society brother put on his uniform and attended an official function, he was usually expected to refrain from drinking beer, wine, or spirits. At first glance, this stress on temperance may seem at-odds with a black masculinity that prized all-male comradeship. Emptying glasses of wine or tumblers of whisky would seem a fitting activity for many men's groups in the late 1800s. Certainly some white lodges, especially in the North, functioned as rough-and-tumble spaces where men drank freely.[54] Yet unregulated alcohol consumption by black men in the Delta, like most areas of the South, carried the potential for disaster. Intoxicated African American men carousing in public seemed to confirm stereotypes of blacks as incapable of acting orderly or carefully managing their money. They also contradicted fraternal efforts to promote discipline among members. Worse still, tipsy black men might be tempted to push the public boundaries of racialized sexual politics and leer at, whistle at, chat openly with, sidle next to, or even physically touch white women—actions that promised swift and sure retribution from law enforcement or vigilantes, including the possibility of being killed. Thus it is not surprising to note that black Mississippi ministers with the ME Church, at their 1881 state conference, lauded the temperance work of one of their peers and his local lodge: "Resolved, That we heartily approve of all organized efforts to promote the Temperance reform, and especially the Independent Order of Good Templars, of which Rev. D. A. Williams is a representative."[55] Or that the Knights of Pythias in southwestern Tennessee required aspiring members to sign a pledge of absolute temperance and undergo "a careful inquiry as to the character of the applicant and his health habits and standing in the community."[56]

Yet fraternal parades, drills, picnics, uniforms, and codes of temperance also represented something greater than the sum of their individual parts. They collectively stood for a special version of visual culture in the post-Reconstruction Delta, one that publicly staged African American discipline, social worth, and organizational talent for blacks and whites. Open displays of black fraternal culture, while not novel in postbellum southern history, surged in cultural significance during the late nineteenth and early twentieth centuries because they acted as a powerful rejoinder to popular spectacles of white southern life that marginalized blacks on the basis of their supposed depravity and disorder. They contradicted, though never erased nor adequately compensated for, the tragic public scenes unfolding with depressing regularity in which blacks were forcibly excluded from schools, compelled to sit in segregated compartments while traveling by train, denied access to the ballot box, and hunted down by vigilante mobs. Indeed, they celebrated and advanced public images of decorous and orderly African Americans at a time when few existed.

The appeal of fraternal visual culture also rose as other forms of African American public festival declined. Starting after the Civil War, black civic leaders organized annual parades and political speeches to honor key turning points in black history, like the signing of the Emancipation Proclamation and the fall of the

Confederacy. These events were wildly popular during the 1860s and early 1870s, often drawing thousands of African Americans. Yet after Reconstruction, their popularity shrunk dramatically. The decline reflected a general sense of despair and anxiety among black southerners as white supremacists regained control over local and state governments and initiated campaigns of disfranchisement; many simply felt they had less to celebrate as their freedoms came under attack. Although commemorative celebrations would rebound in popularity during the 1910s and especially World War I, their shrinking presence during the post-Reconstruction era made fraternal orders all the more vital as sources of positive exhibitions of black character.[57]

Complementing fraternal practices of public performance and behavior were more mystical ones that achieved similar effects of heightening racial pride and demonstrating community decorum by teaching members a burnished version of their African past. Fraternal orders frequently required brethren to memorize vivid chronicles of ancient times unlike any learned in school, stressing that civilization sprang forth from the brilliance and cultural achievements of a free African people hundreds of years earlier. In contrast to white southern stories of the past that debased or dismissed the role of blacks in world or national histories, lodges presented chronicles that memorialized and consecrated black accomplishment.

Most famously, the Prince Hall Masons preached that the roots of black Masonry reached back to King Solomon, who integrated the knowledge of the ages into a new physical science that became the moral and intellectual basis for sustaining human civilization. Solomon's corpus of "eternal truths" was slowly revealed in consecutive stages to individual Masons as they progressed through the levels of initiation. Masonic teachers, however, were careful to stress that the wisdom collected by Solomon began not with him but with the African cultures that preceded him. In this telling of history, the "new" science was actually a product of the efforts of a free and powerful black people that predated the rise of Western culture (figure 2.3).[58]

By claiming Africa as a physical locale and cultural emblem of black success in their institutional genealogies, fraternal orders tapped a powerful ideal with deep roots in the Delta and the South generally. Indeed, their triumphant histories of Africans and African Americans gave members a means of embracing the popular fascination with Africa as both a real and imagined site of black liberty. During slavery, the Civil War, and Reconstruction, blacks viewed Africa with mixed emotions. They saw it, on the one hand, as their ancestral homeland, beckoning them, its forcibly displaced sons and daughters, to return. Once in Africa, they would finally leave racism behind, live safely, and employ their knowledge about and experience with modern civilization to better them financially and improve the continent as a whole. This was the Africa of unlimited possibility and freedom and, for black

Figure 2.3. This tableau integrates a range of African American fraternal images, including symbols of Africa such as the lion in the center and African travelers in the upper right (Odd Fellows Print, Black Print Collection, Manuscript, Archive, and Rare Book Library, Emory University).

Christians, of ready converts to the gospel. On the other hand, blacks worried that by fleeing to Africa to escape racial repression they announced America's failure to live up to its democratic mission. Even more troubling, they feared that their emigration to Africa, especially when championed by whites who doubted their very right or even ability to live as legitimate American citizens, represented a convenient way for the nation simply to banish its black people and sidestep the thorny political and moral issue of how the races could coexist on equal terms.[59]

The advance of Jim Crow in the late nineteenth century only intensified the hopes and fears that southern blacks had long invested in Africa by compelling them to question anew their dreams of ever fully realizing autonomy in America. In the middle and late 1870s, scores of them, seeking practical advice and aid in moving to Africa, wrote letters to the American Colonization Society. It was founded in 1816 as the American Society for Colonizing Free People of Color in the United States and was the most famous and powerful organization dedicated to facilitating black emigration to Africa.[60] To be sure, few black southerners living after Reconstruction ever relocated to Africa, but many sustained the hope of someday living in a place of greater liberty. In 1879 and 1880 upwards of eight thousand blacks from the Delta and the Louisiana parishes lining the Mississippi River channeled their emigrationist wishes into a migration to Kansas.[61] During the 1880s and 1890s, about six hundred black Arkansans, some from the Delta, departed for Liberia. Hundreds more clamored to join them. Stoking their dreams were ministers like Reverend Henry McNeil Turner, the fiery AME cleric who, upon becoming a bishop in 1880, was assigned to lead the Eighth District of his church, which consisted of Arkansas, Mississippi, and the Indian Territory (now Oklahoma). Tennessee. Born free in 1834 in Newberry Courthouse, South Carolina, Turner received his license to preach in 1853. Shortly after the start of the Civil War, he organized the First Regiment of the U.S. Colored Troops of the Union Army and served as its chaplain. During Reconstruction, he was a member of the Georgia House of Representatives as a Republican and helped draft the state's new constitution. As a preacher and bishop, Turner openly addressed the failures of Reconstruction, most notably the violent capping of African American liberties, and frequently urged black southerners to seek out better opportunities for themselves by migrating to safer regions of the country or even to Africa.[62]

In addition to advancing racial order and pride and teaching members a celebratory version of African and African American history, lodges offered a breadth and variety of leadership opportunities unavailable in any other black institution, including black churches. In doing so, they formed new and flexible type of black male political space, one that provided a critical alternative to the ongoing expulsion of black men from electoral and party politics. This space never replaced traditional politics as a forum for addressing and resolving issues matters of community concern and, more broadly, black freedoms. But it did present a limited means for brethren to structure their lives and better their communities in small ways that earned them a fresh degree of social authority when the white public generally accorded them very little.[63]

Within secret societies, individual authority and prestige correlated directly with the number of years of faithful service and the successful completion of officially proscribed fraternal tasks and duties. Black men advanced through an elaborate system of responsibility and privilege organized and supervised by other black men. The top position in most lodges was either the "Most Worthy Grand Master" or "Grand Knight." He delegated authority through an elaborate chain of command that included dozens of subsidiary positions, such as high-ranking assistants, financial secretaries, membership officers, and uniform inspectors. He also oversaw the key ways that fraternal orders affected their local communities and emerged as a new center of community affairs, such as the disbursement of death benefits, assigning of loans and job training to members, and the awarding of small sums of money to black organizations like local schools. Consequently, and as a sign of their growing social importance in the decades after Reconstruction, lodges attracted the most successful and ambitious black male businessmen and politicians in their local area. During the 1880s, the membership rolls for Stringer Prince Hall Mason Lodge in Greenville, Mississippi, included James Lynch, a member of the Mississippi House of Representatives from 1871 to 1874 and the state's Secretary of State from 1875 to 1878; and Isaiah Montgomery, founder of the all-black community in the Delta, Mound Bayou, in 1887.[64]

Beginning in the early 1880s, however, a spirit of antagonism between black churches and lodges blew across the Delta and chilled the mutual respect characterizing their relationship until then. During the next twenty years, many ministers and congregants withdrew their public support of lodges, discontinued the practice of sharing meeting spaces with them, and stopped constructing buildings to be used jointly by houses of worship and secret societies. The key reason for the shift was the swelling popularity of fraternal order, which, by the late nineteenth century, prompted many churchgoers to wonder about long-term effect of secret societies upon the organizational character of African American spiritual life. Black Baptists and Methodists openly questioned whether the growth of lodges was a step forward for black culture or represented something more ambiguous and possibly deleterious, such as a decline in the historical role of churches as the main social and moral force in black life. William Wells Brown spoke for many black critics of secret societies in 1880 when he bemoaned that "the beginning... and the end of the desires of the colored people of the South" seemed to revolve around membership in a fraternal order. In a review of the religion of southern blacks, he complained of this single-mindedness: "[t]o get religion, [they] join a benevolent society that will pay them 'sick dues' when they are ill, and to bury them when they die. . . ."[65]

During these two decades of tension between lodges and churches, a few black ministers occupied the middle ground. While sensitive to the attraction of fraternal culture and the material and spiritual wants of their congregants, they strove to control the passion of their followers by channeling it to the proper institution. Lodges were for improving the quality of a man's social and political life; churches were too, but they bore primary responsibility for nurturing and safeguarding the state of his soul. In an address to the Knights of Pythias of Tennessee in 1887, Charles Phillips, still an active fraternal member and now officially a reverend with CME church, informed his fellow brethren that "[y]ou are doing a work that God never intended his Church to do. There should be no conflict between Christianity and secret societies. The work of each is different and there is no need of fighting."[66] Moderate religious voices like Phillips', though, were rare in the 1880s and 1890s. Far more common were ones denouncing secret societies.

Chief among the earliest protestors were black women, who, according to an official history of the Knights of Pythias, "were skeptical about lodges or secret societies."[67] Although the publication failed to state why black women suddenly grew suspicious of African American fraternal orders, it is not hard to determine two main causes and thereby gain a sharper appreciation for the origins of the emerging rift between lodges and churches. The first is fairly straightforward: many women grew wary of lodges because they represented a black cultural space reserved predominantly for men. Fraternal culture included women but only in a highly segregated and regulated manner: it banned them from all lodge functions except special fraternal balls and events, when they were escorted by male members. Most orders set up women's auxiliaries, but they never achieved the size, organizational sophistication, or independence of the male lodges.[68] They operated under the close supervision of fraternal men as well, despite being run and staffed mainly by women. In Mississippi in 1903 at the annual state meeting of women of the Household of Ruth, which was affiliated with the Odd Fellows, male lodge officials sat in the seats of honor and Brother G. W. Harris presided as Master of Ceremonies.[69] Membership in auxiliaries was also strictly limited; successful candidates to the Household of Ruth filled out an application, secured the endorsement of five members in good standing, and passed a physical exam.[70]

The second reason focuses on how black women gradually came to perceive fraternal orders as a threat to their local social and spiritual influence. During the years immediately following the Civil War, black women in the Delta and across the South attended political rallies, organized community forums and election-day gatherings, campaigned for the Republican Party, openly supported candidates, and even manipulated how black men voted.[71] They found these activities, however, impossible to sustain to the same degree as the laws and culture of Jim Crow solidified. Confronting the reality of political marginalization during the 1880s and 1890s, black women started to view black fraternal orders with suspicion. Lodges seemed to represent yet another social institution constraining their ability to take part in public affairs. To be sure, black women certainly did not see fraternal orders as directly supporting Jim Crow like the judicial system and white vigilantism did. But they did view them as restricting their full and free involvement in black society by excluding them from their front ranks and most of their benefits.

One significant illustration of the changing nature of black women's political and religious power in the Delta and its relationship to their growing mistrust of fraternal orders is a little-known Arkansas trial convened in the state capitol in July 1889, just as the tide of disfranchisement began to wash across the state. The trial centered on allegations of black voter fraud in the Delta and the pivotal role that black churches and especially black women played in it. At its heart was the testimony given by nearly two dozen black men, who swore under oath that they were socially ostracized and physically threatened by family and friends for voting Democratic in the state elections held in the fall of 1888.[72] Most were Baptist and Methodist sharecroppers from the Delta who complained that, because of their Democratic loyalty, local churches and fraternal orders shut their doors to them while women harassed, cajoled, and browbeat them to switch their political allegiances. Many of the black Democrats who took the stand freely admitted that they "turned" or renounced the Democratic Party because they feared persecution from their wives, sisters, and mothers. This legal episode captures some of the important ways that black women historically participated in local politics in the Delta, just before Jim Crow would render those ways ineffective. It also intimates how Jim Crow would spark not only anger and fear in black women over a disappearing political world but also frustration over the rise of secret societies. For between the two remaining large-scale black institutions capable of organizing and shaping local affairs after disfranchisement, they could exercise influence of any significance only in churches, not fraternal orders.

The 1889 Little Rock trial ostensibly focused on alleged accounts of voter abuse committed by black Republican men and women against black Democrats during the fall of the previous year. But it was embedded within a larger web of statewide political tensions whose tendrils reached every county in the Arkansas Delta and affected every black person living in it. In 1888, white Arkansas Democrats looked nervously over their shoulders at Republicans preparing to mount their first serious bid for political control in fourteen years. Since the end of Reconstruction in 1874, the Democrats ruled the State House and governorship, successfully thwarting every Republican challenge. Searching for ways to regain power, Republicans built coalitions with white and black farmers distraught over declining crop prices and persistent deflation. They allied with various agrarian protest groups, such as the Grangers and the Greenbackers. Nothing worked, however, until they threw their full support behind an upstart political party called the Agricultural Wheel. The Wheel, which blamed the historical woes of farmers on the Democrats and called for an expanded money supply and silver standard to counteract deflation, was a biracial alliance. It boasted 1,747 white chapters and 200 black chapters in 1888. In May of that year in Little Rock, the Wheelers changed their name to the Union Labor Party to reflect an alliance with the Knights of Labor and nominated Charles M. Norwood as their gubernatorial candidate.

Norwood nearly won the race for governor. He officially polled 84, 213 votes to Democrat James P. Eagle's 99,214. More frightening for the Democrats, black voters made a difference in the election. In the black majority counties in the Delta, African Americans overwhelmingly supported Norwood and sent eight black Republicans to the State House as legislators, doubling the total from the last election.[73] One Democratic response to these Republican victories was to orchestrate the trial in Little Rock. The goal was clear: to expose black Republicans as brutes highly skilled at physically intimidating or "bulldozing" black Democratic voters, thereby forcing the 1888 election results to be voided on grounds of voter fraud and demonstrating African Americans, a cornerstone of the Republican electorate, to be unfit to vote. The key to pulling it off was finding and putting black Democrats on the stand—a task easier said than done given their small numbers.

Most African Americans, whether northern or southern, were Republicans and shared a bifurcated sense of American political history that pitted the Democrats and coercion in a constant battle against the Republicans and freedom. During the antebellum and Civil War eras, Democrats had defended states rights and the practice of human bondage; Republicans had fought to free the slaves. During Reconstruction, Democrats had passed black codes, enacted crop lien policies, and formed the Ku Klux Klan; Republicans had welcomed blacks into the rank and file and supported civil rights legislation at the federal and state levels. And most recently, Democrats ran national and regional politics with little regard for black liberties.[74] Indeed, most blacks, whether living in the Delta or some other area of the South, experienced a profound sense of alienation from the Democratic Party. It was a national feeling of despair captured by a southern black newspaper editor writing in 1880.

> Everybody knows that the [D]emocratic party is a bad party. It is a party of hate, of secession, of treason, a party opposed to progress, opposed to a free ballot, opposed to universal education, and the advocate of State rights; a party associated with the Ku Klux in the South that has murdered thousands of colored people in cold blood since the war. In a word, it is a party opposed to everything that is good and associated with most every- thing that is bad. Now, we hold that preachers should denounce any such party. . . . because the prophets of old did it. Elijah did, so did John the Baptist, the Savior of the world, and the apostle Paul.[75]

For this journalist, as for many black southerners, the political lines between right and wrong were plainly drawn and no well-intentioned African American could support the Democratic Party.

To be sure, black Republicans in the Delta had at times worked openly with white Democrats after Reconstruction and temporarily preserved a degree of political power by working out a fusion agreement. The terms of the pact reflected, on the one hand, the need of white Democrats for legitimacy and popular influence among African Americans and, on the other hand, the black demand for skills of political brokering and high-level governmental and business contacts enjoyed by white politicians. Under the agreement, the two parties ran complementary fusion tickets during local elections, in which white Democrats traded an open endorsement from leading black Republicans in exchange for a promise that all black Republicans could campaign free from Democratic harassment. The tickets, though generally unpopular with black voters, sometimes worked and "fusion candidates" won elections in Arkansas and Mississippi during the late 1800s.[76] But even in these cases of deal making, black Republicans still swore fealty to the party of Lincoln. It was a far more radical step to join the Democratic Party wholeheartedly.

But a small handful of blacks did go against the grain of African American public opinion for pragmatic reasons and became Democrats. They explained their actions by stressing feelings of loyalty to kindhearted white Democrats and a firm, if shortsighted, belief that the advancement of the race depended on joining the party in power. For example, one black who testified in the 1889 Little Rock trial, W. H. Furbush, directly linked his support for the Democratic Party to a longstanding and financially beneficial friendship with its local leaders. In 1874, Furbush was the sheriff of a mostly black county in the Arkansas Delta, Lee County, when the Democrats regained political control of the State House. Although many white Democrats demanded that Furbush be fired on account of his race, the Democratic governor intervened on his behalf.[77] It was an act of goodwill that this law enforcement officer never forgot. On the witness stand fifteen years later, Furbush, now a farmer, stated that he and his friends voted Democratic because of ties to the candidates. Some, like him, owed their jobs to white Democrats; others, particularly black agricultural workers, lent political support because of their past experience with a white Democratic landowner who treated them fairly. When asked in court if the Democratic office-seekers were popular among his friends, Furbush answered yes. "[T]hey told me their reasons for wanting to vote for [the Democrat]. They said that [he] never required them to mortgage their crops and land and advised them not to mortgage to anybody; he would help them all the time and he was every colored man's friend down there. That was the general sentiment among all that knew him. All the colored men felt kindly towards him."[78]

Among black Democrats like Furbush and his associates, the sense of being well-treated by their party deepened in the 1880s when they watched the growth of the Republican "lily-white" movement. In summer 1886, prominent white Republicans openly worried that their party's sympathetic affiliation with black voters undercut its ability to attract greater numbers from the ever-growing faction of white voters for whom any association with African Americans was anathema. These Republican politicians, hoping to make the party as white as a lily, publicly demanded that African Americans be expelled from their ranks and made a great fuss about founding a whites-only political club in the state capital. Although the lily-white movement drew few Republican supporters, black Democrats could point to these racial tensions as a reason for their politics.[79]

Most black Democrats in Arkansas, though, emphasized simple expediency as the major reason for their party affiliation. Black physician Jerome R. Riley of Jefferson County was a good example. Riley bolted the Republican Party soon after the Democrats came into power. He explained his move in his 1895 book, *The Philosophy of Negro Suffrage,* in which he argued that blacks were better off as Democrats. He pointed out, mistakenly, that "more colored men were elected and commissioned to offices of trust and pay" under the current Democratic administration than the previous Republican one. It made no sense, advised this doctor, for blacks to cast their lot with the party out of power. Rather, "Negro Voters" must "Seek Strength from Those Best Able to Render It."[80] According to Riley, though, this was more than a matter of sheer opportunism. He asserted his belief in a society run by prominent, well-educated elites. The doctor confided to his readers that "My own experience has been that white [Democratic] leadership is preferable [to black Republican], in that it is the most capable from its long training, especially when it possesses the strong sense of fairness, freedom, and equality under the law."[81]

The most famous black Republican-turned-Democrat in the Delta was Hiram Rhodes Revels. Born in 1822 in Fayetteville, North Carolina, to free parents, a graduate of Knox College in Galesburg, Illinois, and an ordained AME minister, Revels helped recruit and organize regiments of black Union soldiers from Maryland and Missouri during the Civil War. In 1864 he served as a chaplain to a black regiment in Mississippi and founded AME churches in Jackson and Vicksburg. After the war, he settled in Mississippi and served briefly as a Republican state senator from Adams County before being selected to represent the state as a United States Senator, where he replaced ex-Confederate president Jefferson Davis. In 1871, Revels became president of Alcorn University in Oakland, Mississippi, a new school for freedmen. Yet the post was a political appointment, and when he challenged local black Republican officials and the state Republican Party he lost the presidency. In reponse, Alcorn threw his full political support to the white Democractic Party, a move that eventually paid off handsomely. Once the white Democrats seized control of the state, leaders reinstalled Revels as president of Alcorn.[82]

Betting their political survival on joining the party of the former Confederacy, however, earned Revels and the other Democratic blacks few lasting political dividends. They ultimately fared no better than Republican African Americans in the battle for local political power because every black man in the Delta was eventually disfranchised. And in some ways they actually fared worse. For black Democrats became *persona non grata* to their African American neighbors and the objects of derision and punishment meted out by black churches and particularly women.

Black Democrats in central and eastern Arkansas were well aware that their political allegiance could quickly make them targets of public ridicule and even harassment. In the weeks leading up to the 1888 election, the hottest topic of conversation in many black churches tended to be who among them was a turncoat—that is, who among them harbored Democratic sentiments. It was not unheard of for some Republicans churchgoers, male and female, to stake out suspected Democrats and spy on them to learn if they attended Democratic meetings or spoke with Democratic politicians. As Reverend James Fleshman, a Baptist minister from Eastman Township, a cotton community northeast of Little Rock, informed the Court, congregants "told me that we have been watching you ever since the Democrats came into power, but we could never catch up with you; but this [election] time we are going to catch you, and when we do we will do you up!"[83]

The hope of "catching" or positively identifying black Democrats was not left to chance by black Republicans on Election Day 1888. Historically, the process of voting was a loud, boisterous, public affair in Arkansas, as it was in other southern states. Party leaders marched friends and neighbors to the polls and let them enter only if they carried printed "tickets" listing their preferred candidates. Men went into the voting area with their ears ringing from the sharp cries of partisans telling them one last time who to support. The level of public commotion surrounding voting in 1888 in central and eastern Arkansas, however, hit a frantic high with the possibility of political change riding on the outcome. Black Republican men and women surrounded voting stations, bellowed encouragement to colleagues, and scanned the queues for would-be Democratic voters.[84] It was not hard to identify them, according to testimony offered in the Little Rock trial. By prior arrangement, black Republican voters revealed themselves through a secret code: they held the party ticket open in the palm of one of their hands while standing in line waiting to vote. Men who did not hold up the ticket were quickly yanked from the line and interrogated by black Republican strongmen. If the rousted men convinced their questioners that they were really dyed-in-the-wool Republicans and simply had forgotten their tickets, they got back in line, unharmed. If not, Republicans cursed them, chased them home, and promised to beat, drown or hang them.[85]

The black Democrats' woes only began at the polls. Once publicly identified, they quickly learned that the price of their politics was the loss of some level of communal status and church privilege. Their neighbors and fellow congregants now shunned them and their families. "I belonged to the Methodist Church" before I voted, testified Nathan Clifton, "but I haven't been in there since." When pressed by an attorney to explain his action, he replied that black churchgoers "didn't speak to a [Democratic] man anymore. They had the children worked up about it. They would throw it up to the children that there is the Democrat nigger's child. They treated me so when I went to the Church that I would not go there anymore. It was the same with my wife. . . . They would not speak to me when I met them in the street."[86] Other black Democrats faced a direct loss of spiritual privileges. Solomon Riddick left his Baptist chapel when the pastor reportedly decreed that all Democrats "ought not be allowed to pray in the church."[87] George Jackson could not even enlist fellow Baptist congregants to help bury his deceased child.[88]

When it came to tracking down and punishing black Democrats, no group was more instrumental than black churchwomen. They held black Democrats individually responsible for the recent decline in their physical safety and the security of their families.[89] Indeed, black women commonly identified the black Democrats with their loss of freedom. In political meetings in Arkansas, according to the testimony of one black Democrat, black women leaped to their feet in anger and began to "fuss" during Republican gatherings when a speaker likened the act of black men voting Democratic to "putting their wives and children back in bondage again. . . ."[90] Another reported that when black political leaders depicted a world run by Democrats as a new slave state, they grabbed the attention of the women in the audience. By arguing that black women "were enslaving themselves" when they permitted a black man to oppose the Republican party, by stressing to them that "your husband is enslaving you and your children when your husband votes the Democratic ticket," these orators appealed to women by connecting the act of voting to enacting their own subjugation.[91]

The black Democrats at the 1889 Little Rock trial described three different ways that black women punished them. First, and most commonly, black women openly scorned and harassed them. One witness from the Little Rock trial, Ed Malone, complained that women refused him everyday acts of hospitality because of his politics. Malone recalled that "I was coming long the road and I ask[ed] a lady for a drink of water and she said 'no Democratic nigger is going to drink out of my well.'"[92] Another black Democrat stated that, before Election Day, "the women got terribly hot. They would not speak to the Democratic women if their husbands were supporting the Democratic ticket, and some of them would go to the houses of the wives of the Democratic niggers and raise a row with them about their husbands supporting the Democratic ticket."[93] At bipartisan black political meetings near the Mississippi River in northeast Arkansas, one man witnessed groups of Republican wives "fussing" with the wives of alleged Democrats, seeking to persuade them to challenge their husbands' politics.[94] Sandy Barron recalled that black women unsuccessfully tried to force him to switch his vote by physically threatening his wife, who subsequently "beg[ged] him to leave the township."[95] And Sam Johnson remembered that, in his neighborhood, wives of Republicans "would not go with my wife because I voted the Democratic ticket" and "would have nothing to do with her."[96]

Second, women threatened to "quit" or "to not associate" with Democratic husbands, fathers, or brothers—an act of defiance that received the public blessing of sympathetic Republican clerics.[97] Just what a woman conveyed to a Democratic man when she swore to "quit" him is unclear, but she probably vowed to act distantly or uncooperatively with him or even to withhold a degree of sexual favor. Or perhaps she pledged to abandon him; at least one witness in the Little Rock trial testified that he knew of a woman who left her husband because he was a Democrat. Whatever the exact meaning of the phrase, she who uttered it publicly identified herself as a vocal—and often successful—critic of the Democratic Party. Indeed, several witnesses claimed that Democratic men refused to vote because they feared that their wives or other female relatives might "quit" them. As one man put it, women "even said that if their husbands would do it [vote Democratic] they would quit them. They kept a great many from voting that way, too."[98]

Third, and most effectively, black women made it difficult for black Democrats to worship at local churches. They repeatedly stopped Democrats from participating in sacramental activity and drove them away from church gatherings. Black churchwomen, according to one witness, broke up prayer meetings when Democrats were present by loudly declaring that anti-Republican voters were "unworthy of any conference."[99] At other times, they directed fellow congregants to shun Democrats and their relatives.[100] By treating unbowing Democratic congregants as sinners of the most serious sort, black church women made the act of voting against the Republican Party into a local crime.

What is missing from the black Democrats' description of the range of actions undertaken against them by black women in the Delta, however, is any mention of any exploit performed in concert with a fraternal official. This absence, obviously, is a product of women's severely proscribed role in the government and daily life of secret societies; it primarily reflects their inability to acquire much sustaining influence within lodges and bring it to bear on black members of the Democrat party. Yet it also points to a crucial fact of local political culture, one that would grow in importance as all African Americans became disfranchised; namely, that women could not participate in the new black public space created within fraternal orders and thus could not play a role in one of the few remaining institutional forums for structuring African American civic life.

The 1889 Little Rock trial produced no quick change in local politics. No election was overturned, no one went to jail, and no black man immediately lost the franchise. In fact, the white Democrats who intended the trial to lift their party's fortunes were sorely disappointed by the results of the next round of state elections in 1890. For that year the Republicans again fared very well and the number of black legislators increased from eight to eleven. This election, however, would be high point of black representation in the Arkansas State House for over eighty years. Moving swiftly after the votes were tallied in 1890, angry Democrats effectively disfranchised most black male voters by implementing the "Australian ballot," a system of centralized election controls. It put a Democratic official in charge of every political race, no matter how small or local; curtailed politicking at the polls; and introduced lengthy ballots that required a basic degree of literacy to comprehend. These coercive measures sharply reduced the power of local black churches and women to monitor and influence the political behavior of their members. Legally, only the most educated black men could now vote, but even they struggled in the face of increased vigilantism by white Democratic supporters. The impact of the Australian ballot upon the political fortunes of Arkansas blacks was made painfully obvious in the 1892 state election, when Democrats won nearly every local and statewide race, black Republicans secured only two seats in the State House, and a poll tax amendment was ratified that would soon make it practically impossible for any black man to vote.

Disfranchisement laws and customs slowly eliminated black men from electoral and party politics and, with it, the chance for black women to affect local politics by influencing how men voted. The degree of political activity practiced by black women during the first decades of freedom now became much harder to maintain. No longer would they monitor Democratic sympathizers, ferret them out among the ranks of black men lining up to vote on Election Day, ostracize them, and deny them sacramental privileges on account of their politics; no longer would they enjoy the same voice in community affairs. Against this backdrop of political transformation, the rise of secret societies turned the screw of political marginalization even tighter for black women. Fraternal orders offered disfranchised men a chance to participate in new forms of black civic life, but not women. As lodges developed into a powerful presence in black communities, black women, not surprisingly, came to see them as another symbol and source of their decreasing political power, one made all the more insulting because they were peopled by their male relatives and friends.

Black women, then, likely supported the many ministers who also started to publicly question whether lodges were growing too numerous and dangerous during the 1880s. Clerics, however, voiced a distinctive list of grievances that reflected their particular social position and wants. They complained that congregants gave more money and personal attention to their lodges than their churches and thereby risked the financial health and overall cultural influence of black denominations. As early as 1883, a reverend with the AME Church argued that lodges are "leading many who before have been true and tried adherents and supporters of the church, to . . . diminish their contributions, in order to be regular in attendance upon 'lodge meetings,' and remain 'financial.'"[101] Similarly, an 1884 resolution passed by black elders of the Mississippi Conference of the ME Church roundly criticized "[t]he over number of secret societies that are now existing in our state" and asserted "that the financial failures in the churches . . . are due mainly to the assessments and dues in many of these secret societies."[102] Bolder still was a CME preacher, who protested in 1887 that fraternal orders "compel all who join them to pay dues, assessments, etc. They require each to attend their meetings. They inculcate the idea that the societies are doing more for the members than the church can do, therefore, thousands will pay dues and assessments into these lodges and refuse to pay dues to the church of Christ."[103]

In retrospect, however, the popular apprehension among ministers that the increasing popularity of fraternal orders registered the imminent demise of black churches seems misplaced. Indeed, Delta churches did not widely collapse during the late nineteenth century for lack of congregants or any other reason. Any drop in the weekly collections probably reflected the steep and steady decline in cotton prices in the area during the 1890s and the lingering effects of the economic depression of 1893 and 1894.[104] What more likely enflamed clerical fears of empty pews was a sneaking suspicion that many male congregants increasingly depended on the lodge as their main source of spiritual guidance and sustenance. As a clergyman with the CME Church grumbled in 1891, "some men will allow themselves to think that he is good enough already providing that he stands well in his Lodge. For instance, a man was asked whether or not he belonged to the Church, and his answer was 'no, but I belong the Masons. . . .' You see that he believed that to be a Mason was sufficient to warrant him a home in heaven."[105] Still, there is no evidence to suggest that droves of black men exchanged their memberships in a church for one in a lodge; instead, they continued their habit of maintaining dual institutional affiliations.

Although preachers falsely anticipated an exodus of male congregants to local lodges, they correctly sensed that the rapid growth of secret societies carried potential risks of racial violence for their communities. Clerics likely recognized that fraternal orders, in their efforts to organize black men and pool members' money, could easily appear related to the Colored Farmers Alliance, which was a popular target of white vigilantism in the Delta during the 1890s. The Colored Farmers Alliance, though officially allied with the larger all-white Southern Farmers' Alliance and its political support for the subtreasury plan and cooperative agricultural stores, was distinctive in its demand for protection of the black franchise and, in 1891, its proposal for a cotton pickers' strike for better working conditions. In 1889, Oliver Cromwell, an Alliance leader, came to Leflore County in the Mississippi Delta and pushed black farmers to spend their money and sell their crops in a local cooperative store. By avoiding local white storeowners and merchants and pooling their orders for supplies, taught Crowell, African Americans could improve their profits and reshape the economy more to their favor. Predictably, white citizens, fearing a loss of control over black dollars and the rise of new class of politically aggressive black agricultural workers, quickly went to work dismantling the community chapter of the Alliance. The centerpiece of their response was the effort of the local sheriff, who, with the full backing of soldiers from the National Guard dispatched by the governor, John M. Stone, sought to punish the leaders and supporters of the Alliance. Violence quickly ensued. A race riot broke out, killing an estimated twenty-five blacks and crushing the local Alliance.[106]

The tensions between churches and fraternal orders, however, did not burn brightly forever. In the third stage of the relationship between the two institutions, fraternal officials, denominational ministers, and black women reached an uneasy détente in which all parties basically agreed on the enduring value of lodges to black culture and religion. Lodge leaders moved first to establish the compromise. To dampen the recent history of heated disagreements with ministers, they stressed the inherent compatibility between fraternal culture and churches and banned certain controversial practices. In 1897, the Supreme Chancellor of the Knights of Pythias explained that a man joined a secret society because "[t]here is a goal to be reached as beautiful as the goal of Christ's life. . . ."[107] And Charles H. Brooks, in an 1899 article about the history of his order, the black Odd Fellows, pointed out that fraternal membership "requires no surrender of political or religious faith. . . . We receive with reverence the teachings of God's Holy Word. . . . [We] acknowledge individually the authority of the church and in most perfect obedience . . . unite to do precisely what the teachings of the church command to be done."[108]

Fraternal leaders matched their words with deeds designed specifically to pacify their detractors. In 1899 the Arkansas Masons took the unusual step of publishing the travel accounts of the state's top-ranking official, the Grand Master, after he visited each of the 153 lodges in the state. This small book, published as part of the official proceedings of the annual Masonic meeting for that year, included a catalogue of disciplinary activities taken against reprobate members found guilty of stealing, drinking, cussing, brawling, and committing adultery. In effect, it demonstrated how the Grand Master meted out punishment to any Mason guilty of behavior that most Baptists and Methodists would deem sinful.[109] Charles Brooks, speaking in 1902 now as a newly appointed regional leader of the United Brotherhood of Friendship, argued that "some . . . churches are injured by our orders and societies; members fail to perform their church vows and the society is esteemed higher than the church. This should not be so. The Church of God should be held and appreciated above all other things of human inventions." To ensure that church laws took precedent over fraternal activities, his order banned all funeral processions, parades, and memorials on Sundays.[110] And in 1903, the Stringer Grand Lodge of the Prince Hall Masons of Mississippi pledged six hundred dollars to Natchez College, the only black Baptist school for aspiring ministers in the state. It was an important gesture of friendship. The money underwrote the cost of a new laundry facility in the hope that it would become a standing memorial to the lodge.[111]

Some reforms to fraternal culture that helped to soothe its critics, though, were ones that brethren had little control over. By the turn of the century, many lodges had collapsed under the weight of financial pressures. For instance, the Grand Master of the Arkansas Masons glumly reported in 1899 on the flagging vitality of one Delta lodge. It recently hit on hard times because of "the low price of cotton—all had a tendency to retard the progress of this lodge and the people generally."[112] In this case, the decline in agricultural prices had crippled the ability of member to support their society financially. A few lodges fell into ruin after too many members joined the fledgling African American Holiness movement, which, as chapter five explores, began in the Delta in the 1890s and forbid its believers to be part of any secret society.[113] More commonly, lodges were forced to close their doors because of a legacy of poor investment decisions. During the 1870s and 1880s, many lodges in their rush to expand had implemented unsound insurance programs. Ignoring or distrusting actuarial principles, leaders had enrolled members with little regard to age or health condition. Now they faced mounting claims from aged and infirm brethren and from the families of deceased members. To avoid defaulting on their obligations, lodge officials were forced to raise monthly dues and assess new charges, which measures prompted some brethren to resign and drove away prospective applicants, especially younger ones. Still confronting the same financial burdens but now with a reduced membership, fraternal officials levied even higher fees upon members, which compelled even more of them to leave. This cycle continued until individual lodges folded.[114]

The sight of lodges being forced to shut their doors because of poor management of their life insurance programs prompted some secret societies to reexamine their liberal policies of enrollment. A case in point was the Odd Fellows of Mississippi, who attacked the problem of insuring members advanced in age and of questionable health head on after experiencing an upsurge in death claims. From 1899 to 1900, they processed only three of them. But from 1900 to 1901, they handled thirty-three. More distressingly, the deceased for this later year only paid about thirty dollars in premiums, yet their benefactors collected an "assessment" or death benefit of about 323 dollars each. They were policy holders for four years on average, though twelve of them failed to reach even their one-year anniversary. In light of these figures, E. H. McKissock, Secretary-Treasury of the state lodge, sounded an alarm over "financial members who have not paid ONE CENT. . . and probably never will." He added that "men who are too old by many years are taken in the Order—policies gotten for them [and] after but a few months an assessment to be issued." McKissock then ordered that older men be charged higher premiums for their insurance policies.[115]

Part of the reason that some fraternal orders experienced monetary difficulties specifically in the Mississippi Delta was based on changes in the local economy. During Reconstruction, whites regularly rented land to blacks on favorable terms or sold it to them at attractive rates as a strategy to lessen the crushing burden of property and levee taxes. From 1865 to 1875, for example, state and county property tax rates jumped by at least 750 percent and the levee tax averaged $4.15 per acre while the price per acre of improved land remained fairly constant, fetching only for ten to thirteen dollars. Even when taxes dropped after Reconstruction, many white land-owners continued to rent to blacks in the hope of keeping them as inexpensive workers and selling land to them. Railroad and timber companies also offered excess land to black buyers at inexpensive prices as well. Delta blacks, in turn, took advantage of these opportunities to climb a few rungs up the economic ladder by buying property with extra money they earned by farming efficiently, partnering with other African Americans farmers and renters to improve their crop yield, and working for the lumber and logging industries. As a result, nearly two-thirds of farm owners in the Mississippi Delta were African American in 1900.

This trend toward greater wealth among blacks living in the Mississippi Delta, however, slowed considerably during the first years of the twentieth century. Whites responded to plummeting cotton prices by replacing the practice of renting and selling land to blacks with a strict policy demanding that blacks work as share-croppers, a form of labor that theoretically promised property owners the lowest cost and best crop yield per acre of farmland. They also greatly tightened access to credit for blacks. Consequently, the number of new black farm owners dropped precipitously after 1900 while the ranks of black tenant farmers and sharecroppers rose sharply.[116] This fall in black income and livelihood was a key factor limiting the ability of local lodges to recruit and sustain members, who now struggled to a greater degree than before to pay their dues and monthly insurance premiums. From 1900 to 1910, Stringer Prince Hall Grand Lodge experienced a record decline in financial contributions, membership totals, and the rate of participation in fraternal activities. Its affiliate lodges across the Delta battled similar problems and many became inactive.[117] In light of this recent history, many Baptist and Methodist leaders, not surprisingly, softened their opinion of fraternal culture. Publicly committed to respect the authority of churches in moral matters, shorn of many of their most objectionable features, and susceptible to financial failure, lodges simply posed a far lesser degree of danger to the public influence of churches.

At a broader level, national African American politicians contributed to the lessening of conflicts between lodges and churches at the turn of the century by contending that racial progress depended on unwavering racial solidarity and programs of self-help. At the forefront was Booker T. Washington, architect of the Tuskegee Institute of Alabama and black America's most prominent spokesman. In his 1905 Atlanta Exposition address, he urged blacks to unite behind his accommodationist program that emphasized industrial education and material development, rather than the pursuit of immediate political equality, as the best way to "bring into our beloved South a new heaven and a new earth."[118] In his philosophy, cooperation between African Americans was an essential component in helping the masses learn occupational skills, acquire habits of thrift and economy, and develop the capital necessary for social and moral uplift. Only by earning and saving more money, instructed Washington, would blacks ultimately command greater economic power with white society and be in a better position to demand the full extent of their civil rights.[119]

Black religious and fraternal leaders in the Delta repeated Washington's call for cooperation between black organizations. Editors at the *Southwestern Christian Recorder* told their readers in 1899 that, "[a]s a people, we are now at a critical period of our history, and we have got to make a business of race building. The church and societies must join hands with the family, and whenever an entertainment of any kind is planned, the very first question to be asked by each is, 'What will be the moral effect upon the people?'"[120] That same year, a committee of Pythian Knights declared that "[i]f the men composing the leading organizations among us could lay aside selfishness and unite and do battle for our common cause . . . the walls of prejudice would transform . . . as nothing under God could hinder the onward march of ten million people."[121]

At the same time that national and local black religious leaders encouraged a spirit of partnership between black institutions, most black women apparently started to accept fraternal orders as a legitimate black organization, though they did so reluctantly and without gaining any new degree of power or authority within them. Central to their consent was their success in creating alternative ways of achieving moral authority in their communities. During the late nineteenth century, black women, as we shall see in later chapters, greatly expanded and enhanced the social and religious significance of their roles as mothers, guardians of the home, and consumers partly as strategies to compensate for their increasing political marginalization.

The decline of fraternal orders as a direct threat to churches' social sway was not, by itself, enough to change the hearts and minds of many of their critics. Before a new era of cooperation between the two institutions could begin, suspicious ministers and congregants needed to make sure that they had an answer to some of the lodges' main sources of public appeal, such as the insurances and regalia. And so, at the turn of the century, they worked feverishly to implement programs to care for their sick and bury their dead and to design pins and emblems publicizing denominational identity. Such internal changes promised that churches would be able to reestablish their rank as the principal voluntary institution in black religious life. They marked as well the extent to which churches incorporated aspects of fraternal culture.

Churches' widespread realization of the value of offering fraternal-style insurance opportunities, of course, originated not only in the pressure exerted upon them by lodges. It also reflected the influence of the small number of mutual aid societies existing within some black southern churches and the local political clubs. The calls for programs of racial self-help sounded by area and national black leaders were significant factors, too. Still, churches' interest in forming relief societies was mainly a reaction to the massive growth of the lodges during the first decades after Reconstruction and the obvious role that the insurance programs played in it. Miss Celestine M. Johnson, for example, bluntly asserted in 1897 that "[o]ur lodge members visit us, they care for us and if we die they bury us. Sad to say, as a whole our church does not do this. . . . But we do ask you to visit your sick, help your poor and needy, and help to bury your dead. . . ."[122] Equally forceful was A.D. Wilson of the CME Church, who, in an article titled "The Church Should Bury Its Dead" published in the *Christian Index* in 1898, demanded that black church leaders must match the insurance programs of the lodges. "The secret societies are playing their part in caring for their members and burying their dead; and for this reason thousands are rushing therein. . . . Therefore, the church ought not to be behind in this good work."[123] Echoing Wilson, fellow Colored Methodist Episcopalian J. C. Powell declared that "[i]t is the duty of the church to see after her poor, needy, and distressed ones; relieve and comfort them as much as possible. If this is done the secret organizations would have less of a hold upon the church members."[124]

As these appeals for institutional transformation thickened and as religious leaders embraced them, black churches started to form religious societies that assured dues-paying members a small stipend when they fell ill and a proper burial at little or no cost when they died. At the turn of the century in Memphis, Baptist preacher T. O. Fuller recalled in his memoir that "members were not received into the Tabernacle Baptist Church . . . if they held membership in a secret society. As a substitute, the Church undertook to care for the sick and bury the dead."[125] Also in the early 1900s, black ministers with the ME Church in the upper part of the Mississippi Delta began a concerted effort to implement programs to provide succor to needy congregants. Surveying the results of this labor years later, a group of ministers cheerfully reported that "all of the churches . . . are conducting a help department for the sick and poor. . . ."[126]

Besides founding their own programs of financial assistance, church leaders, taking cues from the obvious delight that fraternal members took in wearing uniforms, devoted more attention to the role of insignia in public life. They began to broaden the range of their own institutional paraphernalia offered to congregants. By the turn of the century, Baptist ministers from the southern region of the Arkansas Delta popularized membership in local Baptist Young People Unions (BYPU) by encouraging boys and girls to purchase a range of buttons and badges. These adornments ranged in price from the affordable to the expensive. Selections included plain buttons for five and ten cents, gold-rimmed ones for twenty-five cents, and special enamel ones for fifty cents. Those interested in badges could buy a plain one for ten cents or one with the name of the local society emblazoned in gold for fifty cents.[127]

Similarly, black clerics with the ME Church drew attention to their program for children, the Epworth League, by advertising its eye-catching collection of charms for watch chains, lapel buttons, pin clasps, and long pins for neck scarves. The decorations varied widely by level of embellishment and price. Most were simple and unadorned, able to be had for a few pennies. But those cast in sterling silver cost thirty cents; sterling silver and enamel, seventy-five cents; gold and enamel, one dollar and twenty-five cents. At the high end were buttons and charms set in fourteen-carat gold, which carried a price tag of two dollars and fifty cents apiece.[128] These gold trinkets were beyond the reach of most Delta blacks, and likely were produced in the hope that a group of congregants might combine their money and purchase one as a special gift for their minister or church.

The institutional reforms implemented by both lodges and churches ultimately smoothed the way for the new ethos of collaboration that took hold during the early twentieth century. Most church leaders and congregants now readily admitted the enduring value of fraternal orders to black spiritual life. Reverend J. C. Rogers, testifying at the 1903 Annual Session of the Arkansas Central Baptist District

Association in Pine Bluff, claimed that "the principal foundation of secret orders is right; that the intention is to better the moral and social condition of man."[129] Rogers sensed, correctly, that by the twentieth century most Delta blacks demanded a religious life that integrated the rituals and programs found in both churches and fraternal orders.

The cooperative spirit manifested itself in a resurgence of the earlier Delta tradition of building a single structure to house both a church and a lodge. Although suspended during the decades of fraternal and church conflict, it once again became commonplace after 1900. The Baptists and Methodists of Crossett, Arkansas, united with a local fraternal order and "[i]n 1905 a two story building [was] erected . . . for Church and Lodge purposes. There the Methodist Sunday School would meet in the morning and the Baptists in the afternoon at 2:30 P.M."[130] In other communities which could not afford to build a church, congregations rented lodges for worship services. Without a building of his own, the minister of Walnut Grove AME Church in Walnut Grove, Arkansas, "[p]reached in [the] Knights of Pythias Hall from 1902–1913."[131]

This new ethic of inter-institutional harmony was also apparent in burial ceremonies, which openly mixed church and lodge symbols in new and eclectic ways. Sometime in the early twentieth century, the Sir Knights and Daughters of the Tabernacle of Bolivar County, Mississippi, began a tradition of funeral rites that caught the eye of a local historian. In it, he reported, they usher the body of a deceased brother to a local church, where they sit solemnly until the pastor finishes the eulogy and delivers the final blessing. Then "[t]he daughters[,] wearing black dresses and veils edged in white with white gloves, assemble around the caskets in Church in formation." Once arranged, they "march around and clap hands three times, and cross in front of the body, flapping their arms to stimulate angel's wings." At that point, brethren transport the corpse to the grave. Once the body is lowered into the ground, the women again approach the coffin and "walk around [it] three times and sing 'Till We Meet Again[.]'"[132]

Perhaps the best example of the broad public acceptance of both black churches and fraternal orders as vital components to African American religion in the Delta, though, came from the most unexpected source, the Catholic Church. Throughout the post-Reconstruction era, Catholic leaders were the staunchest opponents of black secret societies—one possible explanation for the low number of black Catholics in the Delta and most southern areas outside of the heavily Catholic cities, such as Baltimore and New Orleans. In 1886, Bishop Francis Janssens of Mississippi flatly dismissed lodges as irreligious and irrational. He claimed that "equal temporal and social advantages may be enjoyed in societies fostered by the approval and commendation of the Church."[133] By 1904, however, Janssens had relented in his criticism. He confided to his diary that the "[black] Catholics belonging to them . . .

seek only Insurance and Commercial advantages."[134] Several years later, in a black missionary parish in Pine Bluff, Arkansas, Father John Albert, a white priest, tried a radical experiment. Frustrated by his inability to increase the small number of blacks who celebrated weekly Mass with him, Albert struck on a new tactic. He realized that "[o]ne of the chief obstacles to greater progress among Colored people is the fact that so many of them are members of societies condemned by the church." "These societies mean much to them," continued Albert, "especially in trying times as sickness and death" and do not transform them into moral miscreants, as many white Catholics feared. "After considerable observation I am convinced that the majority of them would make good Catholics."[135] As a result, Albert took the unusual step of formally requesting that his superior, the Bishop of Arkansas, Reverend John Morris, petition the Holy See at the Vatican to permit black Catholics to join secret societies.

Yet Albert's pleas fell on deaf ears. Bishop Morris, after promising to consult about the matter with his fellow southern prelates, kept the strict ban against Catholics of any color joining a fraternal society. In response, Albert quietly started his own black Catholic secret society to help members defray the future cost of burial. It was a short-lived effort, however, and never developed to the point where final decisions were made about uniforms and initiation ceremonies. Bishop Morris soon learned of Albert's experiment, publicly remonstrated him for his blatant disregard of pastoral authority, and shut down the society.[136] Still, Albert's efforts disclosed that, by the early 1900s in the Delta, most black and white southerners grasped that African American spiritual life involved symbolic and structural resources drawn from both churches and secret societies.[137]

It would be historically inaccurate, though, to suggest that the birth of the new century marked the start of an era of utter accord between lodges and churches. Points of tension still lingered between them and occasionally flared into open controversy. For those churchgoers that continued to worry that the lines separating societies and churches were too blurry, especially in matters of worship, there was plenty to complain about on occasion. In his 1902 general survey of southern black churches, W.E.B. Du Bois reported on how fraternal gatherings continued to adopt the look and feel of rituals commonly found in a denominational worship service. One of Du Bois' students described a Baptist minister addressing a gathering of the Knights of Pythias. In front of five hundred people gathered in his own church, the preacher "began by telling the history of the Knights of Pythias." But things changed quickly. The pastor "shut the Bible and began to preach. As soon as I could distinguish between the words and the peculiar sound made by the intaking of his breath, I found myself listening to what the people called 'a good sermont [sic].'" Eventually the observer grew convinced that the lodge meeting had become a church service. "After the sermon there were speeches by several laymen and then the deacons, gathering around the table in front of the pulpit, began to call for the collection. Then the choir sang...."[138] At other times recalcitrant critics condemned what they claimed were fresh examples of persistent fraternal wrongdoings, such as members squandering money and time on celebrations and uniforms. Seeking to tamp down rising public outcries about secret society extravagances in 1909, for example, Edward Lampton, then the Grand Master of the Stringer Lodge of Prince Hall Masons in the Mississippi Delta, issued a stern warning to his followers about the politics of public consumption and one that strongly echoed admonishments delivered by his predecessors during the 1880s and 1890s. Lampton openly counseled members that "the street parade and this costly regalia are not the principal features of the Masons...." Neither this fraternal leader nor any other, however, could pacify the most stubborn protestors, who joined upstart religious movements hostile to secret societies beginning to ripple across the Delta.

The development of secret societies cannot be understood apart from the evolution of black spiritual life during the decades following Reconstruction. Each influenced the growth of the other. In particular, fraternal orders borrowed liberally from African American Protestant theology and rituals while their surging popularity compelled black churches reevaluate their assumption that they were the dominant purveyors of social and spiritual identity and broaden the scope of their institutional offerings to match those found in lodges. As a result, many black churches eventually featured new or expanded burial and aid societies and experimented with ways of enhancing denominational identity through the wearing of domestic commodities styled as religious ornaments.

Ultimately, however, to study the interlocking historical relationship between black fraternal orders and black churches in the Delta is to recall certain basic truths about the institutional arc of African American religion in the post-Reconstruction South—truths all too often missed when historians focus on black churches as the crucial site for the expression of black spiritual life. Most obviously, it testifies to the role of fraternal culture in enlarging the range of financial, social, and psychological resources available to black men attempting to improve their lot, preserve a degree of mastery over their lives, and construct and join a new type of black civic space during Jim Crow. It bears witness to the slow casting out of women from much of traditional political culture in the Delta and their exclusion from the civic space embedded in fraternal culture, thereby setting up the question of how women would eventually refigure social and religious life to include them more fully. Perhaps most significantly, though, it teaches us about the diversity, flexibility, and subtlety of black spiritual life—about how its boundaries extended far beyond the physical walls of its churches and how its beliefs and practices were fruits borne of vines rooted in multiple institutional contexts.

3

THE INTERSECTING RHYTHMS OF SPIRITUAL
AND COMMERCIAL LIFE

*My greatest pleasure was independence—make my money, go and spend it as
I see fit.*

—Irene Robinson in *The American Slave: A Composite Autobiography,
Supplement, Series 1, Arkansas Narratives, Vol. 10,
Parts V and VI*, ed. George Rawick, p. 51

⸺⸺⸺⸺⸺

Leroy Percy was not a man to be trifled with. In the Delta at the turn of the
nineteenth century, few outranked him in terms of power and stature. Born six
months after the start of the Civil War to one of the Mississippi Delta's most powerful
white families, he followed a path well trod by planter elites. After completing his
undergraduate education at University of the South in Sewanee, Tennessee, he attended
the University of Virginia law school, as had his father and grandfather. Returning to his
hometown of Greenville on the banks of Mississippi River where it dipped below the
midline of the state, he quickly established himself as a successful lawyer and hard-nosed
businessman. By the turn of the century, he ran plantations in the Mississippi Delta
totaling nearly twenty thousand acres and counted among his friends Supreme Court
jurists, leaders of Congress, and President Theodore Roosevelt. His political authority
would soon earn him a seat in United States Senate, in 1910.[1]

Yet for all his influence and status in the Delta, Percy was at wits end in late 1906
as he struggled to restrain the buying habits of some of the black laborers on one of
his plantations, Trail Lake, in Greenville. Percy traditionally forced black workers to
spend their every penny at the commissary on his plantation, especially during
Christmas when they tended to purchase more food and personal items than
usual. But during this year's holiday season, Aaron Fuller openly protested the

measly terms of the "advance" offered to him and apparently had begun to shop elsewhere. In a nervous letter to one of his white overseers in charge of Fuller, Percy worried that Fuller's effort to defy his authority on matters of consumption might inspire others to do the same. "I don't think its [*sic*] a good idea to let Aaron Fuller get his supplies anywhere else except at the store. The fact of it is, it will lessen your control over him, and then it puts notions in the heads of other Negroes." Any objection voiced by Fuller about the enforcement of this policy or the size and creditworthiness of his advance in the future, penned Percy, was to be dealt with swiftly and severely. "You can tell him how you are going to advance and that I say advancing him from the store is exactly like advancing him from here [Percy's home]. . . . If this does not suit him, I would not take him [as a worker]. He has nothing and is not in a position to dictate terms."[2]

Percy's letter revealed two cultural dynamics operating at cross-purposes in the Delta during the decades after Reconstruction, each of which carried profound consequences for the evolution of black religious life: blacks seeking greater power over how and where they spent their money, and whites hoping to control it. African Americans usually could secure what they needed to subsist on either at the commissary, at the general store, or, less frequently, from a commercial salesman. But obtaining basic literary and consumer goods not directly tied to daily living or work—such as books, Bibles, hymnbooks, pictures, lithographs of Jesus, curtains, dress clothes, or hair ribbons—was a different matter. Blacks frequently lacked enough money or credit to purchase them. Even when they could afford these commodities, they battled whites like Percy who eagerly denied them the freedom to see, touch, smell, inspect, and acquire them.

These barriers, however, did not mean that Delta blacks were unaware of the rapidly expanding consumer market in the late nineteenth South; they still saw, read about, and heard about it. The garb of a wealthy landowner and his kin on a holiday; a shelf bowing under the weight of manufactured goods in a general store or plantation commissary; an illustration of fancy shoes or a sewing machine in a local newspaper or trade journal; a conversation with a traveling salesman about his wares: each was a window onto the market. There were other sources of information, too. Remembering her childhood in the Mississippi Delta during the late 1800s and early 1900s, one white woman described town squares bursting with brightly colored posters and boldly lettered signs announcing an eclectic mix of consumer products. Tacked to the sides of buildings and hung on the walls and over the doors of saloons, bars, banks, and cotton gins, they advertised "Bull Durham and Old North State smoking tobacco, plug cut chewing tobacco, Levi Garret and Primrose snuff, Wine of Cardui for women, Castoria for children, Grove's Chill Tonic, and the detergent of the day, Gold Dust Twins Washing Powder."[3] The growth of the railroad during this period and the popular excursion cars allowed ever larger numbers of Delta blacks to visit nearby cities like Memphis and Little Rock, where they enjoyed a more complete view of what the market offered. A few Delta blacks successfully opened small mercantile stores in towns with heavy African American populations, such as Greenwood, Mississippi, and Pine Bluff, Arkansas, and usually permitted locals to inspect and examine goods freely. Uniformed, bejeweled fraternal brethren marching in a parade offered yet another public example of manufactured clothing and trinkets, one that embodied associations between racial dignity and material goods and publicized the importance of specialized clothing to notions of racial progress.

In addition to knowing a great deal about the market's many products, a few Delta blacks, when they could, entered the market with extra money to spend. Many agricultural workers strove to supplement their incomes by doing extra jobs on and off the farm. They took on short-term employment especially during the periods of slow activity on the farm, such as the months between planting and harvesting. One key employer was the developing timber industry. In the heavily forested interior counties of the Mississippi Delta, such as Sunflower and Bolivar counties, blacks cut wood, built fences, and carved gates for white neighbors to earn money. Sometimes they felled hardwood trees for storekeepers and lumbar companies.[4] The story was similar in the Arkansas Delta. Among a group of 256 older black agricultural workers from Arkansas interviewed about their lifelong work histories in 1935 and 1936, nearly 45 percent reported that they had boosted their earnings by laboring for a railroad or timber company.[5]

When black Baptists and Methodists in the Delta imagined the consumer market or actually accessed it, they gradually learned about new ways to construct religious identity.[6] Even though the tremendous growth of the national and southern consumer market after Reconstruction introduced novel ideas and practices about segregation to the Delta, it also created limited opportunities for African Americans to explore new dimensions to their faiths. Building on older traditions that integrated spiritual life, work, and consumption, Delta blacks steadily experimented with contemporary advertising schemes and marketing ploys to devise new religious rituals and retool old ones. Appropriating modern techniques of buying and selling, they invented new methods of raising money and public support for their rapidly growing local networks of denominational churches, schools, newspapers, presses, publishing houses, women's associations, and young peoples' unions. These innovations, however, were not always met with open arms. Wedding religion and the market together in complicated and unprecedented ways, they compelled Delta blacks to determine the proper relationship between modern black spiritual and commercial life. Many drew a thick line between them and charged the champions of the market's new place in black sacred life with the sins of pride and worldliness, setting off a series of public debates and controversies that brought some local congregations to the breaking point.

The desire and ability of Delta blacks in the post-Reconstruction era to incorporate literary and consumer goods into their religion was not, of course, entirely new. Slaves, when allowed to make extra money for themselves, often had bought a new pair of shoes, a suit, or a dress to be worn to Sunday church services.[7] Frederick Law Olmsted, while traveling across northern Mississippi, reported bonds people treasuring religious books purchased from peddlers.[8] This braiding of the market and religion reflected a broad historical understanding of the relationship between liberty and consumption. Slaves hungered to sample and own literary and consumer goods and transgress the cultural spaces where they were exchanged because such activities often resonated with the thrill of emancipation. Their appetites as buyers reflected a conception of political identity that loosely combined the role of citizen and consumer: to be free was to be able to buy what they wanted and could afford.[9] Emancipation intensified this link. In the months following the Civil War in Mississippi, for example, black farm workers from across the state demanded labor contracts stripped of clothing provisions. They preferred to wear vestments of their own choosing or design largely because the pants and shirts provided to them by white landowners too closely resembled, in many cases, the quality and style of slave clothing.[10] Making what they wore also offered the exciting potential of fashioning extra shirts, pants, and socks and selling them to kith and kin.

The market's role in black spiritual life in the Delta after Reconstruction, however, grew at once broader and denser. During the 1880s and 1890s, the number of commercial stores in the Delta soared, making it easier for residents to learn about manufactured products. By 1900, each county in Arkansas and Mississippi averaged 144 stores, nearly all white-owned. Typically they were small businesses—saloons, barber-shops, drug stores, and furniture shops—grouped in threes and fours in rural towns. The most important was the general store, where visitors viewed an expanding range of agricultural and consumer products.[11] One turn-of-the-century store near Percy's hometown in the Mississippi Delta sold "[p]lows, harnesses, bridles, saddles, rolls of rope and barbed wire, and chains ranging in size from log chains to trace chains. . . . Inside were barrels of flour, molasses, and sugar, crates of sardines, salmon and potted meat, drums of coal oil, and other staples." Others stacked display cases with fancier goods, such as bolts of gingham cloth, belts with silver buckles, patent leather shoes, pearl-handled parasols, plumed bonnets, and mosquito netting (figure 3.1).[12]

The increase in the number of southern stores and variety of domestic commodities during the late nineteenth century was the result of a series of broad shifts in the national and southern economies, especially in rural areas. From 1860 to 1890, agricultural employment rose nationally by one-half while the

Figure 3.1. Plantation Store, Sunnyside Plantation, Sunnyside, Arkansas, circa 1900 (courtesy of the Mississippi Department of Archive and History).

total amount of newly tilled land increased by 431 million acres, helping to boost the yield on cotton, wheat, and corn by 150 percent by the century's end. This rising supply of raw materials helped to lower production costs and boost the total output of manufactured clothing and foods. The new products moved from the warehouse to the market faster and more easily because of the concomitant expansion of railroads. New policy directives created by the federal government contributed to the increase in the flow of goods and services, as well. The founding of the Federal Bureau of Public Roads in 1893 helped ensure the expansion and upkeep of roads and turnpikes. The U.S. Post Office greatly enhanced the widespread success of mail order buying by implementing a one-cent advertisers' postcard in 1871, rural free delivery in 1898, which provided a new point of access to consumer goods for many blacks, and finally the national parcel post program in 1912.[13] The rise of rural agricultural newspapers kept the public up to date about the latest piece of farm equipment or home utensils, while a slow but steady rise in national rates of overall farm family incomes from 1880 to 1920 made it more possible to buy them.

Improvements in the transportation system and the consumer economy caused a surge in the supply of peddlers in the Delta, especially those who traveled by one-horse wagons. Frequently called "drummers" because of the shape of their wagons, they were a welcome sight to rural residents. A vital link to manufacturers in northern and southern cities, drummers, recalled one white Delta woman, "carried an unbelievable assortment of merchandise-bed spreads, lace curtains, pillow cases, sheeting, towels, men's shirts, undershirts and drawers." She wrote that "[t]hin cotton blankets, which kept a baby warmer than quilts, were sold along with outing yardage for boys' shirts and girls' underskirts, and cotton flannel for thick warm diapers." Sewing supplies for sale included needle and thread along with bits of "lace, embroidery, insertion, rickrack braid, and ribbons of various widths...." What drummers lacked they usually could order through the mail for their customers. Drummers eventually competed for business with their occupational cousins, the "commercial traveler," whose ranks thickened as the railroad penetrated the Delta. Compared to simple foot peddlers or drummers, he usually represented more manufacturers and offered a greater range of finished goods, such as curtains, frames, prints, medicines, and shoes. By the 1910s they were the dominant type of mobile merchant in the Delta.[14]

The growth of the consumer market in the Delta after Reconstruction, however, did not mean that it was immediately more accessible for blacks. Quite the opposite was true. Indeed, for blacks, the cultural spaces of the market became more degrading and difficult to enter than ever before because southern whites strove to etch their vision of a racially stratified society onto the modernizing experience of consumption.[15] Motivating whites was a powerful fear that blacks, emboldened by new market opportunities, might mount specific forms of challenge to the ideology of white supremacy. The market, by furnishing an unprecedented range of domestic goods to all who lived in the Delta, theoretically presented blacks with the physical ingredients from which to create the appearance of a refined lifestyle that comported with white ideals. If blacks suddenly dressed in sophisticated suits, fashionable hats, and well-heeled shoes, decorated their churches with custom-made drapes and electric chandeliers, and adorned their homes with elegant prints, pictures, and books, they threatened to destabilize white efforts to project an image of racial superiority based on the ownership and display of distinctive consumer commodities.

To counter these pressures, white storeowners and customers often embellished stock racist stereotypes by eagerly displaying new commercial advertisements and products that explicitly linked images of blackness to servility, social awkwardness, and filth. For example, wholesalers and manufacturers widely distributed trade cards, which were pocket-sized pieces of laminated cardboard with grotesque characterizations of African Americans. Published first in the 1870s and widely used until the 1920s, the cards pictured blacks as grinning servants and social buffoons aping the conventions of white middle-class society. Campaigns for soaps and other cleaning products conveyed their effectiveness and appeal to white shoppers by showing black people "washing away" their color. Starting about 1905 and continuing until the 1920s, advertisers commonly selected labels for their brands of household and personal goods that included the word "nigger," as in "Nigger Head Tobacco."[16]

These types of advertisements garlanded Delta general stores, with the exception of the very few owned by blacks. They formed a visual backdrop against which whites stylized local customs of segregation and invented new ones that shaped much of the public experience of consumption for African Americans. White shop-owners regularly compelled blacks to enter through their rear doors, sold them shoddy or damaged products, refused them the full amount of credit they needed to purchase what they wanted, and attended to them only after serving every other white customer. Many were also local creditors, which simplified the task of closely monitoring and controlling what blacks purchased and reporting about it to nearby plantation bosses and white landowners.[17]

White mistreatment and surveillance of blacks while they shopped continued at a stricter level in plantation commissaries, which, like general stores, also featured racialized advertisements. After picking cotton, for instance, it was common for sharecroppers to bring their sacks to the local plantation gin, where they received a small slip of paper with a sample of the cotton affixed to it. At this point, the croppers' sample was graded, priced, and recorded in the account book. Then the entire amount of picked cotton was stored. On settlement day, the croppers went to the landowner's office, presented the slips of paper indicating the value of their cotton, earned a credit against their debt, and received cash for amounts beyond what they owed. But even if sharecroppers were fortunate enough to earn money above their debts, landowners like Leroy Percy insisted that workers spend it at the plantation commissary where the latest consumer items were routinely kept from them.[18] Drummers theoretically promised relief from this spectacle of observation and restraint, but in practice they rarely offered a wider or fairer selection of goods or more generous terms of credit to blacks.

In the Delta's growing consumer economy at the turn-of-the-century, therefore, blackness was relentlessly experienced as a limit to commodity experimentation and accumulation. Whatever the mode of shopping or consuming, blacks regularly endured the indignity and danger of being overcharged, ignored, refused credit, and sold inferior products. Race was the most obvious and fundamental factor that influenced the contours of economic exchange for African Americans in the Delta; it directly affected what products they bought, what they paid for them, and what terms of credit they were offered. Some blacks fared better than others, of course. Black doctors, dentists, clerics, merchants and teachers living in larger towns and cities stood a decent chance that, because of their status and income, a drummer would visit them or a white merchant attend to their needs.[19] But even then the hope of fair treatment usually went unfulfilled.

Despite the racial discrimination they faced in the market, black Baptists and Methodists in the Delta persisted in demanding ever-greater entry to it. Much of their interest, of course, was historical: Delta blacks, like African Americans from across the South, traditionally sought to announce and extend their liberty and livelihood by buying and selling consumer goods. But it also reflected an amplification of a long-standing habit of integrating the shifting rhythms of economic and spiritual life. Throughout the first decades of freedom, black Baptists and Methodists liberally mixed the patterns and pressures of agricultural and commercial life into many of their religious practices. These practices lacked any extensive use of manufactured goods or marketing schemes, which is not surprising given the state of the southern consumer market before 1900. Yet they signified a popular willingness and general interest among black in braiding the spiritual with the economic, characteristics that underlay their future efforts to combine the commodities of the market with their sacred lives.

For example, black religious newspapers in the Delta sometimes published letters from readers living across the South that featured special rituals that explicitly mixed agricultural and liturgical activity. These letters effectively served as instructional guides on how to construct ceremonies that blended the seasonal nature of farming with religious ritual. In 1891, the *Southwestern Christian Recorder* reported on a black ME Church that celebrated the gathering of the crop in autumn by erecting a "harvest tree" in the northwest corner of their church and loading it "with offerings from this year's harvest, such as cotton, potatoes, cane, etc."[20] Delta blacks likely recognized the event as a symbolic gesture that recalled a specific testimony by Moses in the book of Deuteronomy. In the twenty-sixth chapter, Moses advised the Israelites to give thanks to God for leading them from Egypt to Canaan Land. He directed them to "take some first fruits of various products of the soil which you harvest from the land which the Lord, your God, gives you and put them in a basket and go to the place which the Lord, your God, choose for the dwelling place of his name. . . . The Priest shall then receive the basket from you and shall set it in front of the altar."[21]

More commonly, Delta blacks made decisions about when to conduct religious celebrations and gatherings based on the crop schedule. Mississippi Baptists living in Tunica County, a sinuous stretch of rich farmland encoiled by the Mississippi River in the northwestern tip of the state, regularly "had a vacation" from all society and missionary unions during the long days of "cotton-readying" in the spring.[22]

Experienced clergy typically planned revivals and denominational conferences with one eye trained on the farmers' calendar, carefully choosing the end of the harvest season in the fall as the ideal time. It was only then that rural agricultural workers had a little time and extra cash on hand. Evangelists and missionaries foolish enough to ignore this agricultural cycle of work typically failed to raise as much money or to save as many souls as they wanted. Baptist minister J. E. Knox could not squeeze a penny from Arkansas sharecroppers while soliciting for Arkansas Baptist College in early summer 1894. It was planting time and, as Reverend Knox complained, "[t]he people . . . are farmers and of course a large contribution at this season is impossible."[23]

On a more literal level, African Americans frequently integrated the physical elements of their labor as farmers and sharecroppers directly into their sacred lives. When crops were poor and cash was scarce, blacks in the Arkansas Delta built churches from whatever resources were at hand. In 1892, founding members of the Zion Wheel Baptist Church outside of Little Rock put up a rough-and-tumble church made of tree limbs and discarded lumber. It sat in the middle of the cotton field that they tilled.[24] During the busy weeks of planting season, it was common for farmers to use every available structure for storage, including their churches. The sight of cattle feed and cotton seed scattered about the pulpit initially puzzled Reverend J. W. E. Bradley when he began to preach in churches throughout Mississippi in June 1895. Bradley, a missionary with the CME church who apparently was not from the area or an agricultural family, penned a letter to his denominational weekly expressing his astonishment and curiosity. I "went to the church and to my surprise I beheld on one side about 200 bundles of fodder, in another about three loads of hay and around the pulpit about 100 bushels of cotton seed."[25] Bradley soon learned that this was a common way that Delta blacks mixed the competing demands of church and work during the early summer in cotton-growing areas.

These examples, while illuminating a history of the porous cultural boundaries between African American spiritual and economic life in the Delta, do not shed new light directly on the question of why, at the turn of the century, blacks suddenly strove to incorporate modern consumer goods as well as techniques of buying and selling into their religion to an unprecedented degree. The key to illuminating the answer lies in recognizing the new consumer market's growing allure as a reservoir of practical aid and inspiration for Delta blacks eager to drum up dollars and public support for their growing number of new churches and denominational organizations. Starting in the late 1870s, black Baptists and Methodists slowly started to expand their local networks of religiously based institutions by constructing new houses of worship and, often for the first time, allied primary schools, district associations, women's conventions, Sunday schools, newspapers, presses, and pastors' and young people's "unions."[26]

Yet their survival required a steady supply of care and cash, prompting many black ministers and laypeople to consider how they might profit from the growing southern consumer market by adopting versions of its advertising tactics and peddling some of its goods.

Fortunately, the new denominational networks developed structurally in ways that facilitated solving some of the financial challenges that they raised. Many of the new schools and associations were tightly clustered in neighborhoods or small towns, met frequently, were part of larger district and state conventions whose delegates gathered as regularly as every two weeks, and published minutes, proceedings, newspapers, and pamphlets. As a result, black Baptists and Methodists saw, heard from, read about, met, and corresponded with each other in greater and more intimate detail than ever before. In effect, they created and participated in nexuses of modern communication that were crucial contexts for the flow of information about the market: through them, African American consumer desire and demand partly took shape and circulated through the Delta. Equally important, entrepreneurial black church leaders tapped them to promote and sell manufactured goods whose proceeds promised to fund part of the expense of their expanding list of denominational institutions.

The associational history of the black Baptists of the Arkansas Delta during the late nineteenth and early twentieth centuries is broadly representative of the costly and intense associational development experienced by all of the major black denominations in the Delta. It provides a valuable window onto the ways in which the growth of African American religion slowly led to a growing involvement by blacks in the consumer market, transforming preachers and churches into important sources of information about modern consumption. It also shows how the boundaries of sacred and commercial life were in constant tension, steadily overlapping and intersecting in ways that reshaped black political and spiritual identity.

The Arkansas State Baptist Convention (ASBC) officially began in 1867 inside First Baptist Church in Pine Bluff. The ASBC devoted its first decade to accomplishing the twin tasks of winning members and setting up churches. It enjoyed smashing success on both fronts, according to the official history of the Convention, as "during this period thousands of converts were born into faith and hundreds of churches organized. . . ." By the late 1870s, however, the roughly thirty thousand Arkansas Baptists started to organize their individual churches into small, interlocking local district associations. These associations, in turn, founded their own clubs, unions, and primary and secondary schools. Among these small grassroots institutions the school was arguably the most important because it offered an alternative to inadequate black public educational facilities and stood as a highly visible badge of local denominational identity. For instance, the Southeast District

Baptist Association in the Arkansas Delta, composed of Ashley, Chicot, Desha, and Drew counties, began making plans for its first school in the mid-1880s. Motivating its members, explained district president Reverend Isaac Bailey, was the grave concern that "[t]he public's school terms were so short and the schools poorly supplied with teaching force." Equally compelling was a fear of falling behind other black churches in the drive to recruit and sustain congregants. "[O]ther denominations were opening little schools all around us. For thus we thought it wise to rise up and do some thing to save our children and denomination."[27]

Smaller associations like Southeast District Baptist often teamed up with neighboring ones to form statewide governing structures for their schools and other associations. Baptist primary schools pooled their resources to support Arkansas Baptist College, the first college established by ASBC, in 1882. Two years later it housed the state's first black Baptist press and published the state's first black Baptist newspaper, *The Baptist Vanguard*. In 1881, leaders of local Sunday schools in the Delta began to draw up plans for the Arkansas Sunday School Convention. Their efforts came to full fruition in 1887, when they elected the first president of the Convention. And Baptist women built on their successes at forming church and district level women's associations and established the Women's State Convention in 1888 and, for their children, the Baptist Young People's Union in 1898.[28]

Embodying the growth and organizational development of the Arkansas State Baptist Convention was the pastoral career of its most famous leader, E. C. (Elias Camp) Morris, who was the most powerful black cleric in the Delta by the twentieth century. Born a slave in 1855 in Murray County, Georgia, Morris went no further than high school in his education. At age nineteen he began preaching at a Baptist church near his birthplace. In 1877 he accepted a call to pastor at Centennial Church in Helena, Arkansas. Three years later Morris' peers in Arkansas elected him secretary of the ASBC and president shortly thereafter. He helped establish Arkansas Baptist College and served as the Chairman of its Board of Trustees for sixteen years. At the national level, Morris was elected as the first president of the all-black National Baptist Convention (NBC), begun in 1895 in Nashville, Tennessee, as the governing body for all black Baptists. He served in this office until his death in 1922. He also was a founding member of the National Baptist Publishing House, begun in 1896 as the publishing arm of the NBC, and coedited one of its quarterly publications, *The Teacher* (figure 3.2).[29]

The efforts of Baptists in the Arkansas Delta to create an extensive network of local denominational organizations with ties to larger state, regional, and national ones were matched, with varying degrees of success, by the other major black religious groups in the Delta. Each created its own set of associations that formed a vital forum for the elaboration of black sacred life and its intersection with the

Figure 3.2. E. C. Morris, 1901. E. C. Morris, *Sermons, Addresses, and Reminiscences and Important Correspondence, with a Picture Gallery of Eminent Ministers* (National Baptist Publishing Board, 1901).

consumer market. In 1883, the black Baptists of the Mississippi Delta took control of the struggling Natchez Seminary in Natchez, Mississippi, their only religious school in the state at that time. In a bid to raise its profile and attract more students, they relocated it to the state capitol and renamed it Jackson College. The Mississippi Baptists lacked a local newspaper and relied on their brethren in Arkansas and the *Baptist Vanguard* for much of their weekly news. Their difficulty in establishing a denominational voice probably stemmed from their fractured organizational structure and young national governing body. The Mississippi Baptist Convention, formed in 1869, oversaw the western part of the state while the Greater Missionary Baptist Union, established in 1872, presided over the central and northern regions of Mississippi. The groups only united in 1890, under the banner of the General Baptist Missionary Convention of Mississippi.[30]

The three major black Methodist churches in the Delta enjoyed greater success than the Mississippi Baptists in establishing and sustaining local colleges. Their superior achievements stemmed from the financial and logistical support provided by their older national church organizations or, in the case of the Colored Methodist Episcopalians, the substantial patronage of white Methodist leaders of the Methodist Episcopal Church, South. The national church bodies underwrote and published the main newspapers used by the local denominational churches and helped fund their schools. The AME Church sponsored the *Christian Recorder*. Its schools in the area were Shorter College, begun in 1886 in Little Rock, and Campbell College, started in 1887 and boasting two campuses based in the Mississippi Delta, at Vicksburg and Friar's Point. In 1898, however, Campbell closed its Delta schools and established a single campus in the state's capitol, Jackson.[31] Black members of the ME Church in Arkansas and Mississippi looked to the ME Church and the *Southwestern Christian Advocate* for their news. First published in 1868 in New Orleans, a regional head-quarters for the ME Church, the *Southwestern Christian Advocate* served black members throughout the Southwest and employed blacks as editors and agents. Black ME ministers regularly read the newspaper from pulpit in order to deliver its stories to the illiterate.[32] In 1887 in Little Rock, Arkansas, church members founded Philander Smith as a school to train ministers. In Mississippi, local leaders joined national church officials and began Rust College in 1868 in Holly Springs with the goal of making it the premier school for black Methodists in the Delta.[33]

Colored Methodist Episcopalians patronized Lane Institute, which opened in 1882, and read the *Christian Index,* founded in 1868. Both institutions were located in the spiritual seat of the denomination, Jackson, Tennessee, about sixty miles northeast of Memphis. Lane benefited handsomely from the patronage of white leaders of the Methodist Episcopal Church, South: they provided the first president of the school, a white minister who served for twenty-one years, and a gift of $7,000 in 1911. Their generosity stemmed from what CME bishop Lucius Holsey described as their moral requirement to help his church. "Although we have become two bands, yet it is, and was understood that this does not, in any sense, release the Methodist Episcopal Church, South, from those duties and obligations that Providence seems to have imposed upon her, in aiding the American African [*sic*] in his Christian development."[34] The Christian Methodist Episcopalians of Mississippi opened Mississippi Industrial College in 1905 in Holly Springs, about fifty miles northwest of the Delta.[35]

This thickening of black denominational culture in the Delta was part of the general growth of southern black organizational life as a whole. Starting shortly after the Civil War and accelerating during the 1880s and 1890s, African Americans steadily built colleges and presses that produced a slow but constant rise in the rate of black literacy, the enrollment of black students in schools of all levels, and the number of black newspapers and journals.[36] Skillful black leadership was the key ingredient in the spread of these new organizations, although support from white philanthropists and white Protestant churches from the North was an important factor at times. Nationally, the most famous examples of interracial educational partnership were Tuskegee University, built by Booker T. Washington with the patronage of Andrew Carnegie and John D. Rockefeller; and Fisk University, heavily sponsored by the Congregational Church and its teachers.[37]

Significantly, black Baptists and Methodists in the Delta viewed their networks of churches, schools, and newspapers as far more than public gauges of denominational progress. They saw them as incubators of racial advancement and religious freedom, places where they worshipped their own God, congregated freely, learned to read, and chronicled and published their own histories. Had they not, few would have worked so tirelessly to ensure their survival and explored so intently the consumer market as a source for their success. Reverend Richard Sinquefield, a divine with the Arkansas Conference of the AME Church, captured the dominant public view of the fundamental role played by these religious institutions in the advancement of black spiritual culture in the Delta in his 1907 autobiography. He wrote, "[h]ere I am on the mountain of seventy-six years and I can look down in the valley and view every path that leads to the summit. I know them for I have traveled them." The "path" guided blacks to the denomination's primary schools, college, and churches. "I know when there was not a Negro school house, when there was not a Negro Church building" continued Sinquefield. "But glory to God the black night is past, the sunlight of God's blessings is shining everywhere. We have schoolhouses everywhere, colleges such as our own dear Shorter, we have church buildings from log cabins to rock edifices, and . . . we can go at all times to serve our God."[38]

Many black Baptists and Methodists in the Delta also steadfastly backed their denominational networks because they saw them as a vital tool in lessening the threat of racial violence, but in conservative ways that did not always attack the problem aggressively or directly. A key spokesman for this point of view was Reverend E. C. Morris. Speaking at the 1908 annual meeting of the Arkansas Baptist State Convention shortly after a lynching of a black man, Morris first voiced disbelief and horror over the act. "Lawless mobs have frequently entered the safety vaults of our temples of justice and pulled from the cells helpless prisoners, and almost in sight of the church and the schoolhouse, have shot to death or roasted alive cringing wretches who may have deserved death, but not until tried and convicted under the laws of our country." Morris quickly calmed himself, however, and devoted the next part of his address to soothing his audience. A cautious and conservative man by nature, he struck one of his familiar themes—that the best solution to the problem of "lawless mobs" was for blacks to seek justice patiently and sustain their denominational schools. These schools, counseled Morris, promised to raise up disciplined black Christians whose industry and sterling character would overturn the chief cause of racial violence: white fears of African Americans as lewd, ill-tempered creatures subject to fits of uncontrollable passion. Not surprisingly, Morris highlighted the efforts of Arkansas Baptist College in the work of improving race relations, implying that it offered its students and supporters the surest route to a safe and prosperous future. "The education work of the Convention is yet the central and principal work before us, and I am pleased to say that it has a warm place in the heart of every lowly Baptist in the State."[39]

Morris's opinion on the subject of racial violence was not the only one in the Delta. Sharply differing with him was Henry McNeil Turner, the outspoken AME bishop who brooked no compromise with white vigilantism. As the bishop over Mississippi and Arkansas during the early 1880s and from other pulpits in the South later on, he steadily encouraged blacks to fight threats to their physical safety and protect their families at all costs. There was little to lose by openly challenging one's oppressor. Turner, of course, also favored black emigration to the northern states or, more radically, to the west coast of Africa as another strategy of survival in the post-Reconstruction South. Movement away from the former Confederacy, he advocated, was the best way to regain a sense of liberty and reestablish, especially for African American men, a sense of pride and control over their lives. Yet Turner's views, however bold and exiting, won few committed followers in the Delta while Morris's less controversial ideas did.[40] Delta blacks tended to react to Jim Crow not so much by contesting it in the ways outlined by Turner but by following Morris' lead and attempting to become educated, to work harder, and to save more.

Another reason for the popularity of the local associations was their role in promoting worldly success. Morris' close friend and associate, Reverend John A. Robinson, testified that his participation in the Arkansas Baptists' network of churches and schools was a primary reason for his rise from slave to high-ranking preacher. As he recounted in a tract published in 1911, he grew up as a slave on a cotton plantation in northeastern Mississippi. After the Civil War, he worked as a sharecropper and learned to read and write by attending a local Baptist school. Eventually Robinson became the teacher at the school, a job he held until 1878, when he officially joined the Baptists and became an itinerant preacher traveling up and down the banks of the Mississippi River. Eight years later he accepted an offer to pastor the Arkansas' oldest black Baptist church, First Baptist, founded by slaves in

1845 in Little Rock. Shortly afterward he enrolled in Arkansas Baptist College and became its first graduate in 1900.[41]

In his tract, Robinson hit upon a final factor for why black Baptists and Methodists went to great lengths to build their associations and networks when he stressed their role in establishing religious newspapers and presses. They not only boosted rates of black literacy, readership, and authorship, he pointed out, but also countered efforts by Democratic politicians to whitewash black contributions to the making of the Delta and the United States. He wrote that "our words and deeds [must] be printed so that the unborn generations in their flight of triumph to glorious achievements may sing, not of sorrow, but of joy." He warned that if newspapers like the *Baptist Vanguard* ever collapsed blacks risked losing a sense of their own past. "Our name and worth to the American civilization, unless we bestir ourselves, will be blotted out." Indeed, Robinson added, "[n]o race can ever amount to much . . . [unless] it takes to make history for themselves that others may read it in the time to come with pride. . . ."[42]

Robinson's belief in the critical value that black religious literature played in creating and representing African American accomplishments was part of a broader strain of conviction shared by many black ministers and congregants about the need to improve the overall quality of public literature for blacks through strong denominational presses. Along with many white church officials and laymen, African American Baptists and Methodists generally feared that most white secular publishers produced pamphlets, books, magazines, and newspapers without fully considering their ethical or moral content; instead, they pandered to the public's prurient impulses and tried to drive up sales by offering sleazy stories, graphic romances, gaudy tales of women corrupted by unrestrained lusts for power and sex, and lurid chronicles of deceit, falsehood, and shame. All too absent was a steady supply of wholesome Christian literature to teach and inspire readers about the redemptive sacrifice of Jesus, the rewards of a life led according to biblical precepts, and the virtues of honesty, chastity, temperance, and fidelity. To be sure, northern-based white religious publishers, such as the American Sunday School Union and the American Baptist Home Mission Society, responded to this perceived lack of proper spiritual literature by expanding the breadth and depth of their own offerings during the 1880s and 1890s. But many black Christians found this new output to be objectionable as well, although for their own reasons: it usually focused on the history of white denominations and either ignored the role of black people in the evolution of Christianity or depicted them in starkly racist terms. Also troubling was the fact that the money black Baptists and Methodists spent on purchasing a Bible or song book or history sold by white religious publishers did little to benefit African American churches or schools.[43] As a result, most Delta blacks shared Robinson's opinion that the best resolution to the problem of offensive religious literature lay in supporting black denominational newspapers and publishing houses.

Reverend E. C. Morris built one of these new church-based publishing houses. After the establishment of the National Baptist Convention in 1895, Morris championed the development of a national publishing house based in Nashville as a way to inculcate racial pride and denominational identity.[44] The task of organizing and running the National Baptist Publishing House fell to Richard Henry Boyd of Tennessee, who was then head of the newly formed NBC Sunday School Union. Under the aegis of the NBC Sunday School Union in 1896, Boyd bought a printing press and building and began producing religious literature for the denomination. A skillful businessman, Boyd incorporated the National Baptist Publishing House under Tennessee law in 1898 and copyrighted material in his own name. By 1905 his company boasted $2.4 million in overall sales; five years later, it counted more than 150 blacks as employees and organized a small savings bank.[45]

Boyd's sparkling success as an entrepreneur, however, raised eyebrows among some clergy curious about where all the money was going and led the NBC to launch a formal investigation into the publishing house's finances. What followed was an episode that split the NBC and serves as a reminder that the process of expanding a denomination's local and regional networks sometimes sparked irreconcilable conflict among members. The first stage of the inquiry discovered evidence suggesting that Boyd was lining his own pockets with the proceeds he earned through the Sunday School Union. Yet when church officials demanded to see all of his record books in 1907, Boyd stonewalled. He steadfastly maintained his innocence and refused to cooperative with investigators for eight years. Tensions boiled over in 1915. Boyd, tired by an unremitting string of allegations of financial impropriety, formally renounced his membership in the NBC. Upon leaving, he, in a move that infuriated his former colleagues, took the publishing house with him and made it the foundation for a new national black Baptist organization, the National Baptist Convention, Unincorporated. Controlling the publishing house in this way was perfectly legal because it was still incorporated in Boyd's name.[46]

Although most Baptists and Methodists strongly endorsed their new institutions, they struggled to find the extra money to stabilize them. As an early strategy of shoring up their denominational associations, church officials simply ordered ministers and congregants to sacrifice financially. In 1878, the AME hierarchy alerted its southern clerics "that they will not be able to get their licenses renewed if they do not take the CHRISTIAN RECORDER and read it."[47] That same year the Bishops of the CME Church, in an attempt to relieve the burden of debt threatening the livelihood of the *Christian Index,* decreed that every preacher subscribe to the newspaper. Those who refused risked being publicly sanctioned.[48] And as late as 1892 blacks from the Upper Mississippi Conference of the ME Church gave money both to Rust College and the *Southwest Christian Advocate* in accordance with a new resolution. It read that "the future prosperity of the Church depends on the development of the whole man, head, hand, and heart" and that "we as a Conference rejoice in the success of establishing institutions of higher learning in the Southern States . . . . [and] work for the interest of that grand and noble cause."[49] As a result, churches organized special events like "Rust Day," when congregants offered special prayers for the success of the college and took up a collection whose final tally was publicly reported at the annual state conference the following winter.[50]

Simply demanding more money from clerics and congregants, however, tended to fall short as a strategy of fundraising. Few of the approximately forty-one black religious newspapers founded between 1880 and 1897 across Mississippi, for example, lasted very long. Nearly every one collapsed within twenty-four months of publishing their first edition.[51] Success rates were no better in Arkansas; only the *Baptist Vanguard* survived more than three years. Typical was the story of the *South-East Advocate,* the short-lived newspaper of the Southeastern Baptist District Association in Arkansas. As reported by the district's president, Reverend Bailey, "[t]his paper was doing fairly well and was keeping the people informed about the work of the District, but a great many of the subscribers got behind and the editor of the paper began to cry out for help but failed to get relief."[52]

Like the denominational newspapers, schools and colleges struggled as well. In 1880 a group of Baptists preachers from the Arkansas Delta formed the Pastor's Union in the hope of building a seminary and university that would be called Helena and based in the Delta town of the same name. But poor fundraising apparently doomed the project from the start.[53] The educational institutions that succeeded often did so only by the narrowest of margins. In April 1895 Arkansas Baptist College, which was the legacy of Helena University, teetered on the verge of collapse and shut its doors for several months because its executive board failed "to raise sufficient means to supplement the tuition and meet the demands of the Institute." It reopened only when it had enough cash on-hand to cover its operating expenses.[54] Lane Institute, the CME college, routinely faced severe budgetary shortfalls that threatened its existence. Its unstable financial condition forced its main spokesman and namesake, Bishop Isaac Lane, to work so doggedly and so aggressively at fundraising that some of his peers privately took to calling him "the beggar."[55]

With the threat of economic ruin hanging over many of their religious institutions, black religious leaders were under continuous strain to find new ways to bring in money. At times they successfully appealed to sympathetic white churches and religious organizations for small amounts of aid and material assistance. For example, when Richard Boyd worked to open the doors of his National Baptist Publishing

House in 1896, he begged his white counterparts with the American Baptist Publishing Society to loan him printing and book plates; when they turned him down for fear of increased competition in the selling of religious literature, he quickly appealed to another white organization, the Southern Baptist Convention, and got what he wanted.[56] Still, blacks, regardless of their denomination, could never completely depend on a steady stream of aid from white benefactors. To ensure the health and longevity of their institutions, they were forced to rely primarily on their own wherewithal. As Reverend E. C. Morris bluntly pointed out, black Baptist organizations in Arkansas desperately and immediately needed to inspire greater levels of public aid because the cost of supporting their growing denominational networks kept spiraling upward. In his 1902 presidential address to the annual meeting of the state's black Baptist leaders, he claimed that "[t]he things which, twenty years ago, would be cheerfully done by the pastors or our churches, without cost, and sometimes at a sacrifice of their personal means, cannot be done now unless the money is in hand to pay for it before the work is done. . . ."[57]

The perpetual need for amassing more money and rallying greater levels of public enthusiasm for their new spiritual associations and networks eventually pushed black Baptists and Methodists in the Delta to explore the expanding consumer market for assistance. This is not to imply that it was the only reason. Delta blacks certainly turned to the market as a cultural site to experience a sense of liberty through acts of consumption, boost entrepreneurial activity as in starting a general store or advertising a new business, and sell self-made goods. These causes, however, were generally not religious ones. The requirement to support the development of denominational schools, newspapers, and presses was, and it led blacks to experiment with ways of integrating the market into their daily spiritual lives.

In one of their earliest instances of selectively borrowing from the consumer economy for the specific purpose of sustaining their religious networks, Delta blacks created a new type of fundraising tactic. To raise cash for Arkansas Baptist College following its near collapse in 1895, the Board of Trustees, composed almost entirely of Baptist ministers, boldly adopted a language of credit and debt as part of their public appeals. They publicly likened their campaigns to attempts by a private business to increase its cash assets by incorporating itself and selling stock to the public. This technique of selling "shares" in the college had been tried several years earlier, but tentatively and with little fanfare. It had been, though, at least partly successful in winning some donations: members of the Arkansas Baptist Sunday School Convention passed a resolution in early 1886 that authorized the treasurer to "purchase five shares of stock in the Arkansas Baptist College."[58] But now, facing mounting bills and living at a time of greater public knowledge about the market and its financing mechanisms, the trustees confidently invited every black Baptist church across the state to join their "Stockholders' Association" by purchasing "shares" at the cost of fifty dollars each. "Stockholders," they advertised, enjoyed the privilege of attending yearly meetings to discuss the financial health of the college. Those churches unable to make a lump sum payment of fifty dollars could elect to use the "installment plan" and enjoy the benefit of spreading the payments out over several months.

The trustees assumed correctly that many black Baptists were familiar with popular commercial ideas about structuring debt, but they badly misjudged how their audience would interpret them. Potential donors, probably influenced by financial depression of 1893 and 1894, believed that the sudden selling of stock by the Trustees indicated that the college was on slippery footing and so they quickly snapped their wallets shut. Trustees responded immediately by assuring local leaders that just the opposite was true: the stock was "benevolent and not speculative." They hastily clarified that "the 'shares' simply means so many units of responsibility for the launching of a first-class Baptist College, and the investments were bread 'cast upon the waters to come back after many days'—not in the form of cash dividends; b[ut] 'dividends' [of] character and religious leadership."[59] The explanations apparently worked. Many church leaders soon became full-fledged stockholders, which allowed for the school to open on schedule.[60]

Although the strategies employed by the Trustees of Arkansas Baptist College were a shaky success, they inspired imitations in later years. When the leaders of the Southeast District Baptist Association in the Arkansas Delta decided to build their school in 1897, they recruited individuals and churches to become members of a fledgling "Stockholders' Association." They met their goal of raising $20,000 by selling "shares of $30 each, which was to be paid by installments of $6 a year."[61] Similarly, in 1900, black Baptists from Pine Bluff, Arkansas, successfully raised money for a grade school based on what they called the "joint stock plan." The ministers were the "trustees" while churches and congregants were the "stock-holders" of the Pine Bluff Normal School. Shares sold at $25 each and, according to a report on the school, "a sufficient number of shares was subscribed and paid for to encourage the leaders in organizing and starting that school."[62]

More commonly, black religious leaders, especially those who were college presidents and newspaper editors, increasingly raised money by treating their constituents as consumers who donated only when given something tangible in return. The Trustees for Arkansas Baptist College awarded a free student scholarship to every church, Sunday school convention, and women's association that contributed at least fifty dollars.[63] Reverend Joseph Booker, the school's president and the editor of the *Baptist Vanguard,* organized alumni to sell pencils stamped with the name of their alma mater. Booker hoped to sell hundreds, delivering them either in person, through a colleague, or through the mail. He believed that the pencils held symbolic significance for sharecroppers and tenant farmers without any formal education as well as for all black people who, "when they buy these pencils, . . . give and yet get something back—that's the only way the majority of our people care to give."[64]

Whether Booker's campaign netted the desired amount of cash is uncertain, but his philosophy of rewarding patrons with a small commodity signaled a subtle shift in the relationship between faith and consumption among Delta blacks in the late nineteenth century. Even though Reverend Booker sold only pencils, his fundraising campaign indicated that his role as a preacher was beginning to encompass a new level of involvement with the commercial market—in this case, the distribution of small manufactured items. It was an idea embedded in a later fundraising effort by Booker. On January 1, 1905, he mailed a special thank-you note to everyone who gave money to Arkansas Baptist College during the previous year. It was a bright red promissory note shaped like an oversized dollar bill, issued by the "Bank of Prosperity" and paying its owner "Three-Hundred and Sixty-Five Happy Days." The note featured a historical panorama of the progress of civilization, represented as a series of small sketches of rural tee-pee dwellers, a mill with a water wheel, a solitary farmer guiding a plow drawn by two horses, a large train running down a track, and finally factories three- and four-stories high with puffing chimneys and a large horn filled with coins (figure 3.3).[65] Sending his supporters this pledge of future prosperity in exchange for their financial assistance was, of course, a clever and eye-catching means of expressing his gratitude. It reminded patrons of the significance of Arkansas Baptist College in advancing the progress of black Baptists and the race in general. Yet in compensating his donors by paying them in a fictitious currency, Booker, however whimsically, reinforced the idea that black preachers were slowly becoming a type of broker of knowledge about the market and some of its products.

Like Booker, other black spiritual leaders began rewarding financial supporters and active workers with small, mass-produced items sometimes marked with recognizable emblems of African American religion or history. In 1896, editors of the *Southwestern Christian Advocate* gave new subscribers a free set of communion implements; two years later, they offered a calendar that recalled their Methodist heritage by featuring a different scene each month from the life of John Wesley.[66] During subscription drives, editors presented the most industrious agents with a new Epworth organ or "fine $75 Mead Bicycle."[67] Similarly, in 1895, the presiding elders and pastors of the ME Church sold pictures of Frederick Douglass for one dollar to raise money for Rust University.[68] And in 1896, men and women scanning the *Baptist Vanguard* learned that a new, leather-bound Bible could be theirs for free if they subscribed (figure 3.4).[69] Or if they preferred, they could receive an "Emancipation Chart," a two-feet high reproduction of the Emancipation Proclamation

Figure 3.3. Bank Note, 1905, Bailey-Thurman Papers (Manuscript, Archive, and Rare Book Library, Emory University).

framed by winged angels and a series of elaborate sketches of blacks progressing from slavery to freedom.[70]

Whether it was a calendar, bike, picture of a famous African American, or wall hanging, blacks began to discover and gain access to a narrow range of consumer goods by patronizing their ministers and denominational newspapers. Even more important, they saw that an act of consumption performed through a black religious institution carried distinctive racial and political meaning. In these examples, Delta black men and women witnessed how their financial support for a beloved cause brought new products into their homes—products that were otherwise difficult, if not impossible, to obtain and which, in their physical makeup (as in the case of the stylized reproduction of the Emancipation Proclamation), often represented a proud moment in their history.

This defining of market behavior as a collaborative statement about religious and racial identification took sharper form as black newspapers began to advise readers directly about how to minimize the problem of racism that they frequently experienced in the marketplace. Increasingly, editors served as guides to the politics of face-to-face shopping by alerting readers about merchants who treated blacks unfairly because of their skin color. In 1894, church leaders listed on the masthead of the *Baptist Vanguard* urged constituents to avoid reading any Arkansas white newspaper or patronizing its advertisers if they failed to oppose lynching or the recent expulsion of local blacks from the rank of postal employees.[71] Likewise, editors at the *Arkansas Mansion,* an independent black newspaper published off and on during the 1880s and 1890s in Little Rock, consistently encouraged their audience to avoid patronizing white businessmen who flatly refused to advertise with them. "In canvassing among the merchants, we find it as a rule, very

A WONDERFUL GIFT!!

It Beats The World

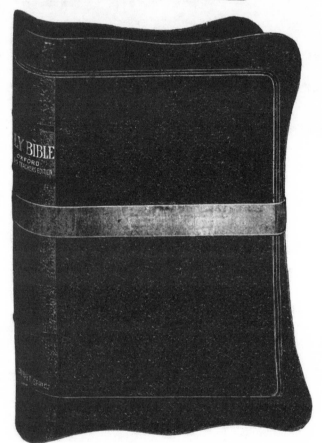

We Have Offered many premiums, but here is some-thing that surprises us. We can put this Oxford Bible and the Vanguard One Year for $2.50 when You Would have TO pay $3.00 FOR THE Bible.

Send Us $2.50 Directly To This Office And We Will Send You The Vanguard ONE YEAR, And At The Same Time SEND you This Oxford Bible.

IT IS A LIBRARY IN ITSELF IT IS A MARVEL THERE IS NOTHING EQUAL TO IT

Figure 3.4. Baptist Vanguard, 30 July 1896.

difficult to secure advertisements," opened an editorial entitled "To the Colored People of Little Rock" in October 1883 and repeated in nearly identical fashion in subsequent editions for years to come, with only the names of the blackballed commercial establishments changing. "The merchants' plea is that the colored people are too ignorant to be guided by advertisements." To prove such ideas wrong and to punish their authors, the editors exhorted readers to shop only at the white-owned stores whose proprietors advertised in their paper. "For the next thirty days patronize Gus Blass & Co, M. M. Cohn & Co., Ottenheimer Bros., M. Stern for dry goods, etc. and every body else whose name appears in the *Mansion*. . . ."[72] Whether these calls for protest became actual boycotts that successfully changed the behavior of white merchants is unknown but probably unlikely.[73] Nevertheless, the editorials enabled black religious organizations to provide an alternate source of knowledge about the market to their readers.

More significantly, editors of black religious presses influenced readers' dealings with the marketplace by transforming sections of their newspapers into abbreviated mail order catalogues. They vouchsafed the quality and fair price of most items advertised in their pages and guaranteed the buyer's full satisfaction with a money back guarantee. Sometimes they even promised to secure fair terms of credit backed by the manufacturer. Interested readers mailed back an order with payment to the editors, who then contacted the wholesaler or manufacturer, arranged for delivery via an itinerant minister or the postal service, and sometimes pocketed a small commission on the sale.

Leading the way were the editors at the *Southwestern Christian Advocate,* who, taking advantage of their publishing house being based in New Orleans as well as their close ties to the white leaders of the ME Church, forged a series of relationships with local and national white manufacturers interested in finding new avenues to reach black consumers. They openly pitched their press as one of the most sensible and economical ways to shop. Subscribers learned that they could buy a twelve-volume encyclopedia at half-off the normal price and with no shipping cost if they placed an order through the newspaper (figure 3.5).[74] If they wanted a new bell for their church, they could entrust their order to an editor who worked closely with a maker in New Orleans.[75] To quell any apprehensions about buying an item advertised through their paper, editors inserted a comforting pledge: "Our readers will please bear in mind that every organ, piano, bell or book purchased through us, helps to swell the profits of the Book Concern; and, further more, we can and do give purchasers better articles at lower prices than if sent elsewhere.[76] One 1894 offer, which simultaneously underscored the newspaper's role as a purveyor of domestic commodities and reminded readers that items purchased through the paper helped it to survive and supported the overall cause of black Methodism, offered a Singer Sewing machine at a steeply discounted price with the word "Advocate" boldly stenciled in big white letters on both sides of its metal casing (figure 3.6).[77]

... THIS $16.00 SET FREE! ...

CHAMBER'S .....
AMERICAN ENCYCLOPEDIA

WHEELER PUBLISHING Co., CONCORD, N.H.

12 Volumes, bound in gilt cloth, well illustrated.

Contains 12,214 pages of important information to every
Student of History and the present times. A valuable
addition to your library, occupying 24 inches of shelf room.

WE have arranged with the publishers of this latest edition of "CHAMBER'S ENCYCLO-
PEDIA " to furnish us with a limited number of sets for our subscribers at a price
within the reach of all.
If you will send us $8.00, we will renew your subscription for one year, and send this
library to your nearest freight or express office. Or, if you will send us 20 new subscribers,
we will send this entire set **absolutely free.**
Address at once, while this offer holds good.

Figure 3.5. Southwestern Christian Recorder, 20 July 1893.

In these examples, black newspaper editors offered a fresh opportunity for their
constituents simultaneously to participate in the consumer economy and shore up
the financial future of their spiritual organizations. Yet some took a more personal
interest in selling and joined the ranks of the small but growing number of itinerant
black ministers who literally scoured the countryside for converts with a Bible in one
hand and a bag of consumer good advertisements and catalogues in the other. These
ministers symbolized the growth of a distinctive breed of black entrepreneur in the
post-Reconstruction South—that of the preacher as peddler. Following traditional
preaching circuits or new ones, they turned their pastoral visits into occasions both
to save souls and to sell a narrow range of literary and consumer goods usually
produced by northern white manufacturers.

THE BEST OF ALL!

The Publishers have recently made arrangements whereby we can furnish the best sewing machine at the lowest price that any paper has yet offered. It is the same or better machine than we have heretofore offered at $20 including the SOUTHWESTERN for a year.

It is made especially for us and named the "ADVOCATE." Here is a correct representation of it:

Figure 3.6. Southwestern Christian Recorder, 20 June 1895.

The phenomenon of black preachers serving as peddlers in the late nineteenth century was not entirely new. Northern black churches had had them for decades. Before the end of the Civil War, they typically were northerners, were few in number, sold only a small selection of religious literature, and rarely ventured into the South. After 1865, though, they pushed into the former Confederacy and there joined forces with local black clerics to build churches and Sunday schools and sell denominational publications. As a book steward with the AME Church in Mississippi during the 1870s, for example, Reverend A. R. Green canvassed homes and houses of worship selling the printed goods of his denomination. In 1878, he traveled across the Mississippi Delta and sold twenty-four hymnbooks, six disciplinary manuals, and twenty-five subscriptions to the *Christian Recorder*.[78]

Like the black churches, northern white churches and religious organizations also employed southern black preachers as peddlers. The story of the American Sunday School Union (ASSU) was typical. Begun in 1824 in Philadelphia by local white businessmen to promote non-denominational Protestant Sunday schools and advertise Christian literature, the ASSU sent white missionaries and white colporteurs, who sold Bibles and tracts, into the South first in 1833. Joining representatives from the ASSU to create an ever-enlarging presence of northern white religious publishers in the region during the antebellum era were those of its competitors, including the American Tract Society (ATS), the American Baptist Publication Society (ABPS), and the American Baptist Home Missionary Society (ABHMS).

During Reconstruction, these white religious groups, along with northern white manufacturers of a wide range of products, sought quick access to the new market for literary and consumer goods represented by freed people. They struck upon the strategy of employing blacks to sell to other blacks, assuming that ex-slaves with little experience with the consumer market would feel more comfortable learning about it from a member of their own race. As a white salesman summarized his plan for slipping goods produced by northern white manufacturers into the hands of black southerners in 1872, "[m]y design is by Negro agents—and I can secure many and enthusiastic ones—to have the books endorsed or noticed by the Negro Conventions, Leagues, Lodges, and their various [religious] societies. . . ."[79] His plan was not unique. In the Delta, the American Baptist Publication Society regularly hired local blacks as salesmen.[80] Its black agents earned money by organizing Sunday schools, inspecting existing ones, and supplying and selling materials to teachers and students.[81] This company heavily solicited African American salesmen through advertisements that ran in denominational publications, including the published minutes of the Arkansas Baptist Sunday School conventions.[82] Other white firms, both religious and strictly commercial, did too. The pages of the *Southwestern Christian Advocate* published entreaties for black agents who would sell an array of goods for a wide range of publishers and manufacturers, including *A Manual for Family Worship and Home Teaching*, distributed by Hunt & Eaton of New York City; Plating Dynamo, a jewelry-making device, crafted in Columbus, Ohio, by an organization of the same name; and Epworth Organs and Pianos, produced and assembled in Chicago.[83]

White manufacturers, however, hired African American salesmen in the hope of doing more than simply bolstering their sales numbers. Many widely acknowledged that God made blacks the inferior race and believed that the increased involvement of blacks in the consumer market, as either buyers or sellers, was a small but important step to stabilizing race relations in the post-emancipation South. For to participate in the market successfully required that individuals to work hard, save, and spend wisely—exactly the traits that some northern manufacturers feared were in short supply among African American southerners and prevented them from becoming industrious and dependable laborers. Ideally, black agents, by instructing fellow blacks about the goods and the ways of the market, would help transmit its habits of discipline to them as well. The market promised to mold freed people into better workers who were content with their bottom rank in South's racial hierarchy.[84]

When recruiting black agents, white manufacturers prized black ministers above any other. The Union Book and Bible House of Philadelphia and the John Hertel Company of Chicago solicited preachers across the South, offering them a small commission of a few cents for every Bible and religious storybook sold.[85] Companies like these viewed African American religious leaders as uniquely positioned to advise members of their race about matters of consumption.[86] It is not hard to see why. Black ministers, because of their status as religious leaders sworn to lead an honest, virtuous, and God-fearing life, enjoyed an unmatched level of public confidence among African Americans. After the mid-1880s, they also traveled for free or at a greatly reduced rate on the railroad, making them more mobile and better able to visit plantations and rural towns than most black travelers.

Still, it seems initially a bit curious that white manufacturers would trust southern black ministers during years of hardening segregation and that, in turn, black ministers would be attracted to this work. But these activities begin to make sense when viewed as two distinct yet complementary types of racial commodification.[87] First, it was a case of white manufacturers commodifying the cultural position of black ministers and editors as the leaders of their communities. Manufacturers employed them to create a small, loosely organized black sales force that they hoped would be capable of easily and quickly tapping the rising interest of Delta blacks for consumer goods. Second, it was a case of black preachers and editors willingly commodifying their own status as local leaders to become salesmen. They primarily aimed to raise money for the support of nascent black institutions, present their congregants with greater access to the world of consumer goods, and hopefully pocket a little extra money for themselves. As salesmen, they hoped not so much to replace the common commercial venues in the Delta as to supplement them with a limited mode of African American consumption whose social environment of buying was arguably safer and fairer than the alternatives for blacks.

One Delta minister who peddled religious goods was Reverend James H. Hoke, an Arkansas Baptist and the General Missionary for the state. In 1895, he scoured the Delta and other regions for converts, subscribers to the *Baptist Vanguard,* and donors to Arkansas Baptist College. Hopping train cars from town to town during the first three months of the year, he battled an unseasonably chilly winter and the poverty of black farmers. He complained bitterly in one of his periodic reports, published in the *Baptist Vanguard,* that, "[o]f the long time I have worked in the field, this quarter has been the hardest. Cold, windy, and rainy. The churches are just as anxious for the work now as when they had plenty of money. All say 'come again.'" Although Hoke was disappointed with the fruits of his labors, it was not for want of effort. By his own account, he covered 1,270 miles, visited forty-one churches, preached fifty-six sermons, delivered twenty-five lectures, attended twenty prayer meetings, and organized six Sunday Schools and one church. Despite his grumbling, he raised $106.70 and sold hundreds of single issues of the *Baptist Vanguard,* several six month and year-long subscriptions to the newspaper, and, most significantly, one hundred "Bibles, Testaments & Books."[88]

Ministers representing religious weeklies usually peddled items in addition to religious tracts and disciplinary manuals. Throughout the 1890s, Reverend Booker, like Reverend Hoke, rapped on the doors of African American churches, homes, and schools across Arkansas to raise money for the two Little Rock institutions under his leadership, Arkansas Baptist College and the *Baptist Vanguard.* During his travels, Booker regularly solicited financial pledges to the college, subscriptions to the newspaper, and mail orders for a wide selection of consumer goods. In person and as editor of the *Baptist Vanguard,* Booker advertised Bibles, pencils, church bells, and organs produced by white manufacturers. Like Booker, Reverend Henry Bullock, a CME missionary and an editor with the *Christian Index* in the late 1890s, was a salesperson who dutifully attended to blacks curious about new manufactured products. Whether working on the road or at his desk, he fielded questions about the value and price of different market items and filled orders for those advertised in his paper. In a letter titled "From the Agent to the Church," Bullock told readers that "[m]any of the patrons write to me for goods we do not carry, and we feel it our duty to get it for them. . . . We have a force of nice workmen and think we can give satisfaction."[89]

Importantly, some black editors and ministers grabbed at the chance to work as salesmen not only for the sake of helping their congregants but also themselves by earning small commissions. Altruism was not their only impetus. Delta ministers, who regularly served without payment for months at a time because their congregations or denominational conferences were too poor to pay them, were always on the lookout for ways to make a spare dollar. Black pastors in northwestern Mississippi traditionally made only a "small salary" and were forced to "farm or do other work" in order to live.[90] Patrick Thompson, chronicling the institutional history of his Baptist faith in Mississippi in 1890, fretted that the paltry sums paid to ministers imperiled the religious health of all local blacks. He spotlighted a fiery speech given at an unspecified Mississippi Baptist Convention by Reverend G. W. Gayles, who argued that "[w]hen ministers are better supported and cared for we will have better churches and congregations."[91] Poverty, however, sometimes sparked creativity and cooperation among some ministers seeking to boost their incomes. In the town of Glen Allan in Washington County, Mississippi, Baptist and Methodist clerics worked closely together when it came time to plan a yearly schedule of "anniversaries," or special days when an individual church honored its preacher by hosting a party and taking up a special monetary collection for him. To maximize the number of celebrants present at each event and thereby ensure the largest possible collection, they arranged their calendars so that individual anniversaries did not overlap and rallied congregants to attend each one.[92]

Similar to black ministers in the Delta, some leading black churchwomen developed a limited commercial role for themselves as peddlers of consumer goods, though of a far more restricted range. They were typically presidents of women's associations and young people's unions as well as the wives of ministers, all prominent social roles that defined them as responsible public figures and brought them into close contact with a wide range of churchgoers. Working mostly as literary agents for northern white religious organizations eager to promote Christianity among African American southerners, they visited local black homes and churches in search of customers and converts. Organizing rural black women into "Bible bands," they created small, interlocking networks of women's religious organizations that promoted literacy, scriptural study, and religious publications. As was the case with white southern women who performed similar labors among whites in the Delta, they earned little, if any, financial reward for their efforts because they often gave away their printed materials or, when they did sell a book of prayers or a yearlong magazine subscription, returned most of the proceeds to the publisher or distributor.[93] Because of their small ranks and limited personal profit, they posed little threat to, and thus sparked no fear of competition with, preachers working as peddlers.

Susie Bailey of Pine Bluff, Arkansas, was an African American colporteur for the American Women's Baptist Home Missionary Society (AWBHMS), a white-run institution based in Nashville, Tennessee, dedicated to spreading the Baptist religion among southern African Americans and other poor groups. Bailey was the wife of Reverend Isaac G. Bailey, the president of Southeastern Baptist District Association, and a leader of local Baptist women's associations. At the turn of the twentieth century, she teamed up with Joanna P. Moore, a white employee of AWBHMS then living in Little Rock, to form Bible bands and distribute Bibles and other religious literature among Delta blacks.[94] Bailey, with Moore's help, quickly became a leading female agent in the region. Many Delta blacks wrote to her for assistance in learning about a new publication or securing a favorite book for themselves, their families, or their church group. "I have had a number of persons who want the 'Little Hand Full of Truth,'" wrote Mrs. S. Bagley of Mars Hill, Arkansas, to Bailey in August 1901, referencing an AWBHMS publication. "Mrs. Bailey[,] if you have any on hand I would be glad to get them—as many as one dozen. . . . If you have them let me know and I will send for them at once."[95] When she didn't have what her customers wanted, Bailey turned to Moore. "We have received your letter, asking for fifty Bibles," acknowledged Moore to a request made to her by Bailey in September 1906. "I have ordered them. [S]ent [to] you from Phil[adelphia] because the Bible we get from them is a much larger type than those at the Nat[ional] Pub[lication] Board."[96] Bailey's success as a colporteur marked her as a favorite target of attention from other white religious organizations, who hoped to use her to further their own evangelical efforts among southern blacks. In a report filed to the AWBHMS, she stated that "[w]e had a goodly number of religious papers that were sent [to] me by the northern circles and some good [C]hristian magazines given by some dear white Christian[s] here in Dermott and we made packages of them and the men started [handing them] out."[97]

Bailey symbolized how some black churchwomen in the Delta forged alliances with white religious publishing companies and sold their spiritual literature to friends, family and neighbors. Along with the male preachers toiling as peddlers, they formed a mobile wing of Baptist and Methodist life that bolstered denominational identities across the Delta; through their actions, individual congregants more readily understood themselves to be not only part of a local house of worship but also a regional church body. Yet the itinerant work of these men and women was not without problems. As it developed and became more of a regular feature in African American religious life, it quickly lead to acts of fraud.

During the 1890s, a rash of black confidence men took advantage of the growing number of black church leaders working as peddlers to swindle black families. They successfully posed as Baptist and Methodist missionaries raising money to help defray the cost of their education and the construction of new schools and churches. In November 1892, a large number of members of the ME Church near Vicksburg fell prey to a wily black couple going by the rakish name of "Mr. and Mrs. Mons Zaro," who repeatedly knocked on the doors of their church and school house and pleaded for gifts of cash to "help him fund his theological studies." The trickery quickly elicited a stern warning from the area's clerics: "Ministers of the gospel and school teachers should be on the lookout for these fak[e]rs, who are little less than highway robbers."[98] Despite the public cautions, it was difficult to expose every imposter. In December 1895, a Baptist minister from outside of Little Rock alerted fellow Baptists to a man traveling across the state claiming to be a replacement for Reverend James Hoke. "I write to inform you that there is a man passing through the country by the name of Wm. James who claims to be the state missionary and whenever he is closely questioned says that Rev. Hoke got into trouble and he is helping him out. . . . Brothers, Elders, watch your step, for the wolf is coming. He has illegal credentials and plenty of blank drafts [that he is] trying to sell to the people for $5.00."[99] To restore popular confidence in his missionaries and reduce the chance of his fellow Baptists becoming the next victim of a smooth-talking charlatan, Reverend E. C. Morris took the unusual steps of publishing a list of official representatives and fundraisers for Arkansas Baptist College and issuing each of them a letter of introduction personally signed by him, which was to be shown to any party doubtful of their official identity.[100] Morris's action calmed public fears about the reliability and fidelity of men claiming to be missionaries and ministers, but incompletely and only for a short time.

A more serious challenge to the public trust of black ministers, and one that prompted Delta blacks to examine in closer detail the connection between people of faith and the consumer market, was the rapid evolution of the social role of preachers as peddlers during the late 1890s. As preachers began to rely less on personal contact and more on print advertisements to reach customers, sell an increasingly eclectic range of fancier and more expensive goods, and hawk goods directly from the pulpit and altar, they faced churchgoers deeply suspicious of their motivations. Scores of critics asked whether too many ministers had become overly concerned with selling to the point where some appeared to act more like men on the make than men of God. They worried that clerics, who had initially entered the broadening consumer market with the honorable intentions of improving their pastoral earnings and helping their communities survive, now sacrificed their moral authority on an altar of personal aggrandizement and acquisitiveness. Importantly, this wave of popular displeasure did not wash over black women colporteurs like Bailey. They failed to spark public controversy because, in comparison to the male preachers, they were few in number, advertised mostly through word of mouth and individual appeals, trafficked mainly in printed religious materials, and registered little or no financial profit.

Of course, the act of a clergyman forcefully advertising a manufactured product and the questions it raised about the line separating religion from the consumer market was part of the life of other religious communities in the late nineteenth and early twentieth centuries. Perhaps the most famous example was the well-known white Congregationalist minister from New York City, Reverend Henry Ward

Beecher, whose campaigns for Pears' Soap elicited cries of blasphemy from some of his peers.[101] Yet underlying the concern of Delta blacks in the late nineteenth century was the distinctive fear that African American preachers who sold goods irresponsibly threatened one of the key values of the market participation for former bondsmen and their families: the opportunity to project images of discipline through consumption. During decades when many southern whites viewed blacks as incapable of social or economic order and frequently judged them by how they handled their money, blacks could ill afford to have their spiritual and social leaders appear as dupes of the market. Indeed, at a time when white supremacists justified the subjugation of African Americans partly on the basis of their supposed inability to exercise the privileges of freedom maturely, including the freedom to enter the market and manage their own financial affairs wisely, Delta blacks could not run the risk of being seen as throwing away precious coin.[102]

Consequently, in the eyes of some black Baptists and Methodists, a dangerous spirit of "vulgar advertising" appeared to haunt their churches, inciting their leaders to care more for the current fashion than the current state of their souls and imperiling the overall progress of the race. "Isn't this rather a new idea—this using our pulpits as an advertising medium for soap?" sneered the Memphis writer known by her pen name of Iola but more famously as Ida B. Wells. Wells, a member of the CME church and a graduate of its flagship school, Rust College in Mississippi, questioned not only the correctness of such behavior but also the incongruity of a black religious leader selling a product frequently marketed as being able to cleanse the "stain" of blackness from its users. She could barely hide her disapproval with recent developments in the ministry. "Some of us never stop to weigh a subject or enterprise in all its bearing . . . but from our pulpits advertise its merits. . . . [T]he pulpit . . . needs raising to a higher level and its sacredness preserved."[103]

Amplifying Wells' concern over the current excesses of clerical advertising were the editors of the *Southwestern Christian Advocate*. In 1902 they sounded an alarm over the burgeoning "commercialism in the pulpit" and broached concerns that too many preachers were engaged in "[q]uestionable methods and entertainments for money getting [which] are robbing the church of its spiritual power and leading the people into actual sin and folly." Though not detailing precisely how ministers erred, the editors did not have to spell it out for their constituency, who knew that clerics sometimes took advantage of their status as community leaders to sell products. It was this particular amalgam of the holy and the profane that so disturbed these church writers and moved them to conclude on a solemn note: "[W]e should be only too glad if all [ministerial advertising] could be dispensed with. We are sure reverence for God's house and a proper regard for sacred things would thus be greatly enhanced."[104]

ads in religious press

The public conflict and confusion excited by African American preachers employing the pulpit as an advertising medium symbolized a deeper political frustration about the role of the consumer market in the spiritual lives of Delta blacks as well. The expanding market, on the one hand, promised African Americans a greater level of entry into the new domain of consumption and the prospect of financing their religious networks and strengthening their denominational identity in innovative ways. Yet on the other hand, the market's customary apparatus of display and delivery—its advertisements, general stores, salespeople, customer service, and use of credit—was heavily racialized and generally designed to limit African American participation. Indeed, white landowners and merchants constrained and manipulated much of the ability of black Baptists and Methodists to exploit the consumer market for their personal advantage, as they did with many of their other social freedoms. In this sense of simultaneously bestowing opportunities for material and spiritual advancement but operating in ways that prevented blacks from taking full advantage of them, the market was an implement of modern society in the post-Reconstruction South that contributed to the overall making of the tenuous political state of African American life.

During this time of heightened sensitivity to public portrayals of black religious leaders and their role in using the market to benefit their communities, the *Baptist Vanguard* ran a new type of advertisement that showcased black ministers selling panaceas. These images concentrated, in miniature relief, the social tensions swirling around the question of the appropriate connection between religion and the market. To be sure, panaceas and their flyers were not new to Delta blacks at the turn of the century: local black newspapers had carried advertisements of them for years. In the mid-1890s, faithful readers of the *Baptist Vanguard* learned about Beecham's Pills, Ripan's Tabules [*sic*], Brown's Iron Bitters, and Kennedy's Medical Discovery, each of which guaranteed to cure of an eclectic group of symptoms ranging from stomach ailments to migraines, breathing problems to skin blemishes.[105] Similarly, the *Southwestern Christian Advocate* published advertisements for Ayer's New Local Remedy, Heiskell's Ointment, and Hood's Sarsaparilla.[106] And anyone skimming the *Christian Recorder* during these years saw like pitches for Booth's Pocket Inhaler, to alleviate all respiratory ills; Parson's Pills, to cure "biliousness and the sick headache;" and Mrs. Winslow's Soothing Syrup, to "regulate the stomach and the bowels."[107] It also offered readers free samples of Dr. Slocum's Treatment, which promised to solve any lung problem.[108] Occasionally it featured advertisements for Rev. A. C. Hamilton, a "minister of the gospel" and physiologist who could magically diagnosis individual illnesses on the spot.[109]

Readers of white religious publications came across advertisements for a variety of cure-alls, too. The inside cover of the December 1892 edition of *The Advanced*

Quarterly, a guide to spiritual living published by the American Baptist Publication Society, featured an eye-grabber for Houten's Cocoa, which promised to "develop digestibility strength," act as a healthy "substitute for Tea and Coffee," and sooth "the Nerves and Stomach." Another, Horsford's Acid, boasted that it "nourishes and invigorates the tired brain and body, imparts renewed energy and vitality, and enlivens the functions." This one also carried a brief written testimonial from Dr. Ephraim Bateman, a white man from Cederville, New York, who submitted that "I have used it for several years . . . and consider it under all circumstances one of the best nerve tonics that we possess."[110]

Some Delta black religious leaders readily accepted the claims of these advertisements for panaceas at face value. In October 1893, Reverend Isaac Bailey, plagued by lingering pulmonary and cardiac problems that restricted his ability to visit to his congregants in Desha County in the Arkansas Delta, ordered a bottle of "Inhaling Balm" from the Office of Child's Catarrh Remedies in Troy, Ohio. It didn't work. Disappointed but still hopeful that another panacea might restore him to full health, he contacted other manufacturers about their remedies.[111] Fortunately, Bailey had his nephew, J. Winston Bailey, to consult. J. Winston ran a mail order business from an office in Spokane, Washington, that, according to his business card, furnished "all kinds of valuable Medical Recipes [and] legitimate trade secrets. . . ."[112]

Although Delta blacks were familiar with panaceas by the 1890s, they saw them marketed in radically different ways by the middle of the decade. The panacea advertisements running in the *Baptist Vanguard,* for example, were distinctive in their use of the themes of trust and authority. They not only featured images of black preachers selling panaceas, which was a novel feature in black religious newspapers, but also cleverly manipulated the religious sensibilities of the public. Indeed, much of their commercial punch depended on the deceptive character of their ministerial portraits and testimonies. An early advertisement for panaceas in the *Baptist Vanguard,* dated April 12, 1895, featured North Carolina Baptist Reverend F. M. Jacobs shilling for Mexican Mustang Liniment, which was produced in Brooklyn, New York (figure 3.7). Here was an instance that revealed the transregional link between northern manufacturers and southern preachers. Spotlessly groomed and impeccably dressed, Singleton communicated a sense of honesty and uprightness that made it easier for the reader to accept his assertion that the liniment possessed an astonishing range of curative powers. "I have had occasions to use it for some years as a general family medicine. It has proven an indispensable thing for the eradications of pains, bruises, and especially for neuralgia, of which my wife was a constant sufferer. . . . I have no hesitancy in recommending it as an indispensable family medicine."[113] Notwithstanding Jacob's

A Pleasure to testify in favor of
MEXICAN
MUSTANG LINIMENT.

Indispensable for the eradication of pains, bruises
and especially neuralgia.

REV. F. M. JACOBS

ASHEVILLE,   N.C.,   APRIL 17, 1896

Lyon Manufacturing Co., Brooklyn, N.Y.

Dear Sirs: I consider it a pleasure to testify to the good qualities of your **Mexican Mustang Liniment.** I have had occasions to use it for some years as a general family medicine. It has proven an indispensible thing for the eradication of pains, bruises, and especially for neuralgia, of which my wife was a constant sufferer. I have tried many liniments, but I may safely say that none has acted so soothingly and successfully as Mustang Liniment. I have no hesitancy in recommending it as an indispensible family medicine.   Yours truly,

REV. F. M. JACOBS,

Pastor Callen St., A. M. E. Zion Church, Asheville, N. C.

25c., 50c., and $1 per bottle. For sale by all Druggists and Storekeepers.
or will be sent by Express, charges paid. For our nearest express office on receipt of price,

Address your letters plainly to

LYON MANUFACTURING CO..
41, 43 & 45 South Fifth St. BROOKLYN, N. Y.

Figure 3.7. Baptist Vanguard, 12 April 1895.

glowing recommendation, however, most panaceas in the late nineteenth century contained high levels of mercury and cocaine that commonly sickened the very patients they were supposed to cure.[114] All too often, the ill would drink up a cure-all only to discover, belatedly, the limits and dangers of placing too much faith in the market and its religious spokesmen. As a result, this advertisement's main, if unintended, effect was to plant doubt in the public's mind about the very credibility of any preacher vouchsafing magical potions.

Like Reverend Jacobs, Reverend A. S. Singleton of Danville, Virginia, sang the praises Mexican Mustang Liniment in the pages of the *Baptist Vanguard*. His endorsement also rang out with the conviction of the newly converted, in this case proclaiming that a little of the special ointment spread on a cloth and applied directly to the head cured all manner of affliction. His accompanying portrait, though, was quite distinctive. Its visual character imbued the advertisement as a whole with a subtle spiritual authority, though one that some viewers, once they noticed it, may have found distasteful. Enhancing Singleton's claims of credibility as a religious salesperson was the illustrator's unusual use of the drawing techniques of shadow and cross-hatching, especially in the space above and behind the minister's shoulders. There, the pen leaves the impression of a pair of angel wings arching over the back of the preacher (figure 3.8).

Similar to the advertisements for Mexican Mustang Liniment, the one for Dr. Miles' Remedies, dated May 18, 1894, featured a clean and well-dressed black minister extolling the virtues of a universal remedy, in this case for heart ailments (figure 3.9). It, too, was deceitful and pushed the issue of just when a minister compromised his trustworthiness when he acted as a pitchman. Its crowning title, "A FOLLOWER OF CHRIST—What Changed His Life," visually supported by the portrait of Reverend M. E. Bell impeccably clad in a starched shirt with a wing collar and a suit coat, mimicked the graphic design of contemporary advertising campaigns for spiritual autobiographies. A hurried reader may have wrongly assumed that Reverend Bell was selling his own story of salvation, in which he detailed when the grace of God "Changed his Life." It was also possible to reach a similar conclusion by glancing only casually at the accompanying endorsement. In it, Bell loosely appropriated literary tropes found in modern conversion narratives, including being made "new" through an encounter with the divine, earning assurance of salvation eternal life, and dedicating one's earthly days to spreading the Gospel. As Bell waxed: "I am a colored clergyman and scarcely know how to thank you for the benefits I have received from your Heart Cure. . . . My heart was so weak with disease that I was not able to preach to my people. I heard of Heart Cure . . . and [used it and] altogether I am an entirely new man."[115] Unlike many conversion narratives, however, the specific agent of transformation here was not

Figure 3.8. Baptist Vanguard, 6 April 1895.

God's love but the Heart Cure, the personal good not salvation but temporary physical respite, and the public benefit not evangelization but simply the sale of a manufactured cure-all. This advertisement, like the ones depicting Reverend Jacobs and Reverend Singleton, compelled readers to ask if too many black religious leaders were trading recklessly on their social and spiritual authority just to turn a sale and make a buck.

A FOLLOWER OF CHRIST.

What Changed His Life.

REV. M. E. BELL

Dr. Miles: May the Almighty bless you for what your medicine has done for me! I am a colored clergyman and scarcely know how to thank you for the benefits I have received from your Heart Cure. Indeed its wonderful merits ought to be blazoned forth in the whole wide world. I can scarcely find words to explain the change it has wrought in me. My heart was so weak with disease that I was not able to preach to my people. I heard of your Heart Cure and bought a bottle and from its use my heart now feels to beat natually and altogether I am an entirely new man. Dr. Hall of the Government Pension Board here, said I could not be cured, but your medicine proved the contrary.

Yours gratefully,
REV. M. E. BELL.

Mt. Vernon, Ill., Sept. 17, 1808.

Dr. Miles' Remedies are sold by all druggists or sent prepaid on reciept of price by the Dr. Miles Medical Co., Elkhart, Ind.

Figure 3.9. Baptist Vanguard, 18 May 1894. (Note the date of the letter is clearly a misprint, given the reference to the Government Pension Board, which was organized after the Civil War.)

These advertisements also represented a thinly veiled threat to a small but growing sector of African American healthcare in the Delta, the black midwife. As access to adequate and reliable medical care persisted as a crucial challenge for Delta blacks, the need for alternative health care providers increased; and as train travel became more widespread and accessible, information about medical care circulated more freely and quickly as did medical personnel themselves. The result was a steady growth in African American midwifes, who, by the early twentieth century, were the most common black healthcare practitioner in the Delta. Yet preachers fronting for a wide range of mail-order panaceas jeopardized the viability of this emerging vocation, promising a quick and easy solution to medical problems that did not require leaving home save to get the postal package. Thus the advertisements of the type seen in the *Baptist Vanguard* not only sparked tensions over the safety of panaceas and the earnestness of their spokesmen but also, and to a lesser extent, the effect of selling them on the ability of black midwives to recruit and sustain patients.[116]

Despite the controversies it generated, the enlarging scope and size of the consumer market was an important, if limited, resource for black Baptists and Methodists desperately in need of ways of supporting and publicizing their multiplying churches and associations in the Delta. Their blending of the commercial and the spiritual certainly built on traditional habits, yet it also marked a new stage in the development of their sacred lives. In it, religious leaders and institutions played a more aggressive role as intermediaries between the market and black consumers and nurtured a form of consumption that invested the act of buying and selling with special significance in their struggle to construct spiritual organizations during segregation. At the same time, churchgoers strove to define the borders dividing the market and the church, but never achieved a clear and lasting public consensus. Their failure to do so ensured that a general state of uncertainty and nervousness over what constituted the appropriate union between modern consumption and African American Christianity would simmer just below the surface in many black Delta faith communities until the early twentieth century, when it mixed with other social and theological disputes and erupted into a large-scale controversy that fundamentally reshaped the religious landscape in the Delta.

The story of intricate relationship between African American consumption and religion in the Delta, however, also transcends its geographic and temporal borders. It reaches out to historians currently practicing their craft, warning them against making sweeping generalizations when assessing and calibrating the degree of social transformation wrought by any one category of culture. In this specific case, it is tempting to be unduly optimistic and overstate the role that the consumer market played in broadening the range of religious experiences and cultural freedoms available to Delta blacks after Reconstruction; in a more universal application, it is enticing to exaggerate the liberating affect of the market on the lives of any oppressed people from the modern era. The key to avoiding these types of sunny interpretations is to frame the place of the market in people's lives comparatively—to situate it among the many different cultural forces that affect the ways in which individuals make decisions—and then determine to what degree, if any, it influenced the ways in which men and women spent their days. In the Delta during Jim Crow, it is critical to recognize that black participation in the consumer market did little to preserve their right to vote, enjoy due process, live free from bodily harm, or secure property. While keeping this reality of African American life in mind, though, one can still observe that, at the level of the local distribution and sale of manufactured consumer goods, Delta blacks sometimes found a small degree of opportunity to exercise a modest degree of new freedom through the liminal figure of the preacher as peddler. They often discovered a greater liberty to sample and purchase goods in an environment not directly controlled by whites, to incorporate trinkets of modernity into practices of racial respectability that defined them as human, and to integrate mass-produced products into fresh expressions of religious belief that at once affirmed their worth as southern consumers and citizens. When analyzed along side of the role of the railroad and fraternal orders in African American religion, the market emerges as one of several key historical factors employed by Delta blacks to attempt to craft lives born of their own ambitions.

4

THE MATERIAL CULTURE OF RELIGION

That the purification of the home must be our first consideration and care. It is in the home where woman is really queen and that she wields her influence with the most telling effect.

—Mary Church Terrell, "The Duty of the National Association of Colored Women to the Race," AME Church Review 12, no.3 (1900): 344

[T]he churches for the poor, as well as for the rich, should pay some attention to beauty as well as to comfort, for this is possible without wealth. Beauty refines and elevates and reacts upon the moral and spiritual life.

—George Henderson, The Southern Workman, 33 (March 190–1): 176

In 1909, members of the Zion Baptist Chapel in Lonoke, Arkansas, tore down their small, crumbling, one-story wooden church. Twenty-three years after building it on a cotton plantation in this small rural town east of the state capitol, congregants wanted to celebrate their growth and health as a spiritual community by constructing a special house of worship. And so they erected an impressive church far larger, more fashionable, and more heavily decorated than most in the Delta. Painted white and boasting a frame construction and a three-story bell tower in the northeast corner, the structure seated about two hundred people in twenty-eight pews carved from golden oak. During services, members sang along with a new Kimball organ and watched the minister consecrate the Lord's Supper upon a raised altar platform rung by three upholstered chairs. Drapes adorned the windows.[1]

By the early twentieth century, most Delta blacks understood the sheer size of Zion Baptist and its design and ornamental features as emblems of a substantial, vibrant, and prosperous congregation. Any black or white visitor to the Delta may have too, but probably without a keen appreciation for how they registered the changing material dimensions to black religion after Reconstruction.[2] In this new culture of church and home adornment, African American Baptists and Methodists, to a degree hitherto unrealized, imbued material things with spiritual meaning and used them to structure, organize, and represent their physical world. They enmeshed architectural forms, church furnishings, and inexpensive literary and domestic consumer commodities in a dense matrix of denominational loyalties and racial associations that provided a valuable means of communicating and constituting sacred belief.[3] For them, corporal objects increasingly symbolized and sustained religious conviction.

The growing infusion of the latest religious literature and domestic goods to the Delta, made possible in part by the rapid development of the railroad and the role of African American preachers and newspapers editors as agents of commodity exchange, introduced many black residents to new styles of personal dress, home life, and church beauty. To be sure, Delta blacks saw and bought only a few of the manufactured items because they usually lacked enough autonomy, money, and credit to acquire what they wanted on a regular basis. Their purchases were primarily limited to simple clothing, home furniture, Bibles, religious tracts, books, lithographs of scenes from the Old Testament, and pictures of black leaders. Still, they made these items the basis of a modern material culture of religion critical in representing their evolving ideas about respectability, domesticity, family, and sacred space.

A crucial local site in the making of this new material culture of religion was the home. Although Delta blacks had always seen it as vital in producing good Baptists and Methodists, the turn of the century witnessed a burgeoning interest in domestic spaces and, more importantly, the development of the ideology of the "black Christian home." The black Christian home was an extension of the church, a place on whose walls hung images of black heroes and icons of African American Protestantism and whose inhabitants dressed tidily and patterned their behavior after the life of Jesus. An idealized setting that theoretically nurtured the manners and morality of all who lived there, it was particularly important in the creation of God-fearing families: here parents developed their households as paragons of sensible consumption, models of cleanliness, and schools for raising law-abiding and devout children.

Admittedly, the task of capturing the look and feel of black Christian homes in the Delta, especially those of its poorest black residents, is a challenge. There are few extant documents directly recording their visual character; instead, much of the evidence about them comes from the extant published writings of black religious leaders. Ministers and prominent church women regularly exhorted their readers to build black Christian homes and proffered exact instructions on how to do so. Yet like other forms of prescriptive literature, these printed missives are characteristically thin on details about how blacks actually responded to the recommendations. Still, much can be gleaned by situating them in the broad context of Delta black society. By doing so, it becomes apparent that they were elements in a wide-ranging conversation rooted in the late nineteenth century about the nature of African American daily living and church decoration—two subjects for which there is ample documentation. When evaluated as part of this broader ongoing dialogue, they appear fairly representative of the cultural hopes and tensions invested in black Christian homes by Delta blacks.

At the heart of the concept of the black Christian home and religious material culture in general in the Delta lay shifting ideas about black women. During the late nineteenth century, many black women echoed religious leaders by proclaiming themselves the chief curators of the black Christian home and, less exclusively, of church decoration. At first glance, their reasoning seems straightforward: the work, particularly in the case of the black Christian home, promised tangible political benefits, such as overturning caricatures of African Americans as profligates, teaching literacy to a new generation of blacks, and instilling boys and girls with a strong knowledge of Scripture. But their labors arguably carried a more immediate and personal payoff, too. By enhancing the cultural significance of their role in establishing the black Christian home and portraying its success as critical to the progress of the black community, black women created a fresh means of earning of social and religious authority at a time when traditional opportunities for gaining them were fast closing.

Fueling broad popular interest in religious material culture as well was its potential to bring a greater level of social order and calm to black congregations recently unsettled by vexing questions of spiritual authenticity and trust. The rapid rise of local and regional associations like primary schools, Sunday schools, women's conventions, and pastors' unions had brought together, in many cases for the first time, large gatherings of black Baptists and Methodists. Now these groups struggled to determine what marked them as a people of faith beyond theological dogma or denominational label. The issue of being able to ascertain readily and publicly a truthful fellow black Christian was made all the more pressing by rising instances of black strangers posing as good-hearted missionaries seeking financial backing in their fight to pull a school or church back from the brink of financial ruin. Canvassing the Delta, these charlatans knocked on the doors of unsuspecting black churchgoers and, with a smile and a good story, quickly secured a donation for their phantom cause. Although bishops and presiding elders issued letters of introduction to their representatives as a way of helping congregants distinguish a legitimate man of God from an imposter, these documents were easily forged and did little to halt swindlers from deceiving the naïve. Complicating matters further were those certified preachers acting in ways that cast shadows over their sincerity. Ministers who peddled expensive goods or panaceas to their followers ignited questions about whether they took advantage of their spiritual status as local leaders just for the sake of earning personal profit. In this environment of uncertain identities and unstable relationships, the material culture of black religion promised a greater level of clarity. Its directives about style and decoration promoted shared experiences of consumption that helped to forge common bonds of denominational identity; its public beliefs and prescribed behaviors openly classified subscribers as reliable, upright Christians.

Significantly, the emergence of African American material Christianity in the Delta coincided with the elaboration of domestic religion among northern white urban Protestants and Catholics, many of whom were first or second generation immigrants from the British Isles and southern Europe. Important similarities existed between them. In both cases, individuals bought objects of religious significance and either wore them or placed them throughout their homes. These objects did not simply mirror a style or mode of religious decoration but served as physical components to rituals and theologies that celebrated the sacredness of the family, promoted middle-class aspirations, and strengthened the moral fiber of the local community and nation. Women chiefly oversaw this aspect of religion.[4]

Yet black Baptists and Methodists in the Delta fostered a distinctive material culture. It was smaller in scope than that nurtured by whites from the urban North: absent was the thick display of embroidered crosses, silver-plated crucifixes, holy water receptacles, and ceramic figurines of saints that crowded the mantles and home altars of Protestants and Catholics living in Boston, New York, and Philadelphia. More notably, Delta blacks carefully selected and utilized their religious objects in ways that reflected their restricted access to the consumer market, their geographic locale, and their specific cultural needs. They relied on them to standardize liturgical practices. They embedded them in overlapping narratives of spiritual and racial improvement that identified the black Christian home as a crucible of moral reform and enlightenment where they learned habits of mind and discipline that armored them for battles against white supremacy. And they situated them in delicate webs of domestic beliefs and practices that enshrined African American women as arbiters of adornment and invested them with racial and moral authority otherwise little attainable in their communities during Jim Crow.

Popular interest in the role of material culture in the making of modern black Baptist and Methodist identities in the Delta soared during the late nineteenth century as changes in the consumer market intersected with new notions about individual and societal respectability and African American domesticity. Sharing the goal of helping Delta blacks mature as Christians and survive Jim Crow, each advised African Americans how they should spend their money, dress, act in public, organize their homes, and raise their children. Collectively, they formed a powerful intellectual environment that shaped how blacks understood the relationship between the material and sacred world.

At the same time that Delta blacks found it easier to inspect and purchase some consumer and literary goods by patronizing their preachers and newspapers, certain ones assumed a fresh degree of spiritual and racial meaning because of their central role in spreading an ethic of respectability. Respectability emerged as a buzzword among many southern black religious and political leaders starting in the late nineteenth century. They widely defined it as a series of conservative moral values and attitudes whose main principles included sobriety, thrift, sexual purity, good hygiene, and politeness. Respectability, although not a universal remedy for poverty or racial conflict, pledged to lift many burdens for its adherents. Chief among its promises was to improve prosperity and challenge popular images of blacks as unruly people incapable of responsibly exercising the privileges of freedom or acting within the boundaries of white bourgeois morality.[5]

Respectability influenced how Delta blacks conceptualized the role of material culture in their religious lives by explicitly linking an ideal of disciplined character to frugal patterns of individual consumption. Proponents legitimated the purchase of a market item only when it directly supported their larger goals of restraint. To convey a public image of economy and self-respect, blacks were encouraged to purchase simple clothing and keep themselves clean and well-groomed; to project an image of a tidy, clean, and orderly people, blacks should buy soap, brooms, mops, and paint and put them to good use.[6] Conversely, advocates of respectability urged blacks never to throw away money on fads or fancies, spend beyond their means, or buy objects of vanity such as lace curtains or extravagant timepieces because any such ill-considered use of income diverted money from church coffers. Only evil came to those who dressed fashionably, especially women, intoned Laura F. Brown at a meeting of Arkansas Baptist mothers held in Pine Bluff in September 1894. "Time is Wasted. . . . Think of the tucks, ruffles, and laces that are sometimes used that are not at all necessary." More seriously, they ran the risk of impoverishing themselves and their loved ones. "Many [of them] are homeless. Many are living in rented homes and on mortgaged farms because of fashionable dress. . . . It leads both men and women into debt."[7]

As was the case in Brown's warning, unstated in many cautions issued to black women about donning immodest clothing was the danger of them falling victim to sexualized stereotypes. As an unnamed columnist for a black monthly opined, "[a]ny woman is too tightly dressed when she cannot raise her arms straight above her head and clasp her hands; who cannot stoop to tie her shoe or pick up a pin without any unpleasant pressure around the waist. Tight lacing is a crime that casts a heavy burden upon the coming generation and makes the present unfit for its duties. It ruins the digestions. . . ."[8] At a practical level, constricting vestments, of course, were uncomfortable. Yet any southern black women would have immediately recognized a more sobering message embedded in this admonition as well. To exhibit garments in public that accentuated the normal curves of their bodies was to run the risk of inflaming views of black woman as promiscuous and immoral. More troubling still was the distinct chance that such attire might catch the roving eye of a white male vigilante, drunkard, or simple aggressor and be interpreted by him as identifying a black woman eager for a sexual encounter or in need of being physically punished for dressing provocatively. In either case, the possible result was some type of sexual assault.[9]

In this sense of promoting orderly consumption and behavior, respectability was part of a larger racial program of social improvement and regimented spending championed nationally by black spokesmen like Booker T. Washington and locally in the Delta by leaders like the Arkansas Delta minister Reverend E. C. Morris, president of the Arkansas Baptist Convention and the National Baptist Convention.[10] In his 1901 address to graduates of Arkansas Baptist College, Morris situated respectability in the context of the wider effort to advance the morality and fortune of Delta blacks. Claiming that the recent progress of the black race was impressive, he boasted that we are now "surrounded with schools and churches, and hav[e] so many educated preachers and competent teachers." Such success, however, required that "much more will be expected of us in the future." And as the twentieth century unfurled, Morris continued, "[w]e will be expected to be better citizens, such as will not dodge the tax collector, no matter if we are discriminated against. We are to be better neighbors by. . . respecting and paying due regard for our neighbors' rights and possessions. Crime among our people must be lessened." Key to a future of continued improvement and acceptance by white Southerners was for the graduates of Arkansas Baptist College to embrace the ethic of respectability—"to be the advocates of purity and right in every quarter," "to teach the people . . . the lessons which will inculcate the habits of cleanliness, economy. . . [and] keep[ing] their surroundings clean."[11]

The notion that respectability could both undercut racism and uplift the black poor threaded its way through the 1910 call of national and local black leaders of the ME Church for their followers to improve their spiritual and social lot. They pushed the social implications of respectability further, however, seeing it as a valuable resource in dispelling persistent white fears over blacks' capacity to handle the privileges of freedom. In a series of essays, they described the recent course of black history in a familiar way, by comparing it to the journey of the ancient Israelites in the biblical story of Exodus. "It was forty years after Israel left Egypt before Canaan could be reached because of unreadiness [*sic*]. It has been about forty-five years since our race left physical slavery and gathered at this Jordan. . . ." They then focused on the present day. Still we have "questions, doubts, and arguments, pro and con, respecting the fitness and ability of the race." The best way to handle these lingering concerns was to act respectably. "Let us decide . . . to enter every sphere and department of American civilization . . . [with] a better appearance" and demonstrate "[g]ood thoughts in the brain and good principles in the soul, together with a clean body, clean teeth, well-combed hair, and clothes on in good shape. . . ."[12]

Implicit in this message, like the one offered by Morris, was the elitist belief that respectability could discipline uncouth and poor African Americans. Black leaders' cries for their followers to live more respectably brimmed with implicit assumptions about class orientation. Many spokespeople were like Morris: literate, educated, and socially prominent men and women. They viewed issues of character and demeanor as vital markers of African American progress, generally approved of Victorian notions of gentility and manners, and clung tightly to the belief that respectable behavior itself could win the admiration of whites and go a long way toward defeating racism.[13] Morris and his ilk further supposed that they, by virtue of their social standing and schooling, were best suited to grasp and implement the ethic in black society. It was their duty to teach respectability to their less fortunate brethren, whose poverty limited their understanding of how it could improve their material condition and character.

By imagining respectability in these ways, elite reformers not only revealed a degree of class tension existing among Delta blacks but also raised the issue of why a sharecropper or tenant farmer would embrace any part of this ethic. The answer is that few likely would have if respectability was only about dignified comportment, vague guarantees of moral and material advancement, and social hierarchy. But because it also carried vital information about disease and illness and taught practical behaviors that promised better health, poorer African Americans in the Delta paid attention. This is not to suggest, however, that when lesser-off Delta blacks embraced respectability that they necessarily accepted its elitist social doctrine that defined them as dependent on leaders like Morris for guidance in matters of public morality and community organization. Rather, it is to point out that the haves and the have-nots among Delta blacks could find common cause in the ethic of respectability but for very different reasons.[14]

Indeed, respectability gained a broad degree of black public approval partly because of its application in advancing wellness. Its stress on habits of cleanliness

<u>and sanitation</u> attacked escalating levels of illness plaguing African American south-
erners. Malaria, typhoid, and the dangers associated with pregnancy and childbirth
exacted an especially severe cost among those living in the most rural areas of the
Delta, where medical care was inadequate or just plain unavailable. Those seeking
aid were all-too-often forced to travel a full day by horseback to reach the nearest
hospital only to be turned away because of their race.[15] Whites owned and operated
every hospital in the Arkansas and Mississippi during this period and strictly limited
the number of beds available to African Americans; as late as 1928, only forty-eight
beds were open to Mississippi's entire black population of nearly one million.[16] Even
when blacks secured admission to white-run hospitals, they received questionable or
ineffective medical treatment. Staff routinely directed black patients to rooms in the
basement, required them to pay for a black nurse if one was not on shift, and
demanded that they provide their own linens, forks, knives, spoons, and tooth-
brushes.[17] The first black-run hospital did not open its doors until the late 1920s,
although a small, eighteen-bed African American infirmary began in Yazoo City,
Mississippi, in 1907.[18] Black physicians may have helped to alleviate the problem of
access to adequate health care for African Americans, but they were few and far in
between. Until the 1940s, Mississippi and Arkansas were among those states with the
worst ratio of black doctors to the black population.[19] Because of these barriers to
medical treatment, Delta black suffered far higher rates of morbidity and mortality
than most Delta whites. In Sunflower County in the Mississippi Delta, the high death
rate hit black children the hardest. By the time most black women had reached forty-
five years old, they had birthed seven or eight children but lost three or four. In
contrast, white women of the same age had generally had birthed five children but
lost only one or two.[20]

The ethic of respectability took root in the Delta for even broader reasons of
health, too. By linking patterns of behavior and consumption to the promise of
renewed bodily vigor, it responded to general anxieties bubbling up through African
American communities across the nation about a future of diminishing vitality and
fertility. National medical and academic leaders triggered these worries by announcing a series of dreadful prophecies for the black race during the 1880s.
Many physicians, black and white, feared that African Americans teetered on the
edge of self-wrought extermination because of their ignorance of standards of proper
cleanliness and sanitation, an opinion that ostensibly gained a measure of credence by
studies documenting a decline in the rate of fecundity among black women. Joining
them were social Darwinists, whose views on evolution and race were starting to
gain a foothold within the university community. They taught that darker-skinned
people were bereft of the character traits of order and industry and therefore unable
to survive in the modern world. Finally, theorists of popular eugenics widely argued

that the sexual habits of blacks were inherently deviant and would soon ruin their capacity to conceive and rear healthy children. Although based on outright faulty data and racist assumptions about the lowly character of African Americans, these highly publicized professional opinions still alarmed black leaders, whose response included embracing respectability because it assured its practitioners a measure of improved health.[21]

In addition to the ethic of respectability, an evolving notion of African American domesticity also concentrated Delta blacks on the expanding role of material culture in their religious lives. The modern history of black domesticity in the South began after the Civil War, when former slaves enjoyed expanded freedom to experiment with notions of home life and family. Like white notions of domesticity, it defined the family as the crucial building block in society; the child as inherently pure in nature; the mother as the spiritual teacher of her family and caretaker of the Christian home; and the father as the material provider for the household. Yet from the start, black southerners imagined domesticity in ways that reflected their particular social and racial status, especially the overwhelming presence of poor agricultural laborers among them. In comparison to whites, black spokespeople for domesticity targeted all African Americans and not just the better off among them. Nor did they encourage black women to dedicate themselves exclusively to the upbringing of their children and the upkeep of their dwellings. Recognizing that most black women labored long hours outside of the home to make ends meet, black leaders urged them to integrate their work with the demands of promoting domesticity within their families.[22]

None was arguably more prominent in defining domesticity for southern blacks living after Reconstruction than Daniel Alexander Payne, the leading bishop of the AME Church during the late nineteenth century. Born free in 1811 to well-off Methodist parents in Charleston, South Carolina, Payne was self-educated. He opened a school for black children in 1829 but shuttered it six years later after the state outlawed the education of blacks. He moved to the North as a twenty-four-year-old and entered the Lutheran Theological Seminary in Gettysburg, Pennsylvania. Poor eyesight, however, prevented his successful completion of study and graduation. He joined the AME church in 1841, became its historiographer in 1848, and rose to the level of bishop in 1852. He led the effort to buy Wilberforce in Ohio in 1856, which was a school for Methodist Episcopal children that he had helped found, transformed it into a university, and served as its president from 1865 to 1876. A prolific author widely considered to be the finest mind in the AME church, he frequently wrote about the themes of African-American respectability and gender roles.[23]

In *Treatise of Domestic Education,* a heavily circulated book published nine years before his death in 1893, Payne popularized a version of the black Christian home that would, in modified form, become quite popular among black men and women in the Delta. He intentionally couched it in strongly gendered terms, seeking to create a conception of African American family, domestic space, and consumption that encompassed much of women's spiritual worth and power. Indeed, one of his implicit goals was to limit women's rising interest in serving in traditionally male positions of clerical leadership, such as bishops and deacons, by channeling their desire for increased authority toward the home.[24]

The immediate spark for *Treatise of Domestic Education* was a recent surge in the number of AME women preaching in public and acting unofficially as deacons and ministers. They built on the long tradition of AME women conducting religious services outside the official bounds of clerical approval and more contemporary changes to denominational policy, such as permitting women to vote for church trustees, serve as an aid to assistants of local pastors in a post officially dubbed "stewardess," and lead missionary societies.[25] Bishops and clergy who gathered in 1884 for the General Conference of the AME Church, which met every four years and was the most important forum for addressing denominational priorities and setting policies, discussed the growing presence of the women preachers.[26] Voting delegates to the Conference passed a resolution recognizing that "[f]emale evange-lists are becoming very numerous and . . . they are not amenable to anyone. . . ." Then, in a surprising move, they ratified the work of these "female evangelists" and, for the first time in AME history, officially cleared a pathway for women to earn a license to preach. "Resolved, that those sisters that have, and who shall receive licenses from the hand of any of our ministers in the future, shall be subject to the same requirements as local preachers, and they shall be amenable to the Quarterly Conference of the church of which they are part of. . . ."[27] As "local preachers," women would stand on the lowest rung on the ladder of formally recognized clergy, below the ordained ranks of deacon and pastor. Yet to attain this status they would only need the consent of a local pastor and his pledge to supervise them.

This 1884 resolution publicly sanctioning women's pastoral abilities promptly elicited an angry backlash from Payne. Penning *Domestic Education* in the immediate aftermath of the conference, the bishop spearheaded an effort to domesticate women's spiritual authority by sharply orientating it within the boundaries of the black family and the black Christian home and connecting it to limited forms of consumption. He conceptualized both institutions as intricately related and collec-tively forming "a miniature Church, with its priest and priestess to train it for the work of Christian life, for its conflicts and its victories." Diurnal prayer was a primary activity. "Let every child, servant, and sojourner within the homestead be assembled early in the morning and early in the evening around the domestic altar there to listen to the word of God—which ought to be read alternately by the father and the mother. . . . " All should have hymnbooks "to join in singing the songs of praise and thanksgiving, of gratitude and love, of penitence and faith, of obedience and hope." Though parents worked cooperatively, women bore the burden of ensuring the success and health of the black Christian home, running its daily operations, and rearing the children. "To teach is as much the duty of the parents as to govern; therefore, co-labor on the part of the father and mother in the training of the intellect of a child will secure a more perfect development. . . . But there is a sense in which the mother is the special teacher and educator of her own child, and every mother ought to be conscious of this truth. . . . " Payne then detailed precisely what black women should do for their young. They must teach them "the difference between what is fit and what is not fit; what is proper and what is not proper for it to do; and what is right and wrong in though, word, or deed." Mothers should also outfit children in clean sensible clothing and make sure that their home featured literature about black heroes and pictures of them. Indeed, moral lessons were "not only to be inculcated by precept, but also by lucid examples drawn from the biographies of the good and great of both sexes. . . ."[28]

Predictably, some AME women resisted Payne's philosophy of domesticity and aggressively tried to expand their opportunities for social and religious leadership on their own terms. They cleverly made Payne's key assertion—that black women were endowed with a God-given ability to shape history by managing the black Christian house—into the basis for claiming the right to a different type of future in which they advanced themselves in occupations other than mother and wife, especially as ordained clergy. They asked if women could use their talents to produce God-fearing husbands and children and better the future of the race, then why not employ them to similar effect as clerics? The most highly celebrated case of southern dissent was that of North Carolinian Sarah Ann Hughes, who, during the mid-1880s, demanded to be ordained as a deacon. She eventually found a sympathetic listener in Bishop Henry M. Turner, appointed as the bishop presiding over the state in 1885. In light of her sparkling skills as an orator and long history of working in churches in North Carolina, including a three-year stint as an unofficial pastor, Turner granted her request at the North Carolina Annual Conference of the AME Church in late November 1885, shortly after the publication of Payne's book.[29]

Hughes' ordination outraged Payne and his supporters, who successfully struck back by organizing local and national efforts to tighten church laws that ultimately stripped her of her title and prevented any other black women from achieving an ordained rank for nearly seventy-five years.[30] In 1887, the all-male North Carolina Conference removed her name from its sanctioned list of deacons, citing her failure to take the examinations and earn the positive testimonials about her character and work from church leaders required of all applicants. The next year, at the Quadrennial

Meeting of the General Conference, delegates took up the issue of women's ordination and, as a matter of official AME policy, forbade it. They overwhelming passed a resolution stating that "Whereas, Bishop H. M. Turner has seen fit to ordain a woman to the order of deacon; and, Whereas, said act is contrary to the usage of our Church, and without precedent in any other body of Christians in the known world, and as it cannot be proved by the Scriptures that a woman has ever been ordained to the order of the ministry; Therefore, be it enacted, That the bishops of the AMEC be and are hereby forbidden to ordain a woman to the order of deacon or elder in the church."[31]

Despite the controversy generated by Hughes' ordination, it is curious that delegates to the general conference in 1888 reversed, in such strong and unequivocal language, the earlier resolution permitting women to be licensed as preachers. Historically, conference resolutions went unchanged for decades. In this case, Payne's opposition clearly made a difference. Yet why it did so and why it acquired broad-based support so quickly are questions whose answers are not so obvious. They turn on the changing racial and political climate in the Delta in the late 1880s and the growing significance of Payne's notion of domesticity and the black Christian home to black men and women. They also reveal some of the reasons behind the growing place of material culture in black religion in the Delta.

Payne's notion about domesticity caught on with men because of its immediate relevance to their personal and political lives in the late 1880s. As African American men experienced at best checkered success in their battles to keep the franchise, receive due process, and protect themselves and their families from racial violence, Payne's idea represented an attempt to preserve the pulpit and upper levels of denominational hierarchy as cultural arenas in which they still exercised a modest degree of mastery and control over their lives.[32] Less obviously, it struck a chord among men critical of the rising popularity of African American black fraternal orders. For them, Payne's efforts effectively sustained and publicized a particular forum of black male leadership and camaraderie, one replete with its own rites and opportunities for social advancement, that was an alternative to secret societies, albeit considerably smaller and more restricted in membership.

Many black women eventually defined themselves as guardians of the black family and Christian home roughly in the provisions outlined by Payne, but not simply because they were told to. Part of the reason they adopted the roles stemmed from their very familiarity; indeed, at first glance, much of the new social value placed upon the construction of the black family and Christian home seemed merely to assign a fresh level of cultural import to black women's long-standing domestic labors. After all, they historically cooked, cleaned, carried water from the well or creek, washed clothes in pots of hot water, nursed the infants, supervised children, and oversaw the general welfare of their loved ones. When part of an agricultural family, they also turned the earth, planted, hoed, weeded, harvested the crops, fed the animals, and tended the vegetable garden.[33] In the eyes of many black women, then, Payne and his supporters appeared simply to add a veneer of moral import to their traditional activities.

Still, something more was at work in black women's general assent to Payne's formulations about domesticity. At an abstract level was the influence of the scholarship of contemporary black Baptist women theologians from across the South. Virginia Broughton, Mary Cook, and Lucy Wilmot Smith, for instance, revised popular views of women's character by speaking out against resilient stereotypes of women as delicate, plastic, and prone to manipulation. Their thinking helped to set the broad intellectual stage for black women to refigure the political worth of their domestic labors during the late nineteenth century. Drawing from a specific exegesis of the Old Testament that emphasized a history of biblical women raising the men who would lead the ancient Hebrews out of bondage, on the one hand, and a burgeoning trend in liberal Protestant theology to ascribe religiosity to women as a distinctive and inviolable trait, on the other, they argued that black women inherently possessed a powerful capacity to shape the thoughts and actions of men, especially within the confines of the home.[34] Katherine Davis Tillman described this special power of black women to affect the development of the black family in an 1885 article penned for the *AME Church Review* after touring the South. "The home is an institution for which we are indebted to Christianity. It is of equal importance with the school and church. . . . It is in the home that our women, and indeed all women, are seen either at their best or their worst."[35]

More notably, black women willingly participated in the act of reevaluating the cultural meaning of their everyday activities because it meshed with their broader efforts to respond to the ongoing transformation of their political influence in the Delta during the 1880s and 1890s. Rising rates of racial violence and the steady and often bloody process of disfranchisement inhibited their ability to exercise political power in the same ways that they had during Reconstruction: no longer did they enjoy the same level of opportunity to participate in political rallies, party hustings, and orchestrated efforts to sway the vote of male friends and relatives. Matters only worsened as fraternal orders emerged as a popular part of the civic culture of the Delta in the late nineteenth century and largely excluded women. In this context of ongoing political disempowerment, black women found modest opportunities to exercise social clout by helping to support and organize the growth of local and regional denominational networks. And as a complement to these public labors, black women sharpened the definition of their role as keepers of the black Christian home and the place of manufactured items in it. They stressed that they shaped the future of their families, communities, and race in their homes; it was here that they influenced the contours of black society in ways that, while unable to fully replace the lost forms of political participation, promised a renewed degree of authority and satisfaction.

It is important to recognize that many black women, while appearing to accept at face value a description of domesticity more or less publicized as by Payne, successfully enlarged its original meaning to encompass a greater range of their personal religious and social experiences. By regularly traveling outside of domesticity's boundaries, they gradually refitted it to meet many of their own aspirations. Central to this effort was their participation in the thickening of black organizational culture in the Delta, particularly the growing density of women's groups. In their conventions, local missions and Sunday school unions, black women directed and planned new dimensions to black sacred culture. Even though the work sometimes carried them far from the hearth and thus ostensibly undercut Payne's circumscribed ideal of domesticity, they usually avoided open opposition from family and pastors. The reasons are instructive: the women typically operated within networks blessed by high-ranking clergy and rarely traveled for more than a couple of days. Most importantly, they frequently used their new associations as public forums to teach about domesticity in ways that Payne generally would have approved of. For example, they argued that black women should police the style of clothing and the types of religious prints and publications that entered the home and ensure that they conformed to frugal, conservative styles.

In 1893 Priscilla Scott delineated black women's preeminence in the black Christian home in a paper she read at the joint meeting of two Arkansas groups, the Women's State Baptist Association and the State Baptist Sunday School Convention. She taught that a black woman's "home ought to be the greatest pleasure and her most precious privilege. Home is the kingdom of women and she should be the reigning Potentate. A father, a mother, children, a house, and its belongings constitute a home [as] the most delightful place in the world."[36] Similar sentiments were expressed by members of the Arkansas Women's Southeast District Association, composed of four central counties from the Delta and formed in 1897. Among its original stated goals was "to get parents interested in daily family devotion; [and] to discuss subjects that will help to raise a higher moral standard in the homes of many of our people. . . ."[37] Echoing Scott, delegates to the annual conferences of the Association regularly identified women's chief obligation to society as creating the black Christian home and educating their children. At the yearly gathering in 1907, the Committee on Mothers and Children reported that "we find that the hand that rocks the cradle rules the world, [and] that the responsibilities of mothers are many in training their children to reach perfect manhood and womanhood. . . ."[38] Several years later at another annual meeting, Mrs. M. B. Hacker argued that "[i]n the making of good citizens we meet with no larger proposition than the making of good men. . . . It hence becomes our duty as mothers to make our boys good. It requires all of their youthful days to do this. The Bible is an excellent agent to use in this great task. It is a standard because all during the ages it has stood the test. . . . Let us teach our boys the precepts of this book." Hacker concluded by reminding her audience of Baptist women that "[g]overnment begins with the family, and law must begin where government begins. Maintain a certain law for your family and see that your boy obeys these laws."[39]

Like this smaller women's group operating at a local level, statewide associations in the Delta also emerged as venues where black women clarified their duties in the black Christian home. On this larger public platform, though, black women regularly seized the opportunity to address bigger audiences, which usually numbered in the hundreds, to deliver bolder assessments of the religious and racial implications of women's domestic work but ones that, again, reinforced Payne's basic ideas. When Sister S. C. Shanks, the president of the Arkansas Baptist Women's Association, summarized the crucial contributions of black women to the progress of the race, she singled out their enduring leadership of the black Christian home as the most important. In her address, which broadly surveyed black women's history of accomplishments since Reconstruction, she stated that "[t]he home and the mother teach the future as well as the present, and their influences must penetrate the very core of our great State." Her main point was that "the call of the mother . . . is not merely to keep watch over her hearthstone, but to prepare the atmosphere in which she lives. . . . If our race is to be reclaimed mentally, morally, spiritually, physically, it must be done through the child . . . [and in] . . . our homes and local churches. . . ."[40]

Two types of assemblies in particular, Bible bands and mothers' meetings, were important vehicles for black women in the Delta to extend their religious leadership. The main goals of these groups reinforced the ideal of the black Christian home and black women's key role in it. Designed and heavily funded by northern white evangelical institutions to improve the "Christian conduct" of former slaves and their families, they sprung up across the area in the 1880s and often spread through interracial partnerships between black and white women. Susie Bailey, the black colporteur for the white American Women's Home Missionary Society (AMHMS) that operated in the Arkansas Delta, for example, worked hand in hand with the white missionary Joanna Moore to form Bible bands and mother's meetings and introduce black women to the concept of the "Fireside School." It was a program of domestic Christian education created by the AMHMS specifically for southern African Americans and one that closely mirrored the ideals of Payne. In the Fireside School, black women pledged to read the bible and pray with their children daily and become public models of conservative temper, disposition, styles of dress, and habits of spending.

Dutiful students of the Fireside School, announced its promotional literature, fulfilled their "responsibility to God for the training of His children in the home" and succeeded in the "purification and elevation of the home life."[41]

In their meetings, Bailey and Moore distributed a variety of instructional pamphlets and tracts to publicize the Fireside School. Along with publications titled *For Mother While She Rocks the Cradle, Conversion of Children,* and *Bible Stories that Entertain and Instruct the Little Ones,* they offered a range of Bibles—including large print, large print with a durable binding, pocket editions, and illustrated—that carried specific recommendations about how to construct a proper black Christian home.[42] In particular, Bailey stressed to her audiences the importance of the School's notion of righteous living, which, in its insistence on the training of children to be moral and on the uplifting power of spiritual books and magazines, closely resembled some of the core principles of the black Christian home. In an unpublished essay, Bailey revealed that she firmly believed "every home should be a place of happiness but it can not be unless there are good rules and the children required to obey them." She continued that mothers "should not neglect the religious training of their children. . . . Every parent should resolve to do his [*sic*] whole duty by . . . carr[y]ing his children to God night and morning. And also buying them good books and subscribing to little religious newspapers. . . . And above all let each child have his own Bible."[43]

Consumed by her mission to spread the message of the Fireside School, Bailey struggled to balance her evangelical and domestic activities. She was not always successful. In 1897 she worked herself to near exhaustion trying to maintain a hectic schedule of meetings and home visits across the Arkansas Delta and care for her seven children. In a report about Bailey filed that year, Moore noted that "[s]he has a large family which she is certainly training for usefulness, and yet she does much Christian work for her neighbors. A Temperance Band for the young people meets at her house weekly. To the Mothers Class . . . [s]he gives a Bible lesson [e]veryday, and the little children meet her each week for a Sunshine Band. She has sold many of our books. I only write this to show how God can use a mother of a larger family, and one who has poor health, and yet she is not idle. . . ."[44]

While many black women like Bailey embraced a version of the Paynian ideal of domesticity in part because it meshed with their ambitions to lead denominational associations and rebuild their religious authority, others pursued alternative paths to spiritual power. African Methodist Episcopal women, for example, successfully lobbied to create the position of "female evangelist" in 1888 and to form and lead new societies, such as the Women's Home and Foreign Missionary Society in 1896.[45] They also helped establish the post of "Deaconess" at the turn of the century, which awarded officeholders broad authority as church leaders but still officially designated them as subservient to men in matters of doctrine and dogma.[46] The other black Methodist groups and the Baptist churches implemented similar positions and programs for black women.[47] Still, more accessible as a way for black women to demonstrate and accrue both spiritual and racial influence was to build the black Christian home.

The ethic of respectability and the idea of domesticity helped prepare black Baptists and Methodists in the Delta to focus more intently on the place of material culture in their sacred lives. Both encouraged African Americans to reconsider the role of consumption in their daily lives: respectability, in its strict insistence on the purchase of specific goods and services that advanced the goal of a disciplined black character; and domesticity, in its stress on the acquisition of spiritual literature and proper clothing that contributed to the making of the black family and Christian home. More broadly, they invited closer attention be paid to the interior and exterior look of individual homes.

Equally important as a factor affecting how Delta blacks viewed religious material culture, though one less heavily publicized, was the effort of some preachers to openly assert that the physical appearance of the home profoundly influenced the overall makeup of its residents. Besides the moral guidance and example of women, they argued beginning in the late 1880s, the material design and decoration of the black Christian home were direct means of personal and communal betterment. The cleanliness of the floors, the selection of the prints and photos hanging on the walls, the decoration of the rooms: each was an important vehicle in forming the residents' values and disposition and, more generally, the collective future of the race. "[Black] Christian homes," opened an 1899 editorial in the *Christian Index,* "have a far greater influence in shaping the destinies of nations and of a people than we commonly imagine."[48] Similarly, in an article whose very title, "Begin a Movement for Better Homes," conveyed its central message, black ministers from the ME Church asserted that "[w]e do not believe one will be either as good a man or as worthy a citizen without the inspiration which a comfortable and happy home lends. . . ."[49]

Part of the reason for the heightened level of attention paid to the social influence of the physical condition of the home was related to African American healthcare. As was the case in the popular backing for of the ethic of respectability, calls for better housing commanded public notice because they responded to a general apprehension that too many blacks lived in substandard living conditions. Fanning that fear was W. E. B. Du Bois. In a series of influential essays published in 1901 in the *Southern Workman,* the monthly magazine published by the Hampton Normal and Agricultural Institute since 1872 and dedicated to documenting black and Native American culture, he summarized the results of his study of contemporary black living conditions in the South. The leading black intellectual of the era found that many rural black southerners lived in shoddily built, dirty, one-room cabins lacking adequate ventilation or plumbing. Overcrowding and a general absence of privacy in them encouraged immodesty and vulgarity among residents. Du Bois also reported that few ate healthy meals, bathed, groomed, scrubbed their floors, washed their dishes, or cleaned their clothes on a regular basis and, as a result, effectively turned their homes into breeding grounds for disease.[50] He concluded that the progress of the race depended in large part on dramatically improving the quality of the black home: "the question of physical homes for nine millions of our fellows . . . is connected with other and pressing questions of health, education, and morals."[51] To save the "country Freedmen" in particular, Du Bois asserted that "[t]he man of right theory, of leading ideas, who can instill into the rural South not only a desire for better homes but definite ideas of betterment will be the missionary who is needed."[52]

In furnishing a home, a few clergy affirmed that religious images themselves literally possessed the power to affect the nature and morality of their viewers. In a front page editorial entitled "The Sacredness of the Home" published in the *Christian Index* in February 1899, an unnamed minister counseled readers on what type of religious pictures to hang in their houses, though in vague and general terms. He told them only to buy "pictures that we will not tire of looking at . . ." and ones that "the more we see [them], the more their beauty grows upon us."[53] Despite never listing his recommended pictures or explaining how they excited change in a viewer, this clergyman obviously believed that one benefited spiritually by regularly gazing at them. Although his opinion was not widespread, it still symbolized the growing public fascination in the religious and social role of material goods.

The increasing clerical attention to respectability, domesticity, and an awareness of the role of material belongings in and the physical condition of black homes in shaping black character eventually merged and swelled into a multidenominational chorus of African American religious and social leaders exhorting congregants to buy and display commercial physical goods wisely. It articulated a specific relationship between black morality and domestic spaces, arguing that an individual's character, ethics, and even education depended greatly on the visual setting of the home. Black Christians must "use money [previously] spent for tobacco, whiskey, and snuff in buying homes and subscribing to books, papers, magazines, etc., for their children," urged Memphis resident Ida B. Wells. In an 1888 article in the *Christian Index,* she argued that blacks "are to be taught personal, individual, family and race pride, the necessity of culture, by beautifying their homes and cultivating their minds."[54] Wells suggested that the most important items for beautifying a black home were religious books and especially pictures. Editors at the *Christian Index* were blunter. In a weekly feature called "Advice," they pointed out that "[i]n the decoration of a home each article tells a story of its own; the small ornaments . . . and especially the kinds of pictures and books. [W]e should always be careful to get good ones, instead of showy ones which are offensive to people."[55]

Because "good" pictures were widely viewed as essential elements in the formation of any black Christian home, clerics did not mince words when describing precisely what types were suitable for hanging. They articulated very specific instructions. "Do not decorate your homes with pictures representing shows, theaters, minstrels and saloons," trumpeted the *Christian Index*'s "Advice" column during the first week of March 1892.[56] Reverend G. I. Izard, in a prescriptive piece bearing the straightforward title "What Kind of Pictures to Hang on Your Walls," published in the *Southwestern Christian Advocate,* declared anathema any depiction of "W. Duke, Sons & Co.'s tobacco manufacturing establishment" or "different theaters, circus shows, [and] base ball playing. . . ." He apparently discovered these types of images papering the walls of some black homes during a preaching tour. They "represent[ed] sin in the blackest form." In their place, Izard admonished that "it is better and will prove more beneficial to the young to have on your walls a picture showing the arrest, crucifixion, burial, resurrection and ascension of our Lord and Savior Jesus Christ."[57]

The strong didactic tone heard in these examples, however, betrayed an anxiety and ambivalence about relying on the market as a key resource to create the black Christian home. For while it supplied visual images helpful in the making of the black Christian home, the market also produced ones that could easily destabilize it. One sign of the pubic awareness of the growing importance of visual images to African American Protestants in the Delta during the 1890s and their dangerous potential was the sudden interest shown by Catholic missionaries in securing supplies of black prints and pictures for use in their evangelical labors. In August 1898, Reverend Thomas Plunkett, a white Josephite brother and director of the Colored Industrial Institute, a small Catholic school in Pine Bluff, Arkansas, filled with mostly non-Catholic children, penned an urgent note to his superior, Reverend Joseph Slattery. Plunkett pleaded not only for items normally used in Catholic worship and devotion—"one dozen rosary beads, two dozen hymn books, and two or three dozen small religious medals"—but also "all the pictures of Colored men and Saints you can afford." These last two items were essential to the goal of winning converts among his young African American charges and their parents, explained Plunkett, because "only by such means [can] we . . . expect to do much with those attending the Institute."[58] Plunkett's demand for black images testified to their expanding significance in the spiritual lives of black Protestants. Yet his efforts also concretized a persistent tension gnawing at many African American Baptists and Methodists over the possible results of increasing the use of mass-produced goods both in the making of black Christian homes and in nurturing greater levels of public refinement.

Not every manufactured religious image—and certainly not one featuring a black Catholic—was appropriate. Even more worrisome was the fear that not every black Protestant possessed the requisite critical faculty necessary to select the proper image for their home.[59]

To counter the market's capacity to undermine the black Christian home and the successful growth of black Protestantism in general, black religious leaders asserted their role as judges and purveyors of what blacks should buy for their houses. As early as 1877, officials of the North Mississippi Conference of the AME Church, a region that included most of the Mississippi Delta, provided pictures of their bishops to congregants who paid their "dollar money," by which they meant their yearly assessment.[60] Other denominations eventually followed suit. The *Southwestern Christian Advocate* sold pictures of their bishops beginning in spring 1891 to members of its ME Churches. "Many of our readers would gladly possess the pictures of our bishops if they only knew where to get them. In order to accommodate them, we have arranged to supply them with a beautiful cabinet group photograph of all our bishops, for the small sum of 25 cents."[61]

For black Christians unable to spare even a few cents to buy portraits, editors started to print them as a regular feature of their newspapers by the end of the century. In this case, they created a visual commodity that was inexpensive, widely available, and fairly easy to distribute and censor. In summer 1894, the *Southwestern Christian Advocate* inaugurated a section called the "Picture Gallery." As its title suggested, this feature offered a picture and brief biography of a different cleric every two to three weeks. They were intended to be cut out and tacked up somewhere inside the home. The portraits quickly became a hit with the readers, according to the newspaper. After surveying preachers and itinerants, it cheerfully reported that "[i]n thousands of the homes of our constituency those pictures with the brief history of their originals will be found." The editors' excitement, however, reflected not only their belief that the popularity of the pictures signaled broad public approval of their version of the proper black Christian home but also more practical financial considerations. They happily pointed out that the Picture Gallery helped to "greatly augment and accelerate . . . the increased circulation of the SOUTHWESTERN."[62] Perhaps spurred by the apparent popular and commercial success of the Picture Gallery, editors at the *Christian Index* inaugurated the similarly titled "Our Picture Gallery" in 1900, but with a twist. They introduced the series by announcing "we shall insert, every week, the portrait of some preacher of our Church, accompanied by a short biography of the same name." They invited all local preachers to mail in a personal history, a portrait, and two dollars.[63] In this case, editors sought to earn extra revenue by assessing those preachers hoping to join the Picture Gallery a promotion fee.

During the 1890s, editors of black religious newspapers published sketches of famous figures in African American history who were not church leaders, too. Readers of the *Southwestern Christian Advocate* enjoyed pictures of Frederick Douglass and Abraham Lincoln, the latter usually printed during the weeks just prior to the anniversary of the Emancipation Proclamation and advertised as a "rugged cut" of the president who freed the slaves.[64] At other times black religious leaders sold mass-produced decorations specifically designed as religious wall hangings. In honor of Thanksgiving in 1895, editors at the *Southwestern Christian Advocate* offered a framed print of a landscape oil painting called "American Beauty." They provided few clues about the print itself, other than it "form[ed] a beautiful ornament for the high, narrow wall spaces for which it is so difficult to obtain pictures of the proper style."[65] Similarly, the editors at the *Baptist Vanguard* offered a wall-hanging of the Emancipation Proclamation in 1896 by stressing its value as "a beautiful ornament for any parlor in the country."[66] The habit of decorating Delta black homes with pictures cut out of black religious newspapers and church publications apparently persisted for years to come. When members of a federal agency investigated the living conditions of black sharecroppers in the Delta during the 1920s, they noted that inhabitants commonly covered their walls with unframed pictures taken from newspapers and magazines.[67]

Moving beyond merely providing visual images to their congregants as a way of influencing black domestic life and uses of material religious culture was the National Baptist Convention, which in 1908 experimented with ways to advertise and produce black dolls. Eager to supply life-like miniatures of well-groomed, well-dressed black girls to black families, President E. C. Morris authored a resolution asking members to establish black dolls as a preferred gift for their children and grandchildren, form black doll clubs, and host "doll bazaars" during the holiday season. That same year Richard H. Boyd, then the head the publishing arm of the Convention (and still a member in good standing), founded the National Negro Doll Company to manufacture black dolls. Many black parents coveted the dolls, believing with their Baptist leaders that they helped their children develop racial pride, self esteem, and proper ideas about hygiene and dress. The dolls were rare in that they didn't ape racial stereotypes of black physical features, as did most commercially produced ones at the time, and they offered a positive commodification of blackness that countered the ugly depictions of African Americans embedded in so many commercial advertisements. Few blacks ever owned one of these black dolls, however, because of their hefty price tag and short supply. The cost of one typically ran at least a dollar, putting it beyond the reach of many Delta consumers.[68]

More successful in publicizing standards of the black Christian home, respectability, and domesticity was the local black parsonage. Of all the black homes in a neighborhood, plantation, or town, it emerged as the most important as a type of community showcase where visitors glimpsed a local model of domestic consumption and organization. It also publicly demonstrated the household work and achievements of the pastor's wife. In an article titled "The Much Needed Parsonage," Mrs. Carrie Mitchell Price, who with her husband, a minister with the ME Church, lived on a cotton plantation in the Mississippi Delta, urged her peers to make "every parsonage in the Mississippi Conference [into] a pleasant place-clean, attractive, and comfortable. . . . Fill its nooks and corners with books and works of art. . . . Let the wives adorn its walls with pictures and surround it with shade trees[,] grass[,] plots and flowers."[69] More boldly, an editorial from the *Southwestern Christian Advocate* published at the turn of the century argued that the parsonage stood as the key visual reminder of how blacks should live at home. "The parsonage . . . [is] the model home of the community. It is more frequently visited than most homes are generally, and from the parsonage the housekeepers of the community not only get the impression of the ability of the preacher's wife to make a home, but get their ideal of home-making. . . ." It concluded by pointing out that "the parsonage represents the community life as no other single home does. It represents the combined industry, home ideals, and aesthetic tastes of the community. . . ."[70]

Delta blacks' desire to refine domestic spaces also extended to more public ones, like their houses of worship. Indeed, at the same time that they fashioned new standards for domestic life they also reinvented norms of decoration and ornamentation for their churches. In both cases they invested certain commercial goods and styles of adornment with spiritual and cultural value and created a religious material culture that communicated their notions of respectability, domesticity, beauty, and progress. By the turn of the century, pastors and their flocks struggled to create houses of worship whose size, design, and number and level of amenities registered the refinement of the community.

When fashioning new standards of church beauty, Delta blacks took cues from changes in style occurring at the national level. During the late nineteenth and early twentieth centuries, leading black evangelical congregations across the country built new churches and refurbished older ones with stained wood, wainscoting, moldings, cornices, frescos, wallpaper, carpet, upholstery, rich color schemes, and modern heating and lighting systems.[71] The parent church for African Methodist Episcopalians, Mother Bethel in Philadelphia, Pennsylvania, underwent a highly celebrated renovation in the late 1880s, as recorded by Bishop Payne. Payne called attention to a national fundraising effort that had successfully transformed the church. No longer was it "as plain as a Quaker's coat, and perfectly free from ornament." The new Mother Bethel contained a magnificent series of stained glass windows done "in the colors of the rainbow, with all the tints and hues of the precious stones mentioned in the Revelation of St. John xxi. 11–21." These windows, claimed Payne, formed "a glorious scene of divine beauty, and so profuse as to resemble the magnificence of the starry heavens."[72] AME church leaders hoped that the new Mother Bethel might inspire similar efforts in congregations throughout the nation and they encouraged members to pay far closer attention to the look of their churches. In 1908 AME clerics attending the General Conference overwhelmingly passed a resolution recognizing that "[a]rchitecture is the art of building according to principles which are determined, not merely by the ends of the edifice it is intended to serve, but by consideration of beauty and harmony."[73]

In the Delta, of course, the majority of black communities lacked the capital to purchase stained glass windows of any type. They simply could not imitate the level of beauty achieved by Mother Bethel. Yet they still participated in a regional variation of the national trend of church adornment. Developing a local visual aesthetic for black Baptist and Methodist churches, they built new houses of worship or renovated old ones, embellished them with richly colored walls and ceilings, and outfitted them with a modest range of handsome furnishings and amenities. As in the case of the black Christian home, it reflected a rising appreciation for, and an ability to take advantage of, the ways in which the built environment and literary and consumer commodities might be used to signal social relations and social values. It also involved women as key leaders in creating this form of religious expression.

First, the emerging visual aesthetic of black churches was in part based on a new definition of pastoral progress. Beginning in the late 1870s, the ownership of a church with a pulpit, a bell, and finished pews was symbolically almost as important an indicator of progress for a minister and his congregation as the number of converts won or backsliders reclaimed. In the yearly reports submitted by itinerants with the AME church beginning in the late nineteenth century, men increasingly framed their accomplishments by cataloguing what they had bought and built. These reports, issued by ministers from the Delta and every corner of the South, were printed in the *Christian Recorder* and demonstrated the growing attention paid to the role of consumer goods in black churches. Presiding Elder R. F. Harley reviewed the labors of an Elder Murry, whose missionary territory included Memphis and western Tennessee, by ticking off the physical improvements made to his church. Harley was extremely specific in his evaluation, measuring the success of his preacher according to the quality of the new church's construction, the size of its overall dimensions, the health of its financial state, and the quality of its ornamentation. He graded Murry quite highly, singling out his "splendid unfinished frame church, 40 × 60, with fourteen feet ceiling." Harley signed off cheerfully, noting that "Elder Murry has succeeded in paying off many of the debts. . . . He has plastered [the church] overhead and has purchased a bell. . . ."[74]

Predictably, the physical appearance and quality of construction of a black church in the Delta depended directly on the financial status of the congregation. The 550 members of the Bethel AME church in Vicksburg, Mississippi, decided to show off their growing membership and prosperity by enriching the visual appeal of the interior in 1880. In this wealthiest of black churches in Vicksburg, one visitor noted that the pastor of the renovated sanctuary preached under "[a]n arched frescoed ceiling with a pale pink background, surrounded with a border of pink and gold[.] [The] seats [had] scrolled ends and straw-colored grainings, the pulpit a deep recess encircled with the motto, 'How amiable are Thy Tabernacles,' &c, with a dark blue cloudy background with a silver lining, and angelic cherubs with wings breaking through the clouds. . . ."[75]

Men and women of means who worshipped at historic Delta churches strove to decorate them ornately as well. Through the addition of fancy wall paintings and new consumer goods, they publicly demonstrated the importance of their churches and hoped to attract new members. In Little Rock, Miles Chapel, the largest CME Church in the state, underwent a major renovation in 1887 to become a badge of "honor" for the denomination and to "make Little Rock a strong hold for us." According to the pastor's wife, Lizzie Johnson, women spearheaded the effort to raise money and purchased "a nice Bible for the church, a fine table, and two [altar] cloths, and the pulpit was beautifully dressed with velvet. . . . A most pleasing feature is noticed on entering the church, that on either side of the pulpit there are two angels nicely adorning the walls, and just above, in the form of an arch, another angel contrasting with the other two, presenting a lovely picture to the eye."[76] Also in Little Rock, worshipers at First Baptist church, the oldest black church in the city, lavished attention upon the construction of a new building in the mid-1880s as part of a public campaign to promote its venerable status and its distinction as the pastorate of the president of Arkansas Baptist College. They built probably the most ornate black Protestant church in the Delta, one constructed from red brick and outfitted "with two front entrances, spires on both sides, a pipe organ, beautifully engraved windows, steam heat, a pool gas, electric lights and fans, a balcony and a large bell that was purchased in 1869." The structure boasted a pastor's study, a choir loft, and a stained glass widow that depicted, somewhat ironically given the lavishness of what surrounded it, "Christ in the Garden of Gethsemane."[77]

When congregants installed a pipe organ in their church, as did members of First Baptist in Little Rock, they selected one of the most sought after material symbols of prosperity for any black religious community in the Delta. It was also one of the most expensive, typically costing between one and two hundred dollars and thus beyond the reach of many groups. During the Third Annual Session of the Arkansas

Baptist Sunday School Convention in June 1886, participants discussed how organs were "really indispensable to denominational progress."[78] Two years later, members of this group again stressed the importance of organs as a badge of progress by including a new statistic in their annual report. Squeezed in between the columns labeled "Converts in S.S. School [sic]" and "Value of Property" was now a new one bearing the heading "Schools with Organs." Out of a total of sixty-seven schools, most of which were located in the Delta and housed in or adjacent to churches, eighteen had organs in 1888.[79] The rising popularity of organs was immediately obvious to anyone who scanned the published minutes for the 1904 Baptist Missionary and Educational Convention of Tennessee, which featured a full-page advertisement for "National Baptist Organs." The promotion appeared opposite the title page and bore the open endorsement of Reverend R. H. Boyd, the secretary of the National Baptist Publishing Board (figure 4.1).[80]

The popular interest in creating fancier and more elaborate churches fired a friendly competition among the leading Baptist ministers in the southern part of the Arkansas Delta. Each scrambled to build a house of worship more beautiful than his colleague's. During the early 1890s, detailed a local black Baptist historian, "[a] great rivalry in church building was begun, and many nice, and some real fine churches were constructed." Though unclear about what "real fine churches" looked like, this writer was certain, if a bit overconfident, about their payoff. The new buildings identified their worshippers as civilized and organized and burnished their image in the eyes of not only their white neighbors but also any local black doubtful the ability of these Baptists to raise a new building and act orderly. The chronicler explained that "Revs. I. G. Bailey, W. H. Allen, W.W. Booker, A. Gross, S. D. Douglass, and others built nice churches and this raised the Baptists very much in the estimation of the public. . . . The Baptists now ceased to be called back numbers [sic], but instead were called a progressive set of church workers."[81]

Few black religious institutions in the Delta were elaborately designed or decorated, of course. Most churches were supported by poor agricultural workers who struggled to raise money to purchase fancy items. Instead congregants usually built simple houses of worship decorated with a few manufactured wall hangings, a string of electric lights, and perhaps a couple of commercially made sketches. Often they balanced store-bought goods with handmade decorations. During his 1883 visit to the Mississippi Delta, New Yorker Clarence Deming reported that "[a]long with every large plantation for hundreds of miles . . . goes the inevitable Negro church." Commonly the structure was a "rough, barn-like exterior, whitewashed, and with seating capacity for perhaps a hundred auditors. Within are coarse benches, cobwebbed board walls, a long desk and platform made of unfinished lumber, a dingy kerosene chandelier with one or two lights, and behind the so-called pulpit a line of tawdry

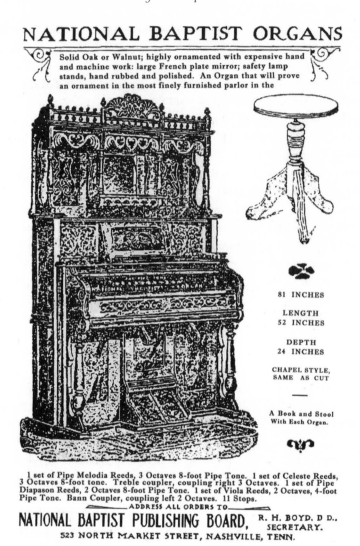

NATIONAL BAPTIST ORGANS

Solid Oak or Walnut; highly ornamented with expensive hand and machine work: large French plate mirror; safety lamp stands, hand rubbed and polished. An Organ that will prove an ornament in the most finely furnished parlor in the

81 INCHES

LENGTH
52 INCHES

DEPTH
24 INCHES

CHAPEL STYLE,
SAME AS CUT

A Book and Stool
With Each Organ.

1 set of Pipe Melodia Reeds, 3 Octaves 8-foot Pipe Tone. 1 set of Celeste Reeds, 3 Octaves 8-foot tone. Treble coupler, coupling right 3 Octaves. 1 set of Pipe Diapason Reeds, 2 Octaves 8-foot Pipe Tone. 1 set of Viola Reeds, 2 Octaves, 4-foot Pipe Tone. Bann Coupler, coupling left 2 Octaves. 11 Stops.

ADDRESS ALL ORDERS TO

NATIONAL BAPTIST PUBLISHING BOARD, R. H. BOYD, D D., SECRETARY.
523 NORTH MARKET STREET, NASHVILLE, TENN.

Figure 4.1. Baptist Missionary and Education Convention of Tennessee, 1904.

colored prints pasted on the boards depicting scriptural themes like Moses and the burning bush, the ark on Ararat, and Daniel with the lions." Although most of the churches surveyed by Deming lacked a bell, he recognized its immense popularity. One poor congregation wanted a bell so badly, he observed, that church members improvised by "substitut[ing] a rusty buzz-saw hung by a rope [that], when stuck by a stone, g[ave] a . . . cracked note to summon worshippers together."[82]

Deming's description of the common black church in the Mississippi Delta loosely matched those found in the Arkansas Delta. Here, a church also tended to be a simple white frame one-story building about 50 × 75 feet in dimension. It usually consisted of a shingle roof, one door that served as the front entrance, and a set of double doors that provided an exit in the back. Four broad windows opened on both sides of the longer walls and provided natural light in the daytime for the one hundred or so people who could sit comfortably in the ten pews. Few of these buildings possessed a bell tower or even a bell. Oil lamps illuminated the interior at night. During the winter months, wood heaters chased away the cold.[83]

Churches of lesser means participated in limited ways in the new material dimension of African American houses of worship. Sometimes they raised money for the sake of adding just one new amenity. A group of women from Gethsemane Baptist Church in Wabbesoke, Arkansas, took it upon themselves to improve the lighting in their house of worship in 1886. They did not buy any run-of-the-mill lighting, however, but instead spent extra money on large, fancy, chandelier-like fixtures. "Today our church is nicely furnished with three Parisian lamps containing 72 Candles," wrote the chair of the women's committee. "We are indeed highly pleased. . . ."[84] At other times poorer congregations turned to more subtle means, such as outfitting their pastors in store-bought clothing. In Greer, Arkansas, in summer 1895, the female members of Morris Chapel Baptist Church "gave a rally to get the pastor a suit of clothes which was a success. [T]hey raised $12.00. . . ."[85]

Although few Delta blacks published accounts during the late nineteenth and early twentieth centuries plainly describing how the material dimension to their faith was changing, much can still be learned about it. The trick is not to confine the search for evidence only to the types of manuscript sources most readily consulted and trusted by scholars: the books, diaries, letters, and personal papers that make up the bulk of any archive. Though some such materials still exist for Delta blacks who lived after Reconstruction, they are scarce and disproportionately representative of the lives of the most privileged African Americans. Relying mainly on them might lead to the false conclusion that only the better-off Delta blacks widely integrated physical objects into their everyday spiritual lives.

To avoid this pitfall, it is important to puzzle over a broad range of sources and particularly to pour over those initially appearing to be ephemeral, such as the letters to the editors, dispatches from traveling itinerants, advertisements for portraits of bishops, and pictures of local clerics. Added to this mix should be more conventional forms of evidence, though ones regarded too lightly at times, like church inventories and pastors' reports on the financial state of their congregations. Buried in these scrapes of history are clues about what Delta blacks, especially those with little money, wanted to wear, read, hang in their homes, and put in their churches; in them are the hidden records of how clothing, prints, pictures, pews, bells, stained glass windows, and electric lights came to carry new religious meaning in the decades after Reconstruction. These documents ultimately cast new light on how Delta blacks transformed their understanding of the relationship between the material and sacred world—how they married new ideas about respectability, domesticity, and the black Christian home to the purchase and display of a highly proscribed range of domestic goods and to strict regimes of conservative behaviors. Similarly, they reveal how African Americans birthed notions of corporate religious sensibility and progress that strongly depended for their realization on the acquisition of domestic furnishings and amenities: by 1900, most black Baptist and Methodist churches in the Delta participated in a local aesthetic of material religious culture in which a house of worship publicly communicated its ambitions and successes through the level of sophistication of its architecture, design, and interior decoration.

In its reading of evidence and selection of interpretative frameworks, however, the story told here about African American religion in the Delta is not terribly new. Instead, it echoes with the strains of religious histories of men and women from other times and places who also left little in the way of traditional archival records yet whose past has still been recovered. Like those histories, the telling of this one depends on reviewing a wide expanse of sources and closely contextualizing them within their local environments. Its visibility requires seeing the past as did the people who originally experienced and preserved it—through an eclectic mix of printed, visual, and physical sources. Finally, its success asks that scholars treat the simple material commodities that constitute so much of the lived reality of sacred belief with as much care and attention as any theological treatise sealed in an airtight vault.

5

THE MAKING OF THE AFRICAN AMERICAN HOLINESS MOVEMENT

I want to tell you some natural facts
Every man don't understand the Bible alike.
But that's all right now, I tell you that's all
But you better have Jesus, I tell you that's all. . . .
Now the Holiness people, when they came in
They said: "Boys, we can make it by livin' above sin."

—Washington Phillips, "Denomination Blues"

In 1889, William Christian, a tall, handsome, thirty-three year-old former slave, threw aside his religious past. Formerly an itinerant Baptist minister who had preached for years in the small towns and cotton plantations strung across the Arkansas Delta, he now embarked on a path revealed in a recent dream and one that guided him toward a new version of African American Christianity. Devoting his days to recapturing the "true" spirit of religion, he built a new type of black church modeled directly on the biblical life of Jesus and his apostles. He called it the "Church of the Living God" and founded it in Wrightsville, Arkansas, a dusty village just east of Little Rock. Like most pastors of any denominational stripe, he strictly forbade members from using liquor, tobacco, and profanity. But Christian's other rules and regulations were unlike anything nearby residents had ever heard of. He referred to his church as a "temple," his followers as "black Jews," and his lieutenants as "chiefs." He celebrated the Sabbath on Saturday. And he instituted a regular foot washing service because "Jesus had done it."

What really turned heads, however, was Christian's bold insistence that God had willed the Church of the Living God into existence as a clear notice of displeasure

sanctified

with Baptist and Methodist churches in the Delta. The key problem with them, Christian revealed in a short autobiographical tract, was that their leaders simply did not understand how one was truly saved. "Now when sinners ask the preachers what they must do to be saved, they tell them to come to the mourners' bench and go get religion. They are telling the poor sinners to do something they never saw in the Bible in their lives." This was poor advice, contended Christian, because merely to "get religion," by which he meant undergoing a conversion, was not enough to earn salvation. Another type of religious experience needed to happen after conversion. "[O]n the day of Penticost [*sic*] sinners asked the apostles what they must do. Peter said repent." Only then would they experience, as had the apostles, the Holy Spirit descending upon them, purifying them of sin, blessing them with supernatural powers, and assuring them of eternal reward. It was an event recorded in the New Testament and popularly known as sanctification. It was also, declared Christian, required of all who would join his church. Perhaps the most remarkable feature about the Church of the Living God, though, was its rapid growth. Sixteen years after its founding, the Church of the Living God had nearly ten thousand members, most drawn from the ranks of black sharecroppers and farmers living in the Delta.[1]

The story of William Christian and the founding of the Church of the Living God, while centered in the Delta, was part of a larger narrative of religious reform that stretched back to the 1740s and John Wesley's teaching on Christian perfectionism in the American colonies. Driven to perfect the human soul and make the body "holy," Wesley and fellow Methodists searched for a way that an individual, after the experience of conversion, might be cleansed of sin. They found it, like Christian did, in the event of the Pentecost and subsequently labeled it "sanctification" or the "second blessing." They called their efforts to popularize it the Holiness movement. During the early republic and antebellum eras, northern white and some black evangelists conducted Holiness revivals. No figure was more important in spreading the movement in northern cities during the 1840s and 1850s than Phoebe Palmer, a white woman. Significantly, it did not penetrate the South to any sizeable degree in the years before the Civil War because of its political affiliation with radical social programs, such as abolitionism. After 1865, though, Holiness spread southward through the teachings, travels, and publications of evangelists such as Joanna Patterson Moore, the white resident of the Arkansas Delta during the 1890s who was employed by the American Baptist Home Missionary Society, and Amanda Berry Smith, a black missionary. Early southern Holiness churches often ignored the color line. The white leaders of the Fire Baptized Holiness Church of Tennessee opened their doors to blacks, while the United Holy Church of America in North Carolina, a predominantly black organization, hosted biracial worship services. Yet over time churches embracing black and white congregants on equal footing bowed to the pressure of public scorn and ridicule and usually forsook this practice.[2]

Although the Holiness movement in America was nearly a century and one-half old by the time Christian renounced his Baptist identity and formed his new church, it had never transformed African American religion in any widespread or lasting manner. That changed at the turn of the twentieth century, however, when Christian and two other erstwhile black Baptist ministers from the Delta birthed the African American Holiness movement. Eventually becoming national in scope, its origins were local and deeply entangled in the post-Reconstruction history of black life in the Delta. Specifically, its taproots lay in the misery generated by the failure of Reconstruction and the rising level of public confusion and dissatisfaction triggered by recent changes in Baptist and Methodist life. First, during the late nineteenth century many black Christians experienced a depth of political despair and power-lessness unmatched since slavery. It was a reaction to the steady deterioration of their citizenship and personal safety. All too common was the lament of an unnamed black man sent forth after he witnessed a public lynching. "What is to become of our poor people under such circumstances? Heaven only knows. We are butchered all over this Southern country by such representatives of 'white supremacy.' . . . My Lord, and my God, where are we? How long, O Lord, how long?"[3] In searching for a reason for their current plight, many Delta blacks openly wondered if they were at least partly guilty for the deplorable state of civic affairs by having unknowingly displeased God in some way. Others were more direct in assigning blame and fingered the contemporary culture of their spiritual life as a key source of their problems.

Indeed, by the 1890s an increasing number of black Baptists and Methodists in the Delta in the 1890s challenged many of the latest changes to their religion. Not every critic condemned every new development, of course, but each articulated a similar uneasiness and frustration over facets of black spiritual life that helped to unite many of them as protestors. For example, a great number dismissed the thousands of men who sustained memberships in fraternal orders and churches at the same time as blasphemers, whose secret oaths, fancy uniforms, elaborate parades, and death benefits betrayed an overweening pride in a human organization and a misplaced confidence in it to care for them in time of need. Others rejected preachers and newspapers editors selling domestic commodities, on the one hand, and the bur-geoning popular interest in adorning black homes and churches with fine furnishings, on the other. Both practices illuminated the presence of a rampant and sinful spirit of idolatry encouraging black Christians to seek purpose and value for their lives not in the word of God but in human organizations and products. Some also identified the recent growth of denominational churches and their attendant presses, schools, and conventions as a source of great harm. These particular detractors took issue with the ordering of Baptist and Methodists houses of worship into districts or regional governing bodies, fearing that it symbolized a growing institutionalization of black religion that would quickly strip local churches of autonomy and excite factionalism over matters of doctrine, liturgy, and worship.

Although critics had questioned the expansion of black sacred culture in the Delta throughout the 1870s and 1880s, their numbers began to swell in the 1890s as a series of conditions came into being that made possible large-scale dissent. The establishment of a modern transportation infrastructure made it easier to organize groups of protestors and disseminate information across rural areas. The expansion of African American print culture facilitated the expansion and popularization of alternative theologies. A new breed of black preacher matured as well, men like Christian who were born at the end of slavery or in freedom, literate, highly mobile, and eager to explore fresh paths of growth for their churches.

This volatile mix of social despair, religious unrest, dramatic improvement in travel and communication, and the coming of age of a new generation of ministers made the Delta ripe for the birth of a religious revival, in this case the African American Holiness movement. Its main leaders were three one-time Baptist preachers who shared a tightly knit world of religion and politics in the Delta: Christian, Charles Price Jones, and Charles Harrison Mason. Jones and Mason were both born in freedom, raised in families of agricultural workers, educated with at least some college training, and fully fledged ministers at a young age. Like Christian, they became Baptist clergy at time when local denominational culture was rapidly expanding. Both men attended Arkansas Baptist College, though only Jones graduated, and participated in Sunday school organizations, Baptist Young People's Unions, and district and state ministerial conventions. With Christian, they were dismissive of many of the popular notions about domestic culture and church adornment and responded by building Holiness congregations partly as a way of breaking away from the modern customs of black religious life in the Delta. Jones and Mason initially collaborated as Holiness ministers but eventually separated and built independent Holiness churches.

Christian, Jones, and Mason preached subtle variations on a central theme—namely, that earthly comfort, security, and authority lay not in the teaching of any denominational church but in the acceptance of their theology of moral perfectionism.[4] At its core lay the idea that Christians of any rank or station in life could suddenly be sanctified and forever washed of sin. Most denominational ministers shared this belief as well, but only as an abstract doctrine of faith with little immediate or practical application to daily life. They typically shunned it as a topic worthy of mention from the pulpit or in a denominational newspaper. When they did discuss it openly, they were usually condemnatory of it. In contrast, Christian, Jones and Mason confidently asserted that God readily and frequently imparted sanctification to his faithful, which earned them the promise of salvation and frequently one or more powers that directly recalled the spiritual gifts that Jesus' apostles had received during the Pentecost, such as the ability to heal bodily ills, cast out evil spirits, testify, or prophesy.

The implications of basing a religious movement on the radical experience of sanctification were far-reaching and, for many traditional Baptist and Methodists, quite threatening. At issue was the legitimacy of many of the contemporary educational and liturgical reforms in denominational life. Holiness leaders constructed churches in which preachers needed not to be formally educated, only sanctified. Women could serve in most high-ranking positions, with the usual exception of pastor. Worship was unrestrained by normal convention and instead made open to the influence and spontaneity of the Holy Spirit, which, as it seized and shook individuals, frequently excited them to leap, twirl, dance, sing lustily, and clutch at the heavens with outstretched arms in ecstatic displays of devotion and praise. As one of Mason's deacons described their unrestrained praise, it "changes as the Spirit changes it. Sometimes when we go in the first thing will be everything [*sic*] in the room weeping, the next thing praying or singing,—the next thing everybody reading the Bible, the next thing all kneeling, all still and quiet."[5] Outside of church, Holiness believers led a "holy life." Placing faith in the Holy Spirit to provide for their needs and wants, they followed a strict disciplinary code characterized by an unswerving devotion to keeping the body pure and the soul sinless. As a result, they avoided dancing, smoking, drinking alcohol, swearing, parading in public, wearing expensive clothes, and decorating with costly goods.

The African American Holiness movement in the Delta quickly established itself and spread east and west of the Mississippi River to become the fastest-growing form of organized black religion in the nation during the early 1900s.[6] Its chief message about the urgent necessity of reform struck a sympathetic chord among Delta blacks disenchanted by recent turns of events in politics and religion. Yet the vow of Holiness leaders to liberate African American Christians fully from the dangers and trappings of modern life was, ultimately, more promise that deliverance. Indeed, the early history of the black Holiness movement was not a straightforward story about a group of Delta blacks breaking ranks with denominational churches and forging a new spiritual community; instead, it was a complicated tale of cultural reconstruction. Christian, Jones, and Mason built their movement in large part by carefully restructuring the engagement between Christian faith and modern society, balancing theological and liturgical innovations against contemporary traditions and customs, and quietly adopting certain dimensions of contemporary Baptist and Methodist life.

William Christian's trajectory from Baptist minister to Holiness preacher preceded the paths taken by his two Delta contemporaries, Charles Price Jones and Charles Harrison Mason, whose successes as evangelists eventually overshadowed his own. Charles Price Jones was born in 1866 in Georgia to a one-time slave. As an adolescent, he worked as an agricultural laborer in different southern and midwestern cities, staying longest in Memphis. At seventeen, he joined the Locust Grove Baptist Church in the Arkansas Delta town of the same name and at twenty-one earned a preaching license. Jones became a member of Centennial Baptist Church in nearby Helena, where he befriended its famous pastor, Reverend E. C. Morris. Morris convinced Jones to pursue an education at Arkansas Baptist College, where he enrolled in January 1888. After completing his course of studies in 1891, he served briefly as an editor of the *Baptist Vanguard* and a trustee of the college. About this time he met Joanna Patterson Moore, the white American Baptist missionary and Holiness evangelist then working in Little Rock. She introduced him to the theology of sanctification and three years later he experienced it personally. Describing the events leading up to it, Jones wrote that, for a long time, he "was not satisfied with a . . . religion that none of the signs spoken of in the Scriptures followed." After fasting and praying for three days, Jones suddenly became sanctified "sweetly in His love. New visions of Christ, of God, of truth, were given me and the earnestness of the Sprit was mine. I was sealed unto the day of Redemption." Jones then began a difficult quest to build Baptist churches that embraced his radical view that only the sanctified were destined for heaven. He pastored congregations first in Searcy and then outside of the Arkansas Delta, in Selma, Alabama, before finally returning to the area after accepting an invitation to lead Mt. Helm Baptist Church in Jackson, Mississippi, in 1895.[7] It was here that he began publishing his Holiness newspaper, *Truth,* met Mason, and with him founded their first African-American Holiness church in 1897 (figure 5.1).

Born in the same year as Jones, Mason spent his first twelve years living on a farm outside of Memphis. In 1878, he and his family fled an epidemic of yellow fever and moved to an agricultural region northwest of the Arkansas Delta, where they worked as tenant farmers. Here, at the Mt. Olive Baptist Church in Preston, Mason was baptized at the age of fourteen. He became an ordained minister at the church in 1891 and two years later discovered the concept of Holiness by paging through the autobiography of Amanda Smith. Shortly after reading her writings in 1893, Mason experienced sanctification. He entered Arkansas Baptist College later that year. During his first few weeks, however, he grew convinced that the college overemphasized classical training in ancient languages and cultures, math, and science as necessary prerequisites for becoming a religious leader. "I entered thinking that education would

Figure 5.1. Rev. C. P. Jones, circa 1900 (Flower Pentecostal Heritage Center).

help me out in preaching. The Lord showed me that there was no salvation in schools and colleges; for the way they were conducted grieved my very soul."

He quickly came to believe that most elements of his education did not adequately prepare him for ministry. Worse still, Arkansas Baptist College, by encouraging a belief that learned abilities were sufficient to lead a church, possibly interfered with it. The only true requirement for an aspiring preacher, Mason decided, was an abiding trust in the Holy Spirit and the experience of sanctification. Not surprisingly, he dropped out of Arkansas Baptist College immediately after finishing his first term. "I packed my books, arose and bade them a final farewell to follow Jesus, with the Bible as my guide." He set out to join the Holiness movement, moved to Jackson, Mississippi, in 1895, and joined forces with Jones (figure 5.2).[8]

Figure 5.2. Rev. C. H. Mason, circa 1910 (Flower Pentecostal Heritage Center).

During the mid 1890s at Mt. Helm Baptist Church, Jones and Mason slowly spread their Holiness teachings and built a small but committed following drawn mostly from the ranks of Baptists and Methodists living in the Delta. In 1895, they hosted a two-week Holiness conference and invited Christians from every denomination. Many attended and joined the movement. Part of their initial success depended, paradoxically, on promoting their work through the recently formed denominational networks of men's and women's organizations. At this early stage of the Holiness movement, Jones and Mason were apparently able to temper their growing frustration with Baptist and Methodist culture in order to take advantage of its organizational culture. It was a type of compromise that they would repeat in the years to come.

For example, one of Jones' earliest converts and closest disciples was Reverend John J. Jeter, also a Baptist minister from the Arkansas Delta. Jones and Jeter stirred up public enthusiasm for their new beliefs by visiting local and state Baptist conventions and there spreading the Holiness message to old friends and strangers alike. Reverend L. W. Blue, the historian of the state's Southeast District Baptist Association and a public skeptic of Holiness, closely monitored their labors. During 1897, recalled Blue in a short book published about 1903, "John A. Jeter, of Little Rock, came to this district and met the Women's Association at Baxter, and introduced [sanctification] in that meeting. He preached several sermons and gave several lectures, from which many of the members of the district thought they too saw the new light and bodily holiness [and] right at once [it] began to take root." Jeter then traveled to the District Association at nearby Monticello, Arkansas, and again won supporters. At this meeting, he actually "succeeded in getting a resolution signed by eight leading ministers and adopted by the association indorsing [sic] this type of sanctification." Jeter stressed that the Holiness movement was "a kind of reformation, or getting closer to the Master, which . . . was much needed, and which all Baptists are in favor of as a part of their doctrine. Some members of First Baptist and Brooks Chapel of Monticello, and a few of the members of First Baptist Dermot, were completely captured by the new faith perspective. Rev. William Collins, a leading minister of the District, was so impressed that he resigned his churches, and now does not pastor at all."[9]

Similarly, sanctification also spread through black women's Bible bands, the groups supported by northern white evangelical organizations seeking to proselytize among southern African Americans and teach them about Scripture. Long before Lizzie Woods became one of the most powerful women in the African American Holiness movement, for instance, she was a well-known Baptist who toiled closely with Joanna Moore and founded and sustained Bible bands in and around Pine Bluff, Arkansas. Wood, born a slave in 1860, visited hundreds of black homes and churches in Arkansas Delta from 1901 to 1909, directing meetings and sharing the bimonthly publication, *Hope*. Ironically, *Hope* introduced her to the Holiness movement and the doctrine of sanctification. As she put it, in 1901 "I received my first *Hope* Paper [sic] in the Bible Band. . . . I studied this paper until the Lord sanctified me." In *Hope*, Woods discovered dozens of testimonies about how prayer and the Holy Spirit could lead one to a state of sinlessness and heal any illness. Studying them and meeting their authors during her work eventually led her to exchange her Baptist church for one run by Mason.[10]

Predictably, not everything went well for the Holiness evangelists during the first years of the movement. Shortly after Jeter's success in the Arkansas Delta, chronicled Reverend Blue, "Rev. J. H. Hoke, [the] state missionary . . . had resolutions condemning it, as a departure from Baptist principles." The resolutions sent a chill across the movement. "A number of leading ministers of Little Rock, Pine Bluff, and other places in the state, that had been deceived by Jones and Jeter returned to the fold, and sanctification as taught by them . . . received such a stunning blow that it at once began to lose ground."[11] Ministerial opposition was far from uniform, though. The president of the Southeast District Baptist Association in the Arkansas Delta, Reverend Isaac Bailey, supported the movement. Jones, writing from Mt. Helm in early 1898, cheerfully reported to his friend Bailey that "God has given us great meetings here lately. Many more have received themselves with the Lord. . . ." Bailey even sought, unsuccessfully, to secure a seat for his son at one of Jones' meetings.[12]

Still, it was only a matter of time until the radical dimensions of Holiness and its objections to the current condition of Baptist and Methodist life drew severe and lasting rebuke from the highest level. By late 1897, Jones and Mason were reeling from an attack against them launched by Baptist leaders in Mississippi. "Between the holiness conventions of 1897 and 1898," reported Jones, "I began to be impressed with the inconsistencies of our Baptist Churches, being myself almost a fanatical Baptist. My attitude brought the severest persecution upon me. . . . Baptist and Methodists held a congress and counsels against me."[13] This period of trial did not end well for the Holiness preachers. The Baptist hierarchy brooked no compromise with them over matters of doctrine and liturgy and forced them to leave the ministry.

In response, Jones and Mason cofounded the first African American Holiness church in the nation, an independent nondenominational fellowship called the Churches of God in Christ in 1897 in Jackson. This act, however, marked the highpoint of their pastoral partnership. In 1907, Mason spent the month of March and part of early April in Los Angeles investigating stories of a great Holiness revival occurring in a ramshackle building on Azusa Street. Led by William Seymour, a thirty-seven year old, half-blind black minister originally from Centerville, Louisiana, but more recently Houston, Texas, the "Azusa Street" revival attracted an interracial crowd. It snared national headlines as tales leaked out of devout white and black Christians entering into trance-like states and uttering a strange language. Participants reported becoming overpowered by the presence of the Holy Spirit and infused with an abundant sense of God's love. As an integral part of this experience, they spoke for a time in a rush of words and phrases unintelligible to all but a small handful of them blessed with the gift of interpretation.[14]

One day at the Azusa Street revival, as he sat cross-legged between two friends, Mason ceased being just an observer of things. Suddenly, he "hear[d] a sound just like the sound of a great wind. I heard the sound like in the Pentecost."[15] Soon "[t]here came wave of glory into me and all of my being was filled with the glory of the Lord. So when He had gotten me straight on my feet there came a light which enveloped my entire being above the brightness of the Sun." Now he, too, spoke for a moment in an unfamiliar language. "When I opened my mouth to say glory, a flame touched my tongue which ran down in me. My language changed and no word could I speak in my own tongue."[16] Mason soon came to believe that "speaking in tongues," as this particular religious act came to be publicly known, was an unmistakable sign of the genuinely saved and more generally represented "a progression in the spiritual life of the membership of the [Christian] church" to a higher level of perfection.[17]

Mason's ideas about speaking in tongues aligned him doctrinally with Pentecostalism, a new religious movement also blossoming in Houston as well as in the midwestern cities of Topeka, Kansas, and Cincinnati, Ohio. Like the Holiness movement, it was based on the story of the Pentecost as recorded in the Bible, but specifically those verses in which Jesus' apostles begin speaking in many "tongues" after receiving the blessing of the Holy Spirit. Pentecostalism taught that the act of speaking in tongues itself occurred after the experiences of conversion and sanctification and was an essential occurrence in the life of any Christian; without this "third blessing," as it was widely dubbed, one was not assured of going to heaven after death. Once back home in Jackson, Mason discussed these theological notions with Jones, who rejected them out of hand. The men soon parted ways, each forming a different branch of the African American Holiness movement in the Delta. Jones began the Church of God (Holiness), while Mason started the Church of God in Christ, known as the first black Pentecostal church because of its teaching that the truly sanctified, like the apostles after the Pentecost, typically spoke in tongues.

Although Christian, Jones, and Mason each ultimately established autonomous Holiness churches at the turn of the twentieth century, they shared an unswerving certainty about the corruption of black religion in the Delta and the urgent need for reform. In their preaching and writings, they collectively mounted a critique of African American spiritual life according to three broad categories—theological, institutional, and cultural—that illuminates the heart of the Holiness message and the main sources of its public appeal. It also sheds light on how the movement grew out of the shifting and often volatile character of black denominational life.

In the post-Reconstruction Delta, most religious leaders loosely agreed on the theological meaning of sanctification. But most Baptist and Methodists clerics typically insisted that individuals underwent sanctification only after enduring long periods of prayer, scriptural study, and self-abnegation; that few Christians ever obtained it; and that even when they did, it brought no guarantee of salvation or supernatural power. Indeed, the rarity of the event rendered it a distant ideal with little relevance to the everyday lives of black Christians. In 1899, Reverend E. C. Morris, at that point the president of the Arkansas Baptist Convention and the National Baptist Convention, summarized the popular meaning of sanctification understood by most of his peers in the Delta and across the nation. "The word 'sanctify' means to set apart, or appoint to service," wrote Morris. It "is a call to service, a getting ready for a meeting in which to worship God; a laying aside of secular matters, that for the time, the whole being may be devoted to the service of God...."[18] A close friend of Morris and fellow national Baptist leader, Reverend J. H. Eason, defined the term more restrictively and openly doubted its claims of moral perfection. Eason submitted that "sanctification is not the product of a single act but a series of progressive acts of faith that successively purify him ever more of sin but never completely."[19]

The lack of public agreement over the meaning of sanctification and to what extent, if any, black Christians ought to incorporate it into their daily religious lives was the main theological reason motivating the Holiness leaders to found new churches. Christian, Jones, and Mason believed that most Baptists and Methodists misinterpreted or simply ignored the obvious precedent for the radical understanding of sanctification, the event of Pentecost, and therefore practiced a religion based on a false reading of the Bible. Only they, as leaders of the African American Holiness movement, captured God's true plans for his people.

Christian, Jones and Mason carefully selected names for their churches that communicated their sense of the backwardness of Baptist and Methodist theology on the matter of sanctification. More generally, in each case the names they chose were meant to tie the Holiness church visibly to the purity of the early Christian church and symbolize the start of a religious community unriven by denominational factions and unadulterated by generations of liturgical and doctrinal invention. Christian took the title "Church of the Living God" because its genealogy traced directly to the New Testament and the early Christian community. In explaining his decision, he wrote that "I know that but God and Christ are one. . . . So when you say the church of God and the church is of Christ, it is all the same. . . . In Paul's teaching in the Cor[inthians] we find that the church was called the Church of God." No other church but his, argued Christian, drew inspiration for its name so literally from the Bible. "Now I want some Catholic pope or priest or a Baptist minister or Methodist bishop or preacher to show [that] the Bible ever called the church a Baptist church, Methodist, Catholic, or any other of these sectarian names they are using." Indeed, he added, "the Catholic and the Baptist is another name altogether, added by men."[20] Similarly, in June 1898, according to the Mt. Helm Minute Book, Jones and Mason "resolved to cut off the name 'Baptist,' and be known as the 'Church of Christ,' separated from all creeds, denominations, associations, and conventions."[21]

The popular allure of the Holiness theology of sanctification to Delta blacks, besides its claims of being rooted in the belief of living out God's actual ambitions for the faithful and the general thrill of joining a new religious movement, also stemmed from practical reasons of safety and health. Many understood that, unlike any event sanctioned by a traditional Baptist or Methodist church, the experience of sanctification promised a measure of physical protection against racial violence. This principle underlay one of the most famous and oft repeated stories about the early history of Mason's Church of God in Christ, one passed down to generations of believers through the present day. "In 1897," recounted Mary Mason, wife of the movement's leader, "the Church of God in Christ established its first church in an old gin on the bank of a little creek in Lexington, Miss[issippi]." As blacks worshipped, a crowd of curious onlookers swelled in this tiny town on the southeastern edge of the Mississippi Delta. Trouble soon broke out. "While the saints were praising the Lord, someone fired several rounds from a shotgun into the building. A few persons were wounded, but no one was killed." The race of the shooter was never identified. He might have been a black Baptist or Methodist outraged over Mason's evangelical success, or, more likely, a white citizen turning to his gun to break up a large assembly of African Americans. Regardless, church leaders quickly claimed that the lack of fatalities was an unambiguous message that God approved of their movement. Mason's wife recalled the episode as a turning point in her husband's ministry, when suddenly his audience began to grow dramatically and his teachings become more popular. "When the reports of this event reached the local newspapers, the worshipping crowds were further increased. Many said: 'If the sanctified people are having meetings under such conditions, truly it must be of the Lord.'"[22]

Mason himself bluntly asserted that God shielded him and his followers from vigilantism. In sermons beginning in the 1910s, he stressed that God would never permit sanctified Christians to be lynched. He told his listeners "all things done in the dark must be brought to light. When you find yourself under the bands of the world, humble yourself and God will take you out of your distresses. . . . He looks on you down in sorrow, without rest, wounded, sore, poor and low, and leads you out. . . . Men are called in the earthquakes and storms, in fires, [and] in lynchings . . . ."[23] Delivering the faithful from the lynch mob became a common subject of Mason's later sermons. In 1925 in Memphis, he affirmed the protection of "the way of holiness" against the "unclean," as recorded in Isaiah 35:8: "And a highway shall be there and a way and it shall be called the holiness way; the unclean shall not pass over it. . . ." Mason then professed that "No coming up there [to the way of holiness] to get a man to lynch. . . . The ready virgins can walk up there, those who are sanctified and baptized with the Holy Ghost."[24]

Just as the theology of sanctification offered to guard relievers from bodily harm, it also carried benefits of wellness. Holiness leaders taught that sanctified Christians, through the power of the Holy Spirit, typically possessed the ability to cure bodily ills without the need to visit a doctor, enter a hospital, or take a pill. Stressing that the power to heal was foremost an act of prayer and supplication to God, they presented a model of health and spiritual authority that was largely independent from the dismal state of medicine and health care services available to Delta blacks. They delivered a sharp message as well to those who hoped to relieve suffering by swallowing a panacea recommended by a denominational minister: faith alone was the better remedy. In one of his books of songs and hymns, Jones bore witness to the healing power of sanctified Christians by recounting a moment when his flagging health was abruptly restored. After suffering through a long night of "fever" and "pains," Jones wrote, an unnamed sanctified person paid him a visit. "I had a servant of the Lord to anoint me . . . and I was shortly well, vigorous in mind, body, and spirit. . . . Glory! Give Jesus a trial in all things, yes, in sickness too."[25] Similarly, Mason described his experience with sickness, only as a healer. Mason recorded that, through the power of God working in him, "[t]umors have been removed from the bodies of women who have been suffering for years, only through [my] faith in God." He openly proclaimed that he had presided over many miracles. "I met with an Elder who had hemorrhages of the lungs. He was a sight to behold. The physicians said that it was impossible for him to live. God, through prayer, rebuked the bleeding. . . . Also through prayer of faith to the Lord, the lame have been able to put down their crutches and walk, and the blind have been made to see; the seemingly dead have been restored to activity again."[26] To remind his audience of his gift, Mason often lined his pulpit and altar with jars filled with tumors he had removed from the sick and with canes taken from the crippled whom he had made to walk.[27] When telling stories about those he had rescued, though, Mason carefully stressed that he was but a vessel through which God's wondrous powers flowed; he himself had no healing abilities. He never charged for his services, either. In these ways, he minimized indictments of self-aggrandizement.

Closely related to the theological category of the Holiness critique was the institutional one. Its main target was the new leadership of denominational churches and its policies on worship and spiritual authority, as exemplified in the case of the black Baptists in Mississippi who united as a single organizational body in 1890 and appointed a handful of ministers to set ecclesiastical policy. Jones and Mason worried that these men possessed too much power and could begin a campaign of religious reform according to their own ambitions. Their fears were not unfounded, as they would soon find out.

The formation of the General Missionary Baptist Convention in Mississippi in 1890 was a fusion of two older groups who had ruled since emancipation, the Baptist Missionary Convention and the General Missionary Baptist Association. Its new leaders were a select group of younger ministers, most born after slavery. Calling themselves the "Progressives," they publicly supported the social vision of Booker T. Washington that stressed racial progress as the product of self-reliance, thrift, and occupational training. Seeking to take advantage of the growing popularity of concepts of respectability and domesticity, they hoped to refine black religion in the Delta and equip fellow Baptists with the values and skills that they believed promised the greatest chance of financial success, social respect, and influence in the post-Reconstruction South.

The Progressives were keen students of recent history. They understood that the tremendous growth of local and statewide denominational organizations in the Delta during the 1870s and 1880s had helped to expand the social services offered by individual churches, organize rural Baptists, and facilitate their access to the consumer market. But it also had brought to light major differences between individual congregations on matters of worship styles and the level of formal training attained by ministers—differences that the Progressives now set out to correct. In their first major action, they took aim at lingering elements of "slave religion," by which they meant practices of ecstatic worship and a popular faith in the supernatural widespread during bondage and still part of many Delta communities. In particular, they desperately wanted members to resist breaking spontaneously into bouts of shrieking, crying, dancing, hand-clapping, and foot stomping during services. Nothing, they asserted, smacked of disorderliness more than impulsive behavior and open exhibits of unchecked emotion. To control worship styles, they suspended the traditional prerogatives of individual Baptist churches to conduct liturgies, appoint preachers, and generally set policies according to the general will of members. They then ordered fellow ministers and deacons to adopt preapproved hymnbooks, train choirs, and enforce rules prohibiting wild "outbursts."[28]

The Progressives also intended to stamp out the tradition of unlettered and untrained men and women serving as unlicensed preachers. Indeed, one of their chief goals was to eliminate the possibility that a person could ever again earn a certificate to preach simply by standing up in a church or at a revival, extemporizing from a biblical passage, and earning popular approval. As a result, they passed rigid guidelines dictating that every candidate for the pulpit be a man, demonstrate a basic level of literacy and ideally have a degree from a college, and pass a written and oral exam on biblical knowledge administered by a seasoned group of pastors drawn from a regional district composed of individual churches from several counties.

In Arkansas, the story of Baptist reform followed a similar path. The history of the Southeastern Baptist District Association in the Arkansas Delta was exemplary in this regard. Between 1889 and 1891, its male leaders enacted "a law forbidding churches to examine and ordain young ministers. . . ." Their objective was to transfer the examination of an applicant for a preaching license from the local congregation to the district level in order to more carefully monitor professional standards and "meet the fast growing demand for a more qualified ministry."[29] In this new organizational structure, leaders of the Southeastern Baptist District Association frequently turned away candidates they deemed illiterate or lacking a sufficient grasp of the Bible. For example, according to the proceedings of the 1906 annual meeting of the Association, those serving on the ministerial qualification board during the previous year had "examine[d] Brother B. J. Cobb for the ministry. After a very [im]partial examination in the branches proscribed by the Association and the Bible, he was pronounced incompetent and referred back for study."[30]

Progressives' hopes for smoothly establishing a new Baptist policy in Mississippi, however, vanished quickly in the face of fierce opposition. As has been the case historically when Baptists of any color from any geographical region seek to build a common denominational culture, some local congregations resisted encroachments upon their autonomy. In the case of black Baptists in the Delta at the turn of the twentieth century, the critics, typically labeled "Conservatives," announced a series of specific demands intended to preserve the individual character and traditions of local churches, some of which harkened back to slavery. They insisted on the right to appoint their own preachers, regardless of educational level; set their own styles of worship and music; and recognize spiritual authority in a variety of ways, including supernatural communication.

Into the fray between Progressive and Conservative Baptists jumped the Holiness leaders, who, surprisingly, offered a compromise position that appealed to moderate men and women who preferred a combination of ideas from both camps.[31] Though more skeptical of Progressive ideas, as might be expected, they did not reject them all. For instance, they supported the Progressives' stress on economy and industry as personal habits that promoted individual well-being and their directive that black churches be actively involved in bettering their communities. Charles Jones, for instance, identified Booker T. Washington as a personal hero and lauded his philosophy of self-help.[32] Washington, he claimed, was a model of success for every black person. "[B]e not impatient, fretful, and envious because you are not as well off today as others," counseled Jones in a series of pithy maxims for the enterprising Holiness believer. "Your day will come. . . . Booker T. Washington won his way into school by sweeping a room. . . . It all came by doing little things and filling menial places well."[33] Indeed, Jones never intended the Holiness way to be cut off from the economic and civil struggles of blacks. In 1906 in *Truth,* he wrote that "[m]ind that God did not teach Israel to have religion apart from a political hope. They were combined. Christ was to reign in their hearts and over their affairs. And so it is yet to be."[34]

Yet at the same time, Holiness leaders openly fretted that the Progressives' vision of a religious culture dangerously insulated men and women from the workings of the Holy Spirit. Indeed, they feared that Progressive policies risked making Christians too dependent on earthly conventions in matters of spiritual belief, education, and personal well-being. Jones evoked part of this position in a letter penned to the General Mississippi Baptist Conference in July 1898, shortly after his dismissal as a Baptist minister. "I beg to say that I am . . . walking but from corrupt and unscriptural denominationalism; from unscriptural names and methods; from man-made constitutions and institutions, and returning to New Testament names and the leadership of the Spirit of God."[35] As an example of the "unscriptural" assertions made by the Progressives, Jones pointed to the issue of ecstatic worship. Far from being an embarrassing atavism of slavery, he argued, it was a central part of the early Christian church and thus worthy of sustaining. To restrain it unjustly limited the ability of Holiness believers to display the physical and emotional signs—the jumping, clapping, yelling, and fainting—recorded in the Bible as the natural behavior of those experiencing sanctification. After Jones realized that the Progressives demanded a type of religion that bore "none of the signs spoken of in the Scriptures," he grew persuaded that they "were not toting fair with Jesus."[36]

Holiness leaders also disparaged the Progressive dictum that a degree from a college or seminary was an important precondition for any minister. Echoing the conclusion drawn earlier by Mason about the value of formal education to a minister while he studied at Arkansas Baptist College, they claimed that an individual's experience of sanctification was the only essential requirement for membership and ministry in a Christian church.[37] This rule enabled the unlettered to serve as pastors, and many did. Most Holiness preachers in the Arkansas Delta, for example, never advanced past high school.[38]

Similarly, Christian, Mason, and Jones upheld their belief that the Holy Spirit commonly spoke to individuals through dreams, visions, and trances despite Progressive views to the contrary. Holiness leaders discarded the opinion that supernatural communication was a vehicle of self-delusion or, as a forceful editorial in the *Southwestern Christian Advocate* described the matter, that it would "produce unnecessary fears and weaken the nervous system . . . , paving the way to hypochondria and often suicide."[39] Instead, Holiness leaders openly validated it as a legitimate and credible source of spiritual empowerment.

The Holiness stance on Progressives' policies was a boon for membership, especially among women. Indeed, at a moment when women watched opportunities for political and spiritual leadership in their communities shrink because of disfranchisement, the growing popularity of fraternal orders, and now the Progressives' qualifications for ministerial leadership, the Holiness movement promised that education and gender were no barriers to advancement within its ranks. This radical position opened the door for black women seeking new ways to establish an additional degree of respect and power in their communities, and many went through it. Even though few of them ever became pastors or elders, Holiness women achieved a visible level of institutional influence and power unrivaled in denominational churches.[40]

The case of "Women's Work" in the Church of God in Christ is instructive. In 1911, Mason created a department of "Women's Work" both as a response to the burgeoning number of female converts and as a statement of confidence in their ability and legitimacy to serve as leaders in his church. Unlike other Baptist and Methodist associations run by women, Women's Work regularly offered its "mothers," as its officers were called, the chance to work, advise, and travel with male preachers and bishops. They enjoyed an unsurpassed freedom to serve as missionaries, teachers, and public models of the Holiness faith. Mason appointed Lizzie Woods as the first "overseer" of Women's Work. She regularly worked elbow-to-elbow with Mason and other bishops in expanding programs for women and children.[41]

Likewise, the Holiness conviction that spiritual authority could be attained through supernatural communication also attracted women. Black women historically experienced the divine and discovered sources of spiritual creativity and power through mystical communions, by receiving instructions from disembodied voices, and by entertaining visits from spirits.[42] Ethel Christian, the wife of William, freely admitted that "in 1889 strange revelations began to unfold to me concerning the Bible and I denounced the sectarian religion and left the Baptist Church and have since preached an unadulterated doctrine." When she eventually assumed a leadership post in the Church of the Living God, she confided that she made decisions by "learn[ing] and receiv[ing] revelations . . . [which] are imparted . . . to the other members."[43]

Because the Holiness movement offered women distinctive pathways to leadership and recognized the supernatural as a valid medium of religious experience and communiqué, women often outnumbered men in its churches. This was the case in Mason's church on Wellington Street in Memphis in 1907, where there were seventy-three female members and forty-three male congregants. Although historically black women formed a majority in black churches, it is important to note here that the ratio of women to men was large, nearly two to one.[44]

In addition to its theological and institutional components, the Holiness critique of black religion in the Delta included an attack on the cultural dimension of contemporary Baptist and Methodist life. It was the most important one in recruiting and retaining followers. Christian, Jones, and Mason gave a powerful voice to the mounting general suspicion that the modern character of denominational churches was illegitimate. They accused Baptist and Methodist houses of worship of nurturing too cozy a relationship with fraternal orders, the consumer market, and material goods and violating a founding principle of the early Christian church—namely, that a complete dependence on the Holy Spirit was the primary source of earthly succor, fellowship, fortune, and power. According to the Holiness leaders, when black Baptists and Methodists joined a fraternal order to find economic security, they sinned grievously because they placed too much of their faith in their fellow man to comfort them in times of distress; when they permitted ministers to act as salesmen to raise money for a church school or newspaper, they relied too heavily on the economics of the market to solve their financial challenges; and when they adorned their homes and churches with expensive commodities, they worshipped false idols.[45]

Surprisingly, Holiness leaders did not condemn the pervasive Baptist and Methodist fascination with the railroad despite its central role in reshaping black spiritual life in the Delta after Reconstruction. Part of the reason was that sanctified Christians, like their denominational counterparts, relied on trains for long-distance travel and communication. But the difference was also a matter of context. Although Baptists and Methodists widely incorporated their experiences with trains into their religion, they did not treat them as objects of public or private devotion. Moreover, denominational leaders quickly and vigorously criticized their followers when they used trains as stages for open displays of extravagance and profligacy, as in the case of Sunday excursions.

The Holiness leaders' lack of criticism of the ways in which Baptists and Methodists made use of the railroad in their religion, however, did not mean that they shared the same appropriations of it. Christian, Mason, and Jones rarely included train references into their sermons, writings, songs, and dreams, possibly because they understood that it was the Holy Spirit and not human technology that was the proper source and symbol of material improvement and change. When invoking trains in their spiritual lives, they did so sparingly and as a basic metaphor for speed and physical strength. For example, in a statement about the need for men and women to slow their lives down so that they could better hear God's voice, Jones wrote that "[t]he world now lived at so high a rate of speed that to stop advancing would itself produce a ruinous, crashing, crushing wreck." And Charles Mason, in an undated sermon, explained the power of a great storm by describing its ability to throw a train off the track. "Locomotives and steel cars were turned upside down, doing His work, His strange work."[46]

In contrast to their benign perception of the relationship between trains and denominational culture, Holiness leaders roundly denounced the men who joined fraternal orders and the women who associated with their female auxiliaries. Echoing earlier detractors of fraternal culture, Holiness officials complained that secret society members, by dutifully paying the dues, wearing the uniforms, memorizing the rules and histories, and attending the many meetings and parades, effectively identified their lodges as the prime source of meaning and sustenance in their lives. Once a person became part of a fraternal order, there was simply too little time or money left over to do much of anything else. Jones was fond of sharing a short personal story that emphasized his conviction that fraternal orders encouraged men to rely exclusively on them for moral guidance and material support. Shortly after experiencing sanctification, Jones recalled, a woman urged him to "join a lodge to take care of him." He brusquely put her off, demanding to know "how could he, being a preacher, teach the *people* to trust God when *he himself* was not trusting God but the lodge?"[47]

Holiness preachers were quick to point out that fraternal members seemed to care more about their reflection in the eyes of their brethren than in the eyes of God. Vanity and concupiscence were common ills afflicting Masons and Odd Fellows, claimed Jones in a sermon in which he juxtaposed the self-centeredness of fraternal brethren with the humility of Joseph, the father of Jesus. "Joseph had none of the man-pleasing, crowd-fearing Spirit which characterizes our day.... Everybody is joining a combination, a brotherhood, a social or religious trust, a mutual help and mutual admiration society.... Every man is closing his eyes and lips to the fault of his brotherhood...."[48] Like Jones, Charles Pleas, one of the first men to join the Mason's Church of God in Christ, recorded in his autobiography that he and his peers "disapprove[d] of [C]hristians connecting themselves with secret, oath-bound societies, as being needless, profitless . . . and not conducive to piety or Christian usefulness."[49] Not surprisingly, it was a common ritual among newly sanctified men to mark their new status by pitching their "secret order pins . . . out the church windows."[50]

The Holiness denunciation of fraternal life sometimes took a devastating toll on individual lodges. When a large number of individuals from a community suddenly joined a Holiness church, local fraternal orders battled collapse. During his tour of Arkansas Masonic lodges in 1899, the Grand Master for the state complained about the havoc caused by the Holiness movement. "Visited Capstone Lodge, No. 125, Monday, July 18, 2 pm. This lodge has lost most of her members, going off in the sanctified movement. It seems that as soon as they become sanctified they are commanded to leave . . . [the] lodge and everything else and get in the go [*sic*] and preach." This Masonic leader could not grasp why his brethren deserted their lodge and forfeited their life and burial insurances. He asked, "[W]hat will we do with this part of the Bible which says, He that does not provide for his own house is worse than an infidel, and that he should leave his father and mother [without aid]. . . ."[51] What this fraternal official apparently failed to understand was that sanctified Christians trusted God wholly and exclusively to "provide" for their needs.

In his 1890 tract, *Notice to All the Free Masons in the World,* William Christian merged a criticism of the affiliation between black denominational churches and black fraternal orders with a broader condemnation of the spending habits of black Christians. Both groups were filled with "merchandisers," whom Christian described as men and women who placed too great a value on the display of fraternal regalia and home decorations purchased from a black preacher or newspaper. Christian argued that there were fundamentally two types of black people in the Delta: those who served money and those who served God. "One grand trouble taken up. I give you to know that money is not God's work. It is the work of man's own hands." Drawing heavily on biblical references, especially from the book of Revelation, he warned of the painful fate that awaited blacks who served money. "Notice another thing. God spoke bitterly against merchandise. Revelations 3.17–18; 9.20. Read the 18th chapter through."

Readers who followed Christian's advice and thumbed through the appointed selections discovered that a painful fate awaited materialistic black Baptist and Methodists. In the first biblical passage, part of a larger two chapter section in which Jesus appeared to John and ordered him to urge sinners to reform, members of the Laodicean church learned that their steady accumulation of wealth led to their spiritual impoverishment. "Because thou sayest, I am rich, and increased in goods, and have need of nothing; and knowest not that thou art wretched, and miserable, and poor, and blind, and naked. . . ." Christian's second reference warned of money's corruptive power. In this selection, a series of "plagues" killed much of mankind as punishment for its wicked idolatry, yet the survivors ignored this lesson about greed and still lusted for luxuries. "And the rest of the men which were not killed by these plagues yet repented not of the works of their hands, that they should not worship devils, and idols of gold, and silver, and brass, and stone, and of wood, which can neither see, nor hear, nor walk." In the last recommended reading, the ultimate consequence of living as a "merchandiser" was revealed. The topic was Babylon and its residents were those "whose sins have reached unto heaven, and God hath remembered her iniquities." In this case, death and destruction befell the Babylonians, who never again enjoyed their "merchandise of gold, and silver, and precious stones, and of pearls, and fine linen, and purple, and silk, and scarlet. . . ."[52]

Like Christian, Jones lashed out at the black public's growing infatuation with money. In 1891, he singled out Baptist and Methodist preachers for criticism.

He believed that they hungered for the things that money could buy and rejected their sworn duty to follow Jesus and live modestly. He protested that "the ministry [was] unconverted, and unreliable, proud, selfish, and even profligate."[53] Jones later concentrated his disapproval on the ethic of respectability. He was careful, however, not to disagree with the ethic's instructions to dress modesty and spend money frugally, which meshed with Holiness injunctions to treat the body as a temple where the Holy Spirit literally dwelled. Indeed, Holiness adherents wore simple clothing partly to signal their dismissal of fashion and fads. When not working, women wore plain dresses, cut straight and without frilly embellishments or lacy embroidery. They selected shoes without heels and avoided the use of make-up. Men donned black or brown suits, white shirts, and simple neckties.[54] Instead, Jones complained that most Delta blacks warped the original intentions of respectability, transforming it from a philosophy that initially sanctioned limited consumption for the purpose of glorifying God and teaching self-discipline into a license to shop, spend, and dream about market fancies. In a poem titled "Memory and Conscience," written when he was learning about "the exceeding sinfulness of sin," he asked that if "respectability/ Is the great thing," then "what means hypocrisy?" Buying goods to "indulge" their "lust," respectable blacks "lose the love of truth and innocence, the fragrant flower of youth." Ultimately the cost of practicing this bastardized form of respectability was a fractured relationship with God. "Our self respect we sell to gratify/The evil tempter, and our God defy."[55]

Unlike the ethic of respectability, Holiness leaders thoroughly damned the emerging standards of beauty embraced by many denominational churches. "These selfish denominational organizations are not Christ's churches," Jones wrote in an editorial on the physical appearance of Baptist and Methodist houses of worship that appeared in *Truth* in 1903. "The church must be sanctified and without spot or wrinkle; her wealth is not that of buildings and money but of faith, and her power is not that of learning and members, but of the Holy Ghost."[56] Holiness sympathizers widely shunned the popular symbols of refinement and importance adorning many Baptist and Methodists churches in the Delta at the turn of the century. They built houses of worship that intentionally lacked stained glass, ornate wall frescos, and velvet altar chair covers. The frugal design and decoration of Holiness churches partly reflected the lean financial times characteristic of the early years of any religious movement, of course, particularly one born during a decade of intermittent economic depression and located in a poor area. Yet the visual culture of Holiness churches was also a reaction to the evolution of contemporary black religious aesthetics. In 1906 in Jackson, Mississippi, Jones constructed the largest black Holiness church to date, the Christ Temple Church. It was sixty feet wide, ninety feet long, and seated one thousand worshippers. Although arguably the showpiece of the Holiness movement, Christ Temple Church was notable for its studied plainness. Its list of features was short and included only smooth-backed benches, a small pastor's study, a secretary's office, and a pipe organ.[57] Smaller Holiness churches mirrored this style of intentional restraint. Just southeast of Christ Temple Church in Jackson sat the Galilee Church of Christ (Holiness). In 1910 members remodeled the eleven-year old building but intentionally decided not to adorn it with fancy additions and accents. The new church, according to a member's matter-of-fact description, had a "floor of rough lumber" and some "very crudely shaped seats."[58] Similarly, Holiness churches built in the Arkansas Delta during the first years of the movement demonstrated simplicity of architecture and interior decoration. Nearly every church was a square, wood-framed building that sat no more than 150 people. Benches and walls were bare, windows uncovered, roofs flat and unbroken by a spire or bell tower. Typically there was only one door, set in the front of the church, to let the faithful in and out. Few had a vestibule or choir loft.[59]

Just as they challenged denominational instructions on personal dress and behavior and models of church design, Holiness believers rejected popular codes regulating public worship. They taught that the body was a medium through which faith might be celebrated in ways that ignored Baptist and Methodist injunctions against uninhibited praise. Holiness men and women were free to respond to the experiences of being filled with God's grace by pounding their feet on the floor, spinning around, beating their chests, and singing at the top of their lungs: giving thanks to Jesus took many forms. Holiness churches also experimented with styles of popular music, much to the consternation of denominational churches. Blues notes and slurry rhythms, guitars, horns, and drums, when used with the proper intention of glorifying God and exciting the congregation to worship ever more energetically, were perfectly acceptable as part of a Sunday morning service or a revival.[60]

In the face of the criticisms hurled at them by Holiness leaders, Baptist and Methodist officials counterattacked but only sporadically and even then in a high-handed and ultimately ineffective manner that betrayed their disbelief that any well-meaning Christian could ever take the Holiness movement seriously. Beginning in the mid-1890s, they replied directly to the charges leveled against them and, not surprisingly, extolled the positive virtues of the recent changes in their spiritual lives. For example, a sharply worded editorial by clerics with the ME Church rebutted accusations that the religious material culture of denominational churches promoted moral lassitude. "It is claimed by some that . . . disloyalty, lack of love for prayer and class meetings . . . are the result of [the] refined and cultured membership of today. Not so. . . . We cannot believe that elegance in church building and decorous deportment in pew and pulpit are indicative of religious laxity."[61] Another public message defended the requirement that all ministers have a formal education. In a review of the essential qualifications for the ministry, editors at the *Southwestern Christian Advocate* urged standards of training equal to other professions. "Has the church a right to demand certain things in the way of preparation for those who seek to enter ministry? Certainly she has; just as much as the state has to make certain demands of the lawyer, the teacher, and the physician."[62] And a third reply supported the practice of barring women from serving as high-ranking leaders on the grounds of moral decency and a version of respectability that frowned on women serving as preachers. This editorial in the *Christian Index* pointed out that "[t]here is often a sect who dominates [*sic*] themselves as holiness people, holding open air meetings, denouncing denominational proclivities, and brand[ing] all other members who are not of the sect as sinners. . . . Very often they have several women preachers to assist them. . . . Seldom if ever [will] a respectable man or woman . . . adhere to such nonsense."[63]

Sometimes denominational spokespeople responded less charitably and portrayed Holiness believers as delusional rabble-rousers. Reverend E. C. Morris, in a sermon titled "Sanctification" delivered before the Arkansas Baptist State Convention in 1899, gruffly cast aside the Holiness complaints about his religion and refused to offer "an answer to that class of persons who are preaching the doctrine of sinless perfection, or bodily holiness. Such an attempt would be only a waste of time in an unsuccessful effort to turn Ephraim from his idols." Morris then dismissed the Holiness definition of sanctification as bankrupt. "Th[eir] call to sanctification, or forming a solemn assembly [based on it], does not imply that the individuals are entirely purged from sin."[64] In a more sarcastic vein, Reverend R. T. Thomas, in a letter about the Holiness movement in Mississippi printed in the *Southwestern Christian Advocate,* mocked members' propensity for outward shows of emotion and belief in the supernatural. "I do not believe in nor can I tolerate the idea of drawing a long face . . . and howling at the mercy seat, falling out prostrate, dead an hour to two; meantime the sinner's spirit leaps out and descends to hell, has a time with the devil, and overcomes him, all hell combined; from thence ascends to heaven and views the situation, gets on a crown, wings, and a heavenly suit and flies to all parts of heaven, sings and is sung to and eventually comes back to earth. . . ."[65]

Although Holiness leaders usually turned a tin ear to these counterattacks, they apparently did take some seriously, especially those focused on the style of their worship services. In 1907, Mason publicly addressed that his preaching and his audience's reaction to it had recently grown more sedate and respectable. He did not attribute the change to any particular cause, and certainly not to public pressure. Yet his statement opens up the possibility that Holiness preachers took to heart some of the criticisms thrown at them by denominational leaders. Earlier in his career as a Holiness minister, Mason claimed that his sermons elicited enthusiastic and physical responses from his congregants. "[S]ometimes they slap their hands; sometimes a fellow gets to running over the floor. . . [or] they crawl sometimes. . . . Sometimes I have seen them lie out all day and night. . . ." But now things were more subdued. Presently, he continued, "[w]e are just a little more orderly." "Now if [members] get happy they stand up and rejoice generally and sit on their seats and rejoice . . . there is not so much slapping now . . . they shout now in a more orderly way than they used to."[66]

The tensions between denominational and Holiness leaders quickly became a hallmark of black religion in the Delta. Both sides refused to negotiate any long-lasting or significant concession over their differences. Instead, they encouraged the public impression that an unbridgeable gulf separated them and that all black Christians had to decide which side to join. The development of these two wings of African American spiritual life, however, should not be viewed simply in anti-thetical terms. Even though Christian, Jones, and Mason swore to build a spiritual movement radically divorced from contemporary Baptist and Methodist traditions in the Delta, there were significant limits to their rhetoric of separation and indepen-dence. For while they avoided many public aspects of Baptist and Methodist life that they deemed profligate and self-centered, they subtly implemented others that fit their needs as a growing religious movement struggling to care for its members, broadcast its doctrines, and win converts. Indeed, the Holiness leaders apparently never intended to split themselves off completely from denominational culture but only to carefully regulate the juncture of black religion with contemporary black religious society in the Delta.

Charles Price Jones, for instance, set aside his complaints about the growing institutionalization of black Baptist life in the Delta in the early 1900s to increase the production and distribution of Holiness literature. Similar to his earlier efforts to spread the Holiness message through local conventions and associational meetings in the Delta in the mid-1890s, Jones now called upon his old network of Baptist leaders and worked hand-in-hand with the National Baptist Publishing House to print large orders of books and his newspaper. In a short autobiographical essay, "The History of My Songs," Jones noted this curious publishing arrangement in a passage chronicling his struggles to sustain his own printing operation. "Our printing office with two thousand new *Jesus Onlies I and II* [sic] just shipped to me from the [National] Baptist Publishing house at Nashville, and a new book of my own not quite finished, and a new issue of *Truth,* a paper I published more than 20 years. . . ." He never fully explained why he cooperated with the Baptists in this way, but he probably sought their aid because of a fire that recently destroyed what he described as "thousands of dollars of office material, type and presses."[67] The National Baptist Publishing House was the largest black religious printer in the South and best equipped to handle large orders. In this case, Jones seemingly distinguished among the types of interactions between the Holiness movement and denominational culture. Although still critical of much of contemporary Baptist and Methodist life, he obviously depended on part of it to help grow his own community.

William Christian struck similar compromises. He openly ridiculed fraternal orders as organizations obsessed with worldly glory but privately taught a glorious version of ancient black history similar to the one learned by the Prince Hall Masons. He told his churchgoers about a long history of black self-reliance and brilliant leadership in which many of the towering figures of biblical times, including Jesus, were dark skinned. The ancestors of Delta African Americans, wrote Christian, included Abraham, David, Job, and Jeremiah—black men whose lives collectively testified to a magnificent tradition of black accomplishment and proved that, when the subject was biblical heroes, "[i]t was as natural to be black as the leopard to be spotted."[68] More significantly, Christian apparently created a network of sick and burial relief societies directly modeled on ones found in black fraternal orders and eventually in some black Baptist and Methodist churches. Several years after founding his church, Christian, according to a national census report of religious bodies, constructed organizations "along the lines followed by fraternal societies . . . [to] render assistance in the care of the sick and the burying of the dead."[69] Christian's actions, however, do not necessarily identify him as a hypocrite in the matter of secret societies. Rather, they point out that he likely distinguished among the social functions of lodges, imitating fraternal narratives that celebrated a rich past of black achievement and social programs that cared for the ill while castigating rituals like parades that he believed only stoked members' egos.

Likewise, Holiness leaders and followers selectively appropriated limited forms of modern religious advertising popular in denominational culture in the Delta. As early as 1889, a publishing firm in Memphis, Tennessee, whose very name—The Living Way Publishing Company—publicly evoked its allegiance to William Christian's Church of the Living God, agreed to print the minutes of the West Tennessee Baptist Conference. Importantly, a conference proceeding was a type of publication that regularly carried a range of advertisements for the latest consumer goods; by publishing one, especially a Baptist one, Christian's followers appeared to be pushing the boundaries that ostensibly separated them from denominational churchgoers. But Living Way was an unusual company. It strictly controlled the nature of its involvement with the Baptists and the consumer market by limiting any association with what it publicly decried as "objectionable" forms of black religious advertising and by openly proclaiming its obedience to the teachings of Christian. It ultimately created an unusually plain booklet notable for its general lack of advertisements and especially the message emblazoned on its back page. In large boldfaced capitol letters, Living Way testified that it was "opposed to all that opposes the Church of the Living God and, in an obvious dig at fraternal orders, "to all secret clans and chambers, being regarded as gospel institutions and advocates." The declaration concluded by calling for "the absolute separation of the Church . . . from these other worldly institutions."[70] Given the company's name and its booklet's multiple references to Christian's church, it is almost certain that Christian himself or one of his high-ranking clerics had sanctioned the publication. The example of Living Way, then, suggests that Holiness leaders were not above making bargains with modern denominational life. In this particular case, they recognized the need of their disciples to make a living and aimed not so much to isolate them from the market as to minimize its negative potential.

A more common way that Holiness leaders imitated their denominational peers was through the use of mass-produced portraits. Recalling a Baptist or Methodist minister showcasing his picture or autobiography in a special section of their religious newspaper and permitting it to be passed out freely or sold to the faithful, Christian, Jones, and Mason frequently printed portraits of themselves and inserted them into pitches for their books and churches. Unlike their denominational brethren, however, they strictly monitored the use and visual composition of their images. They allowed the reproductions to be printed only by church members, published only in authorized books and pamphlets, and distributed only for the purpose of evangelization. Never were the images used as part of a campaign to sell luxury goods. When accompanied by an advertising blurb, the blurb was minimal and focused strictly on the proselytizing mission.

All of the Holiness leaders included pictures of themselves in their early autobiographies that were remarkable for their sameness: all of the men were neatly groomed, formally attired, and rigidly posed in a standing position. Though shadowy and now severely faded, these images still visually register the spirit of modesty and aesthetic minimalism prized by the movement. They shared the basic look of Jones' portrait introducing *The History of My Songs,* published in 1905. Dressed in a buttoned-up white collared shirt and a loose-fitting black topcoat, Jones stood ramrod straight. Positioned sideways to the camera, he stared down and away from the lens. His right shoulder bore the inscription "Jesus Only," as if an epaulet. The only other bit of written material was his title, "Senior Bishop of the Church of Christ," which lay directly below the photo.[71]

As in the examples of Jones and the National Baptist Publishing House, on the one hand, and William Christian and The Living Way Company, on the other, the extensive use of portraits by the Holiness leaders to publicize their work calls to mind the lack of a rigid and complete division between the Holiness movement and Baptist and Methodist society in the Delta. Christian, Jones, and Mason relied on simple contemporary techniques of marketing and conventions of photography to advance their movement and draw attention to it, but in a heavily-controlled approach calculated to avoid the charges of vulgar self-promotion that haunted some denominational preachers who permitted portraits of themselves to become part of advertisements for consumer goods. They clearly gave a nod to the importance of the role of basic forms of modern advertising in the building of religious movements and recognized that black sacred identity after slavery was formed in part through the use of images produced in the market.

Christian, Mason, and Jones developed as promising young Baptist preachers in the Delta during a time of radical change and reorganization in black spiritual life. They watched as the railroad emerged as a prominent site and symbol of spiritual experience, fraternal orders became new components to local black political life and influenced the structural evolution of black churches, and the consumer market sparked new ways of thinking about fundraising, racial progress, respectability, domesticity, and home and church decoration. In contrast to many of their denominational peers, though, they interpreted them as signs of a popular self-centeredness and willful disregard for God's command to trust in the Holy Spirit for every want and need. In response, Christian, Jones, and Mason called for a spiritual renewal based on the doctrine of sanctification, a series of restrictive codes of worldly conduct, and a restoration of the ethos and rituals of the early Christian church. They built the African American Holiness movement, whose core principles resonated deeply with many Delta blacks outraged by decades of racial unrest and more recent institutional and liturgical changes in Baptist and Methodist life.

The development of the Holiness movement in the Delta from the 1890s to the 1910s, however, reflected not only the diversity of black spiritual life but also elements of its shared history. For even as Holiness preachers and sympathizers styled themselves as dissenters from contemporary denominational life, they were, in small yet significant ways, participants in it as well. This is not to suggest that Holiness churches ever became indistinguishable from their denominational counterparts, for they did not: Christian, Jones, and Mason successfully constructed a fresh and durable alternative to established churches in the Delta. But it is to propose that the failure of Christian, Jones, and Mason to fulfill their original pledge and break away fully from the contemporary character of Baptist and Methodist life is not entirely surprising and underscores just how deeply enmeshed certain dimensions of it were in southern African American spiritual life as a whole by the 1910s.[72] While the Holiness leaders certainly challenged many popular African American ideas about theology, religious organization, and spiritual culture, they collectively embraced others. Indeed, their adoption of a belief in a glorious ancient African past, of burial societies, and of restricted forms of commercial advertising and promotion draw attention not only to what sets apart the Holiness movement from denominational churches but also to what unites them. This loose pattern of cultural adaptation, moreover, would continue. The post-World War I generation witnessed Baptist and Methodist congregations successfully experiment with and borrow from Holiness styles of liturgy and worship, including aspects of ecstatic praise and occasionally even speaking in tongues.[73] To a degree unforeseen by Christian, Jones, or Mason at the start of the reform efforts, then, their movement and denominational culture grew not along separate trajectories but ones that periodically intersected and informed each other.

Epilogue

Delta Journeys

Let me tell you what I found
The rooster crowed, to remind Simon and Peter
That he was lying
The rooster crowed, to remind Simon and Peter
That he was lying

—Rosetta Tharpe, *No Room in the Church for Liars*

R osetta Nubin was born in 1921 in the small town of Cottonplant in the
Arkansas Delta. She was raised in the strict Pentecostal traditions of the
Church of God in Christ, though you would never have guessed it by the level of
extravagance surrounding her very public marriage at Griffith Stadium in Washington, D.C., in 1951. Here in the shared home of the Washington Senators professional baseball team and the Washington Redskins football team, in front of twenty
five thousand cheering men, women, and children who had paid a modest entrance
fee to witness the event, Nubin, who had long since changed her name to Rosetta
Tharpe, made her third trip to the altar. Tharpe wed Russell Morrison, the manager
of her career as a singer of sanctified songs, gospel, and blues. It was a fitting
spectacle for a woman who relished her status as a celebrity and what it bought her,
especially heavily embroidered evening gowns, a gold-finished piano, and a home
with mirrored ceilings. Predictably, her latest nuptials elicited howls of disapproval
from some members of Holiness and denominational churches outraged over her
latest affront to their codes of conservative morality.

By the time she took the field to make her vows, Tharpe was growing accustomed
to the adulation of fans as well as the criticism from black Christians incensed by her

casual mixing of the sacred and the commercial. A musical prodigy, she once had all
the markings of becoming a leader with the Church of God in Christ. At four she was
already singing with her mother, evangelist Katie Bell Nubin, widely known as
"Mother Bell," at tent revivals across the Delta. By six she was a skillful guitar player
and developing a clear, powerful voice easily able to bend notes and hold a vibrato for
lengthy stretches. During the 1930s, she and her family relocated to Chicago, where
she experimented with song and sound that blended sanctified church music and the
blues, perfected her skills with the electric guitar, and created a stage presence
marked by flashy clothes and flamboyant jewelry. Tharpe signed with the recording
company Decca in 1938 and quickly rose to fame by singing classic religious songs
like a version of Thomas Dorsey's "Take My Hand, Precious Lord," as well as bluesy
versions of spirituals such as "Down by the Riverside." She made frequent stops at
the most popular African American nightclubs in the country, including the Cotton
Club, Apollo Theater, and Paramount Theater in New York City. By the late 1940s,
she was a top black recording artist heard on the radio across the nation, yet one
hounded by black religious critics fearful that her music and lifestyle challenged the
social values expected of black Christians.[1]

Tharpe's arc from Cottonplant to the forefront of American popular music bore
the imprint of some of the key characteristics of black sacred life that developed in
the Delta during the decades before her birth. She began her career by taking
advantage of the expanded roles for women as leaders in sanctified churches. She
created a hybrid form of music and performance style that embodied the free-
flowing and improvisational nature of Holiness worship. She tested new forms of
technology, in this case radio and records, to spread her music. She also embraced
the consumer market as a way to make money and spread her gospel message, in the
process sparking controversy over the question of whether she bent too far in the
direction of personal aggrandizement.

Tharpe's ascent to stardom prompts us to think broadly about the importance of
the story of African American religion in the Delta from 1875 to 1915 to the modern
unfolding of black and southern history. Indeed, her journey evokes not only
something of the cultural ferment and tensions of the post-Reconstruction era
itself—the transformations in sacred thought and practice that made the Delta a
national center of black religious experimentation—but also its effect on later
articulations of African American identity. This is not to say, however, that the
changes that swept across the Delta contain a transparent outline for African
American life in the mid-twentieth century. Rather, it is to suggest that the character
of these changes at times prefigured and even influenced some of its turning points.

Part of this influence in easy to spot among the tens of thousands of Delta blacks
who, like Tharpe, fled their homes for the promise of a better life in cities like

Great Migration

Chicago. These travelers were part of the "Great Migration" of the early twentieth century, the largest resettlement of people of African descent since the close of the slave trade, involving nearly five hundred thousand black southerners who trekked north from 1915 to 1920 and over one million more during the next decade. Nearly 250,000 black Mississippians and fifty three thousand black Arkansans, most from the Delta areas, emigrated, typically to Chicago.[2] "I want to get my family out of this cursed south land," complained a bitter black farmer from Greenville, Mississippi, desperate to leave. "[D]own here a negro man is not [as] good [as] a white man's dog."[3] A teacher from a nearby town described his frustration with life in the Delta by evoking the spirit of a famous Revolutionary War hero. "I am so sick[,] I am so tired of such conditions that I sometime think that life for me is not worth while [*sic*] and most eminently believe with Patrick Henry[,] "Give me liberty or [*sic*] or give me death."[4] Drawing them northward were glowing reports of racial comity and good paying jobs. Printed in black denominational newspapers and secular presses like the *Chicago Defender* and spun by labor agents, railroad workers, and missionaries, these stories gripped the imagination of many black southerners eager to make a new start for themselves. Though often exaggerated, they contained much truth. Midwestern urban centers were less poisoned by racism than the southern countryside and offered superior jobs. Beginning with the outbreak of hostilities in Europe and accelerating as war clouds gathered over America, their industrial factories and shops grew rapidly to meet the rising demand for war goods. Many companies aggressively recruited southern blacks to fill their assembly lines and manufacturing plants, especially as native-born whites rushed to join the military and Congress reduced the number of immigrants permitted to enter the country.[5]

Delta migrants carried a sharp sense of their recent history with them. In 1916, a group of 147 black Mississippians made up their minds to leave their native homeland for good. They packed up their belongings, made their way to the nearest depot, bought one-way train tickets on the Yazoo and Mississippi Valley Railroad, and rode it to its terminus in Chicago. When their train passed the Ohio River, a topographic feature that they believed to divide the South from the North and mark the end of their lives under segregation, the migrants stopped their watches, knelt in the car, and began to weep openly and sing songs of deliverance that harkened back to slavery.

> I done came out of de land of Egypt/ain't that good news
> O Canaan, sweet Canaan/I am bound for the land of Canaan.[6]

In the language and imagery of their song, these black Mississippians communicated a sense of their redeployment as part of a larger development in African American life. As had previous generations of blacks, they viewed their movement through a lens of sacred history focused on the biblical book of Exodus. Like the ancient Hebrews who, in keeping with God's pledge to care for them, successfully fled persecution in Egypt and eventually found Canaan, blacks from the Delta boarded railroad cars to leave behind the evils of racial violence and discover the fruits of liberty in cities such as Chicago. Nearly forty years had passed since white southerners had brutally ended Reconstruction; now they were ostensibly at a turning point in their lives after redemption when God seemed to be guiding them at last to the Promised Land.[7]

Before Delta blacks ever stepped foot on a train bound for Chicago, of course, they were familiar with the notion of riding the rails to freedom. The explosive growth of the railroad and the declining rate in passenger fares during the 1880s and 1890s had made it possible for many African Americans to board trains for the first time and experience rapid travel. It became both a real and imaginary setting where modern technology intersected with black hopes for a freer life, a location where African Americans underwent conversions and often successfully confronted the rules and customs of segregated travel. In the decades following the migration era, when black artists like Romare Bearden and Jacob Lawrence established the train as a dominant symbol of the black quest for freedom and a hallmark of black modernism, they implicitly recalled its transformative role in the lives of black southerners after Reconstruction.[8]

After joining a church in Chicago, Delta migrants quickly voiced their opinions about how it should operate. They expected their new houses of worship to offer the types of social opportunities they were accustomed to, such as programs to help defray burial costs and financially support the sick; strong connections with civic institutions like fraternal orders; and public campaigns to support black merchants and white storeowners sympathetic to black civil rights. When Chicago's black churches enlarged their social service offerings during the 1920s, then, it was not simply a benevolent response to an influx of the poor and downtrodden in their pews but also an answer to the demands made by southern migrants. Delta travelers transported tensions that had split their denominational churches from Holiness ones as well. The questions of the proper character of liturgy, the level of educational qualification for ministers, the legitimacy of supernatural communication as a source of spiritual authority, and the acceptability of unguarded, unrestrained worship quickly became part of their new churches. Indeed, the conflicts over the comportment and worship style of their southern members that consumed Chicago's African American clerics during the migration era replayed the long-standing divisions that had earlier torn Delta churches apart.[9]

Delta travelers to Chicago approached the issue of consumption in familiar ways, too. They participated and sometimes led efforts to create racial "niche" markets as a way of supporting black commercial ventures. As a result, they often patronized local black merchants, shopkeepers, doctors, lawyers, and funeral directors exclusively.[10] During the 1920s they responded to the problem of racist city stores by organizing boycotts.[11] These forms of behavior, while rising from the new social stresses of urban life, also built on earlier traditions of mixing racial identity with habits of buying and selling. By the turn of the century, Delta blacks already sought greater access to the consumer market through their ministers and newspaper editors. Their leaders arranged for them to buy small literary and consumer commodities outside of stores and commissaries and, by securing a small profit on the transactions, earned money to support black churches, schools, and presses. Their newspapers publicized the names of merchants sympathetic to black liberties and thus deserving of their support—as well as those who did not and should be avoided.

Similarly, the spirit of black nationalism so wildly popular among both black migrants to the urban midwest and to blacks who stayed in the South during the early twentieth century partly sprang from changes to African American southern society in the previous generation, especially the growth of fraternal orders. Black nationalism's most common form, Garveyism, named for its founder Marcus Garvey, directly recalled the fraternal stress on the place of Africa in the African American consciousness, on blacks taking care of blacks, and on the role of ritual in community life. Garvey immigated from Jamaica to New York City in 1916 and quickly set off on a national speaking tour. Within a year he returned to Harlem, founded a chapter of the United Negro Improvement Association [UNIA], and began publishing its official voice, *The Negro World*. UNIA chapters mushroomed in cities and rural areas like the Delta. Garvey preached about racism as a defining experiences of American culture, Africa as a place of refuge for all black people, and the critical need for African Americans to develop their own sources of capital and businesses. He taught that men and women of African descent had once ruled the world's major civilizations. And he commonly wore elaborate, military-style uniforms in public, practiced secret greetings, and crafted elaborate membership ceremonies.[12]

Black nationalism manifested itself in other forms of political organization that also built on a foundation of social order laid previously by fraternal culture. During World War I, many black sharecroppers and tenant farmers from the Arkansas Delta became members of the Progressive Farmers and Household Union of America. Its goal was to leverage the collective economic strength of blacks and earn fairer, more advantageous crop settlement terms with white landowners. This group modeled its internal organization directly after secret societies; observers often remarked how its rituals and ceremonies closely resembled ones long in place in African American orders. More abstractly, the act of joining an organization for the purpose of creating a unified black voice of racial power and dignity echoed one of the primary objectives of black fraternal lodges.[13] An offspring of the Progressive Farmers and Household

Union was the Southern Tenant Farmers' Union, founded during the Great Depression to organize predominantly landless agricultural workers for the purpose of demanding greater financial assistance from the federal and local government. Biracial and open to women, it, too, developed in part because of the experiences of its members in black fraternal orders and houses of worship. As one leader summarized, "because of his long experience in other organizations such as churches, burial, fraternal organizations and the like[,] the Negro generally knows how to run meetings as they should be run."[14]

Black fraternal orders in the Delta contributed more immediately to the formation of black hospitals. The Afro-American Sons and Daughters, a secret society founded in 1924 in the Mississippi Delta, took as its chief mission the construction of the first major black health care facility in the region. Its members, who filled the halls of more than 150 Afro-American lodges, raised $50,000 dollars to make possible the opening of the thirty-two bed Afro-American Sons and Daughters Hospital Yazoo City in 1928. Known simply as the "Afro," it offered fraternal members discount prices for services, though it welcomed all black patients. Similar efforts by other black orders, such as Knights and Daughters of Tabor who opened the forty-two bed Taborian hospital in Mound Bayou, helped establish a small network of black hospitals across the Delta. Crucial to the success of the Taborian hospitals was a high level of cooperation between lodges and churches. Once a year in late June high-ranking fraternal officials with the Knights and Daughters of Tabor held a widely publicized "Sermon Day" at a local church. They hired a cleric to preach his best, most energetic sermon in the hope that it would win new pledges of financial support for the hospital from the audience. "Sermon Day" was quite profitable not only for the Taborian hospitals but for the individual minister, who pocketed half of the money that he raised. During the 1940s and 1950s, these black hospitals become important centers for organizing civil rights protests.[15]

When analyzing the relationship between the post-Reconstruction era and the Great Migration era in black and southern history, however, it is difficult to avoid one recurrent theme, that of racial violence. When African Americans attempted to move out of the "black neighborhoods" in Chicago and into areas populated mostly by whites, they paid a heavy price. From 1917 to 1919, whites bombed the homes of twenty-four African Americans who took up residences in Anglo sections of the city. Public parks were off limits to blacks after dark; those failing to heed this unwritten code faced roving bands of white toughs. In the summer of 1919, a black teenager was murdered after his raft drifted too close to the "white" beach of the South Side. A race riot followed in which twenty-three blacks and fifteen whites died in a weeklong melee quelled only by the intervention of the National Guard.[16] An episode of violence larger in scale erupted in the Delta in 1919 as well. When black members of the

Progressive Farmers and Household Union turned to the courts and publicly threatened to strike as means of obtaining better working conditions, white planters from Phillips County grabbed their guns. Seeking to end this form of black protest once and for all, they staged a bloody attack on supporters and members of the Union in Elaine, Arkansas. When the smoke cleared, between five and twenty whites and at least two hundred blacks lay dead in what was later coined the Elaine Massacre.[17]

The persistent reality of vigilantism shook the popular view that departing the Delta for Chicago was akin to going to the Promised Land. For those that stayed behind, it demonstrated that the loss of so many black laborers would little enhance their ability to wring concessions from white employers. The continuation of extralegal violence as an intimate part of black existence, then, forced African Americans to return again to the question of if they would ever live safely and enjoy a full complement of citizenship rights. For whether they called the Delta, Chicago, or some other corner of the country home, blacks living after World War I still battled for their safety and freedom.

Yet even as the violent capping of African American liberty remained a steady leitmotif of black life, it should not be treated as an overpowering story line when writing about any era. For too long it has been for the post-Reconstruction South, and consequently we have histories that treat racial oppression as a force that flattened much of black society and severely circumscribed if not blocked African American cultural expression, especially among the rural poor and agricultural workers. This book has been an attempt to reveal that the religious transformations in black life after redemption in the Delta constituted a vital chapter in the elaboration of African American culture after slavery. Without grasping what blacks attempted and accomplished during this period, it is difficult to appreciate it as something other than a time when they waited patiently for change to come to their lives; it is hard to see how certain defining features of black life after 1915 took root during these decades.

My objective in this book has not been to sanitize the writing of the past or render it bloodless, but to indicate that while the threat of racial violence certainly hung over Delta blacks, they made decisions about what mattered most to them according to a range of cultural imperatives, especially their ideas about religion. For them, religion was a space where they integrated the realities of second-class citizenship with dreams of overcoming it, where they fashioned ideas and institutions that helped them minimize the ills of segregation and sometimes even overturn them, and where they planned for a future of unchecked liberty even though they knew not when it would come, only that it would. For us, their religion is a subject whose study illuminates strands of African American and southern history hidden too long.

Notes

Prologue

1. E. C. Morris, *Sermons, Addresses, and Reminiscences and Important Correspondence, With a Picture Gallery of Eminent Ministers and Scholars* (Nashville: National Baptist Publishing Board, 1901), 194, 294. Biographical information about Moseley is sketchy; he appears episodically in contemporary books about black southern Baptists and denominational records. His precise date of birth remains undermined, but, based on descriptions and pictures of him, it appears to be around 1860.

2. *Minutes of the Women's State Baptist Association and the State Baptist Sunday School Convention, Held with the St. John Church, New Port, Arkansas, June 19–24, 1893* (n.p: n.d.), *Records of Annual Reports, Minutes, and other publications of selected Arkansas African-American Baptist Associations, and other organizations, 1867–1951*, microfilm, rolls 14, 19, AHC.

3. On the exodus motif among black Americans during slavery, see Eddie Glaude, *Exodus! Religion, Race, and Nation in Early Nineteenth-Century Black America* (Chicago: The University of Chicago Press, 2000); Albert J. Raboteau, *Slave Religion: The Invisible Institution in the Antebellum South* (New York: Oxford University Press, 1978), 311–321; Eugene Genovese, *Roll, Jordan, Roll: The World the Slaves Made* (New York: Oxford University Press, 1972), 253–281; and Timothy L. Smith, "Slavery and Theology: The Emergence of Black Christian Conscience in Nineteenth-Century America," *Church History* 31 (December 1972): 502–503. On its usage during and after slavery, see Raboteau, "African-Americans, Exodus, and the American Israel," *African-American Christianity: Essays in History,* ed. Paul E. Johnson (Berkeley: University of California Press, 1994), 1–17; idem, *Fire in the Bones: Reflections on African American Religious History* (Boston:

Beacon, 1995), 17–37; David W. Wills, "Exodus Piety: African American Religion in an Age of Immigration," *Minority Faiths and the American Protestant Mainstream*, ed. Jonathan Sarna (Urbana: University of Illinois Press, 1998), 136–188; and Floyd T. Cunningham, "Wandering in the Wilderness: Black Baptist Thought after Emancipation," *American Baptist Quarterly* 4 (1985): 268–281.

4. *Minutes of the Women's State Baptist Association and the State Baptist Sunday School Convention, Held with the St. John Church, New Port, Arkansas, June 19–24, 1893*, 20, AHC.

INTRODUCTION

1. "Jesus Handed Me a Ticket," in *God Struck Me Dead: Religious Conversion Experiences and Autobiographies of Ex-Slaves,* ed. Clifton H. Johnson (1969; repr. Philadelphia: Pilgrim Press, 1993), xix, 145, 147.

2. W. E. B. Du Bois, *The Souls of Black Folk* (1903; repr., New York: Dodd and Mead, 1961), 144.

3. On theoretical definitions of popular religion in North America, see Peter Williams, *Popular Religion in America: Symbolic Change and the Modernization Process in Historical Perspective* (Englewood Cliffs, N.J.: Prentice Hall, 1980), 7; Charles Lippy, *Being Religious American Style: A History of Popular Religiosity in the United States* (Westport, Conn.: Greenwood, 1994), 18; Robert Orsi, "Everyday Miracles: The Study of Lived Religion," in *Lived Religion in America: Toward a History of Practice,* ed. David Hall (Princeton: Princeton University Press, 1997), 11; and Colleen McDannell, *Material Christianity: Religion and Popular Culture in America* (New Haven: Yale University Press, 1995), 4.

4. Jon Butler, "Jack in the Box Faith: The Religion Problem in Modern American History," *JAH* 90 (March 2004): 1357–1378; and John M. Giggie, "America's Third Great Awakening: Religion and the Civil Rights Movement," *Reviews in American History* 33 (June 2005): 254–262. In its effort to integrate approaches to the study of American religion and culture and avoid the use of overarching interpretative schemas, this book echoes calls by Robert Orsi and Leigh Schmidt to think of history as being "braided"—or, as Orsi put it, of recognizing "that the linear narratives so beloved of modernity . . . mask the sources of history's dynamics, culture's pain and the possibilities of innovation and change." In place of narratives and conventions that can forcibly shape the telling of history, one needs to be open to and searching for "improbable intersections, incommensurable ways of living, discrepant imaginings, unexpected movements of influence, and inspirations existing side by side. . . . " Robert Orsi, *Between Heaven and Earth: The Religious Worlds People Make and the Scholars who Study Them* (Cambridge: Harvard University Press, 2005), 9; and Leigh Schmidt, *Hearing Things: Religion, Illusion, and the American Enlightenment* (Cambridge: Harvard University Press, 2000).

5. Martin Delany, untitled, *The North Star* (16 February 1849), (23 March 1849), and (13 April 1849). Delany, in these examples of his writing, went on to criticize black churches for not inspiring congregants to resist oppression more openly. Part of the quote is taken from Eddie Glaude, *Exodus! Religion, Race, and Nation in Early Nineteenth-Century Black America* (Chicago: The University of Chicago Press, 2000), 19.

6. E. Franklin Frazier, *The Negro Church in America* (New York: Schocken, 1963; repr., 1974).

7. Judith Weisenfeld, *African American Women and Christian Activism: New York's Black YMCA, 1905–1945* (Cambridge: Harvard University Press, 1997), 3–8, makes a similar point.

8. On the liberating function, see Joseph Washington, Jr., *Black Religion; The Negro and Christianity in the United States* (1964; repr., Lanham, Md.: University Press of America, 1984) and James M. Washington, *Frustrated Fellowship: The Black Baptist Quest for Social Power* (Macon, Ga.: Mercer University Press, 1986); on the prophetic function, see Cornel West, *Prophesy Deliverance! An Afro-American Revolutionary Christianity* (Philadelphia: Westminster, 1982) and Glaude, *Exodus*, who adds the importance of the black church in formulating national forms of black political identity; on the dialectical purpose, see C. Eric Lincoln and Lawrence H. Mamiya, *The Black Church in the African American Experience* (Durham, N.C.: Duke University Press, 1990); Evelyn Brooks Higginbotham, *Righteous Discontent: The Women's Movement in the Black Baptist Church, 1880–1920* (Cambridge: Harvard University Press, 1993), especially the introduction; Jurgen Habermas, "The Public Sphere: An Encyclopedia Article (1964)," *New German Critique,* 1 (Fall 1974): 49–55; and Habermas, *The Structural Transformation of the Public Sphere: An Inquiry into a Category of Bourgeois Society,* trans. Thomas Burger with the assistant of Frederick Lawrence (Cambridge: MIT Press, 1989). For an extended commentary on Higginbotham's idea of the black church, with a eye cast toward its repercussions for notions of the black political state, see Glaude, *Exodus,* 19–43. For a perceptive historiographical review of definitions of the black church, see Judith Weisenfeld, "On Jordan's Stormy Banks," in *New Directions in American Religious History,* ed. Harry Stout and Darryl Scott (New York: Oxford University Press, 1997), 423–427.

9. See, for recent examples, Steven Hahn, *A Nation Under Our Feet: Black Political Struggles in the Rural South from Slavery to the Great Migration* (Cambridge: Harvard University Press, 2003); Nan E. Woodruff, *American Congo: The African-American Struggle for Freedom in the Delta* (Cambridge: Harvard University Press, 2004); J. William Harris, *Deep Souths: Delta, Piedmont, and Sea Island Society in the Age of Segregation* (Baltimore: Johns Hopkins Press, 2001); Jane Dailey *Before Jim Crow: The Politics of Race in Postemancipation Virginia* (Chapel Hill: University of North Carolina Press, 2000); *Jumpin' Jim Crow: Southern Politics from Civil War to Civil Rights,* ed. Jane Dailey, Glenda Gilmore, and Bryant Simon (Princeton: Princeton University Press, 2000); Stephen Kantrowitz, *Ben Tillman and the Reconstruction of White Supremacy* (Chapel Hill: University of North Carolina Press, 2000); Grace Hale, *Making Whiteness: The Culture of Segregation in the South, 1890–1940* (New York: Pantheon, 1998); Leon Litwack, *Trouble in Mind: Black Southerners in the Age of Jim Crow* (New York: Knopf, 1998); and Glenda Gilmore, *Gender and Jim Crow: Women and the Politics of White Supremacy in North Carolina, 1896–1920* (Chapel Hill: University of North Carolina Press, 1996).

10. Works that focus wholly or in large part on rural blacks for this period, but pay little attention to the role of religion, include Woodruff, *American Congo;* Greta de Jong, *A Different Day: African American Struggles for Justice in Rural Louisiana, 1900–1970* (Chapel Hill: University of North Carolina Press, 2002); Harris, *Deep Souths;* John Willis, *Forgotten Time: The Yazoo-Mississippi Delta after the Civil War* (Charlottesville: University of Virginia Press, 2000); Jeannie M. Whayne, *A New Plantation South: Land, Labor, and Federal Favor in Twentieth Century Arkansas* (Charlottesville: University of Virginia Press, 1996); Cobb, *The Most Southern Place on Earth;* Litwack, *Trouble in Mind;* and Neil McMillen, *Dark Journey: Black Mississippians in the Age of Jim Crow* (Urbana: University of Illinois Press, 1988). Important exceptions include Wills, "Exodus Piety"; William E. Montgomery *Under Their Own Vine and Fig Tree: The African-American Church in the South, 1865–1900* (Baton Rouge: Louisiana State

University Press, 1993); Stephen Ward Angell, *Bishop Henry Turner and African-American Religion in the South* (Knoxville: University of Tennessee Press, 1992); Nell Irvin Painter, *Exodusters: Black Migration to Kansas after Reconstruction* (New York: Knopf, 1977); and Hahn, *Under Our Feet.*

11. Rayford W. Login, *The Negro in American Life and Thought: The Nadir, 1877–1901* (New York: Dial, 1954), is credited with dubbing the phrase "the nadir"; Litwack, *Trouble in My Mind*; Hahn, *A Nation Under Our Feet,* 413.

12. Carl H. Moneyhon, *The Impact of the Civil War and Reconstruction on Arkansas* (Baton Rouge: Louisiana State University Press, 1994; repr., Fayetteville: University of Arkansas Press, 2000), 243–264; and John Graves, *Town and Country: Race Relations in an Urban-Rural Context, Arkansas, 1865–1905* (Fayetteville: University of Arkansas Press, 1990), 40–55. For a broad study of Reconstruction era, see Eric Foner, *Reconstruction: America's Unfinished Revolution, 1863–1877* (New York: Harper and Row, 1988).

13. Cobb, *The Most Southern Place on Earth,* 59–68; and Willis, *Forgotten Time,* 61–62, 115–117. See also Bradley G. Bond, *Political Culture in the Nineteenth-Century South: Mississippi, 1830–1890* (Baton Rouge: Louisiana State University Press, 1995); and Albert D. Kirwan, *Revolt of the Rednecks: Mississippi Politics, 1876–1925* (Lexington: University of Kentucky Press, 1951).

14. Steward E. Tolnay and E. M. Beck, *A Festival of Violence: An Analysis of Southern Lynchings, 1882–1930* (Urbana: University of Illinois Press, 1995), 45–46. For lynching statistics on the Arkansas Delta, see the National Association for the Advancement of Colored People [NAACP] study, *Thirty Years of Lynching, 1889–1918* (New York: The National Association for the Advancement of Colored People, 1919), 48–52. For the purpose of calculations, I included all counties composing the Arkansas Delta. For lynching statistics on the Mississippi Delta, see *Thirty Years of Lynching,* 74–80; Willis, *Forgotten Time,* 152–157, 225–226; and Harris, *Deep Souths,* 343.

15. Stephen Cresswell, *Rednecks, Redeemers, and Race: Mississippi after Reconstruction, 1877–1917* (Jackson: University of Mississippi Press, 2005), 64.

16. J. Todd Moye, *Let the People Decide: Black Freedom and White Resistance Movements in Sunflower County, Mississippi, 1945–1986* (Chapel Hill: University of North Carolina Press, 2004), 4–21, provides the best account of the lynching. See also Nick Salvatore, *Singing in a Strange Land: C. L. Franklin, the Black Church, and the Transformation of America* (New York: Little, Brown, 2005), 9–10; Cobb, *The Most Southern Place on Earth,* 113–114. The quotes from *The Vicksburg Evening Post* are from Cobb.

17. U.S. Department of Commerce, Bureau of the Census, *The Social and Economic Status of the Black Population in the United States: An Historical Overview, 1790–1978* (Washington, D.C.: Government Printing Office, 1979), Current Population Reports, Special Studies Series P-23, No. 80 [1979], 13–20. In 1870, 91 percent of all black Americans lived in the South; in 1910, the number was 89 percent. [n.b.: for the purpose of their report, the Census Bureau defined the "South" as a region encompassing all of the former Confederacy plus Delaware, Maryland, West Virginia, Kentucky, Oklahoma, and the District of Columbia.]

18. U.S. Bureau of the Census, *Negro Population, 1790–1915* (Washington, D.C.: Government Printing Office, 1918), 35–36, 46–49, 51, 115, 125, 127, 129, 131, 569–573, 777, 782, 784, 787–788. For population and agricultural census data for 1870–1920, I also relied on the University of Virginia Geospatial and Statistical Data Center, *United*

States Historical Census Data Browser, ONLINE, 1998, University of Virginia. Available: http://fisher.lib.virginia.edu/census/. Accessed July 5–15, 2004. Thanks to Patrick Murphy for his assistance in retrieving and tabulating this data.

19. Rev. John J. Morant, *Mississippi Ministers* (New York: Vantage, 1958), 9–10. Like Morant, an unnamed black man confided to an interviewer in 1941 that he moved from the northwestern Mississippi hill country to the Delta in the late 1870s because of the tall tales spun by land agents. "They come to the hills and make folks think greenbacks grew on trees and they had ponds of molasses here, and folks in the hill believed it." Lewis Wade Jones, "The Mississippi Delta," in John W. Work, Lewis Wade Jones, Samuel C. Adams, Jr., *Lost Delta Found: Rediscovering the Fisk University-Library of Congress Coahoma County Study, 1941–1942,* ed. Robert Gordon and Bruce Nemorov (Nashville: Vanderbilt University Press, 2005), 42.

20. Only 10 percent of the Mississippi Delta was classified as "cleared" in 1860; the figure was 12 percent in 1880. In 1870, only 26 percent of land in the Arkansas Delta was classified as "improved" or cleared; the percentage was basically unchanged in 1880. E. L. Langsford and B. H. Thibodeaux, *Plantation Organization and Operation in the Yazoo-Mississippi Delta Area* (Washington, D. C.: United States Department of Agriculture, 1939), Technical Bulletin No. 682, May 1939, 12–13; Robert L. Brandfon, *Cotton Kingdom of the New South: A History of the Yazoo Mississippi Delta from Reconstruction to the Twentieth Century* (Cambridge: Harvard University Press, 1967), 40.

21. Clarence Deming, *By-Ways of Nature and Life* (New York: G. P. Putnam's Sons, 1884), 332, 343. See also Ernst von Hesse-Wartegg, *Travels on the Lower Mississippi River, 1879–1880: A Memoir by Ernst von Hesse-Wartegg,* ed. Frederick Trautman (Columbia: University of Missouri Press, 1990), 76, 94; and *The Mississippi Delta and the World: The Memoirs of David L. Cohn,* ed. James C. Cobb (Baton Rouge: Louisiana State University Press, 1995), 5.

22. L. A. Rankin, "From Mississippi," *BV* (2 March 1894). Next to his name appeared the name of a town in Mississippi, yet it is difficult to read it. It appears to be "Makan" or "Maran," yet no such Mississippi town exists. Most probably, the town was Marks, from the Delta county of Quitman, or possibly Maud from the Delta county of Tunica. Similarly, black Christians of every stripe read *The Christian Recorder,* the national newspaper of the African Methodist Episcopal Church. It helped readers of all faiths learn about religious, political, and economic developments in the Delta, according to Mississippian B. F. Watson. In his statement about black life along the banks of the lower Mississippi River to members of an 1879 Senate Committee investigating historical causes of southern black migration, Watson testified ". . . the [African Methodist Episcopal] church paper is the usual method of communication among our people." Testimony of B. F. Watson, 46th Congress, 2nd Session, Senate Report 693, *Report and Testimony of the Select Committee of the United States Senate to Investigate the Causes of the Removal of the Negroes from the Southern States to the Northern States* (Washington, D.C.: Government Printing Office, 1879), II, 342.

23. Cobb, *The Most Southern Place on Earth,* 3–4; Thibodeaux and Langsford, *Plantation Organization and Operation,* 6–9; Thomas Foti, "The River's Gifts and Curses," in *The Arkansas Delta,* ed. William Gatewood and Jeannie Whayne (Fayetteville: University of Arkansas Press, 1993), 30.

24. E. A. Boeger and E. A. Goldenweiser, *A Study of the Tenant Systems of Farming in the Yazoo-Mississippi Delta* (Washington, DC.: United States Department of Agriculture,

1916 USDA Bulletin No. 337 (10 February 1916), 3. In 1906, a geologist studying the soil along Deer Creek, Mississippi, reported that "[t]aken as a whole the plant-food percentages in this soil are probably unexcelled by any soil in the world thus far examines," U.S. Congress, House, A. F. Crider, *Geology and Mineral Resources of Mississippi*, 59th Cong., 1st Sess. (1906), House Doc. 831, Serial 5016, 71, as quoted in Brandfon, *Cotton Kingdom of the New South, 29*.

25. William Alexander Percy, *Lanterns on the Levee: Recollections of a Planter's Son* (New York: Knopf, 1941), 1. Similarly, William Faulkner, in the opening pages to *Big Woods: The Hunting Stories,* writes of Mississippi and the Delta region first by describing "[t]he rich deep black alluvial soil which would grow cotton taller than the head of a man. . . ." William Faulkner, "Mississippi," *Big Woods: The Hunting Stories* (New York: Random House, 1931; repr., New York: Random House, 1994), 1–2.

26. On the Mississippi Delta, see Harris, *Deep Souths*; Willis, *Forgotten Time*; Brandfon, *Cotton Kingdom of the New South*; Cobb, *The Most Southern Place on Earth*; Valerie Grim, "Black Farm Families in the Yazoo-Mississippi Delta, 1920–1970" (Ph.D. dis., Iowa State University, 1990); and Sidney Nathans, "'Gotta Mind to Move a Mind to Settle Down': Afro-Americans and the Plantation Frontier," in *A Master's Due: Essays in Honor of David Herbert Donald,* ed., William J. Cooper, Jr., Michael F. Holt, and John McCardell (Baton Rouge: Louisiana State University Press, 1985), which focuses on Tunica County. The literature on the Arkansas Delta is not as large. See Fon Gordon, *Caste and Class: The Black Experience in Arkansas, 1880–1920* (Athens: University of Georgia Press, 1995), which concentrates on blacks in the Delta; Whayne, *A New Plantation South*; the essay collection by Willard B. Gatewood and Jeannie M. Whayne, eds., *The Arkansas Delta: Land of Paradox* (Fayetteville: University of Arkansas Press, 1993); William Gatewood, "Sunnyside: The Evolution of an Arkansas Plantation, 1848–1945," *AHQ* 50 (1991): 5–29; Donald C. Alexander, *The Arkansas Plantation, 1920–1942* (New Haven: Yale University Press, 1943). For studies that treat both the Mississippi and Arkansas Deltas, see Nan E. Woodruff, "African-American Struggles for Citizenship in the Arkansas and Mississippi Deltas in the Age of Jim Crow," *Radical History Review* 55 (Winter 1993): 523–554; and idem, *American Congo.*

27. Willard B. Gatewood, Jr., "The Arkansas Delta: The Deepest of the Deep South," in *The Arkansas Delta,* ed. Gatewood and Whayne, 3–4; Gerald T. Hanson and Carl H. Moneyhon, *Historical Atlas of Arkansas* (Norman: University of Oklahoma Press, 1989), 2–4; Foti, "The Rivers Gifts and Curses," 41.

28. Brandfon, *Cotton Kingdom of the New South,* 24–25; Boeger and Goldenweiser, *A Study of the Tenant Systems of Farming,* 3; Cobb, *The Most Southern Place on Earth,* 3.

29. The Mississippi Delta includes ten Mississippi counties that lay wholly within it parts of nine others. The ten counties are Bolivar, Coahoma, Humphreys, Issaquena, Leflore, Quitman, Sharkey, Sunflower, Tunica, and Washington. The nine counties laying partly within the Mississippi Delta are De Soto, Tate, Panaola, Tallahatchie, Grenada, Carroll, Holmes, Yazoo, and Warren. Humphreys County was created in 1918. The Arkansas Delta includes seventeen Arkansas counties that lay wholly within it and parts of eight others. The seventeen counties are Arkansas, Chicot, Clay, Craighead, Cross, Crittenden, Desha, Jackson, Greene, Lee, Lonoke, Mississippi, Monroe, Phillips, Poinsett, Prairie, and St. Francis. The eight counties laying partly with the Arkansas

Delta include Ashley, Drew, Independence, Jefferson, Lincoln, Randolph, Pulaski, White. When I used sources from the counties laying partly within the Delta, I limited my selection to those whose origins could be traced to one of the counties laying wholly within the region.

30. In Arkansas, the counties with the heaviest black population are Ashley, Chicot, Crittenden, Desha, Drew, Lee, Monroe, Phillips, St. Francis, and parts of those lying near Arkansas, St. Francis, and Red Rivers, such as Jefferson, Pulaski, and Jackson. See the census work and diagrams of M. Langley Biergert, "Legacy of Resistance: Uncovering the History of Collective Action by Black Agricultural Workers in Central East Arkansas from the 1860s to the 1930s," *Journal of Social History* 32 (Fall 1998): 77. Nan Woodruff also demonstrates that the northeastern Arkansas Delta counties of Clay, Craighead, Greene, and, to a smaller degree, Poinsett and Mississippi, were centers of white immigration from the midwest and Tennessee. These settlers typically began as sharecroppers and eventually progressed to landowners and cultivated rice. Many created agricultural communities just for themselves and other white citizens, a project made possible in large part by lumbar companies who sold their cutover lands only to whites. As a result, few blacks lived in many of these counties. In 1910, only 4.8 percent of the population in Craighead was black; 16.6 percent in Poinsett, 43.6 percent in Cross, and 4.2 percent in Mississippi. These numbers were basically the same a decade later. Woodruff, *American Congo,* 30–31.

31. For a general accounting of the evolution of southern black religion during the Civil War and Reconstruction, see Daniel Stowell, *Rebuilding Zion: The Religious Reconstruction of the South, 1863–1877* (New York: Oxford University Press, 1997), 7, 65–79; Montgomery, *Under Their Own Vine and Fig Tree*; and Paul Harvey, *Freedom's Coming: Religious Culture and the Shaping of the South from the Civil War through the Civil Rights Era* (Chapel Hill: University of North Carolina Press, 2005), 5–46. For the different black Methodist churches, see Jualynne E. Dodson, *Engendering Church: Women, Power, and the AME Press* (New York: Rowman & Littlefield, 2002), 7–22; Reginald F. Hildebrand, *The Times Were Strange and Stirring: Methodist Preachers and the Crisis of Emancipation* (Durham, N.C.: Duke University Press, 1995), xii–xxi; Katherine L. Dvorak, *An African-American Exodus: The Segregation of the Southern Churches* (Brooklyn: Carlson, 1991); Clarence E. Walker, *A Rock in a Weary Land: The African Methodist Episcopal Church during the Civil War and Reconstruction* (Baton Rouge: Louisiana State University Press, 1982); Angell, *Bishop Henry McNeal Turner*; William B. Gravely, "The Social, Political, and Religious Significance of the Formation of the Colored Methodist Episcopal Church (1870)," *Methodist History* 18 (Oct. 1979): 3–25. For black Baptists, see Washington, *Frustrated Fellowship*; and Paul Harvey, *Redeeming the South: Religious Cultures and Racial Identities among Southern Baptists, 1865–1925* (Chapel Hill: University of North Carolina Press, 1997).

32. George P. Rawick, ed., *The American Slave: A Composite Autobiography,* 19 (Westport: Greenwood, 1972–79), vol. 4, pt. II, *Texas Narratives,* 92, as quoted in Stowell, *Rebuilding Zion,* 69.

33. For notable exceptions, see the work of black Catholics and black members of the Methodist Episcopal Church in New Orleans in James Bennett, *Religion and the Rise of Jim Crow in New Orleans* (Princeton: Princeton University Press, 2005).

34. Harvey, *Freedom's Coming,* 7, 8.

35. Stowell, *Rebuilding Zion,* 7, 73–78.

36. Harris, *Deep Souths,* 366; U.S. Bureau of the Census, *Census of Religious Bodies* (Washington, D.C.: Government Printing Office, 1919), vol. 2, 240–242, 278–279.

37. Albert J. Raboteau, *Slave Religion: The "Invisible Institution" in the Antebellum South* (New York: Oxford University Press, 1978), x, makes a similar point but in regard to reading historical sources for information about slave religion and dismissing the long-standing notion that slaves had an "invisible" spiritual life.

38. On the creation of community and identity through the publication and exchange of letters, see Walter Johnson, *Soul to Soul: Life inside the Antebellum Slave Market* (Cambridge: Harvard University Press, 1999), 13; Richard Bushman, *The Refinement of America: Persons, Buildings, Cities* (New York: Vintage, 1992), 215.

39. Rawick, *The American Slave.* Rawick subsequently published two supplemental series of interviews unearthed later. Full texts of the interviews are now available on the Library of Congress website, "Born in Slavery: Slave Narratives from the Federal Writers' Project, 1936–1938," http://memory.loc.gov/ammem/snhtml/snhome.html.

40. David L. Cohn, *Where I Was Born and Raised* (Cambridge: Beacon, 1948), 37.

41. See, for example, David P. Henige, *Oral Historiography* (New York: Longman, 1982).

42. Andrea Cantrell, "WPA Sources for African-American Oral History in Arkansas: Ex-Slave Narratives and Early Settlers' Personal Histories," *Arkansas Historical Quarterly* vol. 63, no. 1, (Spring 2004): 44–50; John W. Blassingame, *The Slave Community: Plantation Life in the Antebellum South* (New York: Oxford University Press, 1972), xlvii, as cited in Cantrell, "WPA Sources," 40n20.

43. Thanks to Andrea Cantrell for calling my attention to these documents.

CHAPTER I

1. Ruby Sheppeard Hicks, *The Song of the Delta* (Jackson, Miss.: Howick House, 1976), 3, 46.

2. For theoretical work on how the advent of the railroad generated multiple questions of cultural change, see Leo Marx, *The Machine in the Garden: Technology and the New Pastoral Ideal in America* (New York: Oxford University Press, 1964); Wolfgang Schivelbusch, *The Railroad Journey: The Industrialization of Time and Space in the 19th Century* (Berkeley: University of California Press, 1986); and Amy Richter, *Home on the Rails: Women, The Railroad, and the Rise of Public Domesticity* (Chapel Hill: University of North Carolina Press, 2005).

3. Testimony of Mose Banks, in George Rawick, ed., *The American Slave: A Composite Autobiography, Arkansas Narratives,* vol. 1, pt. I, 101–103.

4. "Prominent Man Arrested," *Indianapolis Freeman* [(3 February 1894). [n.b.: title is a misnomer; the article actually concerns Arkansas sharecroppers.]

5. Testimonies of Augustus Wilson, Boston Blackwell, Henry Russell, and Julia A. White, in *Bearing Witness: Memories of Arkansas Slavery Narratives from the 1930s WPA Collection,* ed. George E. Lankford (Fayetteville: University of Arkansas Press, 2003), 52, 188, 300, 346.

6. Michelle Mitchell, *Righteous Propagation: African Americans and the Politics of Racial Destiny after Reconstruction* (Chapel Hill: University of North Carolina Press, 2005), 17–21.

7. James Grossman, *Land of Hope: Chicago, Black Southerners, and the Great Migration* (Chicago: The University of Chicago Press, 1989), 18–29, esp. 28.

8. William Cohen, *Freedom's Edge: Black Mobility and the Southern White Quest for Racial Control 1861–1915* (Baton Rouge: Louisiana State University Press, 1991), 29–30, 241–242.

9. Nan Woodruff, *American Congo: The African American Freedom Struggle in the Delta* (Cambridge: Harvard University Press, 2004), 28.

10. I. H. Anderson, "The Editor on the Wing," *CI* (18 October 1890).

11. Eric Arnesan, *Brotherhoods of Color: Black Railroad Workers and the Struggle for Equality* (Cambridge: Harvard University Press, 2001), 5–41; and idem, "Like Banquo's Ghost, It Will Not Down: The Race Question and the American Railroad Brotherhoods, 1880–1920," *AHR* 99 (December 1994): 1601–1633, offer the best summary of race and the railroad during the nineteenth and twentieth centuries. Barbara Y. Welke, "When All the Women Were White, and All the Blacks Were Men: Gender, Class, Race, and the Road to Plessy, 1855–1914, *Law and History Review* 13 (Fall 1995): 261–316; and Richter, *Home on the Rails*, 46, 47, 53–55, 85, 99–104, provide an introduction to the history of black women and the railroad.

12. W. E. B. Du Bois, *Darkwater: Voices from Within the Veil* (New York: Harcourt, Brace, and Howe, 1921; repr., Millwood, N.Y.: Kraus-Thompson, 1975), 230.

13. Norm Cohen, *Long Steel Rail: The Railroad in American Folklore* (Urbana: University of Illinois Press, 1981), 619–623, 629–632; and Robert Brandfon, *Cotton Kingdom of the New South: A History of the Yazoo Mississippi Delta from Reconstruction to the Twentieth Century* (Cambridge: Harvard University Press, 1967), 82–90.

14. Cohen, *Long Steel Rail,* 12–14.

15. Richter, *Home on the Rails,* 36, 38–40.

16. Although professional collecting and transcribing of them didn't begin until the 1840s and it is difficult to determine their precise origins, slave spirituals still offer a valuable window onto black religious life under the lash and show the train as an occasional metaphor for religious journey. See John W. Work, *American Negro Songs and Spirituals* (New York: Bonanza Books, 1940), 1; and more generally, James Weldon Johnson, ed., *The Book of American Negro Spirituals* (New York: Viking, 1925), 11–50; and James Weldon Johnson, ed., *The Second Book of Negro Spirituals* (New York: Viking, 1926), 11–23.

17. R. Nathaniel Dett, ed., *Religious Folk-Songs of the Negro, As Sung at Hampton Institute* (Hampton, Va: Hampton University Press, 1927), 131; idem, ed., *The Book of American Negro Spirituals,* 126–127; Norm Cohen, *Long Steel Rail,* 619–624. For another example, see "Same Train," Johnson, ed., *The Second Book of Negro Spirituals,* 60–61.

18. Catherine Clinton, *Harriet Tubman: The Road To Freedom* (New York: Little, Brown, 2004), 36–38, 61–70, 72–78. Wilbur Siebert, *The Underground Railroad: From Slavery to Freedom* (New York: MacMillan, 1898), 195, indicates that most of the runaway slaves that used the Underground Railroad came from the Border States. Correspondingly, Charles L. Blockson, *The Underground Railroad* (New York: Prentice Hall, 1987), 31, noted that the level of escape by slaves from Mississippi was very low.

19. Jesse Hutchinson Jr., *Get off the Track* (Boston: Thayer & Company, 1844), American Antiquarian Society, Worcester, Massachusetts. Thanks to David Morgan for bringing this document to my attention.

20. Testimony of Railroad Dockery, in *Bearing Witness,* ed. Lankford, 65.

21. John F. Stover, *The Railroads of the South, 1865–1900: A Study in Finance and Control* (Chapel Hill: The University of North Carolina Press, 1955), 39, 45. Stover's book

focuses mostly on the southern states east of the Mississippi River. However, the evolution of the railroad in Arkansas follows the same basic trajectory of failure, reform, and recovery laid out by Stover during the years 1865–1900. See A. B. Armstrong, "Railway Systems in Arkansas" (M.A. Thesis, University of Arkansas at Fayetteville, 1923); Dallas T. Herndon, ed., *Annals of Arkansas* (Hopkinsville, Ky.: The Historical Record Association, 1947), vol. 1, 384–391, 480–502; Stephen E. Wood, "The Development of Arkansas Railroads," *AHQ* 7 (Autumn 1948): 137–140, 156–193; Willard B. Gatewood, "The Arkansas Delta: The Deepest of the Deep South," in *The Arkansas Delta: Land of Paradox,* ed. Jeannie M. Whayne and Willard B. Gatewood (Fayetteville: University of Arkansas Press, 1993), 8, 20–21; Carl H. Moneyhon, "Delta Towns: Their Rise and Decline," Whayne and Gatewood, eds., *The Arkansas Delta*, 211–213; Jeannie M. Whayne, *A New Plantation South: Land, Labor, and Federal Favor in Twentieth Century Arkansas* (Charlottesville: University of Virginia Press, 1996), 12, 15–17, 42, 62–63, 97.

22. Herndon, *Annals of Arkansas*, 1: 346.
23. Stover, *The Railroads of the South,* 47, 61, 123–125.
24. Marie M. Hemphill, *Fevers, Floods, and Faith: A History of Sunflower County, MS., 1844–1976* (Indianola, Miss.: Sunflower County Historical Society 1980), 105–106.
25. Moneyhon, "Delta Towns," 212; Wood, "The Development of the Arkansas Railroad," 133.
26. Peter L. Benoit, "Diary of a Trip to America. Jan. 6, 1875 to June 8, 1875," 233–234, CB6-CB7-CB8, Mill Hill Fathers Archive, JFA. Italics and underline in the original.
27. Y. A. Etheridge, *A History of Ashley County, Arkansas* (Van Buren, Ark.: Press-Argus, 1959), 45; Herndon, *Annals of Arkansas,* vol. 1, 379–383; Moneyhon, "Delta Town," 211; Brandfon, *Cotton Kingdom of the New South,* 67–68.
28. Hicks, *Song of the Delta,* 29, 30.
29. Thomas Buchanan, *Black Life on the Mississippi: Slaves, Free Blacks, and the Western Steamboat World* (Chapel Hill: University of North Carolina Press, 2004), 77.
30. "Macedonia Baptist, Pulaski County," box 417, folder 3, "Baptist," WPA-HRS, UAK-F. Likewise, when the Primitive Baptist Church in Stuttgart, Arkansas, was too poor to build a new church its congregation met for services in an old station house on the Cotton Belt Railroad; "Primitive Baptist. Stuttgart, Arkansas," box 416, folder 19, "Colored Primitive Baptist," WPA-HRS, UAK-F.
31. W. E. B. Du Bois, *The Negro Church* (Atlanta: Atlanta University Press, 1903), 72.
32. "Bethel AME Church," box 435, folder 3, "Methodist," WPA-HRS, UAK-F. See also "St Paul's AME Church," box 435, folder 2, "Methodist," WPA-HRS, UAK-F.
33. C. Vann Woodward, *Origins of the New South* (Baton Rouge: Louisiana State University Press, 1971), 146–147; James M. McPherson, *Ordeal by Fire: The Civil War and Reconstruction* (New York: McGraw-Hill, 1982), 599–600. On the New South business ideology, see Paul M. Gaston, *The South Creed: A Study in Mythmaking* (New York: Knopf, 1970); Raymond B. Nixon, *Henry W. Grady: Spokesman of the New South* (New York: Knopf, 1943); Brandfon, *Cotton Kingdom of the New South,* 12.
34. Stover, *The Railroads of the South,* 135, 186–196; Woodward, *Origins of the New South,* 120; McPherson, *Ordeal by Fire,* 600; Edward Ayers, *The Promise of the New South: Life After Reconstruction* (New York: Oxford University Press, 1992), 9; Brandfon, *Cotton Kingdom of the New South,* 5.

35. Woodruff, *American Congo*, 10, 14, 23, 26, 32. Woodruff points out that flood control projects in Mississippi were built slightly earlier than in Arkansas. Mikko Saikku, *This Delta, This Land: An Environmental History of the Yazoo-Mississippi Floodplain* (Athens: University of Georgia Press, 2005), 152, 154–156, notes that by 1912 the levee system along the Mississippi and its tributaries was about fifteen hundred miles and that the average size of levees in the Mississippi Delta had increased by about one-third. See also John C. Willis, *Forgotten Time: The Yazoo-Mississippi Delta after the Civil War* (Charlottesville: University Press of Virginia, 2000), 6, 7–8; J. William Harris, *Deep Souths: Delta, Piedmont, and Sea Island Society in the Age of Segregation* (Baltimore: Johns Hopkins University Press, 2001), 42–43, 44, 47, 81, 213; Whayne, *A New Plantation South*, 1, 3, 14, 14, 103, 116; Gatewood, "The Arkansas Delta," 21; Thomas Foti, "The River's Gifts and Curses," in *The Arkansas Delta*, eds. Whayne and Gatewood, 37, 42, 48.

36. Hicks, *Song of the Delta*, 6.

37. Woodruff, *American Congo*, 11–12, 15–17; Willis, *Forgotten Time*, 9, 53–55, 56, 175, 190; Harris *Deep Souths*, 41–41; Whayne, *A New Plantation South*, 25–27; Foti, "The River's Gifts and Cruses," 34–35; and Moneyhon, "Delta Town," 215–216.

38. Brandfon, *Cotton Kingdom of the New South*, 68, 75–111; Stover, *The Railroads of the South*, 155–185; Harris, *Deep Souths*, 44–45; James C. Cobb, *The Most Southern Place on Earth: The Mississippi Delta and the Roots of Regional Identity* (New York: Oxford University Press, 1993), 79–81.

39. Herndon, *Annals of Arkansas*, 1: 388; Wayne, *A New Plantation South*, 15–17; Gatewood, "The Arkansas Delta," 8, 20–21; Moneyhon, "Delta Towns," 211–212.

40. Stover, *The Railroads of the South*, 277.

41. Stephen Cresswell, *Rednecks, Redeemers, and Race: Mississippi after Reconstruction, 1877–1917* (Jackson: University of Mississippi Press, 2005), 76; Cobb, *The Most Southern Place on Earth*, 80–81.

42. Woodward, *Origins*, 298; Brandfon, *Cotton Kingdom*, 87–101, 169.

43. New St. Mary's Chapel, Colored Methodist Episcopal Church, box 436, folder 12, "Methodist," WPA-HRS, UAK-F.

44. African Methodist Episcopal Church, box 435, folder 7, "Methodist," WPA-HRS, UAK-F. In 1885, hoping to be "closer to the majority of the members," congregants of the Primitive Baptist Church in Salem, Arkansas, moved their original church on "Griggsby Ford Dirt Road where I[ndependent] M[oun]t[ain] R[ail]R[oad] crosses the same," "Primitive Baptist Church," box 416, folder 19, "Colored Primitive Baptist," WPA-HRS, UAK-F.

45. "Hay's Chapel AME Church," Handwritten church history, "Hay's Chapel," 1, box 431, folder 1, "Methodist," WPA-HRS. UAK-F.

46. John W. Work, untitled manuscript on black life in the Delta, in John W. Work, Lewis Wade Jones, and Samuel C. Adams, Jr., *Lost Delta Found: Rediscovering the Fisk University-Library of Congress Coahoma County Study, 1941–1942,* ed. Robert Gordon and Bruce Nemorov (Nashville: Vanderbilt University Press, 2005), 112. Work never indicated Price's denominational affiliation, but given his steady itinerancy and the strong preference among most black Methodists by the 1930s for a regular preacher, I assumed that he was Baptist.

47. W. A. Spencer, "The Southwestern Empire," *SWCA* (28 July 1892). See also "Letter to the Editor from E. W. Johnson, Little Bay, Ark." 29 October 1891. The general message that

local railroad stations attracted black migrants extended outside of the Delta and was not lost Catholic priest Pierre O. Lebeau, S.S.J., as he scoured the South for a place to begin a new mission. When he began a mission for African American Catholics in Petite Parish, Louisiana, in the late 1890s, Lebeau convinced the Texas Pacific Railroad to build a flag station near the chapel, thinking that such a transportation link would attract black migrants. Pierre Lebeau to J. R. Slattery, *The Colored Harvest* (October 1898): 50–51 and Pierre Lebeau to J. R. Slattery, *The Colored Harvest* (January 1899): 248–49. On Lebeau and railroads, see Dolores Egger, *Jim Crow Comes to Church: The Establishment of Segregated Catholic Parishes in South Louisiana.* (M.A. thesis, University of Southwestern Louisiana, 1958), 37–40. JFA.

48. "Colored Methodist Episcopal Church," box 436, folder 12, "Methodist," WPA-HRS, UAK-F.

49. Rawick, *The American Slave, Arkansas Narratives,* vol. 1, Prt. 2, 350.

50. Vernon Lane Wharton, *The Negro in Mississippi, 1865–1890* (Westport, Conn.: Greenwood, 1984), 269.

51. J. C. Powell, "Sunday Excursions—Their Evils, etc." *CI* (14 July 1888). Lawrence Levine mentions excursions in his *Black Culture and Back Consciousness: Afro-American Folk Thought from Slavery to Freedom* (New York: Oxford University Press, 1977), 263.

52. Cf. Wharton, *The Negro in Mississippi,* 269, who claims that the excursions died out by 1890.

53. "Ministerial Union Condemns Express," *SWCA* (5 June 1902). See also "Negro Excursions," *SWCA* (19 June 1902).

54. Jeffrey Richards and John M. MacKenzie, *The Railway Station: A Social History* (Oxford: Clarendon, 1986), 137; Ayers, *Promise of the New South,* 3–33, 132–159; Grace Elizabeth Hale, *Making Whiteness: The Culture of Segregation in the South, 1890–1940* (New York: Pantheon, 1998), 124–125.

55. Russell Baker, a journalist from the midwest, made a similar observation about streetcars in Atlanta during a visit in the early 1900s. He wrote that "in the street cars [Southerners] touch as free citizens, each paying for the right to ride, the white not in a place of command, the Negro without an obligation of servitude"; Russell Baker, *Following the Color Line, American Negro Citizenship in the Progressive Era* (New York: Doubleday, Page, 1908; repr., New York: Harper and Row, 1964), 30–31. See also Hale, *Making Whiteness,* 132–134.

56. John M. Tillman, untitled, *AG* (30 January 1891), as reprinted in *A Documentary History of Arkansas,* ed. C. Fred Williams, S. Charles Bolton, Carl H. Moneyhon, and LeRoy T. Williams (Fayetteville: University of Arkansas Press, 1984), 152. Defending the proposed bill establishing a separate coach law in Arkansas, Tillman wrote that "[t]his bill is modeled after the Mississippi statue which has been tested in court and proven constitutional."

57. Charles A. Lofgreen, *The Plessy Case: A Legal-Historical Interpretation* (New York: Oxford University Press, 1987), 1–6; Catherine A. Barnes, *Journey from Jim Crow: The Desegregation of Southern Transit* (New York: Columbia University Press, 1989), 6–7; and Otto Olsen, ed., *The Thin Disguise: Turning Point in Negro History—Plessy v. Ferguson: A Documentary Presentation (1864–1896)* (New York: Humanities Press, 1967).

58. Hale, *Making Whiteness,* 130–132.

59. E. W. S. Hammond, "Editorial Perambulation," *SWCA* (23 February 1893).

60. W. H. Heard, "The South by a Southerner," *New York Age* (2 January 1892).

61. Editorial, "The Jim Crow Bill," *The National [Baptist] Pilot* (1 February 1900).

62. Russell Russa Moton, *What the Negro Thinks* (New York: Doubleday, Doran, 1929), 72–73.

63. Elizabeth Dale, "Social Equality Does Not Exist among Themselves, nor among Us': *Baylies vs. Curry* and Civil Rights in Chicago, 1888," *AHR* 102 (April 1997): 311–340; Kevin Gaines, "Rethinking Race and Class in African-American Struggles for Equality, 1885–1941," *AHR* 102 (April 1997): 378–388.

64. Glenda Elizabeth Gilmore, *Gender and Jim Crow: Women and the Politics of White Supremacy in North Carolina, 1896–1920* (Chapel Hill: University of North Carolina Press, 1996), 82–84.

65. Evelyn Brooks Higginbotham, "African-American Women's History and the Metalanguage of Race," *Signs: Journal of Woman in Culture and Society* 17 (Winter 1992): 261–263; Barbara Young Welke, *Recasting American Liberty: Gender, Race, Law, and the Railroad Revolution, 1865–1920* (New York: Cambridge University Press, 2001), 283–299; Richter, *Home on the Rails,* 99–104.

66. Anna J. Cooper, *A Voice from the South* (Xenia, Ohio: Aldine Printing House, 1892; repr., New York: Oxford University Press, 1988), 89–90, as quoted in Richter, *Home on the Rails,* 46.

67. *A Documentary History of Arkansas*, ed. Williams et al., 155.

68. Editorial, "Separating the Races on the Cars," *SWCA* (13 March 1890).

69. Editorial, untitled, *CI* (19 March 1898).

70. C. Vann Woodward, *The Strange Career of Jim Crow* (New York: Oxford University Press, 1974), 23–24, 27–28, 38–40; Woodward, *Origins of the New South,* 216; Ayers, *Promise of the New South,* 16–20, 136–146; Hale, *Making Whiteness,* 127. For theoretical and historical insights into southern railroads and streetcars as sites of interracial tension, see especially Robin D. G. Kelley, "Congested Terrain: Resistance on Public Transportation," in *Race Rebels: Culture, Politics, and the Black Working Class* (New York: Free Press, 1994), 55–77. Also August Meier and Elliot Rudwick, "The Boycott Movement against Jim Crow Street Cars in the South, 1900–1906," in *Along the Color Line: Exploration in the Black Experience,* ed. August Meier and Elliot Rudwick (Urbana: University of Illinois Press, 1977), 16–20; Neil R. McMillen, *Dark Journey: Black Mississippians in the Age of Jim Crow* (Urbana: University of Illinois Press, 1989), 293–295; Lester C. Lamon, *Black Tennesseans, 1900–1930* (Knoxville: University of Tennessee Press, 1977), 20–36; and George C. Wright, *Life Behind a Veil: Blacks in Louisville, Kentucky, 1865–1930* (Baton Rouge: Louisiana State University Press, 1985), 52–55.

71. Moton, *What the Negro Thinks,* 79.

72. "Baldy Taylor Simply Protects Himself," *SWCA* (18 September 1902).

73. Lofgreen, *The Plessy Case,* 22.

74. Amy Robinson, "It Takes One to Know One: Passing and Communities of Common Interest," *Critical Inquiry* 20 (Summer 1994): 715–736.

75. Moton, *What the Negro Thinks,* 80.

76. Daniel A. Rudd and Theodore [Scott] Bond, *From Slavery to Wealth: The Life of Scott Bond. The Rewards of Honesty, Industry, Economy, and Perseverance* (Madison, Ark.: The Journal Printing Company, 1917), 205.

77. Testimony of Charles Dortch, in Rawick, *The American Slave: A Composite Autobiography, Arkansas Narratives,* vol. 1, pt. II, 176–177.

78. J. William Harris, "Etiquette, Lynching, and Racial Boundaries in Southern History: A Mississippi Example," *AHR* 100 (1995): 387–410; Harris, *Deep Souths,* 75–82; Ayers, *Promise of the New South,* 136–146; Hale, *Making Whiteness,* 127–130, 130–132. On the relationship between middle-class identity in the late 1800s and the "visual," see T. J. Jackson Lears, *No Place of Grace: Antimodernism and the Transformation of American Culture, 1880–1920* (New York: Pantheon, 1981), 1–47; and more broadly, Karen Halttunen, *Confidence Men and Painted Women: A Study of Middle Class Culture in Victorian America, 1830–1870* (New Haven: Yale University Press, 1980).

79. Editorial, "Justice Requires the Protection of Both," *SWCA* (3 July 1902).

80. J. R. Howard, "Lincoln's Anniversary in the 'Model City of the South," *SWCA* (5 March 1891).

81. J. M. E., "Separate Coaches," *Arkansas Gazette* (1 July 1890).

82. Glenda Gilmore, *Gender and Jim Crow: Women and the Politics of White Supremacy in North Carolina, 1896–1920* (Chapel Hill: University of North Carolina Press, 1996), 87–88.

83. Editorial, *Arkansas Mansion* (28 July 1893), reprinted from *The Interstate News.*

84. "Deeds of Devils. A Mob of Armed Negroes Rob the Station Agent at Linwood," *AG* (11 December 1891).

85. "Blacks on a Bender. Bloody and Fatal Row on the Alzheimer Branch. One Negro Killed Instantly, and a Woman Slightly wounded in the Fracas," *AG* (22 January 1896). See also "Deeds of Devils. A Mob of Armed Negroes Rob the Station Agent at Linwood," *AG* (11 December 1891). On the idea of manners as a battleground of racial conflict, see Robin Kelley, "We Are Not What We Seem: Rethinking Black Working-Class. Opposition in the Jim Crow South," *JAH* 80 (June 1993): 75–112.

86. C. H. Andrews, Jr., "Discussed: African Migration-Washington's Birthday Celebration," *IF* (24 February 1894). See also the letter to the editor by E. W. Johnson, of Little Bay, Arkansas, *SWCA* (29 October 1891).

87. William Holmes, *History, Anniversary Celebration and Financial Report of the Work of the Phillips, Lee, and Monroe County Missionary Baptist District Association From Its Organization, November 10th, 1879 to November 9th, 1889* (Helena, Ark.: Helena World Job Print, 1890), 70, AHC.

88. J. W. Hudson, "Baton Rouge District, Fourth Rouge," *SWCA* (1 January 1891).

89. "A.C.," *SWCA* (22 June 1898).

90. J. W. Reed, "From Little Rock, Ark.," *CI* (26 July 1902).

91. David Harrison, "Our Own Literature in Preference of any Other an Cost," *SWCA* (4 October 1891).

92. J. H. Agnew, "From the Booneville Circuit," *CI* (18 May 1901).

93. J. W. Spearman, "A Word to the Ministers," *CI* (16 January 1904). The *Southwestern Christian Recorder* openly praised the work of another black minister, Reverend Pierre Landry, pastor of St. Paul's Methodist Episcopal Church in Shreveport, Louisiana, for implementing a similar use of the idea of a railroad trip to develop a fund-raiser for a new church roof in 1890. Landry sold tickets to a fictitious "railroad excursion." These were no ordinary tickets, however, as purchasers found out upon examining them closely, but were actually printed cards that deftly combined references to the church's financial need, the story of Exodus, and experience of train travel. "We are now

passing through the tunnel of Mount Indebtedness with one more river to cross. With your help we will soon bridge the same and extend this line over into the promised land of Free Deliverance. Fare for the round-trip. Pullman palace coaches, $20; vestibule palace coaches, $15; parlor reclining chair, $10; first-class passengers coaches, $5; second class passenger coaches, $1." Editorial [untitled] on Reverend Pierre Landry, *SWCA* (2 January 1890).

94. "North Little Rock Conference," *CI* (13 August 1904).

95. Letter to the Editor, *CI* (24 December 1904).

96. On metaphors as forces that can shape the telling of individual histories, see Mary Hesse, *Revolutions and Reconstruction in the Philosophy of Science* (Bloomington: Indiana University Press, 1980), 111–124; Donald Davidson, "What Metaphors Mean," in *Inquiries into Truth and Interpretation* (Oxford: Oxford University Press, 1984); Bonnie G. Smith, "Gender and the Practices of Scientific History: The Seminar and Archival Research in the Nineteenth Century," *AHR* 100 (October 1995): 1150–1153; and idem, *The Gender of History: Men, Women, and Historical Practice* (Cambridge: Harvard University Press, 1998).

97. B. P. Williamson, Letter to the Editor, *CI* (7 August 1904).

98. Clarence Deming, *By-Ways of Nature and Life* (New York: G. P. Putnam's Sons, 1884), 361.

99. Mary Church Terrell, *A Colored Woman in a White World* (Washington, D.C.: Ransdell, 1940), 15–16, 298. Ida B. Wells, *Crusade for Justice: The Autobiography of Ida B. Wells* (Chicago: University of Chicago Press, 1970), 18–20. For a treatment of Wells' railroad incident and a fine accounting of her life, see Patricia Schechter, *Ida B. Wells-Barnett and American Reform, 1880–1930* (Chapel Hill: University of North Carolina, 2001), 43–48. On Anna Cooper, see her *A Voice from the South*, 91–97. For an insightful analysis on Cooper's life, see Kevin Gaines, *Uplifting the Race: Black Leadership, Politics, and Culture in the Twentieth Century* (Chapel Hill: University of North Carolina, 1996), 128–151.

100. "A Railroad that Protects a Lonely Woman," *SWCA* (29 July 1897).

101. "Mrs. Bishop Cottrell Sues for Damages," *CI* (17 December 1904).

102. *Journal of the Proceedings of the Sixth Session of the Upper Mississippi Annual Conference of the Methodist Episcopal Church Held at Grenada, Mississippi, January 8th-13th, 1896* (Starkville, Miss.: E. I. Reid's Steam Printing Office, 1896), 20, Cain Archives.

103. "Separate Coaches on Railroad," *The [Pine Bluff] Hornet* (5 May 1900).

104. Michelle Mitchell, *Righteous Propagation*, 81–85, 114–117; Gilmore, *Gender and Jim Crow*, 62–63, 75–76, 83, 88; Gaines, *Uplifting the Race*, 12–13, 137–138; Schechter, *Ida B. Wells and American Reform*, 44–48, 51–59; Harris, *Deep Souths*, 152–153, 154–155, 160–164; Hale, *Making Whiteness*, 22, 31–35. More generally, see Paula Giddings, *When and Where I Enter: The Impact of Black Women on Race and Sex in America* (New York: Bantam, 1985); Jacqueline Jones, *Labor of Love, Labor of Sorrow: Black Women, Work, and the Family, From Slavery to the Present* (New York: Vintage, 1986); and Herbert G. Gutman, *The Black Family in Slavery and Freedom, 1750–1925* (New York: Vintage, 1976).

105. Testimony of Peggy Lesure in Mrs. L. D. McAfee, *History of the Woman's Missionary Society in the Colored Methodist Episcopal Church Comprising its Founders, Organizations, Pathfinders, Subsequent Developments and Present Status* (Phenix City, Ala.: Phenix City Herald, 1934; repr., Phenix City, Ala.: Phenix City Herald, 1945), 83–86.

106. Testimony of Mrs. V. K. Glenn in McAfee, *History of the Woman's Missionary Society,* 43–45. In another episode revealing how Lesure conceptualized salvation in the language of the railroad, she detailed a scene in which her train "struck a weak place on the river bridge." "The train was shaking, the passengers began to scream." She quickly jumped into action. "I ran and helped the porter shut down the windows. I sat down and began singing: 'Life's Railway to Heaven.'" The train quickly stabilized. When asked by the conductor how she stayed so calm, Lesure replied, "Sir, when I boarded your train, I had two tickets, and if your train can't make it, thank God, I have a ticket that hasn't been punched." Lesure expressed confidence in her own safety and salvation through common railroad parlance: by invoking the image of an unused ticket, she communicated that it was simply not her time to "punch out" or die. McAfee, *History of the Woman's Missionary Society,* 46.

107. Frances Joseph-Gaudet, *He Leadeth Me* (New Orleans: Louisiana Printing Company, 1913), 13–14.

108. Albert J. Raboteau, *Slave Religion: The Invisible Institution in the Antebellum South* (New York: Oxford University Press, 1978), 236–237; Bruce Rosenberg, *The Art of the American Folk Preacher* (New York: Oxford University Press, 1970).

109. Howard Odum, "Folk Song and Folk Poetry as Found in the Secular Songs of the Southern Negroes," *Journal of American Folklore* 24 (1911): 261.

110. On Gates, see Paul Oliver, *Songsters and Saints: Vocal Traditions on Race Records* (Cambridge: Cambridge University Press, 1984), 160.

111. All lyrics transcribed from Rev. J. M. Gates, *Death's Black Train is Coming*, in *Roots N' Blues: The Retrospective, 1925–1950* (New York: Columbia-Sony, 1992, four compact discs, C4K 479011), Blues Archive, University of Mississippi, Oxford, Mississippi.

112. Rev. A. Nix and His Congregation, *Black Diamond Express to Hell*, in Rev. A. W. Nix, *Complete Recorded Works in Chronological Order* (Vienna, Austria: Document Records, 1995, compact disc, DOCD-5328), Blues Archive. University of Mississippi, Oxford, Mississippi. For background information on Nix, and a partial transcription of the lyrics, see Oliver, *Songsters and Saints,* 150–152.

113. It is difficult to establish precisely when the blues began. Among the earliest scholarly observers was Charles Peabody, who published the results of his fieldwork in 1901 and 1902 in "Notes on Negro Music," *Journal of American Folklore* vol. 16, no. 2 (July–September, 1903): 148–152. Peabody offered evidence of blues style of music performed by Delta blacks in Clarksdale, Mississippi. David Evans, *Big Road Blues: Tradition and Creativity in the Folk Blues* (Berkeley: University of California Press, 1982), 32–40, argues that the blues began in the last two decades of the nineteenth century. See also Jeff Todd Titon, *Early Downhome Blues: A Musical and Cultural Analysis* (Urbana: University of Illinois Press, 1977), 3–34; William Ferris, *Blues From the Delta* (Garden City, N.Y.: Anchor/Doubleday, 1978), 30–34; Oliver, *Songsters and Saints,* 1–17; idem, *Blues Fell This Morning: Meaning in the Blues* (1960; repr., Cambridge: Cambridge University Press, 1990), xix–xxiv, 1–12; William Barlow, *"Looking Up at Down": The Emergence of Blues Culture* (Philadelphia: Temple University Press, 1997), 7–21; and Harris, *Deep Souths,* 186–187.

114. W. C. Handy, *Father of the Blues: An Autobiography by W. C. Handy,* ed. Arna Bontemps (New York: MacMillan, 1941; repr., New York: Collier, 1970), 78, 80–82.

115. Hemphill, *Fevers, Floods, and Faith,* 261.

116. Evans, *Big Road Blues,* 44; Ayers, *The Promise of the New South,* 390; and Oliver, *Songsters and Saints,* 246–47.

117. On the cultural associations between religion and the blues, see Jon Michael Spencer, *Blues and Evil* (Knoxville: University of Tennessee Press, 1999); Robert Sacre, "The Saints and the Sinners under the Swing of the Cross," in *Saints and Sinners: Religion, Blues and (D)Evil in African-American Literature,* ed. Robert Sacre (Leige: Société liégeoise de musicologie, 1996), 3–36; Christopher Lornell, "Barrelhouse Singers and Sanctified Preachers," in *Saints and Sinners,* ed. Sacre, 37–49; Guido van Rijn, "Denomination Blues, Texas Gospel with Novelty Accompaniment by Washington Phillips," in *Saints and Sinners,* ed. Sacre, 135–166; Oliver, *Songster and Saints,* esp. 1–18, 199–229; Ferris, *Blues from the Delta,* 79–85; Paul Garon, "Blues and the Church: Revolt and Resignation," *Living Blues* 1 (Spring 1970): 3–10; James Cone, *The Spirituals and the Blues—An Interpretation* (New York: Seabury, 1972); and Red Gruner, "The Blues as a Secular Religion," *Blues World* (April 1970–June 1970): 29–32.

118. Handy, *Father of the Blues,* 91–92; Oliver, *Songsters and Saints,* 204; Evans, *Big Road Blues,* 107; Paul Harvey, *Redeeming the South: Religious Cultures and Racial Identities among Southern Baptists* (Chapel Hill: University of North Carolina Press, 1997), 115–116, 180.

119. Odum, "Folk-Song and Folk-Poetry," 261.

120. Harris, *Deep Souths,* 188; Robert Palmer, *Deep Blues: A Musical and Cultural History of the Mississippi Delta* (New York: Viking, 1981), 51–53.

121. Lyrics from Palmer, *Deep Blues,* 53–54.

122. Evans, *Big Road Blues,* 45; Lyrics from Titon, *Early Downhome Blues,* 81.

123. David Evans, *Tommy Johnson* (London: November Books, 1971), 19, 63. Blues Archive, University of Mississippi, Oxford.

124. Tommy Johnson, *Delta Slide* in *Some Cold Rainy Day* (Macon, Ga.: Southern Preservation Records, 1972, compact disc, PRP 23582), Blues Archive, University of Mississippi, Oxford, Mississippi.

125. Tommy Johnson, *I Wonder to Myself,* in *Some Cold Rainy Day* (Macon: Southern Preservation Records, 1972, compact disc, PRP 23582), Blues Archive, University of Mississippi, Oxford, Mississippi.

126. Henry Thomas, "When the Train Comes Along," *Henry Thomas Sings the Texas Blues* (Berkley: Origin Jazz Records, *OJL* V3, 331/3 rpm), Blues Archive, University of Mississippi, Oxford, Mississippi.

127. Blind Lemon Jefferson, *All I Want is That Pure Religion,* in *Complete Recorded Works of Blind Lemon Jefferson, 1925–1929* (Vienna, Austria: Document Records, 1990) DOCD 80CD 520, 3 compact disks, Blues Archive, University of Mississippi, Oxford, Mississippi.

CHAPTER 2

1. *Journal of Proceedings of the Twenty-Second Annual Session of District Grand Lodge of Mississippi, no. 10, G.U.O. of O.F.,* comp. by J. G. Turner, District Grand Secretary (Kosciusko, Miss.: Preacher-Safeguard Book Print, 1901), 43, MDAH.

2. Charles H. Brooks, *The Official History and Manual of the Grand United Order of Odd Fellows in America* (Philadelphia: Odd Fellows' Journal Print, 1902), 13.

3. In the literature on black life in either the Arkansas or Mississippi Delta, fraternal culture is either ignored or portrayed, in descriptive terms, as a buffer against racism. See, for example, Fon Gordon, *Caste and Class: The Black Experience in Arkansas, 1880–1920* (Athens: University of Georgia Press, 1995), 4, 94; William Harris, *Deep Souths: Delta, Piedmont, and Sea Islands Society in the Age of Segregation* (Baltimore: Johns Hopkins Press, 2001), 280; and Nan Woodruff, *American Congo: The African American Freedom Struggle in the Delta* (Cambridge: Harvard University Press, 2004), 83–84, who argues for the role of fraternal culture in black political organization but who relies almost exclusively on secondary sources. The main exception is Steven Hahn, *A Nation Under Our Feet: Black Political Struggles in the Rural South from Slavery to the Great Migration* (Cambridge: Harvard University Press, 2003), who closely analyzes black fraternal orders in the context of what he labels a rural African American political culture.

4. On the relationship between fraternal orders and economic enterprise, see the classic statements by Booker T. Washington, *The Story of the Negro: The Rise of the Race from Slavery,* vol. 2 (New York: Doubleday, Page, 1909), 170, 165–169, 171; Carter G. Woodson, "Insurance Business Among the Negroes" *Journal of Negro History* 14 (Jan., 1929): 202; Edward Palmer, "Negro Secret Societies," *Social Forces* 23 (December 1944): 210, 211; E. Franklin Frazier, *The Negro Family in the United States* (New York: MacMillan, 1949), 370; August Meier, *Negro Thought in America: Racial Ideologies in the Age of Booker T. Washington* (Ann Arbor: The University of Michigan Press, 1963), 121, 136, 137; and Joel Walker, "The Social Welfare Policies, Strategies, and Programs of Black Fraternal Orders in the Northeastern United States, 1896–1920" (Ph.D. diss., Columbia University, 1985), introduction. Other authors that note the significance of economic enterprise of black fraternal orders to black life as part of wider studies include David T. Beito, "The Lodge Practice Evil Reconsidered: Medical Care Through Fraternal Societies, 1900–1930," *Journal of Urban History,* 23 (July 1997): 569–600; Dennis N. Minelich, "A Socioeconomic Portrait of Prince Hall Masonry in Nebraska, 1900–1920," *Great Plains Quarterly,* 17 (Winter 1997): 35–47; Beito, "Black Fraternal Hospitals in the Mississippi Delta, 1942–1967," *Journal of Southern History* 65 (February 1999): 109–140; David M. Fahey, *The Black Lodge in White America: "True Reformer" Browne and His Economic Strategy* (Dayton, Ohio: Wright State University Press, 1994); Earl Lewis, *In Their Own Interests: Race, Class, and Power in Twentieth-Century Norfolk* (Berkeley: University of California Press, 1991); Joe William Trotter, Jr., *Coal, Class, and Color: Blacks in Southern West Virginia 1915–32* (Urbana: University of Illinois Press, 1990); Elsa Barkley Brown, "Womanist Consciousness: Maggie Lena Walker and the Independent Order of Saint Luke," *Signs: Journal of Women in Culture and Society* 14 (Spring 1989): 610–633; and David G. Hackett, "The Prince Hall Masons and the African American Church: The Labors of Grand Master and Bishop James Walker Hood, 1831–1918," *Church History* 69, no. 4 (Dec. 2000): 770–802. Historians who treat the importance of black fraternal orders in larger works about postbellum black culture include Harry J. Walker, "Negro Benevolent Societies in New Orleans: A Study of Their Structure, Function, and Membership" (M.A. thesis, Fisk University, 1937); Hylan Lewis, *Blackways of Kent* (Chapel Hill: University of North Carolina Press, 1955); David Gerber, *Black Ohio and the Color Line, 1860–1915* (Urbana: University of Illinois Press, 1976); Peter I. Rachleff, *Black Labor in the South: Richmond, Virginia, 1865–1890* (Philadelphia: Temple University Press, 1984); Claude F. Jacobs, "Benevolent Societies of New Orleans During the late Nineteenth and Early Twentieth Centuries," *Louisiana*

History, 29 (Winter 1988): 21–33; Gordon, *Caste and Class;* Harris, *Deep Souths;* Woodruff, *American Congo;* and Hahn, *A Nation Under Our Feet.* On the relationship between fraternal orders and racial self-help, see specifically E. Franklin Frazier, *Black Bourgeois: The Rise of a New Middle Class in the United States* (New York: Free Press, 1957), 87; William Muraskin, *Middle Class Blacks in a White Society: Prince Hall Free-masonry in America* (Berkeley: University of California Press, 1975), 37; and Loretta J. Williams, *Black Freemasonry and Middle-Class Realities* (Columbia: University of Missouri Press, 1980).

5. I. S. Persons, "The Propriety of Closing the Doors of Various Churches," *CI* (16 May 1891); *SWCA* (9 September 1892).

6. Editorial, "The Church and the Secret Society," *CI* (16 February 1889).

7. Lynn Dumenil, *Freemasonry and American Culture, 1880–1930* (Princeton: Princeton University Press, 1984), 32–42; Mark Carnes, *Secret Ritual and Manhood in Victorian America* (New Haven: Yale University Press, 1989), ix, 24–26, 74–75; and Mary Ann Clawson, *Constructing Brotherhood: Class, Gender, and Fraternalism* (Princeton: Princeton University Press, 1989), 53–76.

8. David G. Hackett, "Gender and Religion in American Culture," *Religion and American Culture* 5 (Summer 1995): 127–157; and idem, "The Prince Hall Masons," 798–800.

9. Palmer, "Negro Secret Societies," 208–209; W. E. B. Du Bois, *Economic Cooperation Among Negro Americans,* (Atlanta: The Atlanta University Press, 1907), 21, 22; Gary B. Nash, *Forging Freedom: The Formation of Philadelphia's Black Community* (Cambridge: Harvard University Press, 1988), 98–101, 210; Hackett, "The Prince Hall Masons," 778. See also William H. Upton, *Negro Masonry* (Cambridge: The Most Worshipful Prince Hall Grand Lodge of Massachusetts, 1902).

10. "Knights of Pythias. The Origin and Growth of the Order among the Colored People," 8 June 1887, *The Boston Herald,* (as reprinted in 11 June 1887), *New York Freeman,* in E. A. Williams, S. W. Green, Jos. L. Jones, *History and Manual of the Colored Knights of Pythias of N.A., S.A., E.A., A, and A.* (Nashville: National Baptist Publishing Board, 1917), 192–195, 223, 302; Du Bois, *Economic Cooperation,* 121–24. At times slight discrepancies existed between these sources of membership totals. In these cases, I used the lowest total.

11. "Masonic Notes. Second Day of Grand Lodge Meeting of Colored Masons," *AG* (15 August 1891), article contained in the Reverend J. Lucey Scrapbook, vol. 1, unnumbered pages, ADLR; *Proceedings of the 21st Annual Convention of the Most Worshipful Grand Lodge of the Free & Accepted Masons for the State of Louisiana, Held at Masonic Hall, New Orleans, Louisiana, Jan. 15th, 16th, & 17th, 1884* (New Orleans: The Lodge, 1884), 54, 71, 22; *Proceedings of the 24th Annual Convention of the Most Worshipful Grand Lodge of the Free & Accepted Masons for the State of Louisiana, 1887,* (New Orleans: The Lodge, 1887), 28, 53, 61; *Proceedings of the 38th Annual Convention of the Most Worshipful Grand Lodge of the Free & Accepted Masons for the State of Louisiana, 1900–1901* (New Orleans: The Lodge, 1901), 31, 180; all three volumes of *Proceedings* are in box 28, folder 8, George Longe, Jr., Papers, Amistad. The rates of increase in lodges in Mississippi and Arkansas roughly correlate with rates of increase nationally. For example, the Odd Fellows, the largest group, claimed 4,000 members and 89 lodges for the entire country in 1868; 36,853 members and 1,000 lodges in 1886; 155,537 members and 2047 lodges by 1896; and about 300,000 members and 4,000 lodges by 1904; see Brooks, *The Official*

History and Manual of the Grand United Order of Odd Fellows, 271; Du Bois, *Economic Cooperation*, 115.

12. *Journal of Proceedings of the Twenty-Second Annual Session of District Grand Lodge of Mississippi, no. 10, G.U.O. Of O.F.,* comp. by J. G. Turner, District Grand Secretary (Kosciusko, Miss.: Preacher-Safeguard Book Print, 1901), 27–28, MDAH.

13. Bishop William Elder to Right Reverend Herbert Vaughn, Bishop of Salford, England, 30 March 1873, Bishop Elder Letter Book no. 14, 1872–1873, ADJ.

14. Quote from John Graham, *Mississippi Circuit Riders, 1865–1965* (Nashville: Parthenon, 1967), 110.

15. Bishop Charles Henry Phillips, *From the Farm to the Bishopric* (Nashville: Parthenon, 1932), 60, TSLA.

16. Alferdteen Harrison, *A History of the Most Worshipful Stringer Grand Lodge: Our Heritage is Our Challenge* (Jackson, Miss.: Most Worshipful Stringer Grand Lodge Free and Accepted Masons Prince Hall Affiliate of the State of Mississippi, 1977), 28–31. Harrison is the only scholar to date who has gained access to the printed records of the Most Worshipful Stringer Grand Lodge. Her book contains numerous excerpts from those records, and I quote from them in this chapter.

17. Rev. Revels A. Adams, *Cyclopedia of African Methodism in Mississippi* (n.p., 1902), 132–137, 190–193; Bishop J. W. Hood, *One Hundred Years of the AME Zion Church* (New York: AME Zion Book Concern, 1895, 1–3. On Hood, see Sandy Dwayne Martin, *For God and Race: The Religious and Political Leadership of AMEZ Bishop James Walker Hood* (Columbia: University of South Carolina Press, 1999); and Hackett, "The Prince Hall Masons and the African American Church," 770–802.

18. H. T. Kealing, "Secret Societies Among the Negroes" *CR* (12 April 1883).

19. Rev. R.S. Williams, "Signs of the Times," *CI* (3 February 1884).

20. J. E. Kuykendall, "From St. Joseph, MO," *CI* (20 February 1897).

21. "St. Luke's African Methodist Episcopal Church," box 435, folder 6, "African Methodist Episcopal Church," WPA-HRS, UAR-F. Similarly, after conducing interviews about the formation of black fraternal orders in the Mississippi Delta with black residents from Coahoma County in 1941, Lewis W. Jones reported that "When the AME Churches had been organized in Reconstruction, the Masonic lodges had been established at the same time. The earliest were two-story, with church on the ground floor and lodge rooms occupying the second story," "Memorandum to Charles S. Johnson from Lewis W. Jones," in John W. Work, Lewis Wade Jones, Samuel C. Adams, Jr., *Lost Delta Found: Rediscovering the Fisk University-Library of Congress Coahoma County Study, 1941–1942,* ed. Robert Gordon and Bruce Nemorov (Nashville: Vanderbilt University Press, 2005), 307. See also Samual C. Adams, "Changing Negro Life in the Delta," in ibid, 236.

22. Rev. W. A. Holmes, *History, Anniversary, Celebration, and Financial Report of the Work of the Phillips, Lee and Monroe County Missionary Baptist District Association, From Its Organization, November 10th, 1879, to November 9th, 1889* (Helena, Ark.: Helena World Job Print, 1890), 28, 72, AHC.

23. *Masonic Hand Book of the Constitution of the Most Worshipful Grand Lodge, as found in Most Worshipful Grand Lodge F. & A.M. of Arkansas. Thirty-Second Anniversary and Reunion, August 8, 9, 10, 11, and 12, 1904* (n.p., 1904), Henry Albro Williamson Collection, box 15, folder 3, "Arkansas," microfilm, Schomburg.

24. Hackett, "Prince Hall Masons," 796.

25. Rev. Moses Dickson, "Installation Ceremony of Lodge Officers," in *Manual of the International Order of Twelve of Knights and Daughters of Tabor, Containing General Laws, Regulations, Ceremonies and Drills* (St. Louis: A.R. Fleming Printing, 1903), 165.

26. Dickson, "Burial Ceremony of the Palestine Guards," in *Manual of the International Order,* 261–63.

27. *The Leading Afro-Americans of Vicksburg, Miss. Their Enterprises, Churches, Schools, and Lodges and Societies* (Vicksburg, Miss.: Biographia [sic] Publishing Co., 1908), 79, MDAH. ˈ

28. A. E. Bush and P. L. Dolman, eds., *History of the Mosaic Templars of America-Its Founders and Officials* (Little Rock: General Printing Company, 1924), 152–154, AHC; and Dallas T. Herndon, ed., *Annals of Arkansas* (Hopkinsville, Ky.: The Historical Record Association, 1947), 1: 563. The practice of finding a name for a society in the biblical history of the Children of Israel was also common for orders headquartered outside the Delta. William Burrell, a member of the Virginia-based United Order of True Reformers, described the founder of his order, William Washington Brown, as a modern Moses. He wrote that "[a]s Moses led the children of Israel from the darkness of Egypt into the sight of the light and liberty of Canaan . . . so did William Washington Brown lead the Negro Race through the Grand Fountain into sight of financial light and liberty. . . ." W. P. Burrell and D. E. Johnson, Sr., *Twenty-Five Years History of the Grand Fountain of the United Order of True Reformers, 1881–1905* (Richmond: by the authors, 1901), 289. Similarly, the official history of the Knights of Tabor urged members to draw courage from the order's name, which recalled the biblical battle at Tabor. "That God was with Barak and Deborah in Israel's great battle with the immense army of Sisera; they, with only ten thousand men, assembled on Tabor, to fight Jabin's army, and, if possible, win the victory and break the bondage of the Israelites. God was with Israel, and gave the victory to the bondsmen, though they were opposed by twenty-five their number." "Believing in 'the justice of the God of Israel' and laboring '[u]nder the old name of Tabor,' [w]e felt sure that the Lord God . . . would help us in our needy time." Dickson, *Manual of the International Order,* 16.

29. *The Leading Afro-Americans of Vicksburg, Miss. Their Enterprises, Churches, Schools, and Lodges and Societies,* 79, MDAH.

30. These names were recorded in the *Proceedings of the Twenty-Seventh Annual Communication of the Most Worshipful Grand Lodge, F. & A. M., State of Arkansas Held in The City of Hot Springs, Arkansas, Commencing August 8th, A. L., 5899* [sic] (Hot Springs, Ark., 1899), 80–83, 101–113, Schomburg.

31. Maurice Wallace, " 'Are We Men?' Prince Hall, Martin Delany, and the Masculine Ideal in Black Freemasonary, 1775–1865," *American Literary History* 9, no. 3 (Autumn 1997): 396–424, touches upon this idea for the antebellum era.

32. *Journal of Proceedings of the Twenty-Second Annual Session of District Grand Lodge of Mississippi, no. 10, G.U.O. Of O.F.,* 46.

33. Walter B. Weare, *Black Business in the New South: A Social History of the North Carolina Mutual Life Insurance Company* (Urbana: University of Illinois Press, 1973), 16n44. Weare notes that white insurance companies insured blacks on an equal basis with whites during Reconstruction. Following a study by the Prudential in 1881 that demonstrated higher mortality rates for blacks than whites, however, insurance companies charged blacks prohibitively high premiums or simply refused to insure them at all.

34. Vernon Wharton, *The Negro in Mississippi, 1865–1900* (Chapel Hill: University of North Carolina Press, 1947), 271.

35. Hahn, *A Nation Under Their Feet,* 416–417.

36. *Constitution of The Most Worshipful Stringer Grand Lodge of Free and Accepted Masons of Mississippi* (n.p., 1904), 31–32, Amistad. The Prince Hall Masons of Mississippi, for instance, paid one dollar per month for a maximum death benefit of $700.00; Harrison, *Stringer Grand Lodge,* 46.

37. Dickson, *Manual of the International Order,* 38.

38. Harrison, *Stringer Grand Lodge,* 46.

39. Testimony of Cinda Johnson, in George Rawick, *The American Slave: A Composite Autobiography, Arkansas Narratives* (Westport, Conn.: Greenwood, 1978), vol. 9, pt. II, 76.

40. Palmer, "Negro Secret Societies," 210n20.

41. "Colored Woodman, Certificate of Insurance, 1910," box 14, folder 22, Black Print Culture Collection, Emory.

42. Bush and Dolman, eds., *History of the Mosaic Templars,* 218, 217. Similarly, the Stringer Prince Hall Masonic Lodge claimed to have retired the home and property loans for over 240 members between 1867 and 1917; Harrison, *Stringer Grand Lodge,* 47.

43. Bush and Dolman, eds., *Mosaic Templars,* 220.

44. Burrell and Johnson, Sr., *True Reformers,* 95–100, 118, 151, 196.

45. Glenda Gilmore, *Gender and Jim Crow: Women and the Politics of White Supremacy in North Carolina, 1896–1920,* (Chapel Hill: University of North Carolina Press, 1997), 120, 121, 147–205.

46. On the political connotations of fraternal parades and other public rituals, see William Muraskin, *Middle-Class Blacks in a White Society: Prince Hall Freemasonry in America* (Berkeley: University of California Press: 1975), chap. 2. On the "performance" of identity, see Judith Butler, *Gender Trouble: Feminist and the Subversion of Identity* (New York: Routledge, 1990); and idem, *Excitable Speech: A Politics of the Performative* (New York: Routledge, 1997).

47. *Arkansas Mansion* (28 July 1883), (4 August 1883), (29 March 1884).

48. *Constitution of the Prince Hall Masons of Mississippi, 1904,* 107–110. For the rules governing Old Fellow parades, see Brooks, *Odd Fellows in America,* 242; and W. H. Gibson, Sr., *United Brothers of Fellowship and Sisters of the Mysterious Ten. In Two Parts* (Louisville: Bradley & Gilbert Company, 1897), 65.

49. On parades and public meaning see Susan G. Davis, *Parades and Power: Street Theater in Nineteenth-Century Philadelphia* (Berkeley: University of California Press, 1988), 1–23; Victor Turner, *The Ritual Process: Structure and Anti-Structure* (Chicago: Aldine, 1969); Turner, *Drama, Fields and Metaphors: Symbolic Action in Human Society* (Ithaca: Cornell University Press, 1974). On black fraternal parades and the seizing of public space, see Elsa Barkley Brown and Gregg Kimball, "Mapping the Terrain of Black Richmond," *Journal of Urban History* 21 (March 1995): 296–346.

50. Dickson, *Manual of the International Order,* 191–192.

51. Similarly, the Knights of Pythias forbid that a member "be allowed to enter the Supreme Lodge when in session, unless properly uniformed and Jeweled, or clothed in the established Regalia of his rank. . . ." Williams et. al., *Pythias,* 36.

52. Gibson, *United Brothers,* 65.

53. *Constitution of the Prince Hall Masons, 1904,* 85.

54. Carnes, *Secret Ritual and Manhood in Victorian America*.

55. *Journal of the Thirteenth Session of the Mississippi Annual Conference of the Methodist Episcopal Church, Held at Canton, Mississippi, January 12–17, 1881* (New Orleans: Willis A. Brainard, 1881), 28, Cain Archives.

56. "Knights of Pythias Membership Application. 1900," MS 267—"Memphis Black Fraternal Orders," box 1, folder 3, Special Collections, The University of Memphis, Memphis, Tennessee. See also Williams et. al., "Membership Committee," in *Pythias*, 481–490.

57. Kathleen Ann Clark, *Defining Moments: African American Commemoration and Political Culture in the South, 1863–1917* (Chapel Hill: University of North Carolina Press, 2005), 189–190, 191.

58. Joanna Brooks, "Prince Hall, Freemasonry, and Genealogy," *African American Review* 34, no. 2 (Summer 2000): 197–198, 199, 201, 203–209; Hacket, "Prince Hall Masons," 782–783, 788–791. The best rendering of this history, as Hackett suggests, is Prince Hall, "A Charge Delivered to the African Lodge, June 24, 1979," reprinted in *Early Negro Writings, 1760–1837*, ed. Dorothy Porter (Baltimore: Black Classics, 1995), 63–69; Martin Delaney, *The Origins and Objects of Ancient Masonry, Its Introduction into the United States and Legitimacy Among Colored Men* (Pittsburgh: W. S. Haven, 1853). On the development of race histories, see Laurie Maffly Kipp, "Mapping the World, Mapping the Race: The Negro Race History, 1874–1915," *Church History* 64 (1995): 610–626.

59. Kenneth C. Barnes, *Journey of Hope: The Back to Africa Movement in Arkansas in the Late 1880s* (Chapel Hill: University of North Carolina Press, 2004), 1–12; Hahn, *A Nation Under Our Feet*, 320–321; James T. Campbell, *Songs of Zion: The African Methodist Episcopal Church in the United States and South Africa* (Chapel Hill: University of North Carolina Press, 1998), 66–75; David W. Wills, "Exodus Piety: African American Religion in the Age of Immigration," in *Minority Faiths and the American Protestant Mainstream*, ed. Jonathan Sarna (Urbana: University of Illinois Press, 1998), 141–143.

60. Hahn, *A Nation Under Our Feet*, 330; Barnes, *Journey of Hope*, 6–7, 69, 79–80.

61. Nell Irvin Painter, *Exodusters: Black Migration to Kansas After Reconstruction* (New York: Knopf, 1976); Robert G. Athearn, *In Search of Canaan: Black Migration to Kansas, 1879–1880* (Lawrence: University of Kansas Press, 1978); William Cohen, *At Freedom's Edge: Black Mobility and the Southern White Quest for Racial Control, 1861–1915* (Baton Rouge: Louisiana State University Press, 1991), 139–197; Hahn, *A Nation Under Our Feet*, 332; Barnes, *Journey of Hope*, 12, 130.

62. Barnes, *Journey of Hope*, 11–12, 42–43, 76, 108–109, 112–117; Stephen Ward Angell, *Bishop Henry McNeil Turner and African-American Religion in the South* (Knoxville: University of Tennessee Press, 1992), especially 157–180.

63. Michele Mitchell, *Righteous Propagation: African Americans and the Politics of Racial Destiny after Reconstruction* (Chapel Hill: University of North Carolina Press, 2005), 58, 81; Gilmore, *Gender and Jim Crow*, 62–63, 75–76, 87–88; Kevin Gaines, *Uplifting the Race: Black Leadership, Politics, and Culture in the Twentieth Century* (Chapel Hill: University of North Carolina Press, 1996), 12–13, 137–138; Harris, *Deep Souths*, 152–153, 154–155, 160–164; Hale, *Making Whiteness*, 22, 31–35.

64. Harrison, *Stringer Grand Lodge*, 44, 50–51; Janet Sharp Hermann, *The Pursuit of a Dream* (New York: Oxford University Press, 1981), 20, 221–223, 233.

65. William Wells Brown, *My Southern Home; or, The South and Its People* (Boston: A. G. Brown, 1880), 191–197, as excerpted in Milton Sernett, *African American Religious History: A Documentary Witness* (Durham, N.C.: Duke University Press, 1999), 258.

66. Rev. Dr. C. H. Phillips, "Sermon on Brotherly Unity," *CI* (19 March 1887).

67. Williams et al., *History and Manual of the Colored Knights of Pythius*, 725.

68. The Knights of Pythias began the all-female Order of Calanthe in May 1885 and aimed "[t]o educate it members, socially, morally, and intellectually. . . ." Its leaders, a group of high-ranking male officials and their wives, designed the rituals and charter. In 1891 the Order reported 906 members nationally; fourteen years later, in 1904, it claimed 39,614 members; Williams, et al., *History and Manual of the Colored Knights of Pythias*, 724, 729, 735–38, 746, 779. In 1875, the United Brothers of Friendship started the Sisters of the Mysterious Ten. Twenty years later, according to their published history, the Sisters numbered in the "thousands," supervised their own rituals, and had raised enough money to build several meeting halls. Gibson, *History of the United Brothers*, 55–7, 97, 109, 104.

69. *Proceedings of the Fifth Grand Session of the District Grand Household of Ruth, no. 14., G.U.O. of O.F. of the State of Mississippi. Convened in the Pythian Hall, Greenville. August 4, 5, and 6, 1903 (Woodville Wilkinson County Appeal*, 1903), 4, 6–7, MDAH. For a general explanation of key labels, names and rituals associated with the Order of the Eastern Star, the women's auxiliary of the Masons, see *Syllabus of the Eastern Star[,] Queen of the South and Amaranth Degrees. Prince Hall Affiliation* (n.p., n.d.); W. J. Colville, *The Pentagram, Its Symbolism, and the Heroines of the Order of the Eastern Star* (New York: Macoy Publishing and Masonic Supply Company, 1911; repr., 1914); and W. J. Colville, *Symbolism of the Eastern Star* (Cleveland: Gilbert, 1956); all in the Mamie Wade Avant Papers, Emory.

70. W. B. Johnson, "Ruth-A Noble Type of True Women," in *The Scourging of a Race, and other sermons and addresses* (Washington, D.C.: Beresford, printer, 1904; repr., Washington, D.C.: Murray Bros. Printing, 1915, 75; M. V. P. James F. Needham, comp, *General laws and Regulations of the Household of Ruth. Grand United Order of Odd Fellows in America and Jurisdiction* (n.p., 1956), 3, Emory.

71. Elsa Barkley Brown, "Negotiating and Transforming the Public Sphere: African American Political Life in the Transition from Slavery to Freedom," *Public Culture* 7 (Fall 1994): 107–146; Glenda Gilmore, *Gender and Jim Crow*, 31–61, 119–131; Tera Hunter, *To 'Joy My Freedom: Southern Black Women's Lives and Labors after the Civil War* (Cambridge: Harvard University Press, 1997), 21–44; Jane Dailey, *Before Jim Crow: The Politics of Race in Postemancipation Virginia* (Chapel Hill: University of North Carolina Press, 2000), 1–14, 22–47; and John M. Giggie, " 'Disband Him From the Church': African Americans and the Spiritual Politics of Disfranchisement in Post-Reconstruction Arkansas," *AHQ* 60, no. 3 (Autumn 2001): 245–264.

72. The background information on the witnesses comes mainly from their legal testimonies, the only source of information on them in most cases. The original transcripts for the trial no longer exist; in fact, few original records of any sort exist for Arkansas trials during the late nineteenth century except at the level of the State Supreme Court. Lengthy excerpts of the proceedings, however, were published in contemporary newspapers, especially the *Arkansas Gazette*, the state's largest newspaper and leading Democratic press. In locating information about the trial, its witnesses, and its place in Arkansas history, I would like to thank in particular Russell Baker, archivist

at the Arkansas History Commission, for his generous assistance and willingness to dig with me through black newspapers and census records.

73. The political summary contained in this paragraph and the previous one is largely derived from John Graves, *Town and Country: Race Relations in an Urban-Rural Context, Arkansas, 1865–1905* (Fayetteville: The University of Arkansas Press, 1990), 40–55. Graves provides the best account to date on African-American life in Arkansas during the postbellum era. Other particularly helpful works include Gordon, *The Black Experience in Arkansas*; James H. Atkinson, "The Arkansas Gubernatorial Campaign and the Election of 1872," *AHQ* 4 (Summer 1945): 288–296; Garland E. Bayliss, "Post-Reconstruction Repudiation: Evil Blot or Financial Necessity?" *AHQ* 13 (Autumn 1964): 243–259; Tom W. Dillard, "'To the Back of the Elephant': Racial Conflict in the Arkansas Republican Party," *AHQ* 33 (Spring 1974): 3–15; Willard B. Gatewood, Jr., ed., "Negro Legislators in Arkansas, 1891: A Document," *AHQ* 31 (Autumn 1972): 220–233; Willard B. Gatewood, Jr., ed., "Arkansas Negroes in the 1890s: Documents," *AHQ* 33 (Winter 1974): 293–325; J. Morgan Kousser, ed., "A Black Protest in the 'Era of Accommodation': Documents," *AHQ* 34 (Summer 1975): 149–178; and Carl H. Moneyhon, "Black Politics in Arkansas during the Gilded Age, 1876–1900," *AHQ* 44 (Autumn 1985): 222–245. See also Theodore Saloutos, "The Agricultural Wheel in Arkansas," *AHQ* 2 (June 1943): 127–140; F. Clark Elkins, "Arkansas Farmers Organize for Action: 1882–1884," *AHQ* 8 (Autumn 1954): 231–248; James Fain Harris, "Political Disfranchisement of the Negro in Arkansas" (M.A. Thesis, University of Arkansas at Fayetteville, 1961); and Tom W. Dillard, "The Black Moses of the West: A Biography of Mifflin Wistar Gibbs, 1823–1915" (M.A. Thesis, University of Arkansas at Fayetteville, 1975).

74. Albert J. Raboteau, *A Fire in the Bones: Reflections on African-American Religious History* (Boston: Beacon, 1995), esp. 17–37.

75. "The Pulpit and Politics," *People's Advocate* [Washington, D.C.] (23 October 1880).

76. On the fusion movement in Arkansas, see Graves, *Town and Country*, 48–55; Moneyhan, "Black Politics in the Gilded Age," 230–235. In Mississippi, see James C. Cobb, *The Most Southern Place on Earth: The Mississippi Delta and the Roots of Regional Identity* (New York: Oxford University Press, 1992), 84–86. On black Republican opinions of it, see editorial, *BV* (16 February 1893).

77. Jerome C. Riley, *The Philosophy of Negro Suffrage* (Hartford: American Publishing Company, 1895), 19–20.

78. Testimony of W. H. Furbush, *AG* (2 August 1889).

79. Gordon, *The Black Experience in Arkansas*, 31–32; Dillard, "'To the Back of the Elephant,'" 3–10.

80. Riley, *The Philosophy of Negro Suffrage*, 19–20, 92.

81. Ibid, 19. This idea was voiced nationally and most famously by Martin R. Delany. For most of his adult life, Delany, a Virginia-born educator, backed first Whig and then Republican causes. In the antebellum era, he was a staunch emigrationist and leader of the African Colonization Society; during the Civil War, he served as a recruiter of black soldiers in New England and as the first-ever commissioned black field officer in the Union Army; during the early years of Reconstruction, he worked as an agent with the Freedmen's Bureau in South Carolina. Yet by the late 1870s, Delany became disenchanted with Republican Party politics. He grew convinced that white

Republicans withheld offices from black constituents while black Republican leaders were ill organized, immoral, and frequently undereducated. Believing that the best society was the one governed by the best educated and the most worldly men, regardless of color, Delany called for blacks to support those men whom he thought best embodied these ideals, men who were Democrats. Only by turning Republicans out of office and voting for Democrats, cautioned Delany, would African Americans ever enjoy a biracial peace and secure at least a modest degree of civil liberty. Nell Irvin Painter, "Martin R. Delany: Elitism and Black Nationalism," in *Black Leaders of the Nineteenth Century*, ed. Leon Litwack and August Meier (Urbana: University of Illinois Press, 1988), 149–171.

82. William Gravely, "Hiram Revels Protests Racial Separation in the Methodist Episcopal Church (1876)," *Methodist History* 8 (April 1970): 13–15.

83. Testimony of Reverend James Fleshman, *AG* (28 July 1989). Reverend Fleshman appeared on the 1880 Census of Pulaski County, Arkansas, as a "C[olored] Minister," *List of Bishops, Ministers, Clergymen, and Preachers as Shown in the U.S. Census Records of 1850–1860–1870–1880. Pulaski County, Arkansas*, AHC.

84. Summarized testimony of Anderson Glasgow, "Paying the Fiddler," *AG* (11 August 1889); testimony of W. R. Griffith, *AG* (8 August 1889).

85. Testimony of Reuben Wyatt, *AG* (3 July 1889); testimony of Nathan Clifton, *AG* (4 July 1889); testimony of Sam Johnson, *AG* (6 July 1889); testimony of James Wyatt, *AG* (9 July 1889); testimony of John Clifton, *AG* (9 July 1889). See also the summarized testimonies in "Bulldozing," *AG* (17 July 1889).

86. Testimony of Nathan Clifton, *AG* (4 July 1889).

87. Summarized testimony of Solomon Riddick, *AG* (17 July 1889).

88. Testimony of George Jackson, *AG* (10 August 1889).

89. Beginning in the late 1870s, the rates of sexual assault, lynching, and battery of black women rose steadily, Evelyn Brooks Higginbotham, *Righteous Discontent: The Women's Movement in the Black Baptist Church, 1880–1920* (Cambridge: Harvard University Press, 1993), 119, 152, 189, 224; Neil McMillen, *Dark Journey: Black Mississippians in the Age of Jim Crow* (Urbana: University of Illinois Press, 1989), 124–127, 159–160, 192, 193, 238–245.

90. Testimony of Nathan Clifton, *AG* (4 July 1889).

91. Testimony of James Freshman, "The Democratic Nigger," *AG* (28 July 1889).

92. Testimony of Ed Malone, *AG* (3 July 1889).

93. Testimony of John Clifton, *AG* (9 July 1889).

94. Testimony of Nathan Clifton, *AG* (4 July 1889).

95. Testimony of Sandy Barron, *AG* (4 July 1889).

96. Testimony of Sam Jones, *AG* (6 July 1889).

97. Testimony of Richard Larkin, *AG* (21 July 1889); testimony of James Freshman, *AG* (28 July 1889); testimony of W. R. Furbush, *AG* (2 August 1889); testimony of W. R. Brown, *AG* (27 July 1889).

98. Testimony of James Wyatt, *AG* (9 July 1889).

99. "Jones-Glidewell," *AG* (18 July 1889).

100. Testimony of James Freshman, *AG* (28 July 1889).

101. H.T. Kealing, "Secret Societies Among the Negroes," *CR* (12 April 1883). See also "Our Secret Societies," *IF* (16 November 1889).

102. *Journal of the Sixteenth Session of the Mississippi Annual Conference of the Methodist Episcopal Church, Held at Jackson, Mississippi, January 16–21, 1884* (Columbus, Miss.: Columbus Dispatch Office, 1884), 16, 17, Cain Archives.

103. "Straws from Uncle Joe," *CI* (9 April 1887).

104. U.S. Bureau of the Census, *Historical Statistics of the United States, Colonial Times to 1970* (Washington, D.C.: Government Printing Office, 1976), vol. 2, K-555, 517–518.

105. I. S. Persons, "The Propriety of Closing the Doors of Various Churches," *CI* (16 May 1891); *SWCA*, (9 September 1892).

106. Stephen Cresswell, *Rednecks, Redeemers, and Race: Mississippi after Reconstruction, 1877–1917* (Jackson: University of Mississippi Press, 2005), 62–63; William F. Holmes, "The Leflore County Massacre and the Demise of the Colored Farmers Alliance," *Phylon* 34 (1973): 267–274; idem, "Whitecapping: Agrarian Violence in Mississippi, 1902–1906," *JSH* 35 (1969): 165–185.

107. E. A. Williams, "The Worth of Secret Societies," *IF* (29 December 1894).

108. C. H. Brooks, "United Order of Odd Fellows," *IF* (20 December 1899).

109. *Proceedings of the Twenty-Seventh [1899] Annual Communication of the Most Worshipful Grand Lodge, F. & A. M., State of Arkansas*, 10, 11, 12–13, 17, 18, 24, 30, 31, 42–43, Schomburg.

110. Brooks, *The Official History and Manual of the Grand United Order of Odd Fellows*, 221–222. Other national lodge leaders echoed these attempts to reform behavior offensive to church leaders. One high-ranking Masonic official proclaimed that any member "who, by denouncing the Bible, would thrust discord into his lodge, and become a disturbing element, will find himself led there from. . . ." Jere A. Brown, "Masonic Department," *Cleveland Gazette* (9 September 1884). Similarly, an official with the International Order of Good Samaritans urged the dismissal of any dissolute member. "Let each lodge begin to cut off all of the dead limbs regardless of who they are. . . . If one of the members is seen drunk on the streets or elsewhere he should be dropped. . . . [If] he should be convicted of any crime he should be dropped out of our ranks." I[nternational] O[rder] of Good Samaritans," *Richmond Planet* (12 June 1890).

111. Harrison, Str*inger Grand Lodge*, 50–51.

112. *Proceedings of the Twenty-Seventh [1899] Annual Communication of the Most Worshipful Grand Lodge, F. & A. M., State of Arkansas*, 29.

113. *Proceedings of the Twenty-Seventh [1899] Annual Communication of the Most Worshipful Grand Lodge, F. & A. M., State of Arkansas*, 42–44.

114. Weare, *Black Businesses in the New South*, 11, 14–15; Meier, *Negro Thought*, 137; Woodson, "Insurance Business Among the Negroes," 208; and see also Du Bois, *Economic Cooperation*, 127. In 1890 the True Reformers discontinued a twelve-year system of offering "loans on [death] policies," apparently because of the difficulty in collecting payments, Burrell and Johnson, Sr., *True Reformers*, 149.

115. *Journal of Proceedings of the Twenty-Second Annual Session of District Grand Lodge of Mississippi, no. 10, G.U.O. of O.F.*, 26, 77, 7.

116. The previous two paragraphs are based on John Willis, *Forgotten Time: The Yazoo-Mississippi Delta after the Civil War* (Charlottesville: University of Virginia Press, 2000), 2, 46, 53–55, 57, 72, 54.

117. Harrision, *Grand Stringer Lodge*, 62–64. Harrison, using the Lodge's 1910 proceedings, points out that the highest-ranking member of the group may have absconded with $500

118. Booker T. Washington, *The Booker T. Washington Papers, vol. 3, 1889–1895*, ed. Louis R. Harlan (Urbana: University of Illinois Press, 1974), 586–587.

119. Meier, *Negro Thought*, 121–139; Louis R. Harlan, "Booker T. Washington and the National Negro Business League," in Raymond W. Smock, ed., *Booker T. Washington in Perspective: Essays of Louis Harlan* (Jackson: University Press of Mississippi, 1988), 98–110; Harlan, *Booker T. Washington: The Wizard of Tuskegee, 1891–1915* (New York: Oxford University Press, 1983); *Booker T. Washington, The Story of My Life and Works* (1900; repr., New York: Negro Universities Press 1969), 362.

120. Editorial, "What Should the Societies Do?" *SWCA* (22 June 1899).

121. Williams et. al., "Special Committee on Pythian Community," *Pythian*, 220.

122. Miss Celestine M. Johnson, "What is Required to Revive the Finances of the Church Throughout the Country," *CI* (20 February 1897).

123. A.D. Wilson, "The Church Should Bury Its Dead," *CI* (29 January 1898).

124. J. C. Powell, "The Church and the Secret Societies," *CI* (16 February 1898).

125. T. O. Fuller, *The Story of the Church Life Among Negroes in Memphis, Tennessee* (Memphis: by the author, 1939), Reading Room, Shelby County Public Library, Memphis, Tennessee.

126. *Official Journal of the Twenty-Seventh Annual Session of the Upper Mississippi Conference of the Methodist Episcopal Church held in Wesley's Chapel Church, Greenwood, Mississippi, January 11th to 15th, 1917* (Grenada, Miss.: Sentinel Print, 1917), 26, Cain. In this study of southern black churches in the early 1900s, W. E. B. Du Bois revealed that one dominant characteristic of a flourishing house of worship in the South was its level of benevolent organization, W. E. B. Du Bois, *The Negro Church* (Atlanta: Atlanta University Press, 1903) 49–80.

127. "Supply Order Form, National Baptist Young People's Union Board," box 5, folder 17, Bailey-Thurman Papers, Emory.

128. Advertisements for the Epworth League. See, for example, *SWCA* (1 January 1894), (11 January 1894), (14 October 1897), (28 October 1897).

129. Rev. J. C. Rogers, "Race Evils," *Proceedings of the 24th Annual Session of the Central District Association, Convened with the Barraque St. Baptist Church, October 14–18, 1903, Pine Bluff, Arkansas* (n.p, 1903), 15, *Records of Annual Reports, Minutes, and Other Publications of Selected African-American Baptist Associations, and other Organizations 1867–1951*, microfilm, roll 2, AHC.

130. "Gates Chapel African Methodist Episcopal Church," *Arkansas Baptist Flashlight* (June 1939). Typed copy in "Gates Chapel African Methodist Episcopal Church," box 434, F, 1, "African Methodist Episcopal Church," WPA-HRS, UAR-F. For similar examples, see "St. James African Methodist Episcopal Church," box 435, folder 4, "African Methodist Episcopal Church;" "St. Paul African Methodist Episcopal Church," box 435, folder 5, "African Methodist Episcopal Church;" all WPA-HRS, UAR-F.

131. "Gates Chapel African Methodist Episcopal Church, "Arkansas Baptist Flashlight, June 183. Typed copy in "Gates Chapel African Methodist Episcopal Church." box 434. folder 1, "African Methodist Episcopal Church." For similar examples, see "St. James African Methodist Episcopal Churc," box 435, folder 4, "African Methodist Episcopal

Church"; and "St. Paul African Methodist Episcopal Church," box 435, folder 5, "African Methodist Episcopal Church;" all in WPA-HRS, UAR-F.

132. "Bolivar County History," record group 60, box 432, folder 10, WPA-HRS, Mississippi, MDAH.

133. Reverend Francis Janssens, *Pastoral Letter of the Right Reverend Bishop of Natchez, 1886.* (Natchez, Miss.: Natchez Democrat Print, 1886), 4–5, ADJ.

134. "Diary of Bishop Janssens, Father Meerschaert, Adm., Bishop Heslin," 249, entry dated 14 April 1904, ADJ.

135. John Albert to John B. Morris, Bishop of Little Rock, Arkansas, 16 May 1914, RG-IV-A-25, box 96, folder 1.2; "Secret Societies. Pine Bluff, Arkansas," John Albert to John B. Morris, Bishop of Little Rock, 1 Jan 1915, RG-IV-A-25, box 96, folder 2; "Secret Society. Father Albert. Pine Bluff, Arkansas;" all in ADLR.

136. John Albert to John B. Morris, Bishop of Little Rock, 19 September 1916; John B. Morris to John Albert, 21 September 1916; both in RG-IV-A-25, box 96, folder 2.1, ADLR; "Burial Society. Father Albert. Pine Bluff, Arkansas," ADLR.

137. When evaluating the shifting opinions of local Catholic leaders on the matter of secret societies, it is important to note also the national context. In the late nineteenth century, the archbishops of the Catholic Church in the United States reviewed their longstanding condemnation of all secret societies. As white working-class Catholics flooded the ranks of the Knights of Labor in the 1880s, the archbishops struggled to distinguish between societies inimical to Catholicism and those dedicated to protecting the civil rights of poor citizens. See "The Pastoral Letter of the Third Plenary Council of Baltimore on Forbidden Societies, December 7, 1884," repr. in *Documents of American Catholic History*, ed. John Tracy Ellis (Wilmington, Del.: Michael Glazier, 1976), vol. 2, 418–421; and Fergus Macdonald, *The Catholic Church and Secret Societies in the United States* (New York: The United States Catholic Historical Society, 1946).

138. Du Bois, *The Negro Church*, 76.

139. Harrison, *Grand Stringer Lodge*, 47.

CHAPTER 3

1. On the Percy family, see Bertram Wyatt-Brown, *The House of Percy: Honor, Melancholy and Imagination in a Southern Family* (New York: Oxford University Press, 1994); and Lewis Baker, *The Percy's of Mississippi: Politics and Literature in the New South* (Baton Rouge: Louisiana State University Press, 1983).

2. Leroy Percy to J. B. Ray, 28 Dec 1906, Leroy Percy Papers, appendix 1, box 1, folder 14, MDAH. Thanks to Clinton Bagley for this citation. Part of this citation appears in Ted Ownby, *American Dreams in Mississippi: Consumers, Poverty and Culture, 1830–1899* (Chapel Hill: University of North Carolina Press, 1999), 68.

3. Ruby Sheppeard Hicks, *The Song of the Delta* (Jackson: Howell House, 1976), 3.

4. John Willis, *Forgotten Time: The Yazoo-Mississippi Delta after the Civil War* (Charlottesville: University of Virginia Press, 2000), 53, 54–57.

5. Jeannie M. Whayne, *A New Plantation South: Land, Labor, and Federal Favor in Twentieth Century Arkansas* (Charlottesville: University of Virginia Press, 1996), 63, 255–48. Whayne also reported that these black workers reported other forms of extra employment under the broad categories of service (6.3 percent), artisan and skilled (5.9 percent), other (1.6 percent), merchant (0.6 percent), white collar (0.6 percent). A total of 8.2 percent listed professional occupations like teacher and minister.

6. On the symbiotic role between religion and commercial culture, see R. Lawrence Moore, "Religion, Secularization, and the Shaping of the Culture Industry in Antebellum America," *American Quarterly* 41 (1989): 216–242; idem, *Selling God: American Religion in the Marketplace of Culture* (New York: Oxford University Press, 1994); Leigh Eric Schmidt, *Consumer Rites: The Buying and Selling of American Holidays* (Princeton: Princeton University Press, 1995); and Diane Winston, *Red Hot and Righteous: The Urban Religion of the Salvation Army* (Cambridge: Harvard University Press, 1999). On the spread of evangelical Christianity through commercial techniques and networks, see Frank Lambert, "'Peddler in Divinity': George Whitefield and the Great Awakening, 1737–1745," *JAH* 77 (December 1990): 812–837; idem, *"Pedlar in Divinity": George Whitefield and the Transatlantic Revivals, 1737–1770* (Princeton: Princeton University Press, 1994); and Harry Stout, *The Divine Dramatist: George Whitefield and the Rise of Modern Evangelism* (Grand Rapids: Eerdmans, 1991).

7. Albert J. Raboteau, *Slave Religion: The "Invisible Institution" in the Antebellum South* (New York: Oxford University Press, 1978), 223. On the theme of slaves owning property, see Dylan Penningroth, *The Claims of Kinfolk: African American Property and Community in the Nineteenth-Century South* (Chapel Hill: University of North Carolina Press, 2003).

8. Frederick Law Olmsted, *The Cotton Kingdom*, 2 vols. (New York: Mason Brothers, 1861), 2: 70–71, as quoted in Raboteau, *Slave Religion*, 240–241.

9. These roles are often presented as analytically distinct or even oppositional, with citizens rejecting luxury as a threat to civic virtue and consumers seeking cultural value and personal satisfaction in a world of material goods. But blacks living after Reconstruction in the Delta combined these roles and defined citizenship partly as the opportunity to access the market freely and consume its goods according to their own standards. See Lizabeth Cohen, *A Consumers' Republic: The Politics of Mass Consumption in Postwar America* (New York: Knopf, 2003), 8–9, on the African-American intersection of citizen and consumers; and her *Making a New Deal: Industrial Workers in Chicago, 1919–1939* (Cambridge: Cambridge University Press, 1990), 148–156, on black uses of the consumer market as a challenge to racism.

10. Ownby, *Dreams in Mississippi*, 65–67.

11. Edward Ayers, *The Promise of the New South: Life After Reconstruction* (New York: Oxford University Press, 1992), 81–104; statistics from 81–83. See also Susan Atherton Hanson, "Home Sweet Home: Industrialization's Impact on Rural Southern Households, 1865–1925" (Ph.D. diss, University of Maryland, 1986), esp. chapter 3; Thomas D. Clark, *Pills, Petticoats, and Plows: The Southern Country Store* (Indianapolis: Bobbs-Merrill, 1944); LeGette Blythe, *William Henry Belk: Merchant of the South* (Chapel Hill: University of North Carolina Press, 1950).

12. Hicks, *The Song of the Delta*, 11.

13. Thomas J. Schlereth, "Country Stores, County Fairs, and Mail-Order Catalogues: Consumption in Rural America," in *Consuming Visions: Accumulation and Display of Goods in America, 1880–1920*, ed. Simon J. Bronner (New York: W. W. Norton, 1989), 339–75. On blacks and their use of mail order, see Ownby, *Dreams in Mississippi*, 75; Grace Elizabeth Hale, *Making Whiteness: The Culture of Segregation in the South, 1890–1940* (New York: Pantheon, 1998), 176–179.

14. On the specific descriptions of drummers and traveling salesmen in the Delta, Hicks, *The Song of the Delta*, 105–106. On the history of commercial salesmen, see Timothy

B. Spears, *100 Years on the Road: The Traveling Salesman in American Culture* (New Haven: Yale University Press, 1995), 2, 6–13, 197–199.

15. Cohen, *A Consumers' Republic,* 42–43; Hale, *Making Whiteness,* 169–170; Ownby, *Dreams in Mississippi,* 72–73.

16. Hale, *Making Whiteness,* 152–153, 155–159, 160–161; Patricia A. Turner, *Ceramic Uncles and Celluloid Mammies: Black Images and Their Influence on Culture* (New York: Anchor, 1994), 45–59; Kenneth W. Goings, *Mammy and Uncle Mose: Black Collectibles and American Stereotyping* (Bloomington: Indiana University Press, 1994), 28–31; Robert Jay, *The Trade Card in Nineteenth Century America* (Columbia: University of Missouri Press, 1987).

17. Ayers, *Promise of the New South,* 81–103; Clark, *Southern Country Story,* 55–59; Hale, *Making Whiteness,* 171–175.

18. Nan Woodruff, *American Congo: The African American Freedom Struggle in the Delta* (Cambridge: Harvard University Press, 2004), 24–28; Ownby, *Dreams in Mississippi,* 67–73, 83.

19. Janet Sharp Hermann, *The Pursuit of a Dream* (New York: Oxford University Press, 1981), 219–246; *The Leading Afro-Americans of Vicksburg, Miss. Their Enterprises, Churches, Schools, and Lodges and Societies* (Vicksburg, Miss.: Biographia Publishing Co., 1908), 1–8, MDAH.

20. Mrs. Lizzie Collins, "Letter to the Editor," *SWCA* (22 January 1891).

21. Deuteronomy 26:1–6, King James Version.

22. Typescript, "Tunica County," 30, record group 60, vol. 415, folder "Churches— Tunica County," WPA-HRS, Mississippi, MDAH.

23. J. E. Knox, "Trip Notes," *BV* (15 June 1894). Campaigning for the same cause a year earlier, Reverend Joseph Booker of Little Rock, Arkansas, met with the same fate as Reverend Knox. During a fundraising trip through central Arkansas, he lodged at the home of Mr. and Mrs. H. B. Bennet in Marianna. Even though these black farmers were financially well-off, Booker detailed in a letter to the *Baptist Vanguard,* they refused to give money and instead "pledged to help us on the building only when they gather up the crop," J. P. Booker, "Trip Notes," *BV* (29 September 1893).

24. "Zion Wheel, Baptist," Box 418, folder 33, "National Baptist Convention of America," WPA-HRS, Arkansas, UAK-F. See also "St. Matthew Baptist Church," box 417, folder 29, "Missionary Baptist," WPA-HRS, Arkansas, UAK-F.

25. J. W. E. Bradley, "Starkville Mission," *CI* (29 June 1895).

26. In this context, "union" was a term synonymous with religious organization or group.

27. Rev. Isaac Bailey to Dr. George Sale, of Atlanta, Georgia, 1 February 1910; Rev. Isaac Bailey to Mrs. L. K. Barnes and Mrs. Cyrus Miller, 2 July 1910; both in box 1, folder 3, Bailey-Thurman Papers, Emory.

28. John Franklin Clark, *A Brief History of the Negro Baptists in Arkansas* (Pine Bluff: n.p., 1940, 20, 22, 23–31, 32, 36, 57–61, 61–63. Information on the founding dates of individual district associations is taken from the list on 23–31.

29. Clark, *Negro Baptist in Arkansas,* 33–38; and E. C. Morris, *Sermons, Addresses and Reminiscences and Important Correspondence, With a Picture Gallery of Eminent Ministers* (Nashville: National Baptist Publishing Board, 1901), introduction; Tom W. Dillard, "Three Important Black Leaders in Phillips County," *Phillips County Historical Quarterly,* 19 no. 1 (December 1980): 10–21, at http://www.cals.lib.ar.us/butlercenter/abho/docs/1980%20Grey%20Donohoo%20and%20Morris%20article.pdf. Clark included

a short biography of Morris and reprints of several of his addresses to the state convention. On the founding of the National Baptist Publishing Board and the National Baptist Convention, see James M. Washington, *Frustrated Fellowship: The Black Baptist Quest for Social Power* (Macon, Ga.: Mercer University Press, 1986), 180–185; and Paul Harvey, "Richard Henry Boyd: Black Business in the Jim Crow South," in *Portraits of African American Life Since 1865,* ed. Nina Mjagkih (Wilmington, Del.: Scholarly Resources, 2003), 56–60.

30. Robert Jenkins, "The Development of Black Higher Education in Mississippi (1865–1920)," *JMH* 45 (November 1983): 276–277; Vernon Lane Wharton, *The Negro in Mississippi, 1865–1890* (Chapel Hill: University of North Carolina Press, 1947), 250–254, 259; Patrick H. Thompson, *The History of Negro Baptists in Mississippi* (Jackson, Miss.: R. W. Bailey Printing, 1898), 146–148, 400–403.

31. Revels Alcorn. Adams, *Cyclopedia of African Methodism in Mississippi* (Natchez, Miss.: A.M.E. Press, 1902; repr., Alexandria, Virginia: Chadwyck-Healy, 1987, 41–42; Wharton, *The Negro in Mississippi,* 251.

32. James Bennett, *Religion and the Rise of Jim Crow in New Orleans* (Princeton: Princeton University Press, 2005), 50.

33. Woodie Daniel Lester, *The History of the Negro and Methodism in Arkansas and Oklahoma: The Little Rock-Southwestern Conference, 1838–1972* (Little Rock, Ark.: [T]he Conference 1979), 20–31; Harry Richardson, *Dark Salvation: The Story of Methodism as it Developed Among Blacks in America* (Garden City, N.Y.: Doubleday, 1976), 249; Wharton, *The Negro in Mississippi,* 250.

34. Lucius Henry Holsey, *Autobiography, Sermons, Addresses, and Essays of Bishop L. H. Holsey* (Atlanta: Franklin Publishing, 1898), 215.

35. Othal H. Lakey, *The Rise of Colored Methodism: A Study of the Background and the Beginnings of the Christian Methodist Episcopal Church* (Dallas: Crescendo, 1972), 102–104. Lakey points out that the Christian Index was briefly published in Memphis, Tennessee, and then Louisville, Kentucky, before moving to its permanent home in Jackson, Tennessee. C. H. Phillips, *The History of the Colored Methodist Episcopal Church In America* (Jackson, Tenn.: Publishing House C. M. E. Church, 1898), 62, 81, 82–92, 113, 127; "W.P.A. Church Records, 1785–1942 Accession 1072," box 7, file 10, section on Lane College History (not paginated), microfilm, reel 3, TSLA; Anna L. Cooke, *Lane College: Its Heritage and Outreach 1882–1982* (Jackson, Tenn.: Lane College, 1987), 1–9, 11–19, TSLA.

36. For a survey on southern black education, see James Anderson, *The Education of Blacks in the South, 1860–1935* (Chapel Hill: The University of North Carolina Press, 1988), 33–148. On the southern black press, see I. Garland Penn, *The Afro-American Press and Its Editors* (Springfield, Mass.: Wiley, 1891), 107–130 (for sketches of black editors in 1890, see 133–332); Penelope L. Bullock, *The Afro-American Periodical Press, 1838–1909* (Baton Rouge: Louisiana State University Press, 1981), 64–205; Henry Lewis Suggs, ed., *The Black Press in the South, 1865–1979* (Westport, Conn.: Greenwood, 1983), 23–65, 151–211; 313–357; Paul R. Griffin, *Black Theology as the Foundation of Three Methodist Colleges: The Education Views and Labors of Daniel Payne, Joseph Price, Isaac Lane* (New York: University Press of America, 1984), 15–16, 38–40, 101–108; and Roland E. Wolseley, *The Black Press, U.S.A.* (Ames: Iowa State University Press, 1971), 24–79. In 1870, 79.9 percent of the national black population was illiterate; in 1900, the figure stood at 44.5 percent; and by 1910, 30.4 percent. The term "national black

population" denoted African Americans over the age of ten years, U. S. Bureau of the Census, *Negro Population, 1790–1915* (Washington, D.C.: Government Printing Office, 1918), 404. On enrollment numbers, see Anderson, *The Education of Blacks in the South, 1860–1935,* 33–78; and James M. McPherson, *The Abolitionist Legacy: From Reconstruction to the NAACP* (Princeton: Princeton University Press, 1975), 146–48. On black journals, Penelope Bullock has demonstrated that of the 97 journals published between 1838 and 1909, 11 began in the antebellum period, only one in the Reconstruction era, and 85 in the post-Reconstruction years. And of the groups that published for the first time after 1877, black churches and educational institutions were the most common. Bullock, *The Afro-American Press,* 1–3. On newspapers, I. Garland Penn noted in 1891 that the total number increased from 31 to 154 during the decade 1880–1890. Many of the newspapers were started in the South and under the auspices of a black church. Penn, *The Afro-American Press,* 106–115.

37. On Washington and his patrons, see Louis Harlan, *Booker T. Washington: The Making of a Black Leader* (New York: Oxford University Press, 1972). On the role of northern white Protestant missionaries, see McPherson, *The Abolitionist Legacy.*

38. Richard Anderson Sinquefield, *Life and Times of Rev. Richard Anderson Sinquefield. African Methodist Church. West Arkansas Conference. Forty-two Years in the Itinerant Work, 1832– 1908* (Nashville: African Methodist Episcopal Sunday School Union, 1907), 28–29, AHC.

39. Morris' speech at the 1908 annual meeting of the Arkansas Baptist State Convention is reprinted in Clark, *History of the Negro Baptist of Arkansas,* 69–70, 71. On Morris' guarded response to racial violence, see Fon Gordon, *Caste and Class: The Black Experience in Arkansas, 1880–1920* (Athens: University of Georgia Press, 1993), 91, 108–109, 123–124.

40. On Turner, see Stephen W. Angell, *Bishop Henry McNeal Turner and African-American Religion in the South* (Knoxville: University of Tennessee Press, 1992), especially 123–157.

41. J. P. Robinson, *Why Believers Should be Baptized and Catholicism Exposed* (Nashville: National Baptist Publishing Board, 1911), introduction, 62–63, UAR-F (the title of Robinson's short tract is misleading; much of its focus is autobiographical); G. P. Hamilton, *Beacon Lights of the Race* (Memphis: F. H. Clarke & Brother, 1911), 175–185; Clark, *History of Negro Baptists in Arkansas,* 42.

42. Robinson, *Why Believers Should Be Baptized and Catholicism Exposed,* 63–64.

43. Sally McMillan, *To Raise Up the South : Sunday Schools in Black and White Churches, 1865– 1915* (Baton Rouge: Louisiana State University Press, 2001), 90–93, 96–97; Ted Ownby, *Subduing Satan: Religion, Recreation, and Manhood in the Rural South, 1865–1920* (Chapel Hill: University of North Carolina Press, 1990), 3–4.

44. Morris, "The Demand for a Negro Publishing House," *Sermons,* 55–58.

45. McMillan, *To Raise Up the South,* 102–103, 111; Joseph Harrison Jackson, *A Story of Christian Activism: The History of the National Baptist Convention, U.S.A., Inc.* (Nashville: Townsend, 1980), 71–78; Washington, *Frustrated Fellowship,* 180–181; Paul Harvey, *Redeeming the South: Religious Cultures and Racial Identities among Southern Baptists* (Chapel Hill: University of North Carolina Press, 1997), 243–247; idem, *Freedom's Coming: Religious Culture and the Shaping of the South from the Civil War through the Civil Rights Era* (Chapel Hill: University of North Carolina Press, 2005), 76, 150–151.

46. McMillan, *To Raise Up the South,* 103n25.

47. Rev. J. B. Webb, "Encouragement," *CR* (5 December 1878).
48. Phillips, *History of the Colored Methodist Episcopal Church*, 113, 127. Similarly, Reverend S. Harris, lectured fellow CME ministers from the central and Delta regions of Arkansas the state "that the law requires that you be a subscriber to the [*Christian*] *Index* before your character can pass and your licenses can be renewed," S. Harris, "From Little Rock, Ark," *CI* (6 October 1888). See also F. M. Hamilton, "An Earnest Appeal to the Presiding Elders and Pastors of the CME Church," *CI* (15 January 1887). On the duty of CME ministers to sell their denominational newspaper, the *Christian Index*, see *CI* (20 August 1888), (31 May 1890), and (21 June 1890). Also note that the Phillips, Lee and Monroe County Missionary Baptist Association in eastern Arkansas announced in 1887 that "we regard the building of the Arkansas Baptist College of paramount importance to all other interests of the Baptists in the State" and that "the *Baptist Vanguard* has been a great educator of our people throughout the State, and has done as much as any other agent in creating a proper missionary spirit among the people." The Association then mandated that churches in the conference pay one dollar per month to Arkansas Baptist College for the support of its teachers. Rev. W. A. Holmes, *History, Anniversary Celebration and Financial Report of the Work of the Phillips, Lee, and Monroe County Missionary Baptist District Association, From Its Organization, November 10th, 1879, to November 9th, 1889* (Helena, Ark.: Helena World Job Print, 1890), 54, 114–115, AHC.
49. *Journal of the Second Session of the Upper Mississippi Annual Conference of the Methodist Episcopal Church, Held at Columbus, Mississippi, February 3–8, 1892* (Columbus, Miss.: Excelsior Book and Job Printing Establishment, 1892), 18, 20, Cain Archives.
50. *Journal of the Ninth Session of the Upper Mississippi Annual Conference of the Methodist Episcopal Church, Held at West Point, Miss., January 11 to 16, 189[9]* (Jackson, Miss.: Press of the Mississippi Sentinel, [1899]), 37, Cain Archives. Black Baptists in Memphis and throughout western Tennessee also held an "education day" every July, when preachers held services to collect donations and to pray for the expansion of one of their regional colleges, Roger Williams College in Knoxville, *Proceedings of the Third Annual Session of the Educational Missionary And Sunday-School Convention of Tennessee Held with the Mt. Zion Baptist Church, Knoxville, Tenn., 8–11, A.D. 1890* (Nashville: Tribune Pub. Co. Print, 1890), 16, in microfilm edition, *State Conventions and General Associations of the Nashville, Tennessee, Area Affiliated with Various National Baptist Conventions, 1865–1929*, TSLA.
51. Julius Thompson, *Black Life in Mississippi: Essays on Political, Social, and Cultural Studies in a Deep South State* (New York: University Press of America, 2001), 14, 40n3. Thompson reports that no copies remain of almost every black newspaper published in Mississippi during the nineteenth century, appendix 1, 150–189. Wharton, *The Negro In Mississippi*, 272–273, is even grimmer in his estimate of the longevity of black newspapers in Mississippi, claiming that they "generally lasted only a few months." See also Neil McMillen, *Dark Journey: Black Mississippians in the Age of Jim Crow* (Urbana: University of Illinois Press, 1989), 72–108.
52. Rev. Isaac Bailey, "Moderator's Report," typescript, 3 November 1909, box 4, folder 23, Bailey-Thurman Papers, Emory.
53. *Minutes of the Proceedings of the Pastors' Union of Arkansas, Mississippi, and Tennessee Held at Helena, Arkansas, March 3, 4, 5, and 6. A.D. 1881* (Little Rock: Dean Adams, 1881), esp. 11 in *"African-American Baptist Associations—Arkansas. 1867–1951," Records of Annual*

Reports, Minutes, and other Publications of Selected African-American Baptist Associations, and other Organizations 1867–1951, microfilm, reel 2, AHC.

54. Clark, *History of Negro Baptists in Arkansas,* 57–58.
55. Cooke, *Lane College,* 18.
56. McMillan, *To Raise Up the South,* 113–114, 190–191.
57. Clark, *History of the Negro Arkansas Baptists,* 75.
58. *Minutes and Statistics of the Third Annual Session of the Arkansas Baptist Sunday School Convention Held at the Centennial Baptist Church, Helena, Ark., on the 10, 11, and 12 Days of June, 1886* (Helena: The Golden Epoch and Job Print, 1886), 7 in *"African-American Baptist Associations—Arkansas. 1867–1951,"* Records of Annual Reports, Minutes, and other Publications of Selected African-American Baptist Associations and other Organizations, 1867–1951, microfilm, reel 2, AHC.
59. *Catalogue of Arkansas Baptist College, 1915–1916,* (Little Rock: The Baptist Vanguard, 1916), 26–27, AHC.
60. For an example of churches buying shares, see *History of Phillips, Lee and Monroe County Missionary Baptist District Association,* 22. On stockholder meetings, see, "The Stockholders," *BV* (19 April 1895). In a similar tactic that also borrowed terms from the market, the Phillips, Lee and Monroe County District Association, in an effort to fill the coffers of Arkansas Baptist College in 1892, urged every house of worship in its province to hold "self-denial week," when supporters foreswore "some of the luxuries of life" for seven days and donated the extra money to their denominational school, "General Church Rally for the Benefit of Arkansas Baptist College," *BV* (27 April 1894); and "Self-Denial Week," *BV* (25 March 1897).
61. L. W. Blue, *History of the Southeast District Baptist Association of Arkansas* (n.p., 1903), box 4, folder 46, Bailey-Thurman Papers, Emory.
62. "Pine Bluff Ministerial Institute," *The Pine Bluff Weekly Herald* (27 January 1900).
63. *Catalogue of Arkansas Baptist College, 1915–1916,* 41. Eventually scholarships were given to any individual or institution that gave at least $15 to the college.
64. Jos[eph] Booker, "An Open Letter to Our Students," *BV* (25 June 1896). Two years later, anyone raising ten cash subscribers for the Christian Recorder earned a 14 karat gold "Christian Recorder Fountain Pen," *CR* (14 April 1898), and also (30 March 1900).
65. "Bank of Prosperity" Promissory Note, box 1, folder 1, Bailey-Thurman Papers, Emory.
66. Subscription advertisement featuring communion implements, *SWCA* (21 April 1896). Subscription advertisement featuring calendar, *SWCA* (28 November 1895).
67. Advertisement, "Prizes . . . Prizes," *SWCA* (23 September 1897). See also "Further Inducements," *SWCA* (23 November 1893).
68. J. C. Hartzell, "Our Southern District Campaign," *SWCA* (27 June 1895).
69. Subscription advertisement featuring Bible, *BV* (30 July 1896) and (8 October 1896). In earlier years, editors offered new subscribers a copy of Webster's Dictionary for one dollar. "Do You Want a Dictionary," *BV* (16 February 1893).
70. Subscription advertisement featuring "Emancipation Chart," *BV* (6 April 1896).
71. Editorial, "The Press and the Colored People," *BV* (14 July 1894).
72. Editorial, "To the Colored People of Little Rock," *Arkansas Mansion* (20 October 1883). See also entries for 10 November 1883 and 9 February 1894.

73. On the limits of black boycotts to change the culture of segregation in the early 1900s, see August Meier and Elliot Rudwick, "The Boycott Movement Against Jim Crow Streetcars in the South, 1900–1906," *JAH* 55 (March 1969): 756–776.

74. Advertisement for Chamber's American Encyclopedia, *SWCA* (20 July 1893).

75. Advertisement for Church Bell, *SWCA* (29 October 1891).

76. Editorial announcement, *SWCA* (20 June 1895).

77. Advertisement for Singer Sewing Machine, *SWCA* (12 April 1894).

77. *Minutes of the First Session of the North Mississippi Annual Conference of the African Methodist Episcopal Church Held in Edward Chapel, Coldwater, Miss., from November 15th to 19th, 1877* (Vicksburg: Rogers & Groome, 1878), 28, MDAH.

79. Letter from Edward Alfred Pollard to Robert Brothers Publishers, 21 May 1872, Edward Alfred Pollard papers, Special Collections Library, Duke University.

80. Harvey, "Richard Boyd," 56.

81. McMillan, *To Raise Up the South*, 32–43.

82. *Eleventh Anniversary of the Arkansas Baptist Sunday School Convention Held with the Second Baptist Church, Helena, Ark., June 18, 19, and 20[, 1891]* (Little Rock: Baptist College Print Job), 11, in "African-American Baptist Associations—Arkansas. 1867–1951," *Records of Annual Reports, Minutes, and other Publications of Selected African-American Baptist Associations and other Organizations, 1867–1951,* microfilm, reel 2, AHC.

83. *SWCA* (4 January 1894), (11 January 1894), (18 January 1894), (25 January 1894), (5 January 1894), and (30 January 1896).

84. McMillan, *To Raise Up the South*, 188, 192–193.

85. Henry T. and Mary Ann Harris papers, no. 4360, box 1, series 3, folder 8, Southern Historical Collection, University of North Carolina, Chapel Hill.

86. McMillan, *To Raise Up the South*, 26–31; Harvey, *Redeeming the South*, 20–22.

87. On the idea of multiple commodifications being performed simultaneously, and how they reflect ideas of power and authority, see Jean-Christophe Agnew, "The Give and Take of Consumer Culture," in *Commodifying Everything: Relationships of the Market*, ed. Susan Strasser (New York: Routledge, 2003), 11–43.

88. J. H. Hoke, "From the Field," *BV* (19 April 1895). For a short biography of Hoke, see Clark, *History of Negro Baptists in Arkansas*, 43. For a similar example of another Arkansas Baptist minister selling subscriptions, see also J. E. Knox, "Trip Notes," *BV* (15 June 1894).

89. H. Bullock, "From the Agent to the Entire Church, *CI* (20 August 1898). See also "Wynne District [Arkansas]," *CI* (11 January 1892). Earlier in 1885 Reverend E. Cottrell, a bishop with the CME church and an agent for the *Christian Index*, sold more than just religious literature. He offered his customers a chance to subscribe to the newspaper and to buy "a large lot of Milk for babes and Children's bread . . . at a reduced rate." All proceeds benefited the CME Church. See E. Cottrell, "Price List of Books for The Agent," *CI* (1 November 1885).

90. "Tunica County," 26, record group 60, vol. 415, folder "Churches—Tunica County." WPA-HRS, Mississippi, MDAH; W. E. B. Du Bois, *The Negro Church* (Atlanta: Atlanta University Press, 1903), 60.

91. Thompson, *Negro Baptists in Mississippi*, 170. Thompson failed to give the year of the Mississippi Baptist Convention at which Rev. Gayles spoke, but it necessarily fell prior to 1890, when the Convention was disestablished. Most likely it was sometime during the late 1880s, when the topic of preachers' income first became a popular theme.

92. Virginia Estes Causey, "Glen Allan, Mississippi: Change and Continuity in a Delta Community, 1900 to 1950" (Ph.D. diss., Emory University, 1983), 61–62.
93. *Price List of Hope, Bibles, Fireside School Books, Etc.* (Nashville, n.d.), box 1, folder 4, Bailey-Thurman Papers, Emory. On southern white and black women working as literary agents, see McMillan, *To Raise Up the South,* 118. On Bible bands, see Anthea D. Butler, " 'Only a Woman Would Do': Bible Reading and African American Women's Organizing Work," in R. Marie Griffith and Barbara Savage, eds., *Women and Religion in the African Diaspora; Knowledge, Power, and Performance.* (Baltimore: Johns Hopkins Press, 2006), 156–157.
94. On Moore, see. Butler, "Only a Woman Would Do," 158–168; and Joanna P. Moore, *In Christ's Stead* (Chicago: Women's Baptist Home Mission Society, 1902).
95. S. Bagley to Susie Bailey, 14 August 1901, box 1, folder 6, Bailey-Thurman Papers, Emory. See also Joanna P. Moore to Susie Bailey, 13 May 1896; and Eva Button to Susie Bailey, 26 February 1897, box 1, folder 5, Bailey-Thurman Papers, Emory.
96. Joanna P. Moore to Susie Bailey, 18 September 1906; Susie Bailey to Sister [Joanna] Moore, 19 July 1907, box 1, folder 7, Bailey-Thurman Papers, Emory.
97. Susie Bailey, Bible Class Report to the American Women's Home Missionary Society, handwritten, c. 1914, box 4, folder 39, Bailey-Thurman Papers, Emory.
98. "To the Public," *SWCA* (1 December 1892).
99. Rev. P. H. Frasier, "Letter to the Editor," *BV* (19 April 1895).
100. E. C. Morris, "Correspondence," *BV* (30 July 1896).
101. On Beecher's role in knitting together religion, advertising, and consumption, see Moore, *Selling God,* 85–96 and 206–208. See also 210–212 for a discussion of popular limits to advertising by churches and church leaders in late nineteenth-century America.
102. On the views of whites and especially white landowners toward the spending habits of blacks, see Ownby, *American Dream in Mississippi,* 62.
103. Iola [Ida B. Wells], "Letter to the Editor," *American Baptist,* reprinted, *New York Freedman* (16 July 1887).
104. Editorial, "The Pulpit Weakness," *SWCA* (23 January 1902).
105. *BV* (30 October 1893), (6 October 1893), (2 March 1894), and (27 April 1894).
106. *SWCA* (13 February 1896), (23 February 1896), and (27 February 1896).
107. *CR* (4 March 1897), (11 March 1897), and (18 January 1898). See also *CR* (23 August 1900).
108. *CR* (12 January 1899).
109. *CR* (12 November 1897).
110. Prof. H. H. Harris, ed., *The Advanced Quarterly: International Lessons, Fourth Quarter, October 1892* (Philadelphia: American Baptist Publication Society, 1892), box 5, folder 2, Bailey-Thurman Papers, Emory. For examples in black newspapers, see *BV* (28 April 1893), Oversized Papers 1, Bailey-Thurman Papers, Emory.
111. Letter from "Office of Child's Cararrh Remedies," T. P. Child's and Co., Troy, Ohio, to I. G. Bailey, of Pine Bluff, Ark., 12 October 1893, box 1, folder 1, Bailey-Thurman Papers, Emory; I. G. Bailey to Mrs. J. Wiley of Leeds, Kansas, 24 June 1912, box 1, folder 3, Bailey-Thurman Papers, Emory.
112. J. Winston Bailey to I. G. Bailey, 8 August 1910, box 1, folder 3, Bailey-Thurman Papers, Emory.

113. Advertisement for Mexican Mustang Liniment, *BV* (25 June 1894). For other advertisements for Mexican Mustang Liniment, though ones that feature different preachers as spokesmen, see *BV* (7 May 1896), (9 July 1896), and (10 September 1896).
114. James Harvey Young, *The Toadstool Millionaires: A Social History of Patent Medicine in America Before Regulation* (Princeton: Princeton University Press, 1961), 190–202, 219–225.
115. Advertisement for Dr. Miles' Remedies, *BV* (18 May 1894).
116. David T. Beito, *From Mutual Aid to the Welfare State: Fraternal Societies and Social Services, 1890–1967* (Chapel Hill: University of North Carolina Press, 2000), 183; Laura D. S. Harrell, "Medical Services in Mississippi, 1890–1970," in *The History of Mississippi,* ed. Richard A. McLemore (Hattiesburg: University and College Press of Mississippi, 1973), 2: 554–559.

CHAPTER 4

1. "Zion Chapel," box 417, folder 29, "Missionary Baptist," WPA-HRS, Arkansas. UAK-F.
2. On the relationship between material things and identity, see Leigh Eric Schmidt, *Consumer Rites: The Buying and Selling of American Holidays* (Princeton: Princeton University Press, 1995), esp. 3–32, 105–175; Grant McCracken, *Culture and Consumption: New Approaches to the Symbolic Character of Consumer Goods and Activities* (Bloomington: Indiana University Press, 1988); and *The Social Life of Things: Commodities in Cultural Perspective,* ed. Arjun Appadurai (Cambridge: Cambridge University Press, 1986). On the multiple links between mass-produced items and popular identity, and on how consumers use market objects in ways unforeseen and unintended by their producers and advertisers, see Lawrence Levine, "The Folklore of Industrial Society: Popular Culture and Its Audiences," *AHR* 97 (1992): 1369–1399; idem, *Highbrow/Lowbrow: The Emergence of Cultural Hierarchy in America* (Cambridge: Harvard University Press, 1988); Clarence Taylor, *The Black Churches of Brooklyn* (New York: Columbia University Press, 1994), xvi-xvii, 24, 69–70; Kathy Peiss, *Cheap Amusements* (Philadelphia: Temple University Press, 1986), 11–15; Roy Rozenweig, *Eight Hours for What We Will* (Cambridge: Cambridge University Press, 1983), 208–221; and John F. Kasson, *Amusing the Millions* (New York: Hill and Wang, 1978).
3. For theoretical insights on religious material culture, I relied on David Morgan and Sally M. Promey, *Visual Culture of American Religions* (Chicago: The University of Chicago Press, 2001); David Morgan, *Visual Piety: A History and Theory of Popular Religious Imagery* (Berkeley: University of California Press, 1998); Schmidt, *Consumer Rites;* Colleen McDannell, *The Christian Home in Victorian America, 1840–1900* (Bloomington: Indiana University Press, 1986); idem, *Material Christianity: Religion and Popular Culture in America* (New Haven: Yale University Press, 1995); Robert Orsi, *Madonna of 115th Street: Faith and Community in Italian Harlem, 1880–1950* (New Haven: Yale University Press, 1990); idem, *Thank You, St. Jude: Women's Devotion to the Patron Saint of Hopeless Causes* (New Haven: Yale University Press, 1998); and Diane Winston, *Red Hot and Righteous: The Urban Religion of the Salvation Army* (Cambridge: Harvard University Press, 1999).
4. McDannell, *The Christian Home in Victorian America,* xiv-xvi, 6–12, 12–16, 21, 26, 35–36, 39, 42, 45–48, 73, 109–114; McDannell, *Material Christianity, Religion and Popular Culture in America,* 2–3, 4–5, 69–72, 223, 271–274; and Anne C. Loveland and Otis B. Wheeler, *From Meeting House to MegaChurch: A Material and Cultural History* (Columbia: University of Missouri Press, 2003), 1–3, 61–62, 240.

5. Evelyn Brooks Higginbotham, *Righteous Discontent: The Women's Movement in the Black Baptist Church, 1880–1920* (Cambridge: Harvard University Press, 1993), 14–15, 145, 185–229. See also Higginbotham, "African-American Women's History and the Metalanguage of Race," *Signs: Journal of Woman in Culture and Society* 17 (Winter 1992): 257–267. On the views of whites and especially white landowners toward the spending habits of blacks, see Ted Ownby, *American Dreams in Mississippi: Consumers, Poverty and Culture, 1830–1899* (Chapel Hill: University of North Carolina Press, 1999), 62.

6. For example, see Mrs. L. C. Thompson, "Women's Work in the Church," *CI* (14 November 1896). Also see the calls for cleanliness issued forth by member of the Baptists Women's Convention in 1905 in Higginbotham, *Righteous Discontent,* 193.

7. *Minutes of the Second Mothers' Conference Held in Pine Bluff, Arkansas, September 8th, 9th, & 10th, 1894* (Atlanta, Ga.: Chas. P. Byrd, 1894), 16–17, in "African-American Baptist Associations—Arkansas: 1867–1952," microfilm, roll 14, AHC.

8. *Hope* (October 1893), 8, box 5, folder 55, Bailey-Thurman Papers, Emory.

9. Michelle Mitchell, *Righteous Propagation: African Americans and the Politics of Racial Destiny After Reconstruction* (Chapel Hill: University of North Carolina Press, 2004), 112, 114, 115, 117.

10. On Washington, see his *Up From Slavery: An Autobiography* (New York: Doubleday, Page, 1907), 163–175.

11. E. C. Morris, "Annual Address at the Closing of the Arkansas Baptist College," in his *Sermons, Addresses, and Reminiscences and Important Correspondence, With a Picture Gallery of Eminent Ministers and Scholars* (Nashville: National Baptist Publishing Board, 1901), 130–131.

12. Reverend C.A. Tindley, "Practical Suggestions Toward Material Progress," in *Methodism and the Negro,* ed. I. L. Thomas (New York: Eaton & Mains, 1910), 300, Schomburg.

13. Kathleen Ann Clarke, *Defining Moments: African American Commemoration and Political Culture in the South, 1863–1917* (Chapel Hill: University of North Carolina Press, 2005), 207–208.

14. Martin Summers, *Manliness & Its Discontents: The Black Middle Class & the Transformation of Masculinity, 1900–1930* (Chapel Hill: University of North Carolina Press, 2004), 34, 43.

15. On death and disease, see Valerie Grim, "Black Farm Families in the Yazoo-Mississippi Delta: A Study of the Brooks Farm Community, 1920–1970" (Ph.D. diss., Iowa State University, 1990), in which she uses a series of extensive interviews with elderly black Delta residents who, in many cases, describe life before 1920. For the Arkansas Delta, see Elizabeth Anne Payne, "'What Ain't I Been Doing?': Historical Reflections on Women and the Arkansas Delta" in *The Arkansas Delta: Land of Paradox,* ed. Jeannie Whayne and Willard B. Gatewood (Fayetteville: University of Arkansas Press, 1993); 129, 131–133. More generally, Marian M. Davis, "Death and Nineteenth Century Arkansas: Frequencies in Causes of Death in Three Arkansas Counties During 1850 and 1880," (Honors thesis, University of Arkansas, 1988); Stewart E. Tolnay, "Fertility of Southern Black Farmers in 1900: Evidence and Speculation," *Journal of Family History* (1983); 314–332; and idem, "Black Family Formation and Tenancy in the Farm South, 1900," *American Journal of Sociology* 90, no. 2 (September 1984): 305–325.

16. Thomas Ward Jr., *Black Physicians in the Jim Crow South* (Fayetteville: University of Arkansas Press, 2003), 153, 160.

17. David Beito, *From Mutual Aid to the Welfare State: Fraternal Societies and Social Services, 1890–1967* (Chapel Hill: University of North Carolina Press, 2000), 183.

18. Ward, *Black Physicians,* 70–71, 162–164, 160.

19. Ibid, 60–62, 70–71.

20. J. William Harris, *Deep Souths: Delta, Piedmont, and Sea Island Society in the Age of Segregation* (Baltimore: Johns Hopkins Press, 2001), 154–156, 160–161, 363 (table 20), 397n19. Census data is based on Harris' research.

21. Mitchell, *Righteous Propagation,* 81, 10–11, 81, 112–117.

22. Bailey, *Around the Family Altar,* 13, 15, 17, 19, 22–27.

23. Daniel Alexander Payne and David Smith, *Biography of Rev. David Smith of the A.M.E. Church; Being a Complete History, Embracing over Sixty Years' Labor in the Advancement of the Redeemers Kingdom on Earth. Including "The History of the Origin and Development of Wilberforce University* (Xenia, O[hio]: Xenia Gazette Office, 1881); idem, *Recollections of Seventy Years* (Nashville: Publishing House of the A.M.E. Sunday School Union, 1888); idem, *History of the African Methodist Church*, ed. C. S. Smith (Nashville: Publishing House of the A.M.E. Sunday School Union, 1891; repr., New York: Arno, 1969); and for a quick biographical blurb, see http://www.pbs.org/thisfarby-faith/people/daniel_payne.html, accessed 31 January 2007.

24. Daniel Alexander Payne, *A Treatise on Domestic Education* (Cincinnati: Cranston & Stowe, 1885; repr., 1889).

25. Martha S. Jones, "'Make Us a Power': African American Methodists Debate the 'Women Question,' 1870–1900," in R. Marie Griffith and Barbara Savage, eds., *Women and Religion in the African Diaspora; Knowledge, Power, and Performance* (Baltimore: Johns Hopkins Press, 2006), 137, 138, 143.

26. Jualynne Dodson, *Engendering Church: Women, Power, and the African Methodist Episcopal Press* (New York: Rowman & Littlefield, 2002), 2–3, 7–22, 41–63.

27. *Journal of the 18th Session and 17th Quadrennial Session of the General Conference of the African Methodist Episcopal Church in the World* (Philadelphia: AME Publishing House, 1884), 253, as reprinted in Bailey, *Around the Family Altar,* 86.

28. Payne, *Domestic Education,* 25, 31, 32, 39, 54–55, 58, 136–137, 163. For general background information on Payne and his notions of domesticity, see Bailey, *Around the Family Altar,* 88–95; and especially David W. Wills, "Womanhood and Domesticity in the AME Tradition: The Influence of Daniel Alexander Payne," in *Black Apostles at Home and Abroad: Afro-Americans and the Christian Mission from the Revolution to Reconstruction,* ed. David W. Wills (Boston: G. K. Hall, 1982), 140–145.

29. For information about Hughes, see Stephen Ward Angell, "The Controversy Over Women's Ministry in the African Methodist Church during the 1880s: The Case of Sarah Ann Hughes," in *This Far by Faith: Readings in African American Women's Religious Biography,* ed. Judith Weisenfeld and Richard Newman (New York: Routledge, 1996), 94–109; Angell, *Bishop Henry McNeal Turner and African-American Religion in the South* (Knoxville: University of Tennessee Press, 1992), 182–184; and Jones, "Make Us a Power," 144.

30. On the historical efforts of AME women to become recognized by the church hierarchy as religious leaders, see Dodson, *Engendering Church,* 1–3, 90–97, 114–118.

31. Payne, *History of the African Methodist Church*, ed. C. S. Smith, 154, as found in Bailey, *Around the Family Altar,* 98.

32. Bailey, *Around the Family Altar,* 37–41.

33. Harris, *Deep Souths,* 154–155; Payne, "'What Ain't I Been Doing?,'" 130, 135–138, 139–143. More broadly on the topic of rural black women's labors, see Jacqueline Jones, *Labor of Love, Labor of Sorrow: Black Women, Work, and the Family from Slavery to the Present* (New York: Basic Books, 1985); idem, *The Dispossessed: America's Underclass from the Civil War to the Present* (New York: Basic Books, 1992); and idem, "Encounters, Likely and Unlikely, between Blacks and Poor White Women in the Rural South, 1865–1940," *Georgia Historical Quarterly* 76 (Summer 1992): 333–353.

34. Higginbotham, *Righteous Discontent,* 128–136.

35. Katherine Davis Tillman, "Afro-American Women and Their Work," *African Methodist Episcopal Church Review* 11 (April 1885): 497–98. See also Mrs. Alice Jean Parham, "The Women We Need," *SWCA* (6 June 1895).

36. *Minutes of the Women's State Baptist Association and the State Baptist Sunday School Convention, Held with the St. John Church, New Port, Arkansas, June 19–24, 1893* (n.p., n.d.), 5, in "African-American Baptist Associations—Arkansas: 1867–1952," microfilm, roll 14, AHC. In 1897 an author known as "Sadie C. M." published an article titled "Women's Education" in which she argued that "[m]an endears himself to his family by his constant endeavors to support it and do that which will promote happiness, but woman is around the hearth implanting in the youthful minds the beauty and obligation of the future life and its responsibilities," Sadie C. M., "Woman's Education," *CI* (26 January 1897).

37. L. W. Blue, *History of the Southeastern District Baptist Association of Arkansas* (n.p., 1903), box 4, folder 46, Bailey-Thurman Papers, Emory.

38. *Minutes of the Eleventh Annual Session of the Women's Southeast District Association Held with the Mt. Carmel Church, Warren[,] Ark. Rev. R. A. Adams, Pastor. Aug. 23–25, 1907* (Little Rock: Baptist Vanguard Power Press, 1908), 4, box 5, folder 52, Bailey-Thurman Papers, Emory.

39. *Minutes of the Seventeenth Annual Session of the Baptist Women's Southeast Arkansas Association held at the First Baptist Church, Crosset, Ark., August 23–26, 1913* (Los Angeles: I. G. Bailey, Printer, 1913), 6–7, box 4, folder 44, Bailey-Thurman Papers, Emory.

40. *Minutes of the Forty-Fourth Annual Session of the Arkansas Baptist Women's Association which convened with the First Baptist Church, Dermott, Arkansas, June 1918.* (Los Angeles: I. G. Bailey, Printer, 1913), 11, box 4, folder 36, Bailey-Thurman Papers, Emory.

41. *Tidings,* February 1911, box 5, folder 50 Bailey-Thurman Papers, Emory.

42. *Price List of Hope, Bibles, Fireside School Books, Etc. Sold at Fireside School Headquarters* (Nashville: n.p., 1908), 1, 2, 3, box 1, folder 7, Bailey-Thurman Papers, Emory.

43. Susie Bailey, "The Training of Children," unpublished, undated essay, box 4, folder 9, Bailey-Thurman Papers, Emory. On the formation of black Bible bands and the work of Moore in particular, see Anthea Butler, "'Only a Woman Would Do': Bible Reading and African American Women's Organizing Work," in *Women and Religion in the African Diaspora,* ed. Marie Griffith and Barbara Savage (Baltimore: Johns Hopkins University Press, 2006): 155–178.

44. J. P. Moore, "Words from Workers," *Hope* 11 (April 1897):81. Thanks to Anthea Butler, who provided me with a copy of this document.

45. Dodson, *Engendering Church,* 90–97.

46. Abraham Grant, *Deaconess Manual of the AME Church* (n.p.: 1902), 108–109; Bailey, *Around the Family Altar,* 109.
47. Jones, "Make Us a Power,"128–131, 142–153; Higginbotham, *Righteous Discontent,* 185–229.
48. Editorial, "The Sacredness of Home," *CI* (16 February 1899).
49. Editorial, "Begin a Movement for Better Homes," *SWCA* (5 July 1900). See also "Iola," "The Minister Out of the Pulpit," *CI* (12 May 1888).
50. W.E. B. Du Bois, "The Problem of Housing the Negro, III: The Home of the Country Freedman" *The Southern Workman,* 30, no. 11 (October 1901): 539–541. See also Michele Mitchell, *Righteous Propagation: African Americans and the Politics of Destiny After Reconstruction* (Chapel Hill: University of North Carolina Press, 2004), 138–146; Dorothy Salem, *To Better Our World: Black Women in Organized Reform,* 1890–1920 (Brooklyn: Carlson Publishing, 1990); and Susan L. Smith, "Welfare Mothers and Children: Health and Home in the American South," *Social Politics,* 4, no. 1 (Spring 1997): 49–64.
51. W. E. B. Dubois, "The Problem of Housing the Negro, I: The Elements of the Problem," *The Southern Workman,* 30, no. 8 (July 1901): 390.
52. Du Bois, "The Problem of Housing the Negro," 542.
53. Editorial, The Sacredness of the Home," *CI* (16 February 1899).
54. Iola, "The Minister Out of the Pulpit," *CI* (12 May 1888).
55. Brunetta, "Aesthetics," *CI* (28 January 1900).
56. "Advice," *CI* (5 March 1892); Iola, "The Minister Out of the Pulpit," *CI* (12 May 1888).
57. Rev. G. I. Izard, "What Kind of Pictures to Hang on Your Walls," *SWCA* (19 June 1900).
58. Rev. Thomas Plunkett to Rev. Joseph Slattery, 31 August 1898, 19-K-8 h, Slattery Papers (before 1904), JFA.
59. Higginbotham, *Righteous Discontent,* 97. On the use of domestic spaces as arenas for the enactments of cultural proscriptions, see Lizabeth Cohen, "Embellishing a Life of Labor: An Interpretation of the Material Culture of American Working-Class Homes, 1885–1915," in *Common Places: Readings in American Vernacular Architecture,* ed. Dell Upton and John Michael Vlach (Athens: University of Georgia Press, 1986), 261–278.
60. *Minutes of the First Session of the North Mississippi Annual Conference of the African Methodist Episcopal Church Held in Edward Chapel, Coldwater, Miss., From November 15th to 19th, 1877* (Vicksburg: Rogers & Groome, 1878), 15, MDAH.
61. "Reading Culture," *SWCA* (21 May 1891).
62. "Picture Gallery," *SWCA* (23 August 1894).
63. "Our Picture Gallery," *CI* (16 February 1900).
64. Douglas print is part of the article by J. Z. Hartzell, "Our Southern District Campaign," *SWCA* (6 June 1895); Lincoln print is found in *SWCA* (30 December 1897), (29 December 1898), and (28 December 1899), on the back pages of each edition.
65. "Our Thanksgiving Gift to Everyone of Our Readers," *SWCA* (23 November 1893).
66. Advertisement for the Emancipation Proclamation Wall Chart, *BV* (6 April 1896).
67. Dorothy Dickens, *A Nutrition Investigation of Negro Tenants in the Yazoo-Mississippi Delta,* Bulletin 254, Mississippi Agricultural Experiment Station (August 1928), 10–11.

68. Mitchell, *Righteous Propagation*, 177–183; Higginbotham, *Righteous Discontent*, 166, 194–195. On the broader topic of dolls, race, and identity, see Doris Y. Wilkinson, "The Doll Exhibit: A Psycho-Cultural Analysis of Black Female Role Stereotypes," *Journal of Popular Culture*, 21, no. 2 (Fall 1987): 19–29; Miriam Formanek-Brunell, *Made to Play House: Dolls and the Commercialization of American Girlhood, 1830–1930* (New Haven: Yale University Press, 1993); and Marilyn Maness Mehaffy, "Advertising Race/Raceing Advertising: The Feminine Consumer (-nation), 1876–1900," *Signs: Journal of Woman in Culture and Society* 23, no. 1 (Autumn 1997): 131–174.

69. Mrs. Carrie Mitchell Price, "The Much Needed Parsonage," *SWCA* (8 June 1899). See also Rev. J. W. Jackson, "A Confidential Talk with Ministers' Wives," *SWCA* (14 June 1900).

70. "Why Improve the Parsonage?" *SWCA*; reprint in *Methodism and the Negro*, 293–294. The date of the editorial is not provided. It was likely published around 1908 or 1909 because it was during these years that the other articles and reprinted editorials in the book were composed or published.

71. Loveland and Wheeler, *From Meeting House to Megachurch*, 34, 46, 48, 53, 57; Jeanne Kilde, *When Church Became Theater: The Transformation of Evangelical Architecture and Worship in Nineteenth-Century America* (New York: Oxford University Press, 2002).

72. Payne, *History of the African Methodist Episcopal Church*), 463, as quoted in Loveland and Wheeler, *From Meeting House to Megachurch*, 58.

73. *Minutes of the Twenty-Third Quadrennial Meeting of the General Conference of the African Methodist Episcopal Churches* (Philadelphia: AME Publishing House, 1908), 64, as quoted in Taylor, *The Black Churches of Brooklyn*, 22.

74. Rev. R. F. Harley, Letter to the Editor, *CR* (10 May 1878). See also Sister Havvy Hill, Letter to the Editor, *BV* (10 December 1896). Outside of the Delta, see B.W. Roberts, "A Word from the Isle of the Sea [Key West, Florida]," *CR* (4 January 1877); and Rev. W. R. Harris, "Letter from Forsyth, Georgia," *CR* (2 September 1880).

75. Rev. George W. Bryant, "On the Wing," *CR* (29 January 1880); Rev. Revels A. Adams, *Cyclopedia of African Methodism in Mississippi* (n.p., 1902), 252.

76. Mrs. Lizzie B. Johnson, "Letter from Little Rock, Arkansas," *CI* (30 April 1887).

77. "First Baptist Church," box 417, folder 31, "Baptist," WPA-HRS, Arkansas, UAK-F.

78. *Minutes and Statistics of the Third Annual Session of the Arkansas Baptist Sunday School Convention Held at the Centennial Baptist Church, Helena, Ark., on the 10, 11, and 12 Days of June, 1886* (Helena, Ark: The Golden Epoch and Job Print, 1886), 6, in "African-American Baptist Associations—Arkansas: 1867–1952," microfilm, roll 14, AHC.

79. *Proceedings of the Eighth Annual Session of the Arkansas Baptist Sunday School Convention Held with the First Baptist Church, Little Rock, August 20th and 21st, 1888* (n.p., n.d.), 16, in "African-American Baptist Associations—Arkansas: 1867–1952," microfilm ed., roll 14, AHC [nb: the title of this publication appears to be a misprint and should read "Proceedings of the Fifth Annual Session"]; Loveland and Wheeler, *From Meetinghouse to Megachurch*, 57.

80. *A Journal of the Proceedings of the Seventeenth Anniversary of the Baptist Missionary and Educational Convention of Tennessee Held With First Baptist Church, Murfreesboro, Tenn., July 13th–19th, 1904* (Nashville: National Baptist Publishing Board, 1904), in the *State Conventions and General Associations of the Nashville, Tennessee Area affiliated with Various National [Negro] Baptist Conventions, 1865–1929*, "West Tennessee Association, 1887–1889," microfilm, TSLA.

81. Blue, *History of the Southeast District Baptist Association of Arkansas*, 18–19.
82. Clarence Deming, *By-Ways of Nature and Life* (New York: G. P. Putnam's Sons, 1884), 359–360.
83. See the following documents, some of which include sketches and rough diagrams of churches: "Salem," box 416, folder 19, "Missionary Baptist"; "Providence," folder 2, box 434, "Methodist [AME];" "Little Bethel," box 435, folder 4, "Methodist [AME];" all in WPA-HRS, UAK-F.
84. Rhoda Nolen, "Letter to the Editor," *BV* (10 December 1896).
85. G. W. Lewis, "From Greer, Ark," *BV* (26 July 1895). Tillman, in "Afro-American Women," 486, noted that in southern states "[i]t is the women in our churches . . . who assume the charge of clothing the pastor and his needy family in a little purple and fine linen occasionally."

Chapter 5

1. William Christian, *Notice to All the Free Masons in the World,* as reprinted in "Dangerous Doctrines," *Arkansas Gazette [AG]* (22 June 1890), microfilm, AHC. See also the comment by Christian as reported in "Turbulent Negroes," *AG* (21 June 1890). William Christian, *Poor Pilgrim's Work* (Texarkana, Texas: Joe Erlich Print, 1896), 15. For a brief account of Christian's life, see Elmer T. Clark, *The Small Sects in America* (Nashville: Cokesbury, 1937, 119, 121–122; and David D. Daniels, III, "The Cultural Renewal of Slave Religion: C. P. Jones and the Emergence of the Holiness Movement in Mississippi" (Ph.D. diss., Union Theological Seminary, 1992), 5–6. Few historical records about Christian's early life exist. On membership numbers for the Church of the Living God, see Department of Commerce and Labor, Bureau of the Census, *Special Reports: Religious Bodies: 1906* (Washington, D.C.: Government Printing Office, 1910), Part 2, 207–209. On the social composition of the Holiness movement, see Daniels, "The Cultural Renewal of Slaver Religion," 220–222.
2. Paul Harvey, *Freedom's Coming: Religious Culture and the Shaping of the South from the Civil War through the Civil Rights Era* (Chapel Hill: University of North Carolina Press, 2005), 126–130,142; Daniels, "Cultural Renewal of Slave Religion," 1–3, who rightly notes that blacks are rarely included in the standard histories of Holiness; Timothy Smith, *Revivalism and Social Reform in Mid-Nineteenth Century America* (New York: Abingdon, 1975); Charles Jones, *Perfectionist Persuasion: The Holiness Movement and American Methodism, 1867–1936* (Metuchen, N.J.: Scarecrow, 1974); Donald Dayton, *Theological Roots of Pentecostalism* (Grand Rapids: Francis Asbury Press, 1987). For an integrated treatment of the black and white Holiness movement, see Jay Riley Case, "Conversion, Civilization and Culture in the Evangelical Missionary Mind, 1814–1906" (Ph.D. diss., Notre Dame University, 1999).
3. "Another Negro Butchered," *SWCA* (29 May 1890). See also Reverend G. A. Mason, "The Negro Problem and How Solved," *SWCA* (15 June 1893); Dr. M C. B. Mason, "A New Century Thanksgiving Offering," *SWCA* (17 December 1896); J. T. Crawford, untitled prayer, *BV* (3 December 1896); editorial, untitled, *CI* (26 November 1896).
4. I use the term "Holiness" to describe the African American religious movement inspired by Christian, Jones, and Mason at the turn of the century in the Delta because it is the term that they generally employed themselves. Other scholars refer to the same movement as the sanctified church movement, in reference to the theology of radical sanctification preached by the three men and embraced by their disciples. See, for

example, Cheryl Townsend Gilkes, " 'Together and in the Harness': Women's Traditions in the Sanctified Church," *Signs: Journal of Woman in Culture and Society* 10 (Summer 1985): 678–695; and idem, "The Role of Women in the Sanctified Church," *Journal of Religious Thought* 43, no. 1 (Spring-Summer 1986): 25–28.

5. *Avant et. al. v. Mason et. al,* Shelby County Court House, Memphis, Tennessee, 1907, number 1447, page 123. The case involved a dispute between Mason and another man over who owned the property upon which one of Mason's churches sat. As part of the case, lawyers interviewed Mason in court about the nature of his beliefs and practices. Thanks to Calvin White, who provided me with a copy of this document.

6. For general treatments of the relationship between the African American Holiness movement and southern society, see Paul Harvey, *Redeeming the South: Religious Cultures and Racial Identities among Southern Baptists, 1865–1925* (Chapel Hill: University of North Carolina Press, 1997), 93–95, 113, 116, 132–34, 239–240; Albert J. Raboteau, "The Black Church: Continuity within Change," in his *A Fire in the Bones: Reflections on African-American Religious History* (Boston: Beacon, 1995), 105–107; Edward Ayers, *The Promise of the New South: Life after Reconstruction* (New York: Oxford University Press, 1995), 398–408; Ian MacRobert, *The Black Roots and White Racism of Early Pentecostalism in the U.S.A.* (London: MacMillan, 1988), 28, 34, 37–42, 50–62; Vinson Synan, *The Holiness-Pentecostal Movement in the United States* (Grand Rapids: Eerdmans, 1971), 78–80, 165–178; Charles Edwin Jones, *Black Holiness: A Guide to the Study of Black Participation in the Wesleyan Perfectionist and Glossolalic Pentecostal Movement* (Metuchan, N.J.: Scarecrow, 1987), 45–47, 59–61, 63–64, 98; Clark, *Small Sects*, 116–123.

7. Charles P. Jones, *An Appeal to the Sons of Africa* (Jackson, Miss.: Truth Publishing Company, 1902), v-xi; Daniels, "The Cultural Renewal of Slave Religion," 27–32; Shalandra Dexter, "Sojourners in a Strange Land: The Impact of Northern Urbanization on Black Pentecostal Identity and Culture in Chicago from 1940 to 1980," (Ph.D. diss., Princeton University, 2001), 62–64. The statement by Jones about his experience of sanctification is from the C. P. Jones autobiography, box 1, folder 12, Sherry Sherrod Dupree Collection, Schomburg, as quoted in Harvey, *Freedom's Coming,* 148.

8. Mary Mason, *The History and Life Work of Bishop C. H. Mason* (Memphis: Church of God in Christ Publishing House, 1925; repr., 1997), 20–24; *Official Manual with the Doctrines and Disciplines of the Church of God in Christ 1973* (Memphis: Church of God in Christ Publishing House, 1973), xxiii-xxxi; Lucille J. Cornelius, *The Pioneer: History of the Church of God in Christ* (Memphis: Church of God in Christ Publishing House, 1975), 1–16; Bishop Ithiel Clemmons, *Bishop C. H. Mason and the Roots of the Church of God in Christ* (Bakersfield, Cal.: Pneuma Life Publishing, 1996), 1–8; Dexter, "Sojourners in a Strange Land," 56–60.

9. L. W. Blue, *History of the Southeast District Baptist Association* (n.p., 1903), 20, 35, 36, Emory.

10. "Mother Lizzie (Woods) Robinson, "History of the Bible Band," reprinted from *Hope* (April 1937), in the 37th Annual Women's Convention booklet of The Church of God in Christ (1988), as quoted in Anthea D. Butler, " 'Only a Woman Would Do': Bible Reading and African American Women's Organizing Work," in R. Marie Griffith and Barbara Savage, eds., *Women and Religion in the African Diaspora; Knowledge, Power, and Performance.* (Baltimore: Johns Hopkins Press, 2006), 175. The insights of this paragraph are drawn from Butler's article, especially pages 174–177.

11. Blue, *History of the Southeast District Baptist Association,* 36–37.

12. Charles P. Jones to Rev. Isaac Bailey, 26 March 1898, box 1, folder 1, Bailey-Thurman Papers, Emory. Jones gave no reason for why he could not provide a seat for Bailey's son. Jones wrote, cryptically, "It has since developed why God did not wish your son to come here this session. But the Lord does not allow me to mention it to you."

13. "An Outline of Mount Helm Baptist Church," unpublished, unpaginated type-written manuscript, c. 1958, MDAH.

14. Frank Bartleman, *Azusa Street* (South Plainsfield, N.J.: Bridge, 1980).

15. *Avant v. Mason*, 100.

16. *History and Formative Years of the Church of God in Christ with Excerpts from the Life and Works of its Founders-Bishop C. H. Mason* (Memphis: Church of God in Christ Publishing House, 1969), 19.

17. *Avant v. Mason*, 89.

18. E. C. Morris, *Sermons, Addresses and Reminiscences and Important Correspondence* (Nashville: National Baptist Publishing Board, 1901), 32–33. For similar views by local black Methodists, see Rev. R. T. Thomas, "'Feeling not Religion,' but Religion and Feeling Combine," *SWCA* (19 October 1902); and the editorial, "Ethics of Sanctification," *CI* (14 May 1904).

19. J. H. Eason, *Pulpit and Platform Efforts. Sanctification vs. Fanaticism* (Nashville: National Baptist Publishing Board, 1899), 54–55, Schomburg. For similar opinions from national black Baptist leaders, see E. M. Brawley, ed., *The Negro Baptist Pulpit. A Collection of Sermons and Papers on Baptist Doctrine and Missionary and Educational Work* (Philadelphia: American Baptist Publication Society, 1890), 89–89, 92–96, 97, 102–103, Schomburg; Richard Boyd, "What Baptists Believe and Practice," 129, in *Once a Baptist: Now a Baptist. Why?* ed. Eugene Carter (Nashville: National Baptist Publishing Board, 1905), Schomburg.

20. Christian, *Poor Pilgrim's Work*, 21–22.

21. Excerpt from Mt. Helm Minute Book, as reported in "Mt. Helm Baptist Church vs. C. P. Jones," case number 10041, 25 March 1901 (filing date), 12 October 1901 (judgment), Mississippi Supreme Court, *Report of Cases Decided Upon by the Supreme Court of Mississippi, 1890–1908* (Philadelphia: T. & J. W. Johnson, 1900), 409.

22. Mary Mason, *The History and Life Work of Elder C. H. Mason, Chief Apostle and His Co-Laborers* (n.p., 1924), 13. The same basic version of this story survived as part of the official Church of God in Christ Web site, as part of a history titled, "The Story of Our Church: The Church of God in Christ," http://www.cogic.org/history.htm, accessed 14 June 2005.

23. "Sermon in part by Elder C. H. Mason," undated, reprinted in Mary Mason, *The History and Life Work of Elder C. H. Mason*, 29–30. Given that Mary Mason organized C. H. Mason's sermons in rough chronological order, it seems likely that this sermon was delivered in the first or second decade of the twentieth century.

24. "Sermon of Elder C. H. Mason, Memphis, Tenn[essee], 28 November 1925," as reprinted in Mary Mason, *The History and Life of Work of Elder C. H. Mason*, 34. Thanks to Clarence Hardy for this reference.

25. Charles P. Jones, *Jesus Only, Songs and Hymns* (Jackson: Truth Publishing Company, 1911), song number 100 [unpaginated], as quoted by Daniels, "The Cultural Renewal of Slave Religion," 196.

26. Undated autobiographical excerpt, as printed in Mason, *The History and Life Work of Elder C. H. Mason*, 27. See also Elsie Mason, ed., *From the Beginning of Bishop C. H. Mason*

and the Early Pioneers of the Church of God in Christ (Memphis: Church of God in Christ Publishing House, 1991), 6; and Cornelius, *The Pioneer,* 14.

27. Thomasina Neely, "Belief, Rituals, and Performance in a Black Pentecostal Church: The Musical Heritage of the Church of God In Christ" (Ph.D diss., Indiana Univeristy, 1993), 75–80.

28. Daniels, "The Cultural Renewal of Slave Religion," 64–79, 178–188. Daniels provides the finest analysis to-date of the internal controversies pulling at the seams of a unified Baptist polity in Mississippi. See also Jerma Jackson, *Singing in My Soul: Black Gospel Music in a Secular Age* (Chapel Hill: University of North Carolina, 2004), 12–14.

29. L. W. Blue, *History of the Southeastern District Baptist Association of Arkansas* (n.p., 1903), 17, box 4, folder 46, Bailey-Thurman Papers, Emory.

30. *Proceedings of the Twenty-Third Annual Session of the South-East Bapt. Asso[ciatio]n. Held with the First Bapt. [sic] Church, Rev. W.W. Booker, Pastor. Wilmot, Arkansas, Nov. 1906* (Little Rock: Baptist College Power Press, 1907), 17, box 5, folder 27, Bailey-Thurman Papers, Emory.

31. The idea that the African American Holiness movement represented a compromise between "Conservative" and Progressive reforms is a recent one in the historiography of the field and directly related to the scholarship of David D. Daniels. Most interpretations reflect the influence of Carter G. Woodson, who posited that a fundamental dichotomy developed in southern black religion in the late 1800s between "Conservatives" and "Progressives." The fault line was the place of folk religion in black churches. Woodson, using terms that tipped his hand as to whom he favored, described the Progressives as the well-educated, better mannered blacks who practiced a taste for refined liturgy and classical music learned from white churches. In contrast, the Conservatives were unlettered, poor, and prone to shriek, yell, jump, and stomp their feet in excitement during worship services. They honored the illiterate minister who preached from memory, chanted his sermons, and relied on "crude" readings of the bible. It was out of the Conservative churches that the Holiness movement was born. While avoiding the disparaging characterizations of the Conservatives, most scholars have absorbed the notion of two distinct traditions evolving in black religion at the end of the nineteenth century and emphasized the Holiness movement as a rejection of Progressive reforms and an effort to preserve or restructure for modern use the worship styles of popular during slavery. Daniels, "The Cultural Renewal of Slave Religion"; Carter G. Woodson, *The History of the Negro Church* (Washington, D.C.: Associated Publishers, 1921). For scholars who have agreed with Woodson's basic framework, see Gilkes, "'Together and in the Harness'"; Gilkes, "The Role of Women in the Sanctified Church"; Gaylord Wilmore, *Black Religion and Radicalism: An Interpretation of the Religious History of Afro-American People* (Garden City, N.Y.: Anchor/ Doubleday, 1972; repr. Maryknoll, N.Y.: Orbis, 1983); Leonard Lovett, "Black Holiness-Pentecostalism: Implications for Ethics and Social Transformation" (Ph.D. diss., Emory University, 1978); James S. Tinney, "A Theoretical and Historical Comparison of Black Political and Religious Movements" (Ph.D. diss., Howard University, 1978); and Cheryl Sanders, *Saints in Exile: The Holiness-Pentecostal Experience in African American Religious Culture* (New York: Oxford University Press, 1996).

32. Raboteau, *A Fire in the Bones,* 102–103; Daniels, "The Emergence of the Holiness Movement in Mississippi," 199–247.

33. Jones, *Appeal,* 81.

34. Jones, *Truth* (15 May 1906), as quoted in Daniels, "The Restructuring of Slave Religion," 201. Currently there are no public copies of *Truth* available; copies only exist in the hands of private individuals.

35. Letter of Charles P. Jones to Elder C. T. Stamps, 20 July 1898, "Exhibit No. 2 to Stamp's Deposition," *Mount Helm Baptist Church et al. vs. C. P. Jones, A. B Essex et al.,* 59, folder "1905," Archival Collection, African-American Religion History: A Documentary History Project [work in-progress], Amherst College, Amherst, Massachusetts. Thanks to David Wills for opening the archive that he oversees to me.

36. Charles H. Pleas, *Fifty Years Achievement From 1906–1956[.] A Period in the History of the Church of God in Christ* (1956; repr., Memphis: Church of God in Christ, 1971), 1, Reading Room, Memphis-Shelby County Public Library, Memphis, Tennessee. Part of this quote also appears in Jerma Jackson, *Singing in my Soul: Black Gospel Music in a Secular Age* (Chapel Hill: University of North Carolina Press, 2004), 16.

37. Leonard Lovett, "Aspects of the Spiritual Legacy of the Church of God in Christ: Ecumenical Implications," *Mid-Stream* 24, no. 4 (1995): 391, makes the point that the spiritual experience of sanctification was and is the *sine qua non* prerequisite for membership in Holiness churches, especially the Church of God in Christ.

38. See, for example, box 428, folder 112, "Church of God in Christ, [no town, but listed in Mississippi County, Arkansas];" box 432, folder 112, "Church of God in Christ, [Luxora, Mississippi Country, Arkansas];" box 428, folder 111, "Church of God in Christ, [indecipherable town name, but listed in Lee County, Arkansas];" box 428, folder 114, "Church of God in Christ [North Little Rock, Arkansas];" box 428, folder 114, "Church of the Living God [North Little Rock, Arkansas] ;" all in WPA-HRS, UAR-F.

39. Editorial, "Some Prevailing Superstitions," *SWCA* (21 June 1894).

40. Riley, "Conversion, Civilization, and Culture," 265–274, 305; Daniels, "The Restructuring of Slave Religion," 90–95; Dexter, "Sojourners in a Strange Land," 188; Gilkes, "Harness," 684–685.

41. Anthea Butler, "A Peculiar Synergy: Matriarchy and the Church of God in Christ (Ph.D. diss., Vanderbilt University, 2002), 1, 2, 5, 10; Mason, *From the Beginning of Bishop C. H. Mason,* 36; *Handbook for the Department of Women, Church of God in Christ, Inc.* (Memphis: Church of God in Christ Publishing House, 1989; rev. ed., 1994), 67, as mentioned in Dexter, "Sojourners in a Strange Land," 85. Part of Mason's willingness to appoint women to high-ranking posts probably reflects his early experience with women as purveyors of spiritual truth. Several of his biographies detail his sanctification experience in which women—not men—counseled and tutored him about the meaning of this type of grace. See Cornelius, *The Pioneer,* 1–16; Mason, *The History and Life of Elder C. H. Mason,* 1924, 26–33.

42. See, for example, Jean M. Humez, ed., *Gifts of Power: The Writings of Rebecca Cox Jackson, Black Visionary, Shaker Eldress* (Amherst: The University of Massachusetts Press, 1981); *Amanda Berry Smith, An Autobiography: The Story of the Lord's Dealings with Mrs. Amanda Smith, The Colored Evangelist* (Chicago: Meyer & Brother, 1893); and Nell I. Painter, *Sojourner Truth: A Life, A Symbol* (New York: W. W. Norton, 1996).

43. Interview with Ethel Christian, brief excerpts published in Clark, *Small Sects,* 1937, 121.

44. *Avant v. Mason,* 51–60. During the trial, a member of the church on Wellington Street provided a list of all members. In cases where first names were abbreviated or difficult to discern whether they indicated a man or woman, I did not include them in the tally.

45. Jones, *Appeal,* 113; and Mrs. Elsie Mason, *The Man, Charles Harrison Mason (1866–1961),* 23.
46. Jones, *Appeal,* 113; and Mrs. Elsie Mason, *The Man, Charles Harrison Mason (1866–1961),* 23.
47. Jones, *Appeal,* xv-xvi. (Italics in the original.)
48. Jones, *Appeal,* 16, 29–30.
49. Pleas, *Fifty Years Achievement,* 78, Reading Room, Memphis-Shelby County Public Library, Memphis, Tennessee.
50. Jones, as quoted in Otho B. Cobbins, ed., *History of the Church of Christ (Holiness) U.S.A., 1895–1965* (New York: Vantage, 1966), 18.
51. *Proceedings of the Twenty-Seventh Annual Communication of the Most Worshipful Grand Lodge, F. & A.M., State of Arkansas Held in The City of Hot Springs, Arkansas, Commencing August 8th, A.L., 5899* (Hot Springs, Ark., 1899), 42–43, Schomburg. This type of phenomenon was not widely reported, probably because the men and women who joined the Holiness movement questioned the spiritual righteousness of fraternal orders well before they became a disciple of Christian, Jones, or Mason and thus never joined a lodge or were members for only a brief time.
52. Rev. 3:17–18; 9:20; 18; Bruce M. Metzger and Michael D. Coogan, eds., *The Oxford Companion to the Bible* (New York: Oxford University Press, 1993), 651–654.
53. Green, introduction to Jones, *Appeal,* xi.
54. Jackson, *Singing in My Soul,* 19–20.
55. Jones, *Appeal,* 38, 42.
56. Jones, *Truth* (10 September 1903), 3, as quoted in Lovett, "Aspects of the Spiritual Legacy of the Church of God in Christ," 390.
57. Report on Church Christ Temple, Jackson, Mississippi, reprinted in Cobbins, *History of the Church of Christ (Holiness),* 128–129.
58. Report on Galilee Church of Christ (Holiness), Hazelhurst, Mississippi, reprinted in Cobbins, *History of the Church of Christ (Holiness),* 128–129.
59. See, for example, box 428, folder 111, "Saints Home Church of God in Christ [Athelstan, Arkansas];" box 428, folder 112, "Church of God in Christ [Osceola, Arkansas]"; box 428 folder 114, "Church of God in Christ [North Little Rock, Arkansas]"; box 432, folder 135, "Church of the Living God, Christian Workers for Fellowship [Wrightsville, Arkansas]"; "The Church of the Living God [Earle, Arkansas]"; "Temple 33, Church of the Living God, Christian Workers for Fellowship [Wynne, Arkansas]"; and "Church of the Living God, Temple No. 75 [Newport, Arkansas];" all in WPA-HRS, UAR-F., In his *The Negro Church* (Atlanta: Atlanta University Press, 1903), 67, W. E. B. Du Bois found a similar style of Holiness churches in Florida in the early 1900s.
60. Davarian Baldwin, *Chicago's New Negroes: Modernity, the Great Migration, & Urban Black Life* (Chapel Hill: University of North Carolina Press, 2007), 167–169.
61. Editorial, "Vital Piety," *SWCA* (28 September 1893).
62. Editorial, "Local Preachers, the Future Pastors," *SWCA* (11 September 1902). See also Joshua O. Williams, "Young Men Should be Educated," *SWCA* (30 November 1893); editorial, "Keep them out of the Pulpit," *SWCA* (23 November 1893). See also editorial, "The Collection Problem," *SWCA* (21 August 1902); and the untitled editorial about the relationship between a good rational sermon and a happy congregation, *SWCA* (4 September 1902).

63. Editorial, "Ethics of Santification," *CI* (14 May 1904).

64. Morris, *Sermons,* 32.

65. Rev. R. T. Thomas, "'Feeling not Religion,' but Religion and Feeling Combine," *SWCA* (19 October 1902).

66. *Avant v. Mason,* 88–89.

67. Jones, "History of My Songs," as reprinted in Cobbins, *History of the Church,* 422; Jon Michael Spencer, *Black Hymnody: A Hymnological History of the African-American Church* (Knoxville: University of Tennessee Press, 1992), 104, 105–119.

68. Christian, *Poor Pilgrim's Work,* 4–10. See also Clark, *Small Sects,* 1937, 121; and Synan, *The Holiness-Pentecostal Movement,* 170. George Eaton Simpson, "Black Pentecostalism in the United States," *Phylon* 35, no. 2 (1974): 203–211, makes the point that Christian emphasized racial pride to combat white Baptist traditions.

69. Department of Commerce and Labor, Bureau of the Census, *Special Reports: Religious Bodies: 1906,* part II, 208; Department of Commerce and Labor, Bureau of the Census, *Special Reports: Religious Bodies: 1916* (Washington, D.C.: Government Printing Office, 1920), part II, 217. Jones and Mason also constructed burial and aid societies, but it is difficult to determine when. The Census Bureau reported that each man's church had fraternal style aid societies but in the 1920s. Department of Commerce and Labor, Bureau of the Census, *Special Reports: Religious Bodies: 1926* (Washington, D.C.: Government Printing Office, 1930, Part II, 382.

70. *Minutes of the 18th Annual Session of the Missionary Baptist State and Sunday School Convention Held at Brownsville, Tennessee, November 12, 1888* (Memphis: Living Way Publishing Company, 1889), final page [unpaginated], in *State Conventions and General Associations of the Nashville, Tennessee Area affiliated with Various National [Negro] Baptist Conventions, 1865–1929,* "West Tennessee Association, 1887–1889," microfilm, TSLA.

71. Jones, *History of My Songs,* 12–13. For similar images of Christian, see the inside cover of *Poor Pilgrim's Work.* For Mason, see James Oglethorpe Patterson., *History of the Formative Years of the Church of God in Christ* (Memphis: Church of God in Christ Publishing House, 1969), vi and x.

72. Grant Wacker, *Heaven Below: Early Pentecostals and American Culture* (Cambridge: Harvard University Press, 2001), suggests that Holiness and Pentecostal followers historically strove to restore the purity of the Christian church but they did so by embracing aspects of modern communication technology that helped spread their message.

73. Daniels, "The Cultural Renewal of Slave Religion"; Michael Mullins, "Re-envisioning the Borders of the Sanctified Church: The Holiness Idea in the African Methodist Episcopal Church," (Bachelor's thesis, Amherst College, 1996); Harvey, *Freedom's Coming.*

EPILOGUE

1. The preceding two paragraphs are based on Jerma Jackson, *Singing in My Soul: Black Gospel Music in a Secular Age* (Chapel Hill: University of North Carolina Press, 2004), 6, 72–75, 77–103, 127–132; Gayle Wald, "From Spirituals to Swing: Sister Rosetta Tharpe and Gospel Crossover." *American Quarterly* 55, no.3 (Sep. 2003): 387–416; idem, *Shout, Sister, Shout! The Untold Story of Rock-and-Roll Trailblazer Sister Rosetta Tharpe* (Boston: Beacon Press, 2007); and Michael Harris, *The Rise of the Gospel Blues: The Music*

of Thomas Andrew Dorsey in the Urban Church (New York: Oxford University Press, 1992).

2. James Grossman, *Land of Hope: Chicago, Black Southerners, and the Great Migration* (Chicago: The University of Chicago Press, 1989), 5–6; and William Cohen, *At Freedom's Edge: Black Mobility and the Southern Quest for Racial Control* (Louisiana: Louisiana State University Press, 1991), 295–296.

3. Emmet J. Scott, "Letters of Negro Migrants of 1916–1918," *JNH* 4 (July 1919): 304.

4. Emmet J. Scott, "More Letters of Negro Migrants of 1916–1918," *JNH* 4 (October 1919): 452.

5. The literature on the Great Migration is extensive. I relied on some of the best recent works, including James Gregory, *Southern Diaspora: How the Great Migrations of Black and White Southerners Transformed America* (Chapel Hill: University of North Carolina Press, 2005); Peter Gottlieb, *Making Their Own War: Southern Blacks' Migration to Pittsburgh, 1916–1930* (Urbana: University of Illinois Press, 1987); Grossman, *Land of Hope;* Joe William Trotter, Jr., *Coal, Class, and Color: Blacks in Southern West Virginia, 1915–1932* (Urbana: University of Illinois Press, 1990); Nicholas Lemann, *The Promised Land: The Great Migration and How It Changed America* (New York: Knopf, 1991); Milton C. Sernett, *Bound for the Promised Land: African American Religion and the Great Migration* (Durham: Duke University Press, 1997); and Kimberley Phillips, *Alabama North: African-American Migrants, Community and Working-Class Activism in Cleveland, 1915–1945* (Urbana: University of Illinois Press, 1999).

6. As quoted in Emmet J. Scott, *Negro Migration During the War* (New York: Oxford University Press, 1920), 45–46.

7. Milton C. Sernett, *Bound for the Promised Land: African American Religion and the Great Migration* (Durham, N.C.: Duke University Press, 1997), 56; Wallace Best, *Passionately Divine, No Less Human: Religion and Culture in Black Chicago, 1915–1952* (Princeton: Princeton University Press, 2005), 22–24.

8. John M. Giggie, "'When Jesus Gave Me a Ticket': Train Travel and Spiritual Journeys Among African Americans, 1865–1917," in David Morgan and Sally Promey, eds., *The Visual Culture of American Religion* (Berkeley: University of California Press, 2001), 249–266, 356–359.

9. Best, *Passionately Human,* 57–60, 89, offers the best treatment of the religious lives of southern migrants and how they impacted the sacred world of black Chicagoans and goes far to demonstrate the ways in which what he calls southern "folk" manifested itself. Still, even he tends to repeat old characterizations of southern black religion as spontaneous and "emotional" and neglects to take it on its own ᴜ. ⁻ᵉ He also downplays the extent to which the religious transformations in Chicago's black churches partly reflected the ability of black southerners to demand that crucial dimensions to their former world be represented and validated in their new environment.

10. Robert L. Boyd, "The Storefront Church Ministry in African American Communities of the Urban North during the Great Migration: The Making of an Ethnic Niche" *Social Science Journal,* 35, no. 3 (September 1998): 324–325; S. C. Drake and H. Clayton, *Black Metropolis* (New York: Harper and Row, 1962), 462.

11. Lizabeth Cohen, *Making a New Deal: Industrial Workers in Chicago, 1919–1939* (New York: Cambridge University Press, 1990), 148–156.

12. Steven Hahn, *A Nation Under Our Feet: Black Political Struggles in the Rural South from Slavery to the Great Migration* (Cambridge: Harvard University Press, 2003), 468–474;

Randall Burkett, *Black Redemption: Churchmen Speak for the Garvey Movement* (Philadelphia: Temple University Press, 1978), 1–26; Lawrence W. Levine, "Marcus Garvey and the Politics of Revitalization," *Black Leaders of the Twentieth Century* ed. John Hope Franklin and August Maier (Urbana: University of Illinois Press, 1982), 105–138; Tony Martin, *Race First: The Ideological and Organizational Struggles of Marcus Garvey and the United Negro Improvement Association* (Westport, Conn.: Greenwood, 1976); and Judith Stein, *The World of Marcus Garvey: Race and Class in Modern Society* (Baton Rouge: Louisiana State University Press, 1986).

13. M. Langley Biegert, "Legacy of Resistance: Uncovering the History of Collective Action by Black Agricultural Workers in Central East Arkansas from the 1860s to the 1930s," *Journal of Social History* 32 (Fall 1993): 73–99; Hahn, *A Nation Under Our Feet,* 473–474.

14. As quoted in Hahn, *A Nation Under Our Feet,* 474; Henry L. Mitchell, "The Founding and Early History of the Southern Tenants Farmers' Union," *AHQ* 32 (1973): 342–369.

15. Thomas Ward, Jr., *Black Physicians in the Jim Crow South* (Fayetteville: University of Arkansas Press, 2003), 159–167; David Beito, *From Mutual Aid to the Welfare State: Fraternal Societies and Social Services, 1890–1967* (Chapel Hill: University of North Carolina Press, 2000), 181–194.

16. Grossman, *Land of Hope,* 174–180.

17. The best account of the Elaine Massacre is Nan Woodruff, *The American Congo: The African American Freedom Struggle in the Delta* (Cambridge: Harvard University Press, 2004), 74–109. The estimates for the number of dead are found on 102–103. See also O. A. Rogers, "The Elaine Riots of 1919," *AHQ* 20 (Spring 1961): 95–104; B. Boren McCool, *Union, Reaction and Riot: A Biography of a Race Riot* (Memphis: Memphis State University Bureau of Social Research, 1970); Fon Gordon, *Caste and Class: The Black Experience in Arkansas, 1880–1920* (Athens: University of Georgia Press, 1995), 81, 83, 136–137; and Jeannie Whayne, *A New South Plantation: Land, Labor, and Federal Favor in Twentieth-Century Arkansas* (Charlottesville: University of Virginia Press, 1996), 75–77.

Selected Bibliography

Primary Sources—Manuscript Collections

The Amistad Research Center, Tulane University, New Orleans, Louisiana

    Collins Funeral Home, Jackson, Mississippi, 1924–1981
    Robert English Jones Papers, 1872–1965
    George Longe Jr. Papers, 1768–1971
    New Hope Baptist Church Records, 1886–1887
    Prince Hall Freemasonry-Stringer Lodge Records (Mississippi)
    Charles Barthelemy Rousseve Papers, 1863–1984
    Sisters of the Holy Family Records, 1892–1987
    Alexander Pierre Tureaud Papers, 1783–1981

University of Arkansas at Fayetteville, Special Collections

    W. P. A. Historical Records Survey, Church Records, 1936–1942
    Church of the Living God Papers, 1903–1905
    Leo M. Favrot Collection, 1913–1915
    Isaac Fisher Papers, 1899–1976
    Daniel W. Lewis Sr., Papers, 1874–1984
    Republican Party, Arkansas, State Committee Records, 1896–1933
    Southland College Records, 1872–1925

ARKANSAS HISTORY COMMISSION, LITTLE ROCK

Records of the Annual Conference of the African Methodist Episcopal Church in
Arkansas, 1868–1895
Baptist Associations Records-Western Arkansas Baptist Association, 1903, 1905
Baptist Associations Records-Western District Baptist Association Women's
Work and Sunday School Convention, 1907, 1909, 1911–1912
Governor Elisha Baxter Papers, 1873–1874
Governor Powell Clayton Papers, 1868–1871
List of Colored Bishops, Ministers, Clergymen, and Preachers as Shown in the
U.S. Census
Records of 1850–1860–1870–1880. Pulaski County, Arkansas
W. P. A. Federal Writers Project Folklore Collection, 1936–1938
W. P. A. Federal Writers Project Folklore Collection, 1935–1941

ARCHIVES OF THE CATHOLIC DIOCESE OF JACKSON, MISSISSIPPI

Clipping File—History
Clipping File—Newspapers
Bishop Thomas Heslin—Letter Books and Diaries
Holy Family Church (Natchez) Papers
Bishop Francis Janssens—Letter Books and Diaries

ARCHIVES OF THE CATHOLIC DIOCESE OF LITTLE ROCK, ARKANSAS

Clipping Files—Colored Industrial Institute of Pine Bluff, Arkansas
Records for Colored Industrial Institute of Pine Bluff, Arkansas
Reverend J. Lucy Scrap Books, Volumes 1 and 2
Bishop John B. Morris—Letters
St. Peter's Parish Records—Pine Bluff, Arkansas

DUKE UNIVERSITY, SPECIAL COLLECTIONS, DURHAM, NORTH CAROLINA

Arthur Andrews Papers
Elizabeth (Johnson) Harris Papers
Winfield Harris Mixon Papers
Edward Alfred Pollard Papers
John K. Smith Papers

EMORY UNIVERSITY, SPECIAL COLLECTIONS, ATLANTA, GEORGIA

Bailey-Thurman Papers
Black Print Collection

Josephite Fathers' Archive, Baltimore, Maryland

Colored Industrial Institute-Pine Bluff, Arkansas
John H. Dorsey Papers
Dyer Papers-Photocopies of the Sulpician Archives
Mill Hill Fathers Papers
Knights of Peter Claver, National Council Minutes, 1901–1921
Stephen Ochs—Research Files
Reverend Roy Pacifique Papers
Printed Files—Arkansas (Little Rock) Catholic Magazines
St. Peter's Mission-Pine Bluff, Arkansas
Joseph Slattery Papers

Louisiana State University, Special Collections, Baton Rouge

Bethel Baptist Church Records, Natchitoches, 1921–28
William H. Harris Papers
Knighton (Josiah and Family) Papers, 1886
Macedonia Baptist Church Minute Books, 1877–1920
Honore P. Morancy Family Papers, 1883
Percy (Leroy & Family) Papers
A.L. Simon Papers, 1907
Daniel Trotter Papers

University of Memphis, Special Collections, Tennessee

Flora Andrews Papers
E. B. Costello Papers
Fletcher and Martin Papers
Papers of Memphis Black Fraternal Organizations

Memphis-Shelby County Public Library, Memphis Room, Memphis, Tennessee

Beale Street Baptist Church Minute Book
Collins Chapel-Christian Methodist Episcopal Church History
Clipping File-Black Churches

Millsaps College, J. B. Cain Archives, Jackson, Mississippi

Journals of the Upper Mississippi Annual Conference of the Methodist Episcopal
    Church, 1891–1919
Journals of the Lower Mississippi Annual Conference of the Methodist Episcopal
    Church, 1880–1904

BLUES ARCHIVE, UNIVERSITY OF MISSISSIPPI, OXFORD

Gates, Rev. J. M. *Death's Black Train is Coming,*, in *Roots N' Blues: The Retrospective, 1925–1950.* New York: Columbia-Sony, 1992. Compact disc. C4K 479011.

Jefferson, Blind Lemon. *All I Want is That Pure Religion,* in *Complete Recorded Works of Blind Lemon Jefferson, 1925–1929.* Vienna, Austria: Document Records, 1990. 3 compact discs.DOCD 80CD 520.

Johnson, Tommy. *Delta Slide,* in *Some Cold Rainy Day.* Macon, Ga.: Southern Preservation Records, 1972. Compact disc. PRP 23582.

———. *I Wonder to Myself,* in *Some Cold Rainy Day.* Macon, Ga.: Southern Preservation Records, 1972. Compact disc. PRP 23582.

Nix, Rev. A. W., and His Congregation, *Black Diamond Express to Hell.* In Rev. A. W. Nix, *Complete Recorded Works in Chronological Order.* Vienna, Austria: Document Records, 1995. Compact disk. DOCD-5328.

Tharpe, Rebecca. *No Room in the Church for Liars,* in *Precious Memories.* Jackson, Miss.: Savoy Records, 1997. Compact disk. SCD 5008.

Thomas, Henry. "When the Train Comes Along." In *Henry Thomas Sings the Texas Blues.* Berkley: Origin Jazz Records. *OJL* V3. 33 1/3 rpm.

SOUTHERN HISTORICAL COLLECTION, UNIVERSITY OF NORTH CAROLINA, CHAPEL HILL

Edward Clifford Anderson Papers, 1813–1882
Elizabeth Hooper Blanchard Papers
Eugene Cunningham Branson Papers, 1895–1933
Chilton Norton and Dameron Family Papers
William Cooper Daniels Papers, 1862, 1865, 1872, 1886
Drury Lacy Papers, 1802–1884
Mary Ann and Henry T. Harris Papers
William Porter Miles Papers, 1784–1906
Wallace-Gage Family Papers, 1846–1901
Matt Whitaker Ransom Papers, 1815–1914

MISSISSIPPI DEPARTMENT OF ARCHIVES AND HISTORY, JACKSON

Alfred Holt Stone Papers
Bertie M. Shaw Rollins Collection
W.P.A. County Histories

TENNESSEE STATE LIBRARY AND ARCHIVES, NASHVILLE

Charles Henry Boone Papers
Jacob McGavock Dickinson Papers
Published Histories, Colored Baptist Churches in Nashville, Tennessee
Records of the Western Tennessee Baptist Conference
W.P.A. County Histories

Public Documents

Report of Cases Decided Upon by the Supreme Court of Mississippi, 1890–1908. Philadelphia: T. & J. W. Johnson, 1909.

Report and Testimony of the Select Committee of the United States Senate to Investigate the Causes of the Removal of the Negroes from the Southern States to the Northern States. Washington, D.C.: Government Printing Office, 1879.

U.S. Congress, House of Representatives, *Testimony Taken by the Subcommittee of Elections in Louisiana,* 41st Cong., 2nd sess., House Miscellaneous Document 154, Washington, 1870.

U.S. Congress, Senate, *Report and Testimony of the Select Committee of the United States Senate to Investigate the Causes of the Removal of the Negroes from the Southern States to the Northern States,* 3 vols., 46th Cong., 2nd sess., Senate Report 693, Washington, 1880.

U.S. Congress, Senate, *Report of the United States Committee to Inquire into Alleged Frauds and Violence in the Elections of 1878, with the Testimony and Documentary Evidence,* 2 vols., 45th Cong., 3rd sess., Senate Report 855, Washington, 1879.

U.S. Congress, Senate, *Testimony Taken by the Joint Select Committee to Inquire into the Condition of Affairs in the Late Insurrectionary States,* parts XI and XII, 42nd Cong., 2nd sess., Senate Report 41, Washington, 1872.

U.S. Department of Commerce, Bureau of the Census, *Census of Religious Bodies.* Washington, D.C.: Government Printing Office, 1919. Vol. 2.

U.S. Department of Commerce, Bureau of the Census, *Historical Statistics of the United States, Colonial Times to 1970.* Washington, D.C.: Government Printing Office, 1976. Vol. 2.

U.S. Department of Commerce, Bureau of the Census, *Negro Population, 1790–1915.* Washington, D.C.: Government Printing Office, 1918.

U.S. Department of Commerce, Bureau of the Census, *Special Reports: Religious Bodies, 1906.* Washington, D.C.: Government Printing Office, 1910.

U.S. Department of Commerce, Bureau of the Census, *Special Reports: Religious Bodies, 1916.* Washington, D.C.: Government Printing Office, 1919.

U.S. Department of Commerce, Bureau of the Census, *Special Reports: Religious Bodies, 1926.* Washington, D.C.: Government Printing Office, 1930.

U.S. Department of Commerce, Bureau of the Census, *Special Reports: Religious Bodies, 1936.* Washington, D.C.: Government Printing Office, 1940.

U.S. Department of Commerce, Bureau of the Census, *The Social and Economic Status of the Black Population in the United States: An Historical Overview, 1790–1978* (Washington, D.C.: Government Printing Office, 1979), Current Population Reports, Special Studies Series P-23, No. 80 [1979].

University of Virginia Geospatial and Statistical Data Center. *United States Historical Census Data Browser.* Online. 1998. University of Virginia. Available: http://fisher.lib.virginia.edu/census/. Accessed July 5–15, 2004.

Unpublished Dissertations and Theses

Armstrong, B. "Railway Systems in Arkansas," Master's thesis, University of Arkansas, Fayetteville, 1923.

Battle, Allen O. "Status Personality in a Negro Holiness Sect." Ph.D. diss., Catholic University of America, 1961.

Bayliss, Garland E. "Public Affairs in Arkansas, 1874–1896." Ph.D. diss., University of Texas, 1972.

Baynor, Karl M. "An Analysis of Newspaper Uses and Gratification by Blacks and Whites in Greenwood, Mississippi." Master's thesis, University of Mississippi, 1981.

Beary, Michael Jay. "Birds of Passage: A History of the Separate Black Episcopal Church in Arkansas, 1902–1939." Master's thesis, University of Arkansas, Fayetteville, 1993.

Beatty, Florence R. "The Negro Under Reconstruction with Special Reference to Arkansas." Master's thesis, University of Illinois, 1936.

Bizzell, William Bennett. "Farm Tenantry In the United States." Ph.D. diss., Columbia University, 1921.

Butler, Anthea. "A Peculiar Synergy: Matriarchy and the Church of God in Christ." Ph.D. diss., Vanderbilt University, 2002.

Butler, Loretta M. "A History of Catholic Elementary Education for Negroes in the Diocese of Lafayette, Louisiana." Ph.D. diss., Catholic University of America, 1963.

Butler, Sister Mary Rosetta. "The Development of Negro Parishes in the Diocese of Lafayette." Master's thesis, Xavier University of Louisiana, 1940.

Carter, Luther C., Jr. "Negro Churches in a Southern Community." Ph.D. diss., Yale University, 1955.

Case, Jay Riley. "Conversion, Civilization and Culture in the Evangelical Missionary Mind, 1814–1906." Ph.D diss., Notre Dame University, 1999.

Causey, Virginia E. "Glen Allan, MS: Change and Continuity in a Delta Community, 1900 to 1950." Ph.D. diss., Emory University, 1983.

Daniels, David Douglas III. "The Cultural Renewal of Slave Religion: C. P. Jones and the Emergence of the Holiness Movement in Mississippi." Ph.D. diss., Union Theological Seminary, 1992.

Davis, Marian M. "Death and Nineteenth Century Arkansas: Frequencies in Causes of Death in Three Arkansas Counties During 1850 and 1880." Honors Thesis, University of Arkansas, Fayetteville, 1988.

Dexter, Shalandra. "Sojourners in a Strange Land: The Impact of Northern Urbanization on Black Pentecostal Identity and Culture in Chicago from 1940 to 1980." Ph.D diss., Princeton University, 2001.

Dillard, Tom W. "The Black Moses of the West: A Biography of Mifflin Wistar Gibbs, 1823–1915." Master's thesis, University of Arkansas, 1975.

Ellenburg, Martha. "Reconstruction in Arkansas." Ph.D. diss., University of Missouri, 1967.

Fain, James Harris. "Political Disfranchisement of the Negro in Arkansas." Master's thesis, University of Arkansas, 1961.

Ferris, William R. "Black Folklore from the Mississippi Delta." Ph.D. diss., University of Pennsylvania, 1969.

Fleming, Cynthia G. "The Development of Black Education in Tennessee, 1865–1970." Ph.D. diss., Duke University, 1977.

Gibson, De Lois. "A Historical Study of Philander Smith College, 1877–1969." Ph.D. diss., University of Arkansas, 1972.

Grim, Valerie. "Black Farm Families in the Yazoo-Mississippi Delta: A Study of the Brooks Farm Community, 1920–1970." Ph.D diss., Iowa State University, 1990.

Hanson, Susan Atherton. "Home Sweet Home: Industrialization's Impact on Rural Southern Households, 1865–1925." Ph.D. diss, University of Maryland, 1986.

Harris, James Fain. "Political Disfranchisement of the Negro in Arkansas." Master's thesis, University of Arkansas, Fayetteville, 1961.

Hill, Arthur Cyrus. "History of the Black People of Franklin County, Tennessee." Ph.D. diss., University of Minnesota, 1982.

Holmes, William F. "The White Chief: James R. Vardaman in Mississippi Politics, 1890–1908." Ph.D. diss., Rice University, 1964.

Kenney, Sister Mary Josephine. "Contributions of the Sisters of the Blessed Sacrament for Indians and Colored People to Catholic Negro Education in the State of Iowa." Master's thesis, Catholic University of America, 1942.

Labbe, Dolares Egger. "Jim Crow Comes to Church: The Establishment of Segregated Catholic Parishes in South Louisiana." M.A. thesis, University of Southwestern Louisiana, 1965.

Lovett, Leonard. "Black Holiness-Pentecostalism: Implications for Ethics and Social Transformation." Ph.D. diss., Emory University, 1978.

Mactavish, Bruce D., "With Strangers United in Kindred Relation: Education, Religion, and Community in Northern Mississippi, 1836–1880." Ph.D. diss., University of Mississippi, 1993.

Minett, Ethel. "A History of the Mississippi Baptist Seminary, 1942–1989." Ph.D. diss., University of Mississippi, 1989.

Mullins, Michael. "Re-envisioning the Borders of the Sanctified Church: The Holiness Idea in the African Methodist Episcopal Church." Bachelor's thesis, Amherst College, 1996.

Neely, Thomasina. "Belief, Rituals, and Performance in a Black Pentecostal Church: The Musical Heritage of the Church of God in Christ." Ph.D diss., Indiana University, 1993.

Roth, Donald F. "Grace, Not Race: Southern Negro Church Leaders, Black Identity, and Missions to West Africa, 1865–1919." Ph.D. diss., University of Texas, Austin, 1975.

Russell, Marvin Frank. "The Republican Party of Arkansas, 1874–1913." Ph.D. diss., University of Arkansas, 1985.

Segraves, Joe Tolbert. "Arkansas Politics, 1874–1918." Ph.D. diss., University of Kentucky, 1973.

Sentilles, Renee M. "Forgotten Pioneers: A Comparative Study of the Sisters of the Holy Cross of Utah and the Sisters of the Holy Family of Louisiana." Master's thesis, Utah State University, 1991.

Sisk, Glenn N. "Alabama Black Belt: A Social History, 1875–1917." Ph.D. diss., Duke University, 1951.

Smith, Therese. "Moving in the Spirit: Music of Worship in Clear Creek, Mississippi, As An Expression of Worldview." Ph.D. diss., Brown University, 1988.

Sparks, Randy Jay. "A Mingled Yarn: Race and Religion in Mississippi, 1800–1876." Ph.D. diss., Rice University, 1988.

Thornberry, Jerry John. "The Development of Black Atlanta, 1865–1885." Ph.D. diss., University of Maryland, 1977.

Toth, John Francis. "Mechanisms that Give Rise to the Formalization of Informal Support Systems in a Black Church: An Ethnographic Study." Master's thesis, Mississippi State University, 1993.

Trey, Elly Wynia. "The Church of God and Saints of Christ: A Black Judeo-Christian Movement Founded in Lawrence, Kansas in 1896." Master's thesis, University of Northern Iowa, Cedar Falls, 1989.

Turner, William C. "The United Holy Church of America: A Study in Black Holiness Pentecostalism." Ph.D. diss., Duke University, 1984.

Van Gilder, Craig E. "Growth Patterns of Mainline Denominations and Their Churches: A Case Study of Jackson, Mississippi, 1900–1980." Ph.D. diss., Southwestern Baptist Theological Seminary, 1982.

Walker, Harry J. "Negro Benevolent Societies in New Orleans: A Study of Their Structure, Function, and Membership." M.A. thesis, Fisk University, 1937.

Walker, Joel. "The Social Welfare Policies, Strategies, and Programs of Black Fraternal Orders in the Northeastern United States, 1896–1920." Ph.D. diss., Columbia University, 1985.

Watson, Andrew Polk. "Primitive Religion Among Negroes in Tennessee." Master's thesis, Fisk University, 1932.

Woods, William Leon. "The Travail of Freedom: Mississippi Blacks, 1862–1870." Ph.D. diss., Princeton University, 1982.

Young, Sister Mary David. "A History of the Development of Catholic Education for the Negro in Louisiana." Master's thesis, Louisiana State University, 1944.

Newspapers

ARKANSAS

Arkansas Freeman (Little Rock)
Arkansas Gazette (Little Rock)
American Guide (Little Rock)
Arkansas Mansion (Little Rock)

Baptist Vanguard (Little Rock)
Daily Gazette (Little Rock)
Forrest City Herald (Forrest City)
The Hornet (Pine Bluff)
Little Rock Reporter (Little Rock)
Pine Bluff Weekly Herald (Pine Bluff)
The Reporter (Helena)
Weekly Herald (Pine Bluff)

DISTRICT OF COLUMBIA

People's Advocate (Washington)
The Colored American (Washington)

GEORGIA

The Augusta Union (Augusta)
The Macon Sentinel (Macon)
The Savannah Weekly Echo (Savannah)
The Weekly Defiance (Atlanta)

INDIANA

Indianapolis Freeman
The Indianapolis World

KANSAS

The National Baptist World (Wichita)

KENTUCKY

The Bulletin (Louisville)
The Lexington Standard (Lexington)

LOUISIANA

The Concordia Eagle (Vidalia)
Southern Republican (New Orleans)
Southwestern Christian Advocate (New Orleans)
Weekly Pelican (New Orleans)

MASSACHUSETTS

The Herald (Boston)

MISSISSIPPI

The Free State (Brandon)
The Jackson Headlight (Jackson)

NEW YORK

The Age (New York City)
The Freeman (New York City)
The North Star (Rochester)

NORTH CAROLINA

The Gazette
The North Carolina Republican and Civil Rights Advocate (Weldon)
The True Reformer (Littleton)

OHIO

The Gazette (Cleveland)

PENNSYLVANIA

Christian Recorder (Philadelphia)

SOUTH CAROLINA

Afro-American Citizen (Charleston)
Afro-American Presbyterian (Charleston)
The Peoples Recorder (Columbia)

TENNESSEE

Baptist (Memphis)
Christian Index (Jackson)
Daily Avalanche (Memphis)
Scimitar (Memphis)

TEXAS

Paul Quinn Weekly (Waco)

VIRGINIA

The Montgomery Enterprise (Richmond)
The National Pilot (Petersburg)

The Richmond Planet
The Southern News (Richmond)
The Southern Workman (Hampton)

Primary Books and Pamphlets

Abbott, Rev. A.R. *The Negro in His Own Defense*. Kosciusko, Miss.: Preacher-Safeguard Book Print, 1902.

Adams, Revels Alcorn. *Cyclopedia of African Methodism in Mississippi*. Natchez, Miss.: A.M.E. Press, 1902. Reprint, Alexandria, Virginia: Chadwyck-Healy, 1987.

Atkins, Julia, J.O. Patterson, and German R. Ross. *History and Formative years of the Church of God in Christ with Excerpts from the Life and Works of Its Founder—Bishop C. H. Mason*. Memphis: Church of God in Christ Publishing House, 1969.

Banks, Charles. *Negro Banks of Mississippi*. Cheyney, Pa.: Committee of Twelve for the Advancement of the Negro Race, 1908.

Beadle, Samuel Alfred. *Sketches from Life in Dixie*. Chicago: Scroll Publishing & Literary Syndicate, 1899.

———. *Lyrics of the Underworld*. Jackson, Miss.: W. A. Scott, 1912.

Blue, L. W. *History of the Southeast District Baptist Association of Arkansas*. N.p., 1903.

Boeger, E. A., and E. A. Goldenweiser. *A Study of the Tenant Systems of Farming in the Yazoo-Mississippi Delta*. Washington, D.C.: United States Department of Agriculture. USDA Bulletin No. 337, 10 Feb 1916.

Boyd, R. H. *The Separate or "Jim Crow" Car Laws or Legislative Enactments of Fourteen Southern States*. Nashville: National Baptist Publishing Board, 1909.

Brooks, Charles H. *The Official History and Manual of the Grand United Order of Odd Fellows in America*. Philadelphia: Odd Fellows' Journal Print, 1902.

Brown, William Wells. *My Southern Home; or, The South and Its People*. Boston: A. G. Brown, 1880.

Burrell, W. P., and D. E. Johnson, Sr. *Twenty-Five Years History of the Grand Fountain of the United Order of True Reformers, 1881–1905*. Richmond, Va.: By the authors, 1901.

Bush, A.E., and P.L. Dolman, eds. *History of the Mosaic Templars of America-Its Founders and Officials*. Little Rock, Ark: General Printing Company, 1924.

Carter, Eugene, ed. *Once a Baptist: Now a Baptist. Why?* Nashville: National Baptist Publishing Board, 1905.

Catalogue of Arkansas Baptist College, 1915–1916. Little Rock, Ark.: The Baptist Vanguard, 1916.

Christian, William. *Poor Pilgrim's Work*. Texarkana, Tex.: Joe Erlich Print, 1896.

Clark, John Franklin. *A Brief History of the Negro Baptists in Arkansas*. Pine Bluff, Ark.: n.p., 1940.

Clayton, Powell. *The Aftermath of the Civil War in Arkansas*. New York: Neale, 1915.

Cobb, James C., ed. *The Mississippi Delta and the World: The Memoirs of David L. Cohn*. Baton Rouge: Louisiana State University Press, 1995.

Cobbins, Otho B. *History of the Church of Christ (Holiness) U.S.A., 1895–1965*. New York: Vantage, 1966.

Cohn, David L. *Where I Was Born and Raised*. Cambridge: Beacon, 1948.

——. *The Mississippi Delta and the World: The Memoirs of David L. Cohn*. Edited by James C. Cobb. Baton Rouge: Louisiana State University Press, 1995.

Colville, W. J. *The Pentagram, Its Symbolism, and the Heroines of the Order of the Eastern Star*. New York: Macoy Publishing and Masonic Supply Company, 1911. Reprinted 1914.

Constitution of The Most Worshipful Stringer Grand Lodge of Free and Accepted Masons of Mississippi. N.p., 1904.

Council, William Hooper. *Lamp of Wisdom; or Race History Illuminated*. Nashville: J. T. Haley & Co., Publishing, 1898.

Delaney, Martin. *The Origins and Objects of Ancient Masonry, Its Introduction into the United States and Legitimacy Among Colored Men*. Pittsburgh: W. S. Haven, 1853.

Deming, Clarence. *By-Ways of Nature and Life*. New York: G. P. Putnam's Sons, 1884.

Dett, R. Nathaniel, ed. *Religious Folk-Songs of the Negro, As Sung at Hampton Institute*. Hampton, Va.: Hampton University Press, 1927.

Dickens, Dorothy. *A Nutrition Investigation of Negro Tenants in the Yazoo-Mississippi Delta*, Bulletin 254, Mississippi Agricultural Experiment Station, August 1928.

Dickson, Rev. Moses. *Manual of the International Order of Twelve of Knights and Daughters of Tabor, Containing General Laws, Regulations, Ceremonies and Drills*. St. Louis: A. R. Fleming Printing Co., 1903.

Du Bois, W. E. B. *The Negro Church*. Atlanta: Atlanta University Press, 1903.

——. *The Negro Church*. Atlanta: Atlanta University Press, 1903.

——. *The Souls of Black Folk*. Chicago: A. C. McClurg and Company, 1903.

——. *Economic Cooperation Among Negro Americans*. Atlanta: The Atlanta University Press, 1907.

——. *Darkwater: Voices from Within the Veil*. New York: Harcourt, Brace, and Howe, 1921. Reprint, Millwood, N.Y.: Kraus-Thompson, 1975.

Duncan, Sara J. *Progressive Missions in the South and Addresses with Illustrations and Sketches of Missionary Workers and Ministers and Bishops' Wives*. Atlanta: The Franklin Printing & Publishing Co., 1906.

Eason, J. H. *Pulpit and Platform Efforts. Sanctification vs. Fanaticism*. Nashville: National Baptist Publishing Board, 1899.

Elder, O.V. *History of the City of Memphis and Shelby County, Tennessee*. Vol. 2. Syracuse: D. Mason & Co., 1888.

Eleventh Anniversary of the Arkansas Baptist Sunday School Convention Held with the Second Baptist Church, Helena, Ark., June 18, 19, and 20[, 1891]. Little Rock, Ark.: Baptist College Print Job.

Embry, Rev. J. C. *Thoughts for Today: Upon the Past, Present, & Future of the Colored Americans*. Fort Scott, Kans.: Pioneer Book and Job Publishing House, 1878.

Etheridge, Y. A. *A History of Ashley County, Arkansas*. Van Buren, Ark.: Argus Press, 1959.

Fulkerson, Horace S. *The Negro; As He Was; As He Is; As He Will Be*. Vicksburg, Miss.: Commercial Herald Printers, 1887.

Fuller, T. O. *The Story of the Negro Baptists of Tennessee*. Memphis: Haskins Print, 1936.

——. *The Story of the Church Life Among Negroes in Memphis, Tennessee*. Memphis: by the author, 1939.

Gibbs, Mifflin Wistar. *Shadow and Light: An Autobiography with Reminiscences of the Last and Present Century*. Washington, D.C., 1902.

Gibson, W. H. Sr. *History of the United Brothers of Friendship and Sisters of the Mysterious Ten. In Two Parts*. Louisville, Ky.: Bradley & Gilbert Company, 1897.

Grant, Abraham *Deaconess Manual of the AME Church*. N.p., 1902.

Green, Elisha W. *Life of the Reverend Elisha W. Green*. Maysville, Ky.: The Republican Printing Office, 1883.

Grimes, Rev. William W. *Thirty-three Years' Experience of an Itinerant Minister of the A.M.E. Church*. Lancaster, Pa.: Em[manue] L. S. Press, 1887.

Haley, James T. *Sparkling Gems of Race Knowledge Worth Reading*. Nashville: J. T. Haley & Co., Publishing, 1897.

Hall, P.C. *A Negro's Opinion in a Little Book on Big Things*. Vicksburg, Miss.: Vicksburg Printing and Publishing Co., 1884.

Hamilton, G. P. *Beacon Lights of the Race*. Memphis: F. H. Clarke & Brother, 1911.

Handy, W. C. *The Father of the Blues: The Autobiography of W.C. Handy*. New York: MacMillan, 1941. Reprint, New York: Collier, 1970.

Haynes, Rev. Joseph E. *The Negro in Sacred History or Ham and His Immediate Descendants*. Charleston, North Carolina: Wallace, Evans, & Cogswell Co., 1887.

Holmes, Rev. W. A. *History, Anniversary Celebration and Financial Report of the Work of the Phillips, Lee, and Monroe County Missionary Baptist District Association From Its Organization, November 10th, 1879 to November 9th, 1889*. Helena, Ark.: Helena World Job Print, 1890.

Holsey, Lucius Henry. *Autobiography, Sermons, Addresses, and Essays of Bishop L.H. Holsey*. Atlanta: Franklin, 1891.

Hood, A. P. *The Negro at Mound Bayou*. Nashville: A.M.E. Sunday School Union, 1910.

Hood, Bishop J. W. *One Hundred Years of the AM Zion Church*. New York: AME Zion Book Concern, 1895.

Hutchinson Jr., Jesse. *Get off the Track*. Boston: Thayer & Company, 1844.

Janssens, Reverend Francis. *Pastoral Letter of the Right Reverend Bishop of Natchez, 1886*. Natchez, Miss.: Natchez Democrat Print, 1886.

Johnson, James Weldon, ed., *The Book of American Negro Spirituals*. New York: Viking, 1925.

——, ed. *The Second Book of Negro Spirituals*. New York: Viking, 1926.

Johnson, W. B. *The Scourging of a Race, and other sermons and addresses*. Washington, D.C.: Beresford, printer, 1904. Reprint, Washington, D.C.: Murray Bros. Printing Co., 1915.

Johnson, W. T. *Historical Reminiscences of the First Baptist Church.* Richmond, Va.: Baptist Reporter, 1903.

Jones, Charles P[rice]. *Jesus Only, Songs, and Hymns.* Jackson, Miss., 1901.

——. *An Appeal to the Sons of Africa.* Jackson, Miss.: Truth Publishing Co., 1902.

——. *The History of My Songs.* Chicago: Church of Christ (Holiness), 1905.

——. *Sermons of Life & Power.* Jackson, Miss.: Truth Publishing Company, 1913.

——. *The Gift of the Holy Ghost in the Book of Acts: A Series of Sermons.* Jackson, Miss.: Truth Publishing Company, 1911.

Joseph-Gaudet, Frances. *He Leadeth Me.* New Orleans: Louisiana Printing Company, 1913.

Journal of Proceedings of the Twenty-Second Annual Session of District Grand Lodge of Mississippi, No. 10, G.U.O. Of O.F. Compiled by J. G. Turner, District Grand Secretary. Kosciusko, Miss.: Preacher-Safeguard Book Print, 1901.

Journal of the 18th Session and 17th Quadrennial Session of the General Conference of the African Methodist Episcopal Church in the World. Philadelphia: AME Publishing House, 1884.

Journal of the Ninth Session of the Upper Mississippi Annual Conference of the Methodist Episcopal Church, Held at West Point, Miss., January 11 to 16, 189[9]. Jackson, Miss.: Press of the Mississippi Sentinel, 1899).

A Journal of the Proceedings of the Seventeenth Anniversary of the Baptist Missionary and Educational Convention of Tennessee Held With First Baptist Church, Murfreesboro, Tenn., July 13th–19th, 1904. Nashville: National Baptist Publishing Board, 1904.

Journal of the Proceedings of the Sixth Session of the Upper Mississippi Annual Conference of the Methodist Episcopal Church Held at Grenada, Mississippi, January 8th–13th, 1896. Starkville, [Miss.]: E. I. Reid's Steam Printing Office, 1896.

Journal of the Second Session of the Upper Mississippi Annual Conference of the Methodist Episcopal Church, Held at Columbus, Mississippi, February 3–8, 1892 (Columbus, Miss.: Excelsior Book and Job Printing Establishment, 1892.

Journal of the Sixteenth Session of the Mississippi Annual Conference of the Methodist Episcopal Church, Held at Jackson, Mississippi, January 16–21, 1884. (Columbus, Miss.: Columbus Dispatch Office, 1884.

Journal of the Thirteenth Session of the Mississippi Annual Conference of the Methodist Episcopal Church, Held at Canton, Mississippi, January 12–17, 1881. New Orleans: Willis A. Brainard, 1881.

Keating, J. M. *History of the City of Memphis and Shelby County, Tennessee.* Vol. 1. Syracuse: D. Mason & Co., 1888.

The Leading Afro-Americans of Vicksburg, Mississippi. Their Enterprises, Churches, Schools, and Lodges and Societies. Vicksburg, Miss.: Biographia Publishing Co., 1908.

Marshall, C.K. *The Colored Race Weighed in the Balance.* Nashville: Southern Methodist Publishing House, 1883.

Mason, Mary Esther, ed. *The History and Life Work of Elder C. H. Mason.* N.p., 1924. Reprint, San Francisco: T. L. Delaney, 1987.

Masonic Hand Book of the Constitution of the Most Worshipful Grand Lodge, as found in Most Worshipful Grand Lodge F. & A.M. of Arkansas. Thirty-Second Anniversary and Reunion, August 8, 9, 10, 11, and 12, 1904. N.p., 1904.

McAfee, Mrs. L.D. *History of the Woman's Missionary Society in the Colored Methodist Episcopal Church Comprising its Founders, Organizations, Pathfinders, Subsequent Developments and Present Status.* 1934. Reprint, Phoenix City, Ala.: Phoenix City Herald, 1945.

Minutes and Statistics of the Third Annual Session of the Arkansas Baptist Sunday School Convention Held at the Centennial Baptist Church, Helena, Ark., on the 10, 11, and 12 Days of June, 1886 (Helena: The Golden Epoch and Job Print, 1886).

Minutes of the Eleventh Annual Session of the Women's Southeast District Association Held with the Mt. Carmel Church, Warren[,] Ark. Rev. R. A. Adams, Pastor. Aug. 23–25, 1907 (Little Rock, Ark.: Baptist Vanguard Power Press, 1908).

Minutes of the First Session of the North Mississippi Annual Conference of the African Methodist Episcopal Church Held in Edward Chapel, Coldwater, Miss., from November 15th to 19th, 1877. Vicksburg, Miss.: Rogers & Groome, 1878.

Minutes of the Forty-Fourth Annual Session of the Arkansas Baptist Women's Association which convened with the First Baptist Church, Dermott, Arkansas, June 1918. (Los Angeles: I. G. Bailey, Printer, 1913).

Minutes of the Proceedings of the Pastors' Union of Arkansas, Mississippi, and Tennessee Held at Helena, Arkansas, March 3, 4, 5, and 6. A.D. 1881. Little Rock, Ark.: Dean Adams, 1881.

Minutes of the Second Mothers' Conference Held in Pine Bluff, Arkansas, September 8th, 9th, & 10th, 1894. Atlanta: Chas. P. Byrd, 1894.

Minutes of the Seventeenth Annual Session of the Baptist Women's Southeast Arkansas Association held at the First Baptist Church, Crosset, Ark., August 23–26, 1913. Los Angeles: I. G. Bailey, Printer, 1913.

Minutes of the Women's State Baptist Association and the State Baptist Sunday School Convention, Held with the St. John Church, New Port, Arkansas, June 19–24, 1893 (n.p., n.d.).

Moore, Joanna P. *In Christ's Stead.* Chicago: Women's Baptist Home Mission Society, 1902.

Morris, E. C. *Sermons, Addresses and Reminiscences and Important Correspondence, With a Picture Gallery of Eminent Ministers.* Nashville: National Baptist Publishing Board, 1901.

Needham, M. V. P. James F., comp. *General laws and Regulations of the Household of Ruth. Grand United Order of Odd Fellows in America and Jurisdiction.* N.p., 1956.

Official Journal of the Twenty-Seventh Annual Session of the Upper Mississippi Conference of the Methodist Episcopal Church held in Wesley's Chapel Church, Greenwood, Mississippi, January 11th to 15th, 1917. Grenada, Miss.: Sentinel Print, 1917.

"The Pastoral Letter of the Third Plenary Council of Baltimore on Forbidden Societies, December 7, 1884." In *Documents of American Catholic History.* Edited by John Tracy Ellis. Vol. 2, pages 418–421. Wilmington, Del.: Michael Glazier, 1976.

Payne, Daniel Alexander. *A Treatise on Domestic Education.* Cincinnati: Cranston & Stowe, 1885. Reprint, 1889.

Payne, Daniel Alexander, and David Smith. *Biography of Rev. David Smith of the A.M.E. Church; Being a Complete History, Embracing over Sixty Years' Labor in the Advancement of the Redeemers Kingdom on Earth. Including "The History of the Origin and Development of Wilberforce University.* Xenia, O[hio]: Xenia Gazette Office, 1881.

——— . *History of the African Methodist Episcopal Church*, ed. C. S. Smith. Nashville : Publishing House of the A. M. E. Sunday-school Union, 1891. Reprint, New York: Arno, 1969.

——— . *Recollections of Seventy Years.* Nashville: Publishing House of the A.M.E. Sunday School Union, 1888.

Pegues, A. W. *Our Baptist Ministers and Schools.* Springfield, Massachusetts: Wiley & Co., 1892. Reprint, New York: Johnson Reprint Corp., 1970.

Phillips, C. H. *The History of the Colored Methodist Episcopal Church In America.* Jackson, Tenn.: Publishing House C. M. E. Church, 1898.

Pleas, Charles H. *Fifty Years of Achievement from 1906–1956: A Period in the History of the Church of God in Christ.* Memphis: Church of God in Christ, 1956.

Price List of Hope, Bibles, Fireside School Books, Etc. Sold at Fireside School Headquarters (Nashville: 1908).

Proceedings of the Third Annual Session of the Educational Missionary And Sunday-School Convention of Tennessee Held with the Mt. Zion Baptist Church, Knoxville, Tenn., 8–11, A.D. 1890. Nashville: Tribune Pub. Co. Print, 1890.

Proceedings of the Eighth Annual Session of the Arkansas Baptist Sunday School Convention Held with the First Baptist Church, Little Rock, August 20th and 21st, 1888. N.p., n.d.

Proceedings of the Fifth Grand Session of the District Grand Household of Ruth, No. 14., G.U.O. of O.F. of the State of Mississippi. Convened in the Pythian Hall, Greenville. August 4, 5, and 6, 1903. Wilkerson County Appeal, 1903.

Proceedings of the 21st Annual Convention of the Most Worshipful Grand Lodge of the Free & Accepted Masons for the State of Louisiana, Held at Masonic Hall, New Orleans, Louisiana, Jan 15th, 16th, & 17th, 1884. New Orleans: The Lodge, 1884.

Proceedings of the 24th Annual Convention of the Most Worshipful Grand Lodge of the Free & Accepted Masons for the State of Louisiana, 1887. New Orleans: The Lodge, 1887.

Proceedings of the 38th Annual Convention of the Most Worshipful Grand Lodge of the Free & Accepted Masons for the State of Louisiana, 1900–1901. New Orleans: The Lodge, 1901.

Proceedings of the 24th Annual Session of the Central District Association Convened with the Barraque St. Baptist Church, October 14–18, 1903, Pine Bluff, Arkansas. N.p, 1903.

Proceedings of the Twenty-Third Annual Session of the South-East Bap[is]t. Asso[ciatio]n. Held with the First Bap[is]t. Church, Rev. W.W. Booker, Pastor. Wilmot, Arkansas, Nov. 1906. Little Rock, Ark.: Baptist College Power Press, 1907.

Proceedings of the Twenty-Seventh Annual Communication of the Most Worshipful Grand Lodge, F. & A. M., State of Arkansas Held in The City of Hot Springs, Arkansas, Commencing August 8th, A. L., 5899. Hot Springs, Arkansas, 1899.

Records of Annual Reports, Minutes, and other Publications of Selected African-American Baptist Associations and other Organizations, 1867–1951.

Riley, Jerome C. *The Philosophy of Negro Suffrage.* Hartford, Conn.: American Publishing Company, 1895.

Robinson, J. P. *Why Believers Should be Baptized and Catholicism Exposed*. Nashville: National Baptist Publishing Board, 1911.

Rudd, Daniel A., and Theodore [Scott] Bond. *From Slavery to Wealth: The Life of Scott Bond. The Rewards of Honesty, Industry, Economy, and Perseverance*. Madison, Ark.: The Journal Printing Company, 1917.

Sesquicentennial Festival of Negro Methodism Celebrated by the AMEC: Memphis, Tennessee, June 22–27, 1937. Memphis: n.p., 1937.

Shorter, Susie I. *The Heroines of African Methodism*. Jacksonville, Florida: Chew, 1891.

Sinquefield, Richard Anderson. *Life and Times of Rev. Richard Anderson Sinquefield, African Methodist Church, West Arkansas Conference. Forty-two Years in the Itinerant Work, 1832–1908*. Nashville: African Methodist Episcopal Sunday School Union, 1908.

Terrell, Mary Church. *A Colored Woman in a White World*. Washington, D.C.: Ransdell, 1940.

I. L. Thomas, ed. *Methodism and the Negro*. New York: Eaton & Mains, 1910.

Thompson, Patrick H. *The History of Negro Baptists in Mississippi*. Jackson, Miss.: R.W. Bailey Printing Co., 1898.

Upton, William H. *Negro Masonry*. Cambridge, Massachusetts: The Most Worshipful Prince Hall Grand Lodge of Massachusetts, 1902.

Von Hesse-Wartegg, Ernst. *Travels on the Lower Mississippi River, 1879–1880: A Memoir by Ernst von Hesse-Wartegg*. Edited by Frederick Trautman. Columbia: University of Missouri Press, 1990.

Washington, Booker T. *The Booker T. Washington Papers*. Vol. 3, *1889–1895*. Edited by Louis R. Harlan. Urbana: University of Illinois Press, 1974.

———. *The Story of the Negro: The Rise of the Race from Slavery*. Vol. 2. New York: Doubleday, Page, 1909.

———. *Up From Slavery: An Autobiography* (New York: Doubleday, Page, 1907.

Wells, Ida B. *Crusade for Justice: The Autobiography of Ida B. Wells*. Chicago: The University of Chicago Press, 1970.

Williams, E. A., S. W., Green, and Jos. L. Jones, *History and Manual of the Colored Knights of Pythias of N.A., S.A., E.A., A, and A*. Nashville: National Baptist Publishing Board, 1917.

Woodard, D. W. *Negro Progress in a Mississippi Town, Being a Study of Conditions in Jackson, Mississippi*. Cheyney, Pa.: Committee of Twelve for the Advancement of the Negro Race, 1908.

Primary Articles

Allen, Isabel Dinghies. "Negro Enterprise: An Institutional Church," *The Outlook* (September 17, 1904): 182.

Coleman, S.H. "Free Masonry as a Secret Society Defended," *AME Church Review*, 14, no. 3 (January 1898): 327–388.

Du Bois, W. E. B. "The Migration of Negroes." *Crisis* 14, no. 2 (June 1917): 63–66.

Du Bois, W. E. B. "The Problem of Housing the Negro, III: The Home of the Country Freedman." *The Southern Workman* 30, no. 11 (October 1901): 535–541.

———. "The Problem of Housing the Negro, I: The Elements of the Problem." *The Southern Workman* 30, no. 8 (July 1901): 390–395.

———. "The Negro in the Black Belt: Some Social Sketches." *Bulletin of the Department of Labor* 9, no. 20 (January 1899): 401–417.

Hartzell, Joseph C. "The Negro Exodus," *Methodist Quarterly Review,* (October 1879): 722–747.

Henderson, George W. "The Colored Ministry. Its Functions and Its Opportunities," *Southern Workman* 33 (March 1904): 176.

Moore, J. P. "Words from Workers." *Hope* 11(April 1897):81.

Odum, Howard. "Folk-Song and Folk-Poetry, as Found in the Secular Songs of the American Negroes," *Journal of American Folklore,* 24 (July-September 1911): 261.

Pinch, Pearse. "The Color Line in Worship: Testimony of the Educated Negro," *The Andover Review* (May 1887): 491–504.

Scott, Emmett J. "Letters of Negro Migrants of 1916–1918," *Journal of Negro History,* 4 (July 1919): 290–340.

———. "More Letters of Negro Migrants," *Journal of Negro History,* 4(October 1919): 412–465.

Testier, W.F. "The Idea of Freemasonry," *AME Church Review,* 12:30 (January 1896): 407–415.

Tindley, Reverend C.A. "Practical Suggestions Toward Material Progress." *Methodism and the Negro,* ed. I. L. Thomas. New York: Eaton & Mains, 1910, 297–304.

Tillman, Katherine Davis. "Afro-American Women and Their Work," *African Methodist Episcopal Church Review* 11 (April 1885): 497–98.

Secondary Sources—Books

Albert, Octavia V. R. *The House of Bondage, or Charlotte Brooks and Other Slaves.* New York: Oxford University Press, 1988; 1890; repr., This fictional book was a compilation of chapters in a serialized story that appeared in successive editions of the *Southwestern Christian Advocate* during the late 1880s.

Alexander, Donald C. *The Arkansas Plantation, 1920–1942.* New Haven: Yale University Press, 1943.

Anderson, James D. *The Education of Blacks in the South, 1860–1935.* Chapel Hill: University of North Carolina Press, 1988.

Anderson, Robert Mapes. *Vision of the Disinherited: The Making of American Pentecostalism.* New York: Oxford University Press, 1979.

Angell, Stephen W. *Bishop Henry McNeal Turner and African-American Religion in the South.* Knoxville: University of Tennessee Press, 1992.

Appadurai, Arjun, ed. *The Social Life of Things: Commodities in Cultural Perspective.* Cambridge: Cambridge University Press, 1986.

Arnesen, Eric. *Brotherhoods of Color: Black Railroad Workers and the Struggle for Equality.* Cambridge: Harvard University Press, 2001.

——. *Waterfront Workers of New Orleans: Race, Class, and Politics, 1863–1923*. New York: Oxford University Press, 1991.

Arthur, George R. *Life on the Negro Frontier*. New York: Association Press, 1934.

Athearn, Robert G. *In Search of Canaan: Black Migration to Kansas, 1879–1880*. Lawrence: University of Kansas Press, 1978.

Ayers, Edward. *The Promise of the New South: Life After Reconstruction*. New York: Oxford University Press, 1992.

Bailey, Julius. *Around the Family Altar: Domesticity in the African Methodist Episcopal Church, 1865–1900*. Gainesville: University of Florida Press, 2005.

Baker, Lewis. *The Percy's of Mississippi: Politics and Literature in the New South*. Baton Rouge: Louisiana State University Press, 1983.

Baker, Ray Stannard. *Following the Color Line*. New York: Doubleday, Page, 1908. Reprint, New York: Harper and Row, 1964.

Baldwin, Davarian. *Chicago's New Negroes: Modernity, the Great Migration, & the Urban Black Life*. Chapel Hill: University of North Carolina Press, 2007.

Barlow, William. *"Looking Up at Down": The Emergence of Blues Culture*. Philadelphia: Temple University Press, 1997.

Barnes, Catherine A. *Journey from Jim Crow: The Desegregation of Southern Transit*. New York: Columbia University Press, 1989.

Barnes, Kenneth C. *Journey of Hope: The Back to Africa Movement in Arkansas in the Late 1880s*. Chapel Hill: University of North Carolina Press, 2004.

Bartleman, Frank. *Azusa Street*. South Plainsfield, N.J.: Bridge, 1980.

Bates, Beth Tompkins. *Pullman Porters and the Rise of Protest Politics in Black America, 1925–1945*. Chapel Hill: University of North Carolina Press, 2001.

Beito, David. *From Mutual Aid to the Welfare State: Fraternal Societies and Social Services, 1890–1967*. Chapel Hill: University of North Carolina Press, 2000.

Bennett, James. *Religion and the Rise of Jim Crow in New Orleans*. Princeton: Princeton University Press, 2005.

Berlin, Ira. *Slaves Without Masters: The Free Negro in the Antebellum South*. New York: Pantheon, 1974.

Best, Wallace D. *Passionately Human, No Less Divine: Religion and Culture in Black Chicago, 1915–1952*. Princeton: Princeton University Press, 2005.

Bethel, Elizabeth Rauh. *Promiseland: A Century of Life in a Negro Community*. Philadelphia: Temple University Press, 1981.

Blassingame, John W. *The Slave Community: Plantation Life in the Antebellum South*. New York: Oxford University Press, 1972.

Blockson, Charles L. *The Underground Railroad*. New York: Prentice Hall, 1987.

Blythe, LeGette. *William Henry Belk: Merchant of the South*. Chapel Hill: University of North Carolina Press, 1950.

Bodnar, John. *Remaking America: Public Memory, Commemoration, and Patriotism in the Twentieth Century*. Princeton: Princeton University Press, 1992.

Bodnar, John, Roger Simon, and Michael P. Weber. *Lives of Their Own: Blacks, Italians, and Poles in Pittsburgh, 1900–1960*. Urbana: University of Illinois Press, 1982.

Boeger, E. A. and E. A. Goldenweiser. *A Study of the Tenant Systems of Farming in the Yazoo-Mississippi Delta*. Washington, D.C.: United States Department of Agriculture, 1916. USDA Bulletin No. 337 (10 February 1916).

Bond, Bradley G. *Political Culture in the Nineteenth-Century South: Mississippi, 1830–1890*. Baton Rouge: Louisiana State University Press, 1995.

Botrin, B. A. and Alvin F. Harlow, eds. *A Treasury of Railroad Folklore: The Stories, Tall Tales, Traditions, Ballads, and Songs of the American Railroad Man*. New York: Bonanza Books, 1953.

Brandfon, Robert L. *Cotton Kingdom of the New South: A History of the Yazoo Mississippi Delta from Reconstruction to the Twentieth Century*. Cambridge: Harvard University Press, 1967.

Brekus, Catherine A. *Strangers and Pilgrims: Female Preaching in America, 1740–1845*. Chapel Hill: University of North Carolina Press, 1998.

Buchanan, Thomas. *Black Life on the Mississippi: Slaves, Free Blacks, and the Western Steamboat World*. Chapel Hill: University of North Carolina Press, 2004.

Bullock, Penelope L. *The Afro-American Periodical Press, 1838–1909*. Baton Rouge: Louisiana State University Press, 1981.

Burkett, Randall. *Black Redemption: Churchmen Speak For the Garvey Movement*. Philadelphia: Temple University Press, 1978.

Burrell, W. P. and D. E. Johnson, Sr. *Twenty-Five Years History of the Grand Fountain of the United Order of True Reformers, 1881–1905*. Richmond: by the authors, 1901.

Bush, A. E. and P. L. Dolman, eds. *History of the Mosaic Templars of America-Its Founders and Officials*. Little Rock, Ark.: General Printing Company, 1924.

Bushman, Richard. *The Refinement of America: Persons, Buildings, Cities*. New York: Vintage, 1992.

Butler, Judith. *Excitable Speech: A Politics of the Performative*. New York: Routledge, 1997.

———. *Gender Trouble: Feminism and the Subversion of Identity*. New York: Routledge, 1990.

Campbell, James T. *Songs of Zion: The African Methodist Episcopal Church in the United States and South Africa*. Chapel Hill: University of North Carolina Press, 1998.

Carnes, Marc. *Secret Ritual and Manhood in Victorian America*. New Haven: Yale University Press, 1989.

Certeau, Mechael de. *The Practice of Everyday Life*. Translated by Steven Rendall. Berkeley: University of California Press, 1984.

Clark, Elmer T. *The Small Sects in America*. Nashville: Cokesbury Press, 1937.

Clark, Kathleen Ann. *Defining Moments: African American Commemoration and Political Culture in the South, 1863–1913*. Chapel Hill: University of North Carolina Press, 2005.

Clark, Thomas D. *Pills, Petticoats, and Plows: The Southern Country Store*. Indianapolis: Bobbs-Merrill, 1944.

Clawson, Mary Ann. *Constructing Brotherhood: Class, Gender, and Fraternalism*. Princeton: Princeton University Press, 1989.

Clayton, H. and S. C. Drake. *Black Metropolis*. New York: Harper and Row, 1962.

Clemmons, Bishop Ithiel. *Bishop C. H. Mason and the Roots of the Church of God in Christ*. Bakersfield, Cal.: Pneuma Life Publishing, 1996.

Clinton, Catherine. *Harriet Tubman: The Road To Freedom*. New York: Little, Brown, 2004.

Cobb, James C. *The Most Southern Place on Earth: The Mississippi Delta and the Roots of Regional Identity*. New York: Oxford University Press, 1993.

Cobbins, Otho B. *History of Church of Christ (Holiness) USA 1895–1965*. New York: Vantage, 1965.

Cohen, Lizabeth. *A Consumers' Republic: The Politics of Mass Consumption in Postwar America*. New York: Knopf, 2003.

———. *Making a New Deal: Industrial Workers in Chicago, 1919–1939*. New York: Cambridge University Press, 1990.

Cohen, Norm. *Long Steel Rail: The Railroad in American Folklore*. Urbana: University of Illinois Press, 1981.

Cohen, William. *At Freedom's Edge: Black Mobility and the Southern White Quest for Racial Control, 1861–1915*. Baton Rouge: Louisiana State University Press, 1991.

Cone, James. *The Spirituals and the Blues—An Interpretation*. New York: Seabury, 1972.

Cooke, Anna L. *Lane College: Its Heritage and Outreach, 1892–1992*. Jackson, Tenn.: Lane College, 1987.

Cooper, Anna J. *A Voice from the South*. Xenia, Ohio: Aldine Printing House, 1892. Reprint, New York: Oxford University Press, 1988.

Cornelius, Lucille J. *The Pioneer: History of the Church of God in Christ*. Memphis: Church of God in Christ Publishing House, 1975.

Creel, Margaret Washington. *"A Peculiar People": Slave Religion and Community Culture Among the Gullahs*. New York: Oxford University Press, 1988.

Cresswell, Stephen. *Rednecks, Redeemers, and Race: Mississippi after Reconstruction, 1877–1917*. Jackson: University of Mississippi Press, 2005.

Crockett, Norman L. *The Black Towns*. Lawrence: The Regents Press of Kansas, 1979.

Dailey, Jane. *Before Jim Crow: The Politics of Race in Postemancipation Virginia*. Chapel Hill: University of North Carolina Press, 2000.

Dailey, Jane, Glenda Gilmore, and Bryant Simon, eds. *Jumpin' Jim Crow: Southern Politics from Civil War to Civil Rights*. Princeton: Princeton University Press, 2000.

Daniel, Pete. *Breaking the Land: The Transformation of Cotton, Tobacco, and Rice Cultures Since 1880*. Urbana: The University of Illinois Press, 1985.

Dann, Martin E., ed. *The Black Press, 1827–90: The Quest for National Identity*. New York: Putnam, 1971.

Davidson, Donald. *Inquiries into Truth and Interpretation*. Oxford: Oxford University Press, 1984.

Davis, Allison, Burleigh B. Gardner, and Mary B. Gardner. *Deep South: A Social Anthropological Study of Caste and Class*. Chicago: The University of Chicago Press, 1941.

Davis, Susan G. *Parades and Power: Street Theater in Nineteenth-Century Philadelphia*. Berkeley: University of California Press, 1988.

Dayton, Donald. *Theological Roots of Pentecostalism*. Grand Rapids: Francis Asbury Press, 1987.

De Jong, Greta. *A Different Day: African American Struggles for Justice in Rural Louisiana, 1900–1970*. Chapel Hill: University of North Carolina Press, 2002.

Detweiler, Frederick G. *The Negro Press in the United States*. Chicago: The University of Chicago Press, 1922.

Deverall, William. *Railroad Crossing: Californians and the Railroad, 1850–1910*. Berkeley: University of California Press, 1993.

Dittmer, John. *Black Georgia in the Progressive Era, 1900–1920*. Urbana: University of Illinois Press, 1977.

Dixon, Robert M. W. and John Godrich, eds. *Blues and Gospel Records, 1890–1943*. Essex, England: Storyville, 1997.

Dodson, Jualynne E. *Engendering Church: Women, Power, and the AME Press*. New York: Rowman & Littlefield, 2002.

Dollard, John. *Caste and Class in a Southern Town*. New Haven: Yale University Press, 1937.

Dvorak, Katherine L. *An African-American Exodus: The Segregation of the Southern Churches*. Brooklyn: Carlson, 1991.

Drago, Edmund L. *Black Politicians and Reconstruction in Georgia: A Splendid Failure*. Baton Rouge: Louisiana State University Press, 1982.

Drake, St. Clair, and Horace R. Cayton. *Black Metropolis: A Study of Negro Life in a Northern City*. New York: Harcourt, Brace, 1945.

Dumenil, Lynn. *Freemasonry and American Culture, 1880–1930*. Princeton: Princeton University Press, 1984.

Dupree, Sherry Sherrod. *African-American Holiness Pentecostal Movement: An Annotated Bibliography*. New York: Garland, 1996.

Duster, Alfreda, ed. *Crusade for Justice: The Autobiography of Ida B. Wells*. Chicago: The University of Chicago Press, 1970.

Ellis, John Tracy, ed. *Documents of American Catholic History*. Wilmington: Michael Glazier, 1976.

Evans, David. *Tommy Johnson*. London: November Books, 1971.

——— . *Big Road Blues: Tradition and Creativity in the Folk Blues*. Berkeley: University of California Press, 1982.

Fahey, David M. *The Black Lodge in White America: "True Reformer" Browne and His Economic Strategy*. Dayton, Ohio: Wright State University Press, 1994.

Fahey, John. *Charley Patton*. London: Studio Vista, 1970.

Faulkner, William. "Mississippi." In *Big Woods: The Hunting Stories,* 3–7. New York: Vintage Book, 1955. Reprint, New York: 1994.

Ferris, William R. *Blues From the Delta*. Garden City, N.J.: Anchor/Doubleday, 1978.

——— . *Mississippi Folk Voices: Text and Photographs*. Somerville, Mass.: Rounder Records, 1972.

Fisher, Miles Mark. *The Master's Slave: Elijah John Fisher, a Biography*. Philadelphia: Judson, 1922.

Fite, Gilbert C. *Cotton Fields No More: Southern Agriculture, 1865–1980*. Lexington: University Press of Kentucky, 1984.

Fitts, LeRoy. *History of Black Baptists*. Nashville: University of Tennessee Press, 1985.

Fligstein, Neil. *Going North: Migration of Blacks and Whites from the South, 1900–1950*. New York: Academic Press, 1981.

Foner, Eric. *Reconstruction: American's Unfinished Revolution, 1863–1877*. New York: Harper and Row, 1988.

Formanek-Brunell, Miriam. *Made to Play House: Dolls and the Commercialization of American Girlhood, 1830–1930*. New Haven: Yale University Press, 1993.

Franklin, Jimmie Lewis. *Journey toward Hope: A History of Blacks in Oklahoma*. Norman: University of Oklahoma Press, 1982.

Franklin, John Hope. *Reconstruction: After the Civil War*. Chicago: The University of Chicago Press, 1961.

Frazier, E. Franklin. *The Negro Church in America*. New York: Schoken Books, 1963. Reprint, 1974.

——— . *Black Bourgeois: The Rise of a New Middle Class in the United States*. New York: Free Press, 1957.

——— . *The Negro Family [ok]in the United States*. New York: MacMillan, 1949.

Fredrickson, George M. *The Black Image in the White Mind: The Debate on Afro-American Character and Destiny, 1817–1914*. New York: Harper and Row, 1971.

Fulop, Timothy E. and Albert J. Raboteau, eds. *African-American Religion: Interpretive Essays in History and Culture*. New York: Routledge, 1997.

Gaines, Kevin. *Uplifting the Race: Black Leadership, Politics, and Culture in the Twentieth Century*. Chapel Hill: University of North Carolina, 1996.

Gaston, Paul M. *The South Creed: A Study in Mythmaking*. New York: Knopf, 1970.

Gatewood, Willard B., Jr., ed. *Slave and Freeman: The Autobiography of George L. Knox*. Louisville: University of Kentucky Press, 1979.

——— . *Aristocrats of Color: The Black Elite, 1880–1920*. Bloomington: Indiana University Press, 1990.

Genovese, Eugene D. *Roll, Jordan, Roll: The World the Slaves Made*. New York: Pantheon, 1974.

Gerber, David. *Black Ohio and the Color Line, 1860–1915*. Urbana: University of Illinois Press, 1976.

Giddings, Paula. *When and Where I Enter: The Impact of Black Women on Race and Sex in America*. New York: Bantam, 1985.

Gilmore, Glenda. *Gender and Jim Crow: Women and the Politics of White Supremacy in North Carolina, 1896–1920*. Chapel Hill: University of North Carolina Press, 1996.

Glaude, Eddie. *Exodus! Religion, Race, and Nation in Early Nineteenth-Century Black America*. Chicago: The University of Chicago Press, 2000.

Goings, Kenneth W. *Mammy and Uncle Mose: Black Collectibles and American Stereotyping*. Bloomington: Indiana University Press, 1994.

Gordon, Fon. *Caste and Class: The Black Experience in Arkansas, 1880–1920*. Athens: University of Georgia Press, 1995.

Gottlieb, Peter. *Making Their Own Way: Southern Blacks' Migration to Pittsburgh, 1916–1930*. Urbana: University of Illinois Press, 1987.

Graham, John H. *A Study of Revel's Methodist Church of Greenville, Mississippi*. Atlanta: Interdenominational Theological Center, 1960.

————. *Mississippi Circuit Riders, 1865–1965*. Nashville: Parthenon, 1967.

Graves, John. *Town and Country: Race Relations in an Urban-Rural Context, Arkansas, 1865–1905*. Fayetteville: University of Arkansas Press, 1990.

Gregory, James. *Southern Diaspora: How the Great Migrations of Black and White Southerners Transformed America*. Chapel Hill: University of North Carolina Press, 2005.

Griffin, Paul R. *Black Theology as the Foundation of Three Methodist Colleges: The Education Views and Labors of Daniel Payne, Joseph Price, Isaac Lane*. New York: University Press of America, 1984.

Griffith, Marie and Savage, Barbara eds. *Women and Religion in the African Diaspora: Knowledge, Power, Performance*. Baltimore: Johns Hopkins University Press, 2006.

Grossberg, James. *Land of Hope: Chicago, Black Southerners, and the Great Migration*. Chicago: The University of Chicago Press, 1989.

Gutman, Herbert G. *The Black Family in Slavery and Freedom, 1750–1925*. New York: Vintage, 1976.

Habermas, Jurgen. *The Structural Transformation of the Public Sphere: An Inquiry into a Category of Bourgeois Society*. Translated by Thomas Burger with the assistantance of Frederick Lawrence. Cambridge: MIT Press, 1989.

Hahn, Steven. *A Nation Under Our Feet: Black Political Struggles in the Rural South from Slavery to the Great Migration*. Cambridge: Harvard University Press, 2003.

Hale, Grace. *Making Whiteness: The Culture of Segregation in the South, 1890–1940*. New York: Pantheon, 1998.

Halttunen, Karen. *Confidence Men and Painted Women: A Study of Middle Class Culture in Victorian America, 1830–1870*. New Haven: Yale University Press, 1980.

Handy, W. C. *Father of the Blues: An Autobiography by W. C. Handy*. Edited by Arna Bontemps. New York: MacMillan, 1941. Reprint, New York: Collier Books, 1970.

Hanson Gerald T. and Carl H. Moneyhon. *Historical Atlas of Arkansas*. Norman: University of Oklahoma Press, 1989.

Harding, Vincent. *There is a River: The Black Struggle for Freedom in America*. New York: Harcourt Brace Jovanovich, 1981.

Harlan, Louis. *Booker T. Washington: The Wizard of Tuskegee, 1891–1915*. New York: Oxford University Press, 1983.

————. *Booker T. Washington: The Making of a Black Leader*. New York: Oxford University Press, 1972.

Harris, J. William. *Deep Souths: Delta, Piedmont, and Sea Island Society in the Age of Segregation*. Baltimore: Johns Hopkins Press, 2001.

Harris, Michael. *The Rise of the Gospel Blues: The Music of Thomas Andrew Dorsey in the Urban Church*. New York: Oxford University Press, 1992.

Harris, William C. *The Day of the Carpetbagger: Republican Reconstruction in Mississippi*. Baton Rouge: Louisiana State University Press, 1979.

Harrison, Alferdteen. *A History of the Most Worshipful Stringer Grand Lodge: Our Heritage is Our Challenge*. Jackson, Miss.: Most Worshipful Stringer Grand Lodge Free and Accepted Masons Prince Hall Affiliate of the State of Mississippi, 1977.

———, ed. *Black Exodus: The Great Migration from the American South*. Jackson, Miss.: University of Mississippi Press, 1991.

Harvey, Paul. *Freedom's Coming: Religious Culture and the Shaping of the South from the Civil War through the Civil Rights Era*. Chapel Hill: University of North Carolina Press, 2005.

———. *Redeeming the South: Religious Cultures and Racial Identities among Southern Baptists, 1865–1925*. Chapel Hill: University of North Carolina Press, 1997.

Hatch, Nathan. *The Democratization of American Christianity*. New Haven: Yale University Press, 1989.

Hemphill, Marie M. *Fevers, Floods, and Faith: A History of Sunflower County, MS, 1844–1976*. Indianola, Miss.: Sunflower Country Historical Society, 1988.

Henige, David P. *Oral Historiography*. New York: Longman, 1982.

Hennessy, James, S. J. *American Catholics: A History of the Roman Catholic Community in the United States*. New York: Oxford University Press, 1981.

Henri, Florette. *Black Migration: Movement North, 1900–1920*. Garden City, N.J.: Anchor/Doubleday, 1975.

Hermann, Janet Sharp. *The Pursuit of a Dream*. New York: Oxford University Press, 1981.

Herndon, Dallas T. ed. *Annals of Arkansas*. Hopkinsville, Ky.: The Historical Record Association, 1947.

Hesse, Mary. *Revolutions and Reconstruction in the Philosophy of Science*. Bloomington: Indiana University Press, 1980.

Hickman, Nollie. *Mississippi Harvest*. Oxford: University of Mississippi Press, 1962.

Hicks, Ruby Sheppeard. *The Song of the Delta*. Jackson, Miss.: Howick House, 1976.

Higginbotham, Evelyn Brooks. *Righteous Discontent: The Women's Movement in the Black Baptist Church, 1880–1920*. Cambridge: Harvard University Press, 1993.

Hildebrand, Reginald F. *The Times Were Strange and Stirring: Methodist Preachers and the Crisis of Emancipation*. Durham: Duke University Press, 1995.

Hudson, Arthur Palmer, ed. *Specimens of Mississippi Folklore Collected with the Assistance of Students and Citizens of Mississippi*. Ann Arbor: University of Michigan, 1928.

Humez, Jean M. ed. *Gifts of Power: The Writings of Rebecca Cox Jackson, Black Visionary, Shaker Eldress*. Amherst: The University of Massachusetts Press, 1981.

Hunter, Tera. *To 'Joy My Freedom: Southern Black Women's Lives and Labors after the Civil War*. Cambridge: Harvard University Press, 1997.

Hurston, Zora Neal. *The Sanctified Church*. Berkeley: Turtle Island, 1981.

Jackson, Jerma. *Singing in My Soul: Black Gospel Music in a Secular Age*. Chapel Hill: University of North Carolina, 2004.

Jackson, John B. *Discovering the Vernacular Landscape*. New Haven: Yale University Press, 1984.

Jackson, Joseph H. *A Story of Christian Activism: The History of the National Baptist Convention, USA, Inc.* Nashville: University of Tennessee Press, 1980.

Jay, Robert. *The Trade Card in Nineteenth Century America.* Columbia: University of Missouri Press, 1987.

Johnson, Charles S. *Patterns of Negro Segregation.* New York: Harper and Brothers, 1943.

———. *The Negro in American Civilization: A Study of Negro Life and Race Relations in the Light of Social Research.* New York: Henry Holt, 1930.

Johnson, Clifton H. *God Struck Me Dead: Religious Conversion Experiences and Autobiographies of Ex-Slaves.* Philadelphia: Pilgrim Press, 1969.

Johnson, Franklin. *The Development of State Legislation Concerning the Free Negro.* New York: Arbor Press, 1919.

Johnson, Gary B., and Howard W. Odum. *Negro Workday Songs.* Chapel Hill: University of Carolina Press, 1976.

Johnson, James Weldon. *Along This Way: The Autobiography of James Weldon Johnson.* New York: Viking, 1933.

Johnson, Walter. *Soul to Soul: Life inside the Antebellum Slave Market.* Cambridge: Harvard University Press, 1999.

Jones, Charles Edwin. *Perfectionist Persuasion: The Holiness Movement and American Methodism, 1867–1936.* Metuchen, N.J.: Scarecrow, 1974.

———. *Black Holiness: A Guide to the Study of Black Participation in the Wesleyan Perfectionist and Glossolalic Pentecostal Movements.* Metuchan, N.J.: Scarecrow, 1987.

Jones, Jacqueline. *The Dispossessed: America's Underclass from the Civil War to the Present.* New York: Basic Books, 1992.

———. *Labor of Love, Labor of Sorrow: Black Women, Work, and the Family from Slavery to the Present.* New York: Basic Books, 1985.

Jones, Leroi [Amiri Baraka]. *Blues People: Negro Music in White America.* New York: William Morrow, 1963.

Jordan, Lewis G. *Negro Baptist History, USA, 1750–1930.* Nashville: University of Tennessee Press, 1930.

Joyce, Donald F. *Gatekeepers of Black Culture: Black-Owned Book Publishing in the United States, 1817–1981.* Westport, Conn.: Greenwood, 1983.

Kantrowitz, Stephen. *Ben Tillman and the Reconstruction of White Supremacy.* Chapel Hill: University of North Carolina Press, 2000.

Kasson, John F. *Amusing the Millions.* New York: Hill and Wang, 1978.

Katz, Bernard, ed. *The Social Implications of Early Negro Music in the U.S.* New York: Arno, 1969.

Kelley, Robin D. G. *Race Rebels: Culture, Politics, and the Black Working Class.* New York: Free Press, 1994.

———. *Hammer and Hoe: Alabama Communists During the Great Depression.* Chapel Hill: University of North Carolina Press, 1990.

Kennedy, Louise V. *The Negro Peasant Turns Cityward: Effects of Recent Migrations to Northern Centers.* New York: Columbia University Press, 1930.

Klein, Maury. *The Great Richmond Terminal: A Study in Businessmen and Business Strategy.* Charlottesville: University of Virginia Press, 1970.

Kilde, Jeanne. *When Church Became Theater: The Transformation of Evangelical Architecture and Worship in Nineteenth-Century America.* New York: Oxford University Press, 2002.

Kirwan, Albert D. *Revolt of the Rednecks: Mississippi Politics, 1876–1925.* Lexington: University of Kentucky Press, 1951.

Kolchin, Peter. *First Freedom: The Responses of Alabama's Blacks to Emancipation and Reconstruction.* Westport, Conn.: Greenwood, 1972.

Kousser, J. Morgan. *The Shaping of Southern Politics: Suffrage Restriction and the Establishment of the One-Party South, 1880–1910.* New Haven: Yale University Press, 1975.

Kusmer, Kenneth L. *A Ghetto Takes Shape: Black Cleveland, 1870–1930.* Urbana: University of Illinois Press, 1976.

Lakey, Othal H. *The Rise of Colored Methodism: A Study of the Background and the Beginnings of the Christian Methodist Episcopal Church.* Dallas: Crescendo, 1972.

Lambert, Frank. *"Pedlar in Divinity": George Whitefield and the Transatlantic Revivals, 1737–1770.* Princeton: Princeton University Press, 1994.

Lamon, Lester C. *Black Tennesseans, 1900–1930.* Knoxville: University of Tennessee Press, 1977.

Langsford, E. L. and B. H. Thibodeaux. *Plantation Organization and Operation in the Yazoo-Mississippi Delta Area.* Washington, D. C.: United States Department of Agriculture, 1939. Technical Bulletin No. 682. May 1939.

Lankford, George E. ed. *Bearing Witness: Memories of Arkansas Slavery Narratives from the 1930s WPA Collection.* Fayetteville: University of Arkansas Press, 2003.

Leach, William. *Land of Desire: Merchants, Power, and the Rise of a New American Culture.* New York: Pantheon, 1993.

Lears, T. J. Jackson. *No Place of Grace: Anti-modernism and the Transformation of American Culture, 1880–1920.* New York: Pantheon, 1981.

Lemann, Nicholas. *The Promised Land: The Great Black Migration and How It Changed America.* New York: Knopf, 1991.

Lester, Woodie Daniel. *The History of the Negro and Methodism in Arkansas and Oklahoma: The Little Rock—Southwest Conference, 1838–1972.* Little Rock, Ark: The Conference, 1979.

Levine, Lawrence W. *Highbrow/Lowbrow: The Emergence of Cultural Hierarchy in America.* Cambridge: Harvard University Press, 1988.

———. *Black Culture and Black Consciousness: Afro-American Folk Thought from Slavery to Freedom.* New York: Oxford University Press, 1977.

Lewis, Earl. *In Their Own Interests: Race, Class, and Power in Twentieth-Century Norfolk.* Berkeley: University of California Press, 1991.

Lewis, Hylan. *Blackways of Kent.* Chapel Hill: University of North Carolina Press, 1955.

Lincoln, C. Eric, and Lawrence H. Mamiya. *The Black Church in the African American Experience.* Durham: Duke University Press, 1990.

Lippy, Charles. *Being Religious American Style: A History of Popular Religiosity in the United States.* Westport, Conn.: Greenwood, 1994.

Litwack, Leon F. *Been in the Storm So Long: The Aftermath of Slavery.* New York: Knopf, 1979.

———. *North of Slavery: The Negro in the Free States, 1790–1860.* Chicago: The University of Chicago Press, 1961.

———. *Trouble in Mind: Black Southerners in the Age of Jim Crow.* New York: Knopf, 1998.

Lofgreen, Charles A. *The Plessy Case: A Legal-Historical Interpretation.* New York: Oxford University Press, 1987.

Logan, Marie T. *Mississippi-Louisiana Border Country: A History of Rodney, Mississippi, St. Joseph, Louisiana, and Environs.* Baton Rouge: Louisiana State University Press, 1980.

Logan, Rayford W. *The Betrayal of the Negro from Rutherford B. Hayes to Woodrow Wilson.* New York: Collier Books, 1965.

———. *The Negro in American Life and Thought: The Nadir, 1877–1901.* New York: Dial, 1954.

Lomax, Alan. *The Land Where the Blues Began.* New York: Pantheon, 1993.

Loveland, Anne C. and Otis B. Wheeler. *From Meeting House to MegaChurch: A Material and Cultural History.* Columbia: University of Missouri Press, 2003.

Luker, Ralph. *The Social Gospel in Black and White.* Chapel Hill: University of North Carolina Press, 1991.

MacDonald, Fergus. *The Catholic Church and Secret Societies in the United States.* New York: The United States Catholic Historical Society, 1946.

MacRobert, Ian. *The Black Roots and White Racism of Early Pentacostalism in the U.S.A.* New York: St. Martin's, 1988.

Malone, Bill C. *Southern Music, American Music.* Lexington: University of Kentucky Press, 1979.

Mandle, Jay R. *Not Slave, Not Free: The African American Economic Experience since the Civil War.* Durham: Duke University Press, 1992.

———. *The Roots of Black Poverty: The Southern Plantation Economy after the Civil War.* Durham: Duke University Press, 1978.

Marchand, Roland. *Advertising the American Dream: Making Way for Modernity, 1920–1940.* Berkeley: University of California Press, 1985.

Martin, Sandy Dwayne. *For God and Race: The Religious and Political Leadership of AMEZ Bishop James Walker Hood.* Columbia: University of South Carolina Press, 1999.

Martin, Sandy O. *Black Baptists and African Missions: The Origins of a Movement, 1880–1915.* Macon, Ga.: Mercer University Press, 1989.

Martin, Tony. *Race First: The Ideological and Organizational Struggles of Marcus Garvey and the United Negro Improvement Association.* Westport, Conn.: Greenwood, 1976.

Marx, Leo. *The Machine in the Garden: Technology and the New Idea in America.* New York: Oxford University Press, 1964.

Mays, Benjamin E. and Joseph W. Nicholson. *The Negro's Church*. New York: Institute of Social and Religious Research, 1933. Reprint, New York: Arno, 1969.

McAfee, Mrs. L. D. *History of the Woman's Missionary Society in the Colored Methodist Episcopal Church Comprising its Founders, Organizations, Pathfinders, Subsequent Developments and Present Status*. Phenix City, Ala: Phenix City Herald, 1934. Reprint, 1945.

McCool, B. Boren. *Union, Reaction and Riot: A Biography of a Race Riot*. Memphis: Memphis State University Bureau of Social Research, 1970.

McCracken, Grant. *Culture and Consumption: New Approaches to the Symbolic Character of Consumer Goods and Activities*. Bloomington: Indiana University Press, 1988.

McDannell, Colleen. *The Christian Home in Victorian America, 1840–1900*. Bloomington: Indiana University Press, 1986.

——— . *Material Christianity: Religion and Popular Culture in America*. New Haven: Yale University Press, 1995.

McMillan, Sally. *To Raise Up the South: Sunday Schools in Black and White Churches, 1865–1915*. Baton Rouge: Louisiana State University Press, 2001.

McMillen, Neil R. *Dark Journey: Black Mississippians in the Age of Jim Crow* Urbana: University of Illinois Press, 1989.

McPherson, James M. *Ordeal by Fire: The Civil War and Reconstruction*. New York: McGraw-Hill, 1982.

——— . *The Abolitionist Legacy: From Reconstruction to the NAACP*. Princeton: Princeton University Press, 1975.

——— . *The Struggle for Equality: Abolitionists and the Negro in the Civil War and Reconstruction*. Princeton: Princeton University Press, 1964.

Meier, August. *Negro Thought in America: Racial Ideologies in the Age of Booker T. Washington*. Ann Arbor: University of Michigan Press, 1963.

Meier, August and Elliott Rudwick. *From Plantation to Ghetto*. New York: Hill and Wang, 1976.

——— , eds. *Along the Color Line: Exploration in the Black Experience*. Urbana: University of Illinois Press, 1977.

Mercer, Dorson Ridmond. *Negro Tales from Pine Bluff, Arkansas, and Calvin, Michigan*. Bloomington: University of Indiana Press, 1948.

Mitchell, Michele. *Righteous Propagation: African Americans and the Politics of Racial Destiny after Reconstruction*. Chapel Hill: University of North Carolina Press, 2005.

Moneyhon, Carl H. *The Impact of the Civil War and Reconstruction on Arkansas*. Baton Rouge: Louisiana State University Press, 1994. Reprint, Fayetteville: University of Arkansas Press, 2000.

Montgomery, William E. *Under Their Own Vine and Fig Tree: The African-American Church in the South, 1865–1900*. Baton Rouge: Louisiana State University Press, 1993.

Moore, R. Laurence. *Selling God: American Religion in the Marketplace of Culture*. New York: Oxford University Press, 1994.

Morant, Rev. John J. *Mississippi Ministers*. New York: Vantage, 1958.

Morgan, David. *Visual Piety: A History and Theory of Popular Religious Imagery.* Berkeley: University of California Press, 1998.

Morgan, David, and Sally M. Promey *Visual Culture of American Religions.* Chicago: The University of Chicago Press, 2001.

Morris, Aldon. *The Origins of the Civil Rights Movement: Black Communities Organizing For Change.* New York: Free Press, 1984.

Morton, Robert R. *What the Negro Thinks.* Garden City, N.Y.: Doubleday, Doran, 1929.

Moton, Russell Russa. *What the Negro Thinks.* New York: Doubleday, Doran, 1929.

Moye, J. Todd. *Let the People Decide: Black Freedom and White Resistance Movements in Sunflower County, Mississippi, 1945–1986.* Chapel Hill: University of North Carolina Press, 2004.

Muraskin, William. *Middle Class Blacks in a White Society: Prince Hall Freemasonry in America.* Berkeley: University of California Press, 1975.

Myrdal, Gunnar. *An American Dilemma: The Negro Problem and Modern Democracy,* 2 vols. New York: Harper, 1944. Reprint, New York: Harper and Row, 1962.

Nash, Gary B. *Forging Freedom: The Formation of Philadelphia's Black Community.* Cambridge: Harvard University Press, 1988.

National Association for the Advancement of Colored People, The. *Thirty Years of Lynching, 1889–1918.* New York: The National Association for the Advancement of Colored People, 1919.

Neverdon-Morton, Cynthia. *Afro-American Women of the South and the Advancement of the Race, 1895–1925.* Knoxville: University of Tennessee Press, 1989.

Newby, I. A. *Jim Crow's Defense: Anti-Negro Thought in America, 1900–1930.* Baton Rouge: Louisiana State University Press, 1965.

Nixon, Raymond B. *Henry W. Grady: Spokesman of the New South.* New York: Knopf, 1943.

Ochs, Stephen J. *Desegregating the Altar: The Josephites And the Struggle for Black Priests, 1871–1960.* Baton Rouge: Louisiana State University Press, 1990.

Oliver, Paul. *Blues Fell This Morning: The Meaning of the Blues.* New York: Horizon, 1960. Reprint, Cambridge: Cambridge University Press, 1990.

——. *The Story of the Blues.* Radnor, Pa.: Chilton, 1969.

——. *Songsters and Saints: Vocal Traditions on Race Records.* Cambridge: Cambridge University Press, 1984.

Olsen, Otto, ed. *The Thin Disguise: Turning Point in Negro History—Plessy v. Ferguson: A Documentary Presentation (1864–1896).* New York: Humanities Press, 1967.

Orsi, Robert. *Between Heaven and Earth: The Religious Worlds People Make and the Scholars Who Study Them.* Cambridge: Harvard University Press, 2005.

——. *Thank You, St. Jude: Women's Devotion to the Patron Saint of Hopeless Causes.* New Haven: Yale University Press, 1998.

——. *Madonna of 115th Street: Faith and Community in Italian Harlem, 1880–1950.* New Haven: Yale University Press, 1990.

Ownby, Ted. *American Dreams in Mississippi: Consumers, Poverty and Culture, 1830–1899.* Chapel Hill: University of North Carolina Press, 1999.

——— . *Subduing Satan: Religion, Recreation, and Manhood in the Rural South, 1865–1920.* Chapel Hill: University of North Carolina Press, 1990.

O'Malley, Michael. *Keeping Watch: A History of American Time.* New York: Viking, 1994.

Painter, Nell Irvin. *Exodusters: Black Migration to Kansas after Reconstruction.* New York: Knopf, 1977.

Palmer, Robert. *Deep Blues: A Musical and Cultural History of the Mississippi Delta.* New York: Viking, 1981.

Patterson, James Oglethorpe. *History of the Formative Years of the Church of God in Christ.* Memphis: Church of God in Christ Publishing House, 1969.

Peiss, Kathy. *Cheap Amusements.* Philadelphia: Temple University Press, 1986.

Penn, I. Garland. *The Afro-American Press and Its Editors.* Springfield, Mass.: Wiley, 1891.

Penningroth, Dylan. *The Claims of Kinfolk: African American Property and Community in the Nineteenth-Century South.* Chapel Hill: University of North Carolina Press, 2003.

Percy, William Alexander. *Lanterns on the Levee: Recollections of a Planter's Son.* New York: Knopf, 1941.

Pettigrew, M.C. *From Miles to Johnson.* Memphis: CME Publishing House, 1970.

Phillips, Charles Henry. *From the Farm to the Bishopric: An Autobiography.* Nashville: Parthenon, 1932.

Phillips, Kimberley. *Alabama North: African-American Migrants, Community and Working-Class Activism in Cleveland, 1915–1945.* Urbana: University of Illinois Press, 1999.

Powdermaker, Hortense. *After Freedom; A Cultural Study in the Deep South.* New York: Russell and Russell, 1939.

Powell, J. C. *Black Culture and Back Consciousness: Afro-American Folk Thought from Slavery to Freedom.* New York: Oxford University Press, 1977.

Raboteau, Albert J. *Fire in the Bones: Reflections on African-American Christianity.* Boston: Beacon, 1996.

——— . *A Fire in the Bones: Reflections on African-American Religious History.* Boston: Beacon, 1995.

——— . *Slave Religion: The "Invisible Institution" in the Antebellum South.* New York: Oxford University Press, 1978.

Rabinowitz, Howard N. *Race Relations in the Urban South, 1865–1880.* New York: Oxford University Press, 1978.

Rachleff, Peter J. *Black Labor in the South: Richmond, Virginia, 1865–1890.* Philadelphia: Temple University Press, 1984.

Randolph, Peter. *From Slave Cabin and Pulpit.* Boston: Earle, 1893.

Rankin, Tom. *Sacred Space: Photographs from the Mississippi Delta.* Jackson: University of Mississippi Press, 1993.

Ransom, Roger L., and Richard Sutch. *One Kind of Freedom: The Economic Consequences of Emancipation.* Cambridge: Cambridge University Press, 1977.

Raper, Arthur F. *Preface to Peasantry: A Tale of Two Black Belt Counties.* Chapel Hill: University of North Carolina Press, 1936.

Rawick, George P., ed. *The American Slave: A Composite Autobiography.* 19 vols. Westport, Conn.: Greenwood, 1972–1979.

Redkey, Edwin S. *Black Exodus: Black Nationalist and Back-to-Africa Movements, 1890–1910.* New Haven: Yale University Press, 1969.

Richards, Jeffrey, and John M. MacKenzie. *The Railway Station: A Social History.* Oxford: Clarendon, 1986.

Richardson, Harry. *Dark Salvation: The Story of Methodism as it Developed Among Blacks in America.* Garden City, N.Y.: Doubleday, 1976.

Richardson, Joe M. *Christian Reconstruction: The American Missionary Association and Southern Blacks, 1861–1890.* Athens: University of Georgia Press, 1986.

Richter, Amy. *Home on the Rails: Women, The Railroad, and the Rise of Public Domesticity.* Chapel Hill: University of North Carolina Press, 2005.

Rollinson, Mary G. *Grassroots Garveyism: The Universal Negro Improvement Association in the Rural South, 1920–1927.* Chapel Hill: University of North Carolina Press, 2007.

Rosenberg, Bruce. *The Art of the American Folk Preacher.* New York: Oxford University Press, 1970.

Rosengarten, Theodore. *All God's Dangers: The Life of Nat Shaw.* New York: Knopf, 1974.

Rozenweig, Roy. *Eight Hours for What We Will.* Cambridge: Cambridge University Press, 1983.

Ryan, Mary. *Women in Public, Between Banners and Ballots, 1825–1880.* Baltimore: John Hopkins University Press, 1990.

Sackheim, Eric, ed. *The Blues Line: A Collection of Blues Lyrics.* New York: Schirmer Books, 1969.

Sacre, Robert ed. *Saints and Sinners: Religion, Blues and (D)Evil in African-American Literature.* Liege: Société liégeoise de musicologie, 1996.

Saikku, Mikko. *This Delta, This Land: An Environmental History of the Yazoo-Mississippi Floodplain.* Athens: University of Georgia Press, 2005.

Salem, Dorothy. *To Better Our World: Black Women in Organized Reform, 1890–1920.* Brooklyn: Carlson, 1990.

Salvatore, Nick. *Singing in a Strange Land: C. L. Franklin, the Black Church, and the Transformation of America.* New York: Little, Brown, 2005.

Sanders, Cheryl J. *Saints in Exile: The Holiness-Pentecostal Experience in African American Religion and Culture.* New York: Oxford University Press, 1996.

Scarborough, Dorothy. *On the Trail of Negro Folk Songs.* Cambridge: Harvard University Press, 1978.

Schechter, Patricia. *Ida B. Wells-Barnett and American Reform, 1880–1930.* Chapel Hill: University of North Carolina, 2001.

Schivelbusch, Wolfgang. *The Railroad Journey: The Industrialization of Time and Space in the 19th Century.* Berkeley: University of California Press, 1986.

Schmidt, Leigh. *Consumer Rites: The Buying and Selling of American Holidays.* Princeton: Princeton University Press, 1995.

———. *Hearing Things: Religious Illusion and the American Enlightenment.* Cambridge: Harvard University Press, 2000.

Scott, Emmett J. *Negro Migration during the War.* New York: Oxford University Press, 1920.

Scott, James C. *Domination and the Arts of Resistance: Hidden Transcripts.* New Haven: Yale University Press, 1990.

Sernett, Milton C. *Bound for the Promised Land: African American Religion and the Great Migration.* Durham: Duke University Press, 1997.

――― . *Afro-American Religious History: A Documentary Witness.* Durham: Duke University Press, 1985.

Sewell, George Alexander. *Mississippi Black History Makers.* Jackson: University of Mississippi Press, 1977.

Siebert, Wilbur. *The Underground Railroad: From Slavery to Freedom.* New York: MacMillan, 1898.

Smith, Bonnie. *The Gender of History: Men, Women, and Historical Practice.* Cambridge: Harvard University Press, 1998.

Smith, Timothy. *Revivalism and Social Reform in Mid-Nineteenth Century America.* New York: Abingdon Press, 1975.

Smock, Raymond W., ed. *Booker T. Washington in Perspective: Essays of Louis Harlan.* Jackson: University Press of Mississippi, 1988.

Sobel, Mechal. *The World They Made Together: Black and White Values in Eighteenth-Century Virginia.* Princeton: Princeton University Press, 1987.

Spain, Refus L. *Ease in Zion: A Social History of the Southern Baptists, 1865–1900.* Nashville: Vanderbilt University Press, 1967.

Sparks, Randy J. *On Jordan's Stormy Banks: Evangelicalism in Mississippi, 1773–1876.* Athens: University of Georgia Press, 1994.

Spear, Allan H. *Black Chicago: The Making of a Negro Ghetto.* Chicago: The University of Chicago Press, 1967.

Spears, Timothy B. *100 Years on the Road: The Traveling Salesman in American Culture.* New Haven: Yale University Press, 1995.

Spencer, Jon Michael. *Blues and Evil.* Knoxville: University of Tennessee Press, 1993.

――― . *Black Hymnody: A Hymnological History of the African-American Church.* Knoxville: University of Tennessee Press, 1992.

Sprigle, Ray. *In the Land of Jim Crow.* New York: Simon and Schuster, 1949.

Stearns, Marshall W. *The Story of the Jazz.* New York: Oxford University Press, 1956.

Stein, Judith. *The World of Marcus Garvey: Race and Class in Modern Society.* Baton Rouge: Louisiana State University Press, 1986.

Stout, Harry. *The Divine Dramatist: George Whitefield and the Rise of Modern Evangelicalism.* Grand Rapids: Eerdmans, 1991.

Stover, John F. *Railroads.* Chicago: The University of Chicago Press, 1961.

――― . *American The Railroads of the South, 1865–1900: A Study in Finance and Control.* Chapel Hill: The University of North Carolina Press, 1955.

Stowell, Daniel. *Rebuilding Zion: The Religious Reconstruction of the South, 1863–1877.* New York: Oxford University Press, 1997.

Suggs, Henry Lewis, ed. *The Black Press in the South, 1865–1979*. Westport, Conn.: Greenwood, 1983.

Summers, Martin. *Manliness & Its Discontents: The Black Middle Class & the Transformation of Masculinity, 1900–1930*. Chapel Hill: University of North Carolina Press, 2004.

Swift, David E. *Black Prophets of Justice: Activist Clergy before the Civil War*. Baton Rouge: Louisiana State University Press, 1989.

Synan, Vinson. *The Holiness-Pentecostol Movement in the United States*. Grand Rapids: Eerdmans, 1971.

Taft, Michael. *Blues Lyric Poetry: An Anthology*. New York: Garland, 1983.

Taylor, Arnold H. *Travail and Triumph: Black Life and Culture in the South Since the Civil War*. Westport, Conn.: Greenwood, 1971.

Taylor, Clarence. *The Black Churches of Brooklyn*. New York: Columbia University Press, 1994.

Thompson, E. P. *The Making of the English Working Class*. New York: Oxford University Press, 1966.

Thompson, Julius. *Black Life in Mississippi: Essays on Political, Social, and Cultural Studies in a Deep South State*. New York: University Press of America, 2001.

Tindall, George B. *The Emergence of the New South, 1913–1945*. Baton Rouge: Louisiana State University Press, 1967.

——— . *South Carolina Negroes, 1877–1900*. Columbia: University of South Carolina Press, 1952.

Titon, Jeff Todd, ed. *Downhome Blues Lyrics: An Anthology from the Post-World War II Era*. Urbana: University of Illinois Press, 1981.

——— . *Early Downhome Blues: A Musical and Cultural Analysis*. Urbana: University of Illinois Press, 1977.

Tolnay, Stewart E. *The Bottom Rung: African American Family Life on Southern Farms*. Urbana: University of Illinois Press, 1999.

Tolnay, Stewart E., and E. M. Beck, *A Festival of Violence: An Analysis of Southern Lynchings, 1882–1930*. Urbana: University of Illinois Press, 1995.

Trotter, Joe William. *Coal, Class, and Color: Blacks in Southern West Virginia: 1915–32*. Urbana: University of Illinois Press, 1990.

Turner, Patricia A. *Ceramic Uncles and Celluloid Mammies: Black Images and Their Influence on Culture*. New York: Anchor, 1994.

Turner, Victor. *Drama, Fields and Metaphors: Symbolic Action in Human Society*. Ithaca: Cornell University Press, 1974.

——— . *The Ritual Process: Structure and Anti-Structure*. Chicago: Aldine, 1969.

Tuttle, William M., Jr. *Race Riot: Chicago in the Red Summer of 1919*. New York: Atheneum, 1970.

Vance, Rupert B. *Human Factors in Cotton Culture: A Study in the Social Geography of the American South*. Chapel Hill: University of North Carolina Press, 1929.

Verde, Max E. *Paramount 12000/13000 Series*. London: Storyville, 1971.

Vincent, Charles. *Black Legislators in Louisiana During Reconstruction*. Baton Rouge: Louisiana State University Press, 1976.

Wacker, Grant. *Heaven Below: Early Pentecostals and American Culture*. Cambridge: Harvard University Press, 2001.

Wald, Gayle. *Shout, Sister, Shout! The Untold Story of Rock-and-Roll Trailblazer Sister Rosetta Tharpe*. Boston: Beacon Press, 2007.

Walker, Clarence E. *A Rock in a Weary Land: The African Methodist Episcopal Church during the Civil War and Reconstruction*. Baton Rouge: Louisiana State University Press, 1982.

Wallace, Les. *The Rhetoric of Anti-Catholicism: The American Protective Association, 1887–1911*. New York: Garland, 1990.

Ward, Thomas Jr. *Black Physicians in the Jim Crow South*. Fayetteville: University of Arkansas Press, 2003.

Washington, James Melvin. *Frustrated Fellowship: The Black Baptist Quest for Social Power*. Macon, Ga.: Mercer University Press, 1985.

———, ed. *A Testament of Hope: The Essential Writings of Martin Luther King*. San Francisco: Harper and Row, 1986.

Washington, Joseph Jr. *Black Religion; The Negro and Christianity in the United States*. Boston: Beacon, 1964. Reprint, Lanham, Md.: University Press of America, 1984.

Weare, Walter B. *Black Business in the New South: A Social History of the North Carolina Mutual Life Insurance Company*. Urbana: University of Illinois Press, 1973.

Weiner, Jonathan. *Social Origins of the New South: Alabama, 1860–1885*. Baton Rouge: Louisiana State Suniversity Press, 1978.

Weisenfeld, Judith. *African American Women and Christian Activism: New York's Black YMCA, 1905–1945*. Cambridge: Harvard University Press, 1997.

Welke, Barbara Young. *Recasting American Liberty: Gender, Race, Law, and the Railroad Revolution, 1865–1920*. New York: Cambridge University Press, 2001.

West, Cornel. *Prophesy Deliverance! An Afro-American Revolutionary Christianity*. Philadelphia: Westminster, 1982.

Wharton, Vernon Lane. *The Negro in Mississippi, 1865–1890*. Chapel Hill: University of North Carolina Press, 1947.

Whayne, Jeannie M. *A New Plantation South: Land, Labor, and Federal Favor in Twentieth Century Arkansas*. Charlottesville: University of Virginia Press, 1996.

Whayne Jeannie M., and Willard B. Gatewood Jr., eds. *The Arkansas Delta: Land of Paradox*. Fayetteville: University of Arkansas Press, 1993.

White, John R. *The American Railroad Passenger Car*. Baltimore: John Hopkins University Press, 1978.

White, Walter. *How Far the Promised Land?* New York: Viking, 1955.

Wiggins, William H., Jr. *O Freedom! Afro-American Emancipation Celebrations*. Knoxville: University of Tennessee Press, 1987.

Williams, C. Fred, S. Charles Bolton, Carl H. Moneyhon, and LeRoy T. Williams, eds. *A Documentary History of Arkansas*. Fayetteville: University of Arkansas Press, 1984.

Williams, Loretta J. *Black Freemasonry and Middle-Class Realities*. Columbia: University of Missouri Press, 1980.

Williams, Melvin D. *Community in a Black Pentecostal Church: An Anthropological Study*. Pittsburg: University of Pittsburg Press, 1974.

Williams, Peter. *Popular Religion in America: Symbolic Change and the Modernization Process in Historical Perspective*. Englewood Cliffs, N.J.: Prentice Hall, 1980.

Williams, Rosalind H. *Dream Worlds: Mass Consumption in Late Nineteenth Century France*. Berkeley: University of California Press, 1982.

Williamson, Joel. *The Crucible of Race: Black-White Relations in the American South Since Reconstruction*. New York: Oxford University Press, 1986.

———. *After Slavery: The Negro in South Carolina During Reconstruction, 1861–1877*. Chapel Hill: University of North Carolina Press, 1965.

Willis, John. *Forgotten Time: The Yazoo-Mississippi Delta after the Civil War*. Charlottesville: University of Virginia Press, 2000.

Wilmore, Gayraud S. *Black Religion and Black Radicalism*. Garden City, N.Y.: Anchor/Doubleday, 1972. Reprint, Maryknoll, N.Y.: Orbis Books, 1983.

Winston, Diane. *Red Hot and Righteous: The Urban Religion of the Salvation Army*. Cambridge: Harvard University Press, 1999.

Witten, Marsha. *All Is Forgiven: The Secular Message in American Protestantism*. Princeton: Princeton University Press, 1993.

Wolseley, Roland E. *The Black Press, U.S.A.* Ames: Iowa State University Press, 1971.

Woodruff, Nan E. *American Congo: The African-American Struggle for Freedom in the Delta*. Cambridge: Harvard University Press, 2004.

Woods, James M. *Mission and Memory: A History of the Catholic Church in Arkansas*. Little Rock, Ark.: Diocese of Little Rock, Arkansas, 1993.

Woodson, Carter. *The History of the Negro Church*. Washington, D.C.: Associated Publishers, 1921.

———. *A Century of Negro Migration*. Washington, D.C.: Association for the Study of Negro Life and History, 1918.

Woodward, C. Vann. *The Strange Career of Jim Crow*. 3rd ed. New York: Oxford University Press, 1974.

———. *Origins of the New South, 1877–1913*. Baton Rouge: Louisiana State University Press, 1971.

Work, John W. *American Negro Songs and Spirituals*. New York: Bonanza Books, 1940.

Work, John W., Lewis Wade Jones, Samuel C. Adams, Jr., *Lost Delta Found: Rediscovering the Fisk University-Library of Congress Coahoma County Study, 1941–1942*. Edited by Robert Gordon and Bruce Nemorov. Nashville: Vanderbilt University Press, 2005.

Wright, Gavin. *Old South, New South: Revolutions in the Southern Economy since the Civil War*. New York: Basic Books, 1986.

Wright, George C. *Life Behind a Veil: Blacks in Louisville, Kentucky, 1865–1930*. Baton Rouge: Louisiana State University Press, 1985.

Wyatt-Brown, Bertram. *The House of Percy: Honor, Melancholy and Imagination in a Southern Family*. New York: Oxford University Press, 1994.

Young, James Harvey. *The Toadstool Millionaires: A Social History of Patent Medicine in America Before Regulation*. Princeton: Princeton University Press, 1961.

Secondary Articles

Agnew, Jean-Christophe. "The Give and Take of Consumer Culture." In *Commodifying Everything: Relationships of the Market,* ed. Susan Strasser, 11–43. New York: Routledge, 2003.

Angell, Stephen Ward. "The Controversy Over Women's Ministry in the African Methodist Church during the 1880s: The Case of Sarah Ann Hughes" In *This Far by Faith: Readings in African American Women's Religious Biography,* ed. Judith Weisenfeld and Richard Newman, 94–109. New York: Routledge, 1996.

Aptheker, Herbert. "Resistance and Afro-American History: Some Notes on Contemporary Historiography and Suggestions for Future Research." In *In Resistance: Studies in African, Caribbean, and Afro-American History,* ed. Gary Y. Okihiro, 10–20. Amherst: University of Massachusetts Press, 1986.

Armstrong, Thomas F. "The Building of a Black Church: Community in Post Civil War Liberty County, Georgia." *Georgia Historical Quarterly* 66 (1982): 346–367.

Arnesen, Eric. "Like Banquo's Ghost, It Will Not Down: The Race Question and the American Railroad Brotherhoods, 1880–1920." *American Historical Review* 99 (December 1994): 1601–1633.

Atkinson, James H. "The Arkansas Gubernatorial Campaign and the Election of 1872." *Arkansas Historical Quarterly* 1 (Winter 1942): 307–321.

Bacote, Clarence A. "Negro Proscriptions, Protests, and Proposed Solutions in Georgia, 1800–1908." *Journal of Southern History* 25 (November 1959): 471–98.

Barjenbruch, Judith. "The Greenback Political Movement: An Arkansas View." *Arkansas Historical Quarterly* 36 (Summer 1977): 107–122.

Bayliss, Garland E. "Post-Reconstruction Repudiation: Evil Blot or Financial Necessity?" *Arkansas Historical Quarterly* 13 (Autumn 1964): 243–259.

Beito, David T. "Black Fraternal Hospitals in the Mississippi Delta, 1942–1967." *Journal of Southern History* 65 (February 1999): 109–140.

——— . "The Lodge Practice Evil Reconsidered: Medical Care Through Fraternal Societies, 1900–1930." *Journal of Urban History* 23 (July 1997): 569–600.

Berkeley, Kathleen C. " 'Colored Ladies Also Contributed: Black Womens' Activities from Benevolence to Social Welfare, 1866–1896." In *The Web of Southern Social Relations: Women, Family, and Education,* ed. Walter J. Fraser, R. Frank Sanders, and Jon L. Wakelyn, 181–203.

——— . "The Politics of Black Education in Memphis, Tennessee, 1868–1891." In *Southern Cities, Southern Schools: Public Education in the Urban South,* ed. Rick Ginsberg and David N. Plank, 199–236. Westport, Conn.: Greenwood, 1980: Athens: University of Georgia Press, 1985.

Biegert, M. Langley. "Legacy of Resistance: Uncovering the History of Collective Action by Black Agricultural Workers in Central East Arkansas from the 1860s to the 1930." *Journal of Social History* 32 (Fall 1998): 77–99.

Boyd, Robert L. "The Storefront Church Ministry in African American Communities of the Urban North during the Great Migration: The Making of an Ethnic Niche." *Social Science Journal* 35, no. 3 (September 1998): 319–322.

Brooks, Joanna. "Prince Hall, Freemasonry, and Genealogy." *African American Review* 34, no. 2 (Summer 2000): 197–216.

Brown, Elsa Barkley. "Negotiating and Transforming the Public Sphere: African American Political Life in the Transition from Slavery to Freedom." *Public Culture* 7, no. 1 (Fall 1994): 107–146.

"Womanist Consciousness: Maggie Lena Walker and the Independent Order of Saint Luke." *Signs: Journal of Women in Culture and Society* 14 (Spring 1989): 610–633.

Brown, Elsa Barkely and Gregg Kimball. "Mapping the Terrain of Black Richmond." *Journal of Urban History* 21 (March 1995): 296–346.

Butler, Anthea D. "'Only a Woman Would Do': Bible Reading and African American Women's Organizing Work." In *Women and Religion in the African Diaspora; Knowledge, Power, and Performance,* ed. R. Marie Griffith and Barbara Savage, 155–178. Baltimore: Johns Hopkins Press, 2006.

Butler, Jon. "Jack in the Box Faith: The Religion Problem in Modern American History." *Journal of American History* 90 (March 2004): 1357–1378.

Cantrell, Andrea. "WPA Sources for African-American Oral History in Arkansas: Ex-Slave Narratives and Early Settlers' Personal Histories." *Arkansas Historical Quarterly* 63, no. 1 (Spring 2004): 44–50.

Clark, Howard L. "Growth of Negro Population in the U.S. and Trend of Migration from the South Since 1860. Economic Conditions the Reason Negroes are Leaving the South." *Manufacturers Record* 83, no. 4 (January 25, 1923): 61–63.

Clark, William A. "Sanctification in Negro Religion." *Social Forces,* 15 (1937): 544–551.

Cobb, James C. "Somebody Done Nailed Us on the Cross: Federal Farm and Welfare Policy in the Civil Rights Movement in the Mississippi Delta." *Journal of American History,* 77 (December 1990): 927–931.

Cohen, Lizabeth. "Embellishing a Life of Labor: An Interpretation of the Material Culture of American Working-Class Homes, 1885–1915." In *Common Places: Readings in American Vernacular Architecture,* ed. Dell Upton and John Michael Vlach, 261–278. Athens: University of Georgia Press, 1986.

Cohen, William. "Black Immobility and Free Labor: The Freedmen's Bureau and the Relocation of Black Labor, 1865–1968." *Civil War History* 30, no. 3 (September 1984): 221–234.

Cunningham, Floyd T. "Wandering in the Wilderness: Black Baptist Thought after Emancipation." *American Baptist Quarterly* 4 (1985): 268–281.

Dale, Elizabeth. "Social Equality Does Not Exist among Themselves, nor among Us: *Baylies vs. Curry* and Civil Rights in Chicago, 1888." *American Historical Review* 102 (April 1997): 311–340.

Davis, P. O. "A Negro Exodus and Southern Agriculture." *American Review of Reviews* 63 (October 1923): 401–407.

De Santis, Vincent P. "The Republican Party and the Southern Negro, 1877–1897." *Journal of Negro History* 45, no. 2 (April 1960): 71–87.

——. Negro Dissatisfaction with Republican Policy in the South, 1882–1884."
Journal of Negro History 36 (April 1951): 148–59.

Dethloff, Henry C. and Robert R. Jones. "Race Relations in Louisiana, 1877–98."
Louisiana History 9 (Fall 1968): 301–323.

Dillard, Tom W. "Three Important Black Leaders in Phillips County." *Phillips County Historical Quarterly* 19, no. 1 (December 1980): 10–21. Available (without the original bibliography) at: http://www.cals.lib.ar.us/butlercenter/abho/docs/1980%20Grey%20Donohoo%20and%20Morris%20article.pdf.

——. "'Golden Prospects and Fraternal Amenities': Mifflin W. Gibbs' Arkansas Years." *Arkansas Historical Quarterly* 35 (Winter 1976): 307–333.

——. "To the Back of the Elephant: Racial Conflict in the Arkansas Republican Party." *Arkansas Historical Quarterly* 33 (Spring 1974): 3–15.

——. "Scipio A. Jones." *Arkansas Historical Quarterly* 31 (Winter 1972): 201–219.

Donald, Henderson H. "The Negro Migration of 1916–1918." *Journal of Negro History,* 6, no. 4 (October 1921): 388–498.

Elkins, F. Clark. "Arkansas Farmers Organize for Action: 1882–1884." *Arkansas Historical Quarterly* 8 (Autumn 1954): 231–248.

Fleming, Walter L. " 'Pap' Singleton, The Moses of the Colored Exodus."
American Journal of Sociology 15, 1 (July 1909): 61–82.

Foti, Thomas. "The Rivers Gifts and Curses." In *The Arkansas Delta,* ed. William Gatewood and Jeannie Whayne, 41–52. Fayetteville: University of Arkansas Press, 1993.

Gaines, Kevin. "Rethinking Race and Class in African-American Struggles for Equality, 1885–1941." *American Historical Review* 102 (April 1997): 378–388.

Garon, Paul. "Blues and the Church: Revolt and Resignation." *Living Blues* 1 (Spring 1970): 3–10.

Garvin, Roy. "Benjamin or 'Pap' Singleton and His Followers." *Journal of Negro History* 33, no. 1 (January 1948): 7–23.

Gatewood, Willard B. Jr. "The Arkansas Delta: The Deepest of the Deep South."
In *The Arkansas Delta,* ed. William Gatewood and Jeannie Whayne, 3–24. Fayetteville: University of Arkansas Press, 1993.

——. "Sunnyside: The Evolution of an Arkansas Plantation, 1840–1945."
Arkansas Historical Quarterly 50 (Spring 1991): 5–29.

——, ed. "Arkansas Negroes in the 1890s: Documents." *Arkansas Historical Quarterly* 33 (Winter 1974): 293–325.

——. "Negro Legislators in Arkansas 1891: A Document." *Arkansas Historical Quarterly* 31 (Autumn 1972): 220–233.

Giggie, John M. "America's Third Great Awakening: Religion and the Civil Rights Movement." *Reviews in American History* 33 (June 2005): 254–62.

——. "'Disband Him From the Church': African Americans and the Spiritual Politics of Disfranchisement in Post-Reconstruction Arkansas." *Arkansas Historical Quarterly* 60, no. 3 (Autumn 2001): 245–264.

——. "'When Jesus Gave Me a Ticket': Train Travel and Spiritual Journeys Among African Americans, 1865–1917." In *The Visual Culture of American*

Religion, ed. David Morgan and Sally Promey, 249–266, 356–359. Berkeley: University of California Press, 2001.

Gilkes, Cheryl Townsend. "The Role of Women in the Sanctified Church." *Journal of Religious Thought* 43 (Spring-Summer 1986): 24–41.

——. "'Together and in Harness': Womens' Traditions in the Sanctified Church." *Signs: Journal of Woman in Culture and Society* 10 (Summer 1985): 678–699.

Goings, Kenneth W. and Gerald L. Smith. "Unhidden Transcripts: Memphis and African American Agency, 1862–1920." *Journal of Urban History* 21 (March 1995): 372–394.

Gravely, William. "The Rise of African Churches in America (1786–1822): Re-Examining the Contexts." In *African American Religious Studies: An Interdisciplinary Anthology,* ed. Gayraud Wilmore, 301–317. Durham, N.C.: Duke University Press, 1989.

——. "Hiram Revels Protests Racial Separation in the Methodist Episcopal Church (1876)." *Methodist History* 8 (April 1970): 13–20.

——. "The Social, Political, and Religious Significance of the Formation of the Colored Methodist Episcopal Church." *Methodist History* 18 (October 1979): 3–25.

Graves, John W. "The Arkansas Separate Coach Law of 1891." *Arkansas Historical Quarterly* 32 (Summer 1973): 148–65.

Gruner, Red. "The Blues as a Secular Religion." *Blues World* (April 1970-June 1970): 29–32.

Habermas, Jurgen. "The Public Sphere: An Encyclopedia Article (1964)." *New German Critique* 1 (Fall 1974): 49–55.

Hackett, David G. "The Prince Hall Masons and the African American Church: The Labors of Grand Master and Bishop James Walker Hood, 1831–1918." *Church History* 69, no. 4 (December 2000): 770–802.

——. "Gender and Religion in American Culture." *Religion and American Culture* 5 (Summer 1995): 127–157.

Hall, Prince. "A Charge Delivered to the African Lodge, June 24, 1979." Reprinted in *Early Negro Writings, 1760–1837,* ed. Dorothy Porter, 63–69. Baltimore: Black Classics, 1995.

Hall, Robert L. "Tallahassee's Black Churches, 1865–1885." *Florida Historical Quarterly* 48 (1979): 185–196.

Harlan, Louis R. "Booker T. Washington and the National Negro Business League." In *Booker T. Washington in Perspective: Essays of Louis Harlan,* edited by Raymond W. Smock. 98–110. Jackson: University Press of Mississippi, 1988.

Harrell, Laura D. S. "Medical Services in Mississippi, 1890–1970." In *The History of Mississippi,* ed. Richard A. McLemore, 2, 554–559. Hattiesburg: University and College Press of Mississippi, 1973.

Harris, J. William. "Etiquette, Lynching, and Racial Boundaries in Southern History: A Mississippi Example." *American Historical Review* 100 (1995): 387–410.

Harvey, Paul. "Richard Henry Boyd: Black Business in the Jim Crow South." In *Portraits of African American Life Since 1865,* ed. Nina Mjagkih, 51–68. Wilmington, Del.: Scholarly Resources, 2003.

Hatch, Roger D. "Integrating the Issue of Race Into the History of Christianity in America." *Journal of the American Academy of Religion* 2, no. 46 (1978): 545–569.

Henderson, George W. "The Colored Ministry. Its Functions and Its Opportunities." *Southern Workman* 33 (March 1904): 176–178.

Higginbotham, Evelyn Brooks. "African-American Women's History and the Metalanguage of Race." *Signs: Journal of Woman in Culture and Society* 17 (Winter 1992): 257–267.

Higgs, Robert. "The Boll Weevil, the Cotton Economy, and Black Migration: 1910–1930." *Agricultural History* 50, no. 2 (April 1976): 335–350.

Holmes, William F. "Labor Agents and the Georgia Exodus, 1899–1900." *South Atlantic Quarterly* 79, no. 4 (Autumn 1980): 436–448.

——— . "The Leflore County Massacre and the Demise of the Colored Farmers' Alliance." *Phylon* 34 (September 1973): 267–274.

——— . "The Arkansas Cotton Pickers Strike of 1891 and the Demise of the Colored Farmer's." *Arkansas Historical Quarterly* 32 (Summer 1973): 107–119.

——— . "Whitecapping: Agrarian Violence in Mississippi, 1902–1906." *JSH* 35 (1969): 165–185.

Jacobs, Claude F. "Benevolent Societies of New Orleans During the late Nineteenth and Early Twentieth Centuries." *Louisiana History* 24 (Winter 1988): 21–33.

Jenkins, Robert. "The Development of Black Higher Education in Mississippi (1865–1920)." *Journal of Mississippi History* 45 (November 1983): 276–277.

Johnson, Charles S. "How Much of the Migration Was a Flight from Persecution." *Opportunity* 1, no. 9 (September 1923): 273–275.

Johnson, Clifton H. "Slavery Was Hell Without Fires." *God Struck Me Dead: Religious Conversion Experiences and Autobiographies of Ex-Slaves*, 162–163, 167. Philadelphia: Pilgrim Press, 1969.

Jones, Jacqueline. "Encounters, Likely and Unlikely, between Blacks and Poor White Women in the Rural South, 1865–1940." *Georgia Historical Quarterly* 76 (Summer 1992): 333–353.

Jones, Martha S. "'Make Us a Power': African American Methodists Debate the 'Women Question,' 1870–1900." In *Women and Religion in the African Diaspora; Knowledge, Power, and Performance*, ed. R. Marie Griffith and Barbara Savage, 128–153. Baltimore: Johns Hopkins Press, 2006.

Kelley, Robin D. G. "Congested Terrain: Resistance on Public Transportation." In *Race Rebels: Culture, Politics, and the Black Working Class*, 55–76. New York: Free Press, 1994.

——— . "Writing Black Working-Class History from Way, Way Below." In *Race Rebels: Culture, Politics, and the Black Working Class*, 1–16. New York: Free Press, 1994.

——— . "We Are Not What We Seem: Rethinking Black Working-Class Opposition in the Jim Crow South." *Journal of American History* 80 (June 1993): 75–112.

——— . "Comrades, Praise Gawd for Lenin and Them!: Ideology and Culture Among Black Communists in Alabama, 1930–35." *Science and Society* 52, no. 1 (Spring 1988): 59–82.

Kennedy, Thomas C. "Southland College: The Society of Friends and Black Education in Arkansas." *Arkansas Historical Quaterly* 42 (Autumn 1983): 207–238.

Kipp, Lori Maffly. "Mapping the World, Mapping the Race: The Negro Race History, 1874–1915." *Church History* 64 (1995): 610–626.

Kirby, Jack T. "The Southern Exodus, 1910–1960: A Primer for Historians." *Journal of Southern History* 49, no. 4 (November 1983): 585–600.

Kousser, J. Morgan, ed. "A Black Protest in the 'Era of Accommodation': Documents." *Arkansas Historical Quarterly* 34 (Summer 1975): 149–178.

Kunkel, Peter, and Gordon D. Morgan. "Arkansas' Ozark Mountain Blacks: An Introduction." *Phylon* 34 (September 1973): 283–288.

Kuyk, Betty M. "The African Derivation of Black Fraternal Orders in the United States." *Comparative Studies in Society and History* 25, no. 4 (October 1983): 572–579.

Lambert, Frank. "Pedlar in Divinity: George Whitefield and the Great Awakening, 1737–1745." *Journal of American History* 77 (December 1990): 812–837.

Leslie, James W. "Fred Havis: Jefferson County's Black Republican Leader." *Arkansas Historical Quarterly* 37 (Autumn 1978): 240–251.

Levine, Lawrence. "Marcus Garvey and the Politics of Revitalization." In John Hope Franklin and August Maier, eds., *Black Leaders of the Twentieth Century*, 105–138. Urbana: University of Illinois Press, 1982.

———. "The Folklore of Industrial Society: Popular Culture and Its Audiences." *American Historical Review* 97 (1992): 1369–1399.

Lewis, Ronald L. "From Peasant to Proletarian: The Migration of Southern Blacks to the Central Appalachian Coalfields." *Journal of Southern History* 55 (February 1989): 77–102.

Litwack, Leon F. "The Ordeal of Black Freedom." In *The Southern Enigma: Essays on Race, Class, and Folk Culture,* ed. Walter J. Fraser, Jr. and Winfred B. Moore, Jr., 5–24. Westport, Conn.: Greenwood, 1983.

Lornell, Christopher. "Barrelhouse Singers and Sanctified Preachers." In *Saints and Sinners: Religion, Blues and (D)Evil in African-American Literature.,* Edited by Robert Sacre. 37–49. Leige: Société liégeoise de musicologie, 1996.

Lovett, Leonard. "Aspects of the Spiritual Legacy of the Church of God in Christ: Ecumenical Implications." *Mid-Stream* 24, no. 4 (1995): 389–397.

Luker, Ralph. "The Social Gospel and the Failure of Racial Reform, 1885–1898." *Church History* 46 (March 1977): 80–99.

Martin, Robert E. "Negro Disfranchisement in Virginia." *The Howard University Studies in the Social Sciences* 1 (1938): 65–79.

Matthews, John Michael. "The Dilemma of Negro Leadership in the New South: The Case of the Negro Young Peoples' Congress of 1902." *South Atlantic Quarterly* 73 (1974): 130–143.

Matthews, Linda M. "Keeping Down Jim Crow: The Railroads and the Separate Coach Bills in South Carolina." *South Atlantic Quarterly* 73 (Winter 1974): 117–129.

McCallum, Brenda. "Songs of Work and Songs of Worship: Sanctifying Black Unionism in the Southern City of Steel." *New York Folklore* 14, no. 1–2 (1980): 9–33.

McPherson, James M. "Abolitionists and the Civil Rights Act of 1875." *Journal of American History* 52 (December 1965): 493–510.

Mehaffy, Marilyn Maness. "Advertising Race/Raceing Advertising: The Feminine Consumer (-nation), 1876–1900." *Signs: Journal of Woman in Culture and Society* 23, no. 1 (Autumn 1997): 131–174.

Meier, August. "Negro Class Structure and Ideology in the Age of Booker T. Washington." *Phylon* 23 (3rd quarter 1962): 258–266.

Meier, August, and Elliot Rudwick. "The Boycott Movement Against Jim Crow Street Cars in the South, 1900–1906." *Journal of American History* 55 (March 1969): 756–775.

Minelich, Dennis N. "A Socioeconmic Portrait of Prince Hall Masonry in Nebraska, 1900–1920." *Great Plains Quarterly* 17 (Winter 1997): 35–47.

Mitchell, Henry L. "The Founding and Early History of the Southern Tenants Farmers' Union." *Arkansas Historical Quarterly* 32 (1973): 342–369.

Moneyhon, Carl H. "Delta Towns: Their Rise and Decline." In *The Arkansas Delta: Land of Paradox,* ed. Jeannie Whayne and Willard B. Gatewood, 211–221. Fayetteville: The University of Arkansas Press, 1993.

———. "Black Politics in Arkansas During the Gilded Age, 1876–1900." *Arkansas Historical Quarterly* 44 (Autumn 1985): 222–245.

Moore, R. Lawrence. "Religion, Secularization, and the Shaping of the Culture Industry in Antebellum America." *American Quarterly* 41, no. 2 (1989): 216–242.

Nash, Horace D. "Blacks in Arkansas During Reconstruction: The Ex-Slave Narratives." *Arkansas Historical Quarterly* 48 (Autumn 1989): 243–259.

Nathans, Sidney. " 'Gotta Mind to Move a Mind to Settle Down': Afro-Americans and the Plantation Frontier." In *A Master's Due: Essays in Honor of David Herbert Donald,* ed. William J. Cooper, Jr., Michael F. Holt, and John McCardell, 204–222. Baton Rouge: Louisiana State University Press, 1985.

Orsi, Robert. "Everyday Miracles: The Study of Lived Religion." In *Lived Religion in America: Toward a History of Practice,* ed. David D. Hall, 3–21. Princeton: Princeton University Press, 1997.

Painter, Nell Irvin. "Martin R. Delany: Elitism and Black Nationalism." In *Black Leaders of the Nineteenth Century,* ed. Leon Litwack and August Meier, 149–172. Urbana: University of Illinois Press, 1988.

Palmer, Edward. "Negro Secret Societies." *Social Forces* 23 (December 1944): 207–212.

Payne, Elizabeth Anne " 'What Ain't I Been Doing?': Historical Reflections on Women and the Arkansas Delta." In *The Arkansas Delta: Land of Paradox,* ed. Jeannie Whayne and Willard B. Gatewood, 128–147. Fayetteville: University of Arkansas Press, 1993.

Peabody, Charles. "Notes on Negro Music." *Journal of American Folklore* 16, no. 2 (July–September 1903): 148–152.

Raboteau, Albert J. "African-Americans, Exodus, and the American Israel." In *African-American Christianity: Essays in History,* ed. Paul E. Johnson, 1–17. Berkeley: University of California Press, 1994.

Reich, Steven A. "Soldiers of Democracy: Black Texans and the Fight For Citizenship, 1917–1921." *Journal of American History* 82 (March 1996): 1478–1504.

Rijn, Guido van. "Denomination Blues, Texas Gospel with Novelty Accompaniment by Washington Phillips." In *Saints and Sinners: Religion, Blues and (D)Evil in African-American Literature,* ed. by Robert Sacre, 135–166. Leige: Société liégeoise de musicologie, 1996.

Robinson, Amy. "It Takes One to Know One: Passing and Communities of Common Interest." *Critical Inquiry* 20 (Summer 1994): 715–736.

Rogers, O. A. "The Elaine Riots of 1919." *Arkansas Historical Quarterly* 20 (Spring 1961): 95–104.

Robinson, Armstead L. "Plans Dat Comed from God: Institution Building and the Emergence of Black Leadership in Reconstruction Memphis." In *Toward a New South? Studies in Post-Civil War Southern Communities,* ed. Orville Yernon Burton and Robert C. McMath Jr, 93. Westport, Conn.: 1982.

Sacre, Robert. "The Saints and the Sinners under the Swing of the Cross." In *Saints and Sinners: Religion, Blues and (D)Evil in African-American Literature.* Edited by Robert Sacre. 3–36. Leige: Société liégeoise de musicologie, 1996.

Saloutos, Thoedore. "The Agricultural Wheel in Arkansas." *Arkansas Historical Quarterly* 2 (June 1943): 127–140.

Schlereth, Thomas J. "Country Stores, County Fairs, and Mail-Order Catalogues: Consumption in Rural America." In *Consuming Visions: Accumulation and Display of Goods in America, 1880–1920,* ed. Simon J. Bronner, 339–375. New York: Norton, 1989.

Schmidt, Leigh Eric. "The Easter Parade, Piety, Fashion, and Display." *Journal of Religion and American Culture* 4 (Summer 1994): 135–165.

Simpson, George Eaton. "Black Pentecostalism in the United States." *Phylon* 35, no. 2 (1974): 203–211.

Sisk, Glenn N. "Negro Migration in the Alabama Black Belt—1875–1917." *Negro History Bulletin* 17 (November 1953): 32–34.

Smallwood, James. "The Black Communists in Reconstruction Texas: Readjustments in Religion and the Evolution of the Negro Church." *East Texas Historical Journal* 16 (1978): 16–28.

Smith, Albert C. "Southern Violence Reconsidered: Arson as Protest in Black Belt Georgia, 1865–1910." *Journal of Southern History* 55 (November 1985): 527–564.

Smith, Bonnie G. "Gender and the Practices of Scientific History: The Seminar and Archival Research in the Nineteenth Century." *American Historical Review* 100 (October 1995): 1150–1184.

Smith, Susan L. "Welfare Mothers and Children: Health and Home in the American South." *Social Politics* 4, no. 1 (Spring 1997): 49–64.

Smith, Timothy. "Slavery and Theology: The Emergence of Black Christian Consciousness in Nineteenth Century America." *Church History* 51 (1972): 497–512.

Spencer, C.A. "Black Benevolent Societies and the Development of Black Insurance Companies in Nineteenth Century Alabama." *Phylon* 46, no. 3 (September 1985): 251–261.

Strickland, Arvarh. "Toward the Promised Land: The Exodus to Kansas and Afterward." *Missouri Historical Review* 69, no. 4 (July 1975): 376–412.

Terrell, Mary Church. "The Duty of the National Association of Colored Women to the Race." *AME Church Review* 12, no. 3 (1900): 344. In *Around the Family Altar: Domesticity in the African Methodist Episcopal Church, 1865–1900,* 104, by Julius Bailey. Gainesville: University of Florida Press, 2005.

Taylor, David. "Ladies of the Club: An Arkansas Story." *Phillips County Historical Quarterly* 23 (June-September 1985): 29–39.

Tolnay, Stewart E. "Black Family Formation and Tenancy in the Farm South, 1900." *American Journal of Sociology* 90, no. 2 (September 1984): 305–325.

———. "Fertility of Southern Black Farmers in 1900: Evidence and Speculation." *Journal of Family History* (Winter 1983): 314–332.

Wald, Gayle. "From Spirituals to Swing: Sister Rosetta Tharpe and Gospel Crossover." *American Quarterly* 55, no. 3 (September 2003): 387–416.

Wallace, Maurice. "'Are We Men?': Prince Hall, Martin Delany, and the Masculine Ideal in Black Freemasonary, 1775–1865." *American Literary History* 9, no. 3 (Autumn 1997): 396–424.

Wardlow, Gayle Dean. "Reverend D. C. Rice—Gospel Singer." *Storyville* 23 (June-July 1969): 164–167, 183.

Weisenfeld, Judith. "On Jordan's Stormy Banks." In *New Directions in American Religious History,* ed. Harry Stout and Darryl Scott, 423–444. New York: Oxford University Press, 1997.

Welke, Barbara Y. "When All the Women Were White, and All the Blacks Were Men: Gender, Class, Race, and the Road to Plessy, 1855–1914." *Law and History Review* 13 (Fall 1995): 261–316.

Wheeler, Elizabeth L. "Isaac Fisher: The Frustrations of a Negro Educator at Branch Normal College, 1902–1911." *Arkansas Historical Quarterly* 41 (Spring 1982): 3–50.

Wilkinson, Doris Y. "The Doll Exhibit: A Psycho-Cultural Analysis of Black Female Role Stereotypes." *Journal of Popular Culture* 21, no. 2 (Fall 1987): 19–29.

Williams, Charles. "The Conversion Ritual in a Rural Black Baptist Church." In *Holding on to the Land and the Lord: Kinship, Ritual, Land, Tenure, and Social Policy,* ed. Robert Hall and Carol Stark, 69–79. Athens: University of Georgia Press, 1982.

Wills, David W. "Exodus Piety: African American Religion in an Age of Immigration." In *Minority Faiths and the American Protestant Mainstream,* ed. Jonathan Sarna, 136–188. Urbana: University of Illinois Press, 1998.

———. "Womanhood and Domesticity in the AME Tradition: the Influence of Daniel Alexander Payne," in *Black Apostles at Home and Abroad: Afro-Americans and the Christian Mission from the Revolution to Reconstruction,* ed. David W. Wills, 110–145. Boston: G. K. Hall, 1982.

Wood, Stephen E. "The Development of Arkansas Railroads." *Arkansas Historical Review* 7 (Autumn 1948): 156–193.

Woodman, Harold D. "Economic Reconstruction and the Rise of the New South, 1865–1900." In *Interpreting Southern History: Historiographical Essays in Honor of Sanford W. Higginbotham,* ed. John Boles and Evelyn T. Nolen, 254–307. Baton Rouge: Louisiana State University Press, 1987.

Woodruff, Nan Elizabeth. "African-American Struggles for Citizenship in the Arkansas and Mississippi Deltas in the Age of Jim Crow." *Radical History Review* 55 (Winter 1993): 33–51.

Woodson, Carter G. "Insurance Business Among the Negroes." *Journal of Negro History* 14, no. 2 (January 1929): 202–226.

Worthman, Paul, and James Green. "Black Workers in the New South, 1865–1915." In *Key Issues in the Afro-American Experience,* ed. Nathan I. Huggins, Martin Kilson, and Daniel Fox, 2, 47–69. New York: Harcourt, Brace, Jovanovich, 1971.

Wynes, Charles E. "The Evolution of Jim Crow Laws in Twentieth Century Virginia." *Phylon* 28 (Winter 1967): 416–425.

INDEX

ABHMS. *See* American Baptist Home
    Missionary Society
ABPS. *See* American Baptist Publication
    Society
The Advanced Quarterly, 129
advertisements
    Holiness-Pentecostal movement and,
        190–91, 192
    for panaceas, 130, *131, 132–33, 133, 134*
    racist stereotypes in, 101–2
    in religious newspapers, *118, 120, 121,*
        129, 157
    trade cards as, 101–2
Africa
    African American emigration to, 74–75
    African Colonization Society and, 225n81
    America Colonization Society and, 75
    American Society for Colonizing Free
        People of Color and, 75
    for Garvey, as refuge, 198
    Jim Crow laws and, 75

Liberia, 75
    as symbol of liberty, for fraternal
        organizations, 73–75, *74*
African American fraternal organizations. *See*
    fraternal organizations, African
    American
African American Holiness-Pentecostal
    movement. *See* Holiness-Pentecostal
    movement, African American
African American males. *See* males, African
    American
African American midwives. *See* midwives,
    African American
African American physicians. *See* physicians,
    African American
African American secret societies. *See* secret
    societies, African American
African American women. *See* women,
    African American
African American women's groups. *See*
    women's groups, African American

Baptists' criticism of, 174
"black Christian home" and, 167
on black ministers, 178–79
on black religious life in Delta, 175–76
Christian and, 165–66, 168–69
on church improvements, 186–87
Church of the Living God and, 165–66
"Conservative" *v.* "Progressive"
    movements and, 247n31
consumerism of African Americans and,
    167–68, 183
founding of, 21
fraternal organizations and, 167, 183–85
institutional critique of black churches
    within, 178–79, 189
Jones, Charles Price, and, 168–69
Mason, Charles Harrison, and, 168–69
materialism as sin for, 183
Methodists' criticism of, 174
music use within, 187
population demographics for, 182–83
"Progressives" and, criticisms of, 181–82
public worship restrictions within, 187
railroad imagery in, 183–84
on religious advertising, 190, 192
religious newspapers and, 167
as religious revival, 168
religious visions and, 181
speaking in tongues as part of, 175
"third blessing" within, 175
on use of leader's images, 191
women's role in, 169, 182, 188, 248n41
Woods' as part of, 173
Holsey, Lucius, 108
Hood, J. W., 64
Hope, 173
The Hornet, 48
hospitals, segregation in, 144
hospitals, African American
    Afro-American Sons and Daughters and, 199
    fraternal organizations' role in, 199
Household of Ruth, 77

Hudson, J. W., 44
Hughes, Sarah Ann, 147–48
Huntington, Colin P., 32
Hurt, "Mississippi John," 55
    "Got the Blues, Can't Be Satisfied," 55
Hutchings, Joe, 47

illiteracy rates, for African Americans,
    232n36
income levels, for African Americans, 89–90
Independent Order of Good Templars
    (fraternal organization), 72
insurance. *See* life insurance
"I Wonder to Myself," 55–56

Jackson College, 107
Jacobs, F.M., 130
Janssens, Francis, 93
Jefferson, "Blind" Lemon, 57
    "All I Want is That Pure Religion," 57
Jeter, John J., 173
Jim Crow laws, 7–8, 19
    Africa as escape from, 75
    on railroads, 25–26
    sexual politics of, 48
Johnson, Celestine, 91
Johnson, Cinda, 68
Johnson, Clifton H., 23
Johnson, Lizzie, 160
Johnson, Sam, 84
Johnson, Tommy, 55–56
    "Delta Slide," 56
    "I Wonder to Myself," 55–56
Jones, Absalom, 62
Jones, Charles Price, 21, 168–72, *171,* 180.
    See also Holiness-Pentecostal
    movement, African American
    "The History of My Songs," 189, 191
    Holiness-Pentecostal movement and,
    168–69
    on institutionalization of religious life, 189
    on respectability, 186

Progressive Farmers and Household Union
of America, 198, 200
"Progressives" movement (among Baptists),
179–82
"Conservatives" *v.,* 180–81, 247n31
Holiness-Pentecostal movement criticisms
of, 181–82
religious training for, 179–80
on "slave religions," 179
Washington and, 179
women's role in, 179, 182
Protestantism
black religious life and, 6, 61, 156
fraternal organization and, 95
religiosity in females within, 149
publishers. *See* American Baptist Home
Missionary Society; American Baptist
Publication Society; American Tract
Society; American Women's Baptist
Home Missionary Society; The Living
Way Publishing Company; National
Baptist Publishing House

racial commodification, 123
"racial passing," 41
racism
in advertisements, 101–2
African American respectability as force
against, 142–43
railroads, 23–58. *See also* segregation laws,
on railroads
in Arkansas, 29, 209n21
in autobiographies, 23–24
black churches at, 31, 33, 212n47
black spiritual press and, as metaphor for,
44, 209n16
black women and, as spiritual metaphor
for, 47–48, 50
book of Exodus and, 26, 53
in chanted sermons, 51–53
after Civil War, in South, 25, 28
cultural meaning of, 25

in the Delta, 29–34, 34*f,* 35*f*
"dummy lines" for, 32
employment discrimination and, 25
"excursion trips" on, 36–38, 37
as form of liberty, 23–24
fraternal organizations and, growth of
from, 60
Holiness-Pentecostal movement and,
183–84
increase in consumerism as result of,
100–101
Jim Crow laws on, 25–26
levee construction and, 32
as location coordinates for blacks, 43–44
migration influenced by, 34–35
missionaries and, 31, 36
in Mississippi, 29
in music, 26
Plessy v. Ferguson and, 38
rural ecumenism influenced by, 36
sectarianism influenced by, 36
segregation laws on, 7, 38–42
sexual harassment of black women on, 25,
27, 40, 48
spiritual transformation and,
as metaphor for, 3, 20, 26, 45–47,
216n106
in "train songs," 54–57
Underground Railroad, 25, 27–28
Rankin, L. A., 12
Reconstruction
African American parades after, 73
fraternal organizations after, 62–63
migration into the Delta after, 10
Reed, J. W., 44
religious life, for blacks in Delta, 6–7
agricultural calendars and, 103–4
autobiographies as source for, 18–19
blues music and, 54
consumerism as influence on, 20–21,
98–136
epistolary history of, 17